SPENSER'S SUPREME FICTION: PLATONIC NATURAL
PHILOSOPHY AND *THE FAERIE QUEENE*

SPENSER'S SUPREME FICTION

Platonic Natural Philosophy and
The Faerie Queene

JON A. QUITSLUND

UNIVERSITY OF TORONTO PRESS
Toronto Buffalo London

© University of Toronto Press Incorporated 2001
Toronto Buffalo London
Printed in Canada

ISBN 0-8020-3505-1

Printed on acid-free paper

National Library of Canada Cataloguing in Publication Data

Quitslund, Jon A.
  Spenser's supreme fiction : Platonic natural philosophy and The
  faerie queene

  Includes bibliographical references and index.
  ISBN 0-8020-3505-1

  1. Spenser, Edmund, 1552?–1599. Faerie queene. 2. Plato –
  Influence. I. Title

  PR2358.Q58 2001   821'.3   C2001-901620-4

The University of Toronto Press acknowledges the financial assistance
to its publishing program of the Canada Council for the Arts and the
Ontario Arts Council.

University of Toronto Press acknowledges the financial support for its
publishing activities of the Government of Canada through the Book
Publishing Industry Development Program (BPIDP).

He had to choose. But it was not a choice
Between excluding things. It was not a choice

Between, but of. He chose to include the things
That in each other are included, the whole,
The complicate, the amassing harmony.

Wallace Stevens, 'Notes toward a Supreme Fiction'

Contents

Acknowledgments

Any scholarly project entails debts more easily acknowledged than repaid. Since mine has involved an unaccountably long duration and has shed several skins, some contributions to it are hard to discern, even for me. First, I would like to express my gratitude to the sources of funds and other support that made my work possible, especially in its early stages. The Woodrow Wilson National Fellowship Foundation provided dissertation year support, having already funded my first year of graduate study. The National Endowment for the Humanities awarded me a summer stipend. I have benefited enormously from the collections and the hospitality of several research libraries: those at Princeton University and Harvard University, the New York Public Library, the Bodleian Library, the British Museum, the Warburg Institute, the Huntington Library, and – by far the most important to my project and my career – the Folger Shakespeare Library. Over the years I received many forms of support (sabbaticals and other leaves, released time, travel funds, and other reimbursements for expenses, including some of the costs of publication) from several administrative units of The George Washington University. I am grateful to all of these institutions for their support of my work, and thankful for many kindnesses shown by individuals within them.

Some who were most helpful to me in early stages or in parts of my research and writing have not lived to see it completed: I think especially of Sears Jayne, Paul Oskar Kristeller, Hugh Maclean, D.W. Robertson, Charles Trinkaus, and D.P. Walker; I also remember gratefully the support of my colleague and Chair for many years, John P. Reesing, Jr. Colin Frank saw me through a period of dejection. John Sekora, a close friend for many years, beyond category in his generosity and empathy, is the one I most miss in my intended audience.

Thomas P. Roche, Jr, was my principal mentor for the project that laid the foundation for this book; his patience, cautionary words, and friendly encouragement date back more years than we care to count. Other friendships within the community of Spenserians have contributed to my thinking in many ways, large and small, mostly as a consequence of the annual meeting in Kalamazoo. Judith H. Anderson, Jane Bellamy, Elizabeth Bieman, Kenneth Borris, Donald Cheney, Patrick Cheney, Jerome Dees, Wayne Erickson, Kenneth Gross, Bert Hamilton, Margaret Hannay, S.K. Heninger, Kent Hieatt, John Hollander, Carol Kaske, Arthur Kinney, Theresa Krier, Roger Kuin, Richard Mallette, Elizabeth Mazzola, David Lee Miller, Richard Neuse, William Oram, Richard Peterson, Anne Lake Prescott, David Richardson, William Sessions, Lauren Silberman, Gordon Teskey, Humphrey Tonkin, Gary Waller, John Watkins, and John Webster may not agree with the use I have made of ideas from their work and from casual conversations, but I expect that they share my grateful awareness of the ways minds touch each other and words summon responses long after being uttered. I owe further thanks to several friends who read chapters of the book at one stage or another and offered helpful comments: Elizabeth Bieman, Michael Bristol, Patrick Cook, Kent Hieatt, Philip Highfill, Theresa Krier, Elizabeth Mazzola, and Claudia Tate identified flaws and gaps in my argument and endorsed the book's potential when it was still in rough shape. Barbara Estrin has been the most faithful of correspondents, the most acute and generous of readers. Michael Allen influenced the scope of the book more than most, during and long after my time at the Huntington Library. Colleagues and friends without a vested interest in Spenser and the Renaissance have nevertheless supplied me with strength and cheered my 'dulled spright': I owe the most to Robert N. Ganz, Judith Harris, Rika Lesser, David McAleavey, Judith Plotz, Ann Romines, and Christopher Sten. Allan Leventhal deserves a sentence to himself in appreciation for his steady counsel. So does my wife, Toby, for many kinds of practical help and personal support, *sine qua non*.

Parts of the book were, in substantially different form, presented as papers in sessions devoted to Spenser at the annual International Congress on Medieval Studies in Kalamazoo, Michigan. A portion of chapter 6 originally appeared, in slightly different form, as 'The Work of Mourning in Spenser's Garden of Adonis,' in *Renaissance Papers* for 1997. Permission to reprint this material has been granted by the Southeastern Renaissance Conference.

Anonymous readers for the University of Toronto Press have, by their judicious attention and various comments, stimulated me to make many changes, large and small, in the text that they read; it is now a much better book than I could have accomplished without their advice. I also wish to thank my editors, headed by Suzanne Rancourt and including, most fortunately for me, Miriam Skey.

Writers sit alone at their desks, but what they write is subject to innumerable influences and expectations, some from far beyond the dispersed community to which a scholarly book is addressed. My mind has been occupied not only with conversation and writing of all sorts, but with paintings and music offering models of creativity and examples to emulate, however distantly, in my own work. Jazz, which of all the arts speaks to me most directly, has been an ambient part of my working environment, not out of harmony with Spenser's eldritch music. In closing I will take from that world, from the saxophonist Charles Lloyd, a dedication: in *All My Relations* Lloyd offers an exemplary tribute to his nameable and unnameable influences, past, present, and future. Here, in turn, is my tribute to all my relations.

Texts and Abbreviations

Spenser's poetry is cited in the editions of A.C. Hamilton (*The Faerie Queene*, Longman Annotated English Poets [London & New York: Longman, 1977]) and William A. Oram et al. (*The Yale Edition of the Shorter Poems of Edmund Spenser* [New Haven & London: Yale University Press, 1989]); I have also consulted *The Shorter Poems*, ed. Richard A. McCabe (London: Penguin Books, 1999). Abbreviations for the titles of individual poems by Spenser follow the example set by *The Spenser Encyclopedia*: e.g., *Colin Clouts Come Home Againe* is *Colin Clout*, and in *Fowre Hymnes* (*FH*), 'An Hymne in Honour of Love' is *HL*. For the Spenser / Harvey *Letters* of 1580 I use the *Prose Works* in the *Variorum Edition*, ed. Edwin Greenlaw et al. (Baltimore: Johns Hopkins University Press, 1932–57).

For references to classical texts I generally use the Loeb Classical Library; for editions of several dialogues of Plato, see below and in works cited. References in parentheses and notes usually provide the author's last name and a short title; for full descriptions of titles not listed below, see works cited.

Some texts are cited with an abbreviation or initial letters standing for the title:

AP   Philip Sidney. *An Apology for Poetry*. Ed. Geoffrey Shepherd. Nelson's Medieval and Renaissance Library. London: Thomas Nelson, 1965.

CHRP   *The Cambridge History of Renaissance Philosophy*. Ed. Charles B. Schmitt et al. Cambridge: Cambridge University Press, 1988.

D   Léon Hébreu [Leo Hebraeus]. *Dialogues d'Amour: The French translation attributed to Pontus de Tyard and published in Lyon, 1551, by Jean de Tournes*. Ed. T. Anthony Perry. University of North Carolina Studies in Comparative Literature, no. 59. Chapel Hill: University of North Carolina, 1974.

On Love   Marsilio Ficino. *Commentary on Plato's Symposium on Love*. Trans. and ed. Sears Jayne. Dallas: Spring Publications, 1985. Ficino's Latin is cited from the edition of Raymond Marcel, Paris: Les Belles Lettres, 1956. References (e.g., VI iii 109) are to speech, chapter, and page in Jayne's translation.

RPM   *The Renaissance Philosophy of Man*. Ed. Ernst Cassirer, Paul Oskar Kristeller, and John Herman Randall, Jr. Chicago: University of Chicago Press, 1948.

SE   A.C. Hamilton, gen. ed. *The Spenser Encyclopedia*. Toronto: University of Toronto Press, 1990.

Sympos.   Plato. *Symposium*. Trans. Alexander Nehamas and Paul Woodruff. Indianapolis: Hackett Publishing Company, 1989.

Sympose   Le Roy, Louis. *Le Sympose de Platon, ov de l'amovr et de beavté, tradvit de grec en François, auec trois liures de Commentaires* ... Paris: for Vincent Sertenas, 1559.

SPENSER'S SUPREME FICTION

Introduction

After years of experience with *The Faerie Queene*, a reader may be so enveloped in the poem and so confirmed in the self-awareness it encourages that Spenser's lines about his 'weary steps' and 'rare thoughts delight' speak across the centuries, describing his own condition:

> The waies, through which my weary steps I guyde,
> > In this delightfull land of Faery,
> > Are so exceeding spacious and wyde,
> > And sprinckled with such sweet variety,
> > Of all that pleasant is to eare or eye,
> > That I nigh rauisht with rare thoughts delight,
> > My tedious trauell doe forget thereby;
> > And when I gin to feele decay of might,
> It strength to me supplies, and chears my dulled spright.   (VI Proem 1)

I would have the reader of this book share in these terms my ambivalence toward all that I have put into it. The poem's spacious ways have drawn me to both labour and delight; I have been called to earnest concentration and tempted into digressive efforts to match Spenser's learning. Whatever knowledge a reader accumulates must be, like the poem at its end, 'vnperfite,' but Spenser teaches us to live with imperfection, and in time *The Faerie Queene* becomes for its devotee, as it was for the poet, a mirror of what he is as well as what he knows.

This book has been long in the making: both error and its avoidance take time. By my project's convoluted passage as well as in its final shape, I hope to render due honour to my subject. Spenser allows us to call his poetry our subject, but of all mastering intellects, his may be the most shadowy, eluding us not like Proteus but like Nature at the end of the *Cantos*, veiled and evanescent. For those who submit to it as I have done, *The Faerie Queene* is a text in which the act of reading is an entertaining fiction: Spenserians, not Spenser, are being read. Having written myself into a corner several times while working on this book, I wish I could hold Spenser responsible for composing a good part of my life's episodic narrative, which has been complicated by frustrated quests, vainly seeking open-endedness through compulsive repetitions, enthralled for years by a colonizing presence.

My understanding of Spenser has changed with the times. I came to *The Faerie Queene* with a mind devoted to close reading, prepared by what now is regarded as old historicism: the history of ideas and topoi, history of forms and styles, and social history treated as the foundation for competing and evolving world views. At first the Renaissance appealed to me, over against the modern world with its moving frontier in the present, as the source for some of the ideals of Modernism and a conspicuously artificial backdrop against which the phenomena of high modernity stood out dramatically. Beginning in graduate school, in an environment where historians of art enjoyed the highest prestige among humanists, I was drawn to scholarship associated with the Warburg Institute and committed myself to the study of cultural history on that model. In my eyes, until some time early in the seventies, Spenser was the last poet for whom C.S. Lewis's 'discarded image' was vital and as big as life, neither fragmented, reduced to miniatures, nor contradicted by empiricism as it was in most seventeenth-century poetry. Motivated in part by nostalgia and antiquarian interests, I tried to understand the larger elements of Spenser's world view and some of its local colour. Parts of this enterprise still seem worth while, although Lewis's model of the old order still evident in the Renaissance has had to compete for some years now with Stephen Greenblatt's different scenario, in which early modern texts such as Spenser's show us the 'structural joints' in social and psychological arrangements that were visible when our world, now 'cracking apart,' was being constructed (*Renaissance Self-Fashioning* 174–5).

It was clear from the beginning of my work on Spenser and the Platonic tradition that although the natural or cosmological order would provide my framework, the microcosmic and psycho-dynamic aspects of Spenser's narrative would always be calling for attention. For years this call was hard to heed, but eventually I saw what I wanted to make of the interplay of macro- and microcosm. Simultaneously, Spenser studies became more sophisticated, meaningfully connected with a growing body of literary theory and psychoanalytically oriented work on early modern culture, and open also to insights from sociology, anthropology, and political theory. I had known for a long time that the analogical nature of *cosmos* and *psyche* was central to Ficino's Platonism: this was clear from his commentary *On Love*, and I found that its elaborate analogies illuminated the eccentric structures of *The Faerie Queene*. The psychoanalytic and social constructionist turns in literary studies were welcome, therefore, and pertinent to interests already established. I also welcomed the new perspectives on Renaissance culture introduced by historically minded studies of gender and sexuality, based on the insights of feminism and leading to a deeper understanding of homosociality and the cultural codes of compulsory heterosexuality. Studies of the equivocal language constituting individual subjects and their public and private *umwelt* are still breaking new ground, and I intend to contribute something to that work with this study.

These excursions have taken me far beyond Plato and the erotic energies that had always been evident in the renaissance of Platonism, but readers of Derrida, Foucault, Lacan, and Cixous all recognize Plato's seminal significance in their work. Wasn't Socrates the original absent presence, and wasn't Plato the first self-effacing and all-embracing Author? *The Symposium* and the *Phaedrus*, two dialogues especially important to Ficino and subsequently to Spenser, are explicitly devoted to locating both homoerotic desire and generative sexuality within a patriarchal cultural economy, and of course gender studies (including queer studies) have linked the Renaissance with ancient Athens, seeing those cultural moments as similarly relevant to the history of the present.

Even in its incomplete state, *The Faerie Queene* is an encyclopedic poem, enfolding in its capacious fiction not only the great and varied repertoire of literary materials and ornaments we would expect from the 'poet's poet,' but symbols and narrative discourse in which lore of all the arts pertinent to 'virtuous and gentle discipline' is reduced to poetic form. The texture and scope of Spenser's poem body forth learning as well as a fertile imagination, and a long look into it inspires admiration of the poet's ability to make his learning into an imagined world. Even if we discount by half all the books and trends of thought that have been claimed over the centuries as Spenser's sources, we are left with a library, and many contributions to exegesis suggest that, whatever our progress, we are still far from understanding fully the scope of his wisdom and ingenuity.

The greatest claims for the learned character of Spenser's poetry have appeared in studies that emphasize the nonpoetic, even extraliterary, sources of his inspiration: the encyclopedias, handbooks, texts, and treatises to which an educated man of the Renaissance went for knowledge of the world and mankind's engagement with it. But both the poem and these tracts are extensive, and the ways through them are, where not unknown, confused by inconclusive and contradictory arguments. Source study, and the larger enterprise of interpretation based upon ideas attributed to the poet's mind or his milieu, are methodologically less respectable and apt to be less helpful to the common reader than informed but frankly subjective 'readings' of a poem. And *The Faerie Queene* presents the student of sources with special problems. Spenser used all of his reading freely, and exerted himself to combine emergent ideas with traditional schemes and tropes. The ideas from which he started can seldom be traced in his text, nor is the subtlety in his handling of learning immediately apparent. Spenser possessed a deeply conservative cast of mind, often indistinguishable from that will-of-the-wisp, the 'spirit of the times,' or that artefact of mid-twentiethth-century culture, 'the Elizabethan world picture,' but he managed his feats of accommodation by a profoundly personal mode of vision. Appearing naive in one passage, ideologically committed in another, he also invites us on many occasions to construe ideas and events from a disengaged perspective, playful or sceptical.

In the earlier stages of my work on Spenser, it seemed important to claim for the author an ambition to encompass the world in his book. And not only that: I believed that 'our sage and serious poet' claimed access to knowledge, if not Truth, of a sort that asked his interpreters to reify abstractions, understanding their content as pre-established. My maturing experience with the poem has not redefined it, but has rendered it less definite, especially where Truth is concerned. The forsaking of Truth is represented early in Book I of *The Faerie Queene* as the grossest of errors, but throughout the Legend of Holiness and its sequels, knowing Truth and acting in accordance with that knowledge are shown to be enormously complex undertakings. Una stands unveiled before Redcrosse at the end of his self-defining and self-excelling quest, but she remains elaborately dressed, and as the narrative proceeds through its several Books, ending posthumously in a coda defined by its incompleteness, the integuments of Truth are multiplied with each episode.

The environment in which I read Spenser today offers some access to clarifications, but they are not the sort I sought in an earlier day. My commitment to an author-centred reading requires a grounding in historicist scholarship even though it no longer promises freedom from the history of the present. The aim of plausibility constrains me rather as

Redcrosse and Guyon were constrained by their willingness to serve Gloriana, but irony adds its darkness to the conceit: the Faerie Queene is even more remote than Una, and the narrative's often unceremonious forsaking of its heroes and heroines contains lessons in their limitations for all its readers.

The distinctive character of *The Faerie Queene* in both its fictive and its rhetorical aspects requires that the student of sources and ideas use tact and imagination. We are called upon to participate in Spenser's vision, and it is difficult to combine this activity with attention to matters outside the poem. Earlier work of the kind I have undertaken is voluminous but in large measure inconclusive, often unsatisfying when judged as interpretation. Accordingly, my study is specialized and exploratory but it also makes some attempt to be systematic, building upon the positive results of earlier scholarship. I have learned from several studies addressing the dynamics of intertextuality; they lead away from the naive tactics found in many studies of sources, influences, and traditions. I have sought to describe the various kinds of texts that can be plausibly identified as contributing to Spenser's conception of the order of nature, and I have paid particular attention to those that are included *within* the economy of *The Faerie Queene*. While commenting at length upon passages in the poem well known for their importance and their complexity, I have also sought to describe some of the structural characteristics that the author's philosophical learning conferred upon the poem as a whole. My interest in Spenser's text and several intertexts, therefore, is both selective and wide-ranging.

Some of the matters I discuss cannot be understood without reference to sources. I offer close readings of texts when they can be placed specifically in the intertextual matrix of *The Faerie Queene*, and I call on voices representative of opinions that were widely held in the author's time. Also, at some points it has seemed appropriate to look ahead from the Elizabethan period to developments that Spenser seems to have anticipated. Recognizing that studies of sources and backgrounds too often overwhelm, obscure, or simplify the literary texts they are supposed to enrich and clarify, I have tried to place *The Faerie Queene* in the midst of other texts, such as Ficino's *De Amore*, that are nonpoetic but full of fictions.

The encyclopedic and erudite character of Spenser's poem is nowhere more apparent than in the various set pieces concerned with nature and its cycles. There, and in related threads of narrative, myth, and imagery dispersed throughout the six Books and the final *Cantos*, Spenser evokes the diversity of the created world, regarded as a *paysage moralisé*; he represents the relationship of the individual psyche, the imagination, and the moral life to the natural order; and he evokes the occult causes by which all created things are endowed with form and vitality. The heroic poem of the Renaissance was supposed to present its readers with a golden image of their fallen world and to offer images of virtuous action through its narrative, so the first two of these undertakings are not unusual or unprecedented. While the third and most philosophical dimension of the poem – revelation of the forces at work in creation, and exposition of the principles evident in their working – is not unrelated to the other two, it is unusual in a poem that is not hexameral but heroic. Homer, Virgil, Ariosto, and Tasso offer passages analogous to Spenser's Garden of Adonis, but no prototypes for its representation of 'the first seminarie / Of all things, that are borne to liue and die' (III vi 30.4–5). For better poetic parallels to the Garden, and to thematically related passages such as the Temple and Marriage cantos concluding Book IV and the *Two Cantos of Mutabilitie*, we must look to poems such as Hesiod's *Theogony*, Ovid's *Metamorphoses*, Dante's *Commedia*, the *Romance of the Rose*, Palingenius's *Zodiac of Life*, the *Divine Weeks* of Du Bartas, and other poems in the traditions of encyclopedia and anatomy. Nor will poetic sources alone explain the ideas Spenser presents in these passages.

Although they may seem out of place in a heroic poem, the cantos I have cited are fundamental parts of Spenser's design, and not the only evidence that he took a philosopher's interest in the secret sources of the world's vitality. 'The strain of cosmogonic myth running through the poem,' which Alastair Fowler has called 'one of the most remarkable features of *The Faerie Queene*' (*Spenser and the Numbers of Time* 213), has attracted the attention of several scholars.[1] This scholarship encourages us to see in a new light what C.S. Lewis claimed long ago, that *The Faerie Queene* is 'like life itself, not like the products of life. It is an image of the *natura naturans*, not of the *natura naturata*' (*Allegory of Love* 358).

Much of my study will focus upon this aspect of Spenser's poetry. I will argue that the prominence of cosmogonic myths in *The Faerie Queene* is indicative of his interest in the Platonic philosophical tradition, and that the content of his myths – indeed, of his fiction as a whole – can be elucidated with reference to that tradition. I agree with Robert Ellrodt's argument that Spenser's fascination with cosmic creative processes, and his praise of God as, above all else, the world's 'Maker' or 'Workmaister,' measures the depth of his roots in the Judaeo-Christian tradition, since an understanding of God as a personal Providence whose love is displayed throughout the created order is not to be found in ancient philosophy, even in Platonism (*Neoplatonism in the Poetry of Spenser* 126, 154–9, 207). A sharp distinction between Judaeo-Christian and Graeco-Roman traditions would not, however, have been meaningful to Spenser. He approached and appropriated the doctrines of ancient philosophy through the mediating interpretations of patristic, medieval, and Renaissance authors, in whose writings a synthesis of traditions was achieved and then taken for granted.[2] It appears that Spenser read ancient texts in search of support for Christian doctrines, and he often added Christian colouring in his use of them. This had been the approach of many thinkers in the early centuries of the Christian era, and in the century preceding Spenser's birth several schools of thought contributed to this syncretism. Support for the creation account in Genesis was sought in Plato's *Timaeus* and *The Symposium*, and ancient cosmogonic myths were adapted to many purposes, with no thought that what they lacked in literal truth should make them unwholesome to good Christian readers. It can also be argued that when Spenser echoed this syncretism in his poem he was not only honouring God as the creator and sustainer of the universe, but appealing to a theme, Neoplatonic in origin and prominent in Renaissance writings about poetry, that the poet is a maker analogous to God. Like other analogies providing the poem's deep structures, however, that between the poet and the divine Maker is equivocal: Spenser cloaks the pride of an ambitious author in humble acknowledgment of his need for favour, order, and vitality external to himself.

Spenser presents his understanding of the created world order primarily in terms of the myths and metaphors of ancient tradition. When he alludes to Genesis, as when he says that the creatures in the Garden of Adonis 'yet remember well the mightie word, / Which first was spoken by th'Almightie lord, / That bad them to increase and multiply' (III vi 34.4–6), much of the effect of the allusion depends upon its presence in a non-Biblical context. Adonis is not to be confused with Adonai, but etymology often provided a leg on which syncretistic curiosity could travel. References to the world's 'great workmaister' carry overtones that are not exclusively Christian; the Demiurge of the *Timaeus* comes into the picture, and a reader familiar with the texts attributed to Hermes Trismegistus, supposed in the Renaissance to date from the time of Moses, might hear allusions to them. Spenser nowhere describes the creation of matter or of light ex nihilo. This does not mean that he doubted that Christian doctrine, but only that such articles of faith are out of place in secular poetry, where the central subject matter is experience within the natural order. He often writes of this order as distinct, though not isolated, from the order of grace, and when doing so he avoids all but decorative appeals to exclusively Christian authority.

Spenser seems, like many humanistic poets before him, to have enjoyed thinking in classical terms, and he was not troubled, as were Tasso and Milton and some Elizabethan puritans, by a need to distinguish explicitly between pagan fables and Christian truths.

Spenser's poetic universe is clearly governed by a Christian Providence, but he does not insist upon the point. He says in *Colin Clouts Come Home Againe* and the first of his *Fowre Hymnes* that Love, not God the Father working through his Son, 'made' the world (*Colin Clout* 841–2, 883–6; *HL* 74–7, 94–8). Spenser's Love is Hesiod's, Empedocles', and Plato's, but also Ficino's, Pico's, Leone Ebreo's, and Louis Le Roy's; Love personified could not have contained the same meaning for him and his readers that it did in antiquity. It is a pagan concept in a Christian context, inflected with some ambiguity. All Christians know from 1 John 4:16 that God is Love. If the Christian idea had not been deeply bred into him, it is doubtful that Spenser would have written as he did of Love as a cosmic principle, but he expects us to remember the biblical dictum without being reminded. He tells us that Venus was Love's 'great mother,' and that he was 'Begot of Plentie and of Penurie' (*HL* 52–3). In Christian terms this is a fiction (two, in fact, for the price of one). Some among Spenser's contemporaries would have called it a lie; others may have read the lines indulgently but in exclusively Christian terms, denying Venus and her son any claim to divinity. But interpretation must allow Spenser's fictions their integrity; in this case it is the integrity of the myth by which Socrates, with the help of Diotima (another fiction), explains the daemonic nature of Love (*Sympos.* 202E–4C). Some of Spenser's readers would have recognized the allusion, whether they had read Plato's dialogue or Ficino's better-known commentary on it – or any in the plethora of derivative discussions of Love's parentage. In the tradition to which Ficino and Spenser were both contributing, such fictions accept Christian interpretation, and were even designed to attract it, but Renaissance interpretations add to classical motifs without transforming them beyond recognition.

It is difficult to define the kind of truth that Spenser would have us find in his fictions, or their relation to his own convictions. He was not an ironist in the usual sense, but rhetoricians classified irony as a trope within *allegoria*, and the spaciousness of Spenser's poetry adds second thoughts to every statement and every narrative moment. Significance in his poetry is always emergent, always attending an end that has been intimated but not yet reached. Perhaps he himself never saw things whole, but everything he saw was part of a world assumed to be whole, with an integrity independent of its observer. So there is truth in his account of Love's making of the world, but it does not contradict what were to him, no doubt, the greater truths recorded in Genesis and the opening of John's gospel. I imagine that Spenser believed no less in the existence of a god of Love than he believed in the natural inevitability of death and seasonal regeneration. Besides being a figure in traditional literary topoi, Love was for him sometimes a person like an angel or a demon, sometimes an aspect of what has been called the life-force, but in any case Love is a name with a referent in the external world as well as in our emotional and imaginative life. Spenser's poetry does not ask our assent, however, in the same way that a natural philosopher demonstrates the dependence of life upon seasonal change and the structure of the elemental world. If it is proper to view him as the prototypical 'right poet' described by Sidney, Spenser 'nothing affirmeth'; the assertions, ideals, and appeals to our ethical sensitivity by which he seeks to teach and move us all arise from consideration of hypothetical circumstances, distinct from the domains of practical life and theoretical discourse.

The theory of fiction of which Sidney provided the classic statement in English was formulated first in Italy, arising directly out of speculation which attended the revival of interest in Plato and the Neoplatonists – a revival that began in erudite circles in Italy, and by the years of Spenser's maturity had influenced many aspects of cultural life throughout Europe. It is part of my thesis that the philosophical doctrines formulated by Ficino and his followers, with Platonic authorities in place of biblical revelation and its interpreters, provided a ready frame of reference for the kind of fiction Sidney and Spenser wished to invent.

Explaining the nature of the doctrines that Spenser alluded to or incorporated in *The Faerie Queene* and making clear in what forms Platonic authorities and opinions were available to Spenser will tax the limits of this book, and a precis of my argument at this point might only make the reader impatient for proof. I should make reasonably clear at the beginning, however, what I mean by the terms 'Platonism' and 'Platonic tradition.'[3] I will attempt to use these terms and others allied to them with something like the meaning that they held for Spenser and his contemporaries, allowing for some loss of precision in the search for authenticity. I will seldom use the term 'Neoplatonism,' which was not current in the Renaissance, although Neoplatonic doctrines were much more accessible and attractive to Renaissance minds than what we now consider the authentic thought of Plato. Some Renaissance scholars recognized that Proclus and Plotinus had introduced both new methods of argument and new doctrines into the Platonic tradition, but they seldom made distinctions between the thought of Plato himself and the systems of his followers.

While they did not use the term 'tradition,' many of the Renaissance followers of Plato were convinced that truths more ancient than Socrates' teachings had been transmitted by a long line of interpreters, with Plato in a key position. They believed that later philosophers had simply codified Plato's teachings, in a progressive and still open-ended unfolding of the truth.[4] Marsilio Ficino undertook to restore the texts constituting this tradition to the light of day in the West, after centuries in which Platonism had been an important factor in theology and philosophy but most ancient sources had been inaccessible. In the work of translation, interpretation, and adaptation, Ficino had many successors and imitators: Cristoforo Landino, Giovanni Pico della Mirandola, Leone Ebreo, Francesco Cattani da Diacceto, Agostino Nifo, Egidio da Viterbo, Symphorien Champier, Jacques Lefèvre d'Etaples, John Colet, H.C. Agrippa von Nettesheim, Agostino Steucho, John Dee, Louis Le Roy, Giordano Bruno, and Francesco Patrizzi are only the most important.

Ficino founded a short-lived academy of brilliant men, and the movement in which he played a central role was both less and more than a school of thought. Platonism was an ideology without any canons of orthodoxy, and without the pedagogical infrastructure that the followers of Aristotle retained in the continental universities and in England. The thought of Plato's most serious followers tended to be eclectic, and as the ideas of the ancients and their modern interpreters were diffused in the courtly and humanistic culture of the sixteenth century (not only in poetry but in prose fiction, commentaries, dialogues, conduct-books, handbooks of philosophy, and compendia on such topics as Greek and Roman mythology), there were new opportunities for departures from an authentically Platonic content.[5] 'Platonic' remained, however, a term with a certain cachet. Its honorific use had roots in the Middle Ages, when educated people wished for more knowledge of Plato's thought than the available texts would allow them, and what was known exercised a strong appeal because it seemed both exotic and germane to Christian theology. Liberal use of the term 'Platonic' was encouraged by the information explosion that began in the second half of the fifteenth century. Toward the end of the sixteenth century there was a reaction in some quarters to lighter-than-air 'Platonism for the ladies' and the kindred phenomena of Petrarchism, but Spenser was not alone in his commitment to what G.A. Gesualdo, in his commentary on Petrarch's *Canzoniere*, had called 'Platonic sentiments.' In Spenser's poetry, more seriously than in any other Elizabethan literature, such idealistic sentiments are grounded in a view of human nature and the world's order that is authentically philosophical.

Spenser's temperament and interests were such that, given the influences at work in his milieu, only the limits of his own erudition kept Platonic doctrines from merging in his mind with others that had through the centuries been associated with them. The unstructured, nonspecific character of his borrowings from the tradition has not prevented critics over the centuries from considering Platonism fundamental to his world view. Kenelm Digby, the founder of Spenser scholarship, observed that 'survaying his works, you shall finde him a constant disciple of *Platoes* School,'[6] and within a broad definition of that 'School,' Digby's statement would be supportable. I am not inclined to approach Spenser as in any sense doctrinaire: the intellectual climate in which he worked did not promote the awareness of competing schools of thought that we find in Digby's *Observations*, composed circa 1628. However, I find that often, in what seems a conscious shaping of his thought and language, Spenser gave a Platonic colouring to his treatment of a traditional theme or topos.[7] It is useful to distinguish between the programmatic Platonic design evident in certain places and the diffuse Platonism that is present in the broad and deep discursive structures of Spenser's poetry. While the deep structures are sourceless, transmitted through Western culture like inherited traits from the gene pool, programmatic Platonism can sometimes be traced to specific sources. Some intertextual connections with Plato's dialogues are as subtle and significant as the allusions and transformations that define Spenser's relations with Virgil, Chaucer, and Ariosto.

Spenser does not as a rule handle commonplaces merely as commonplaces, and some of his ideas were either unfamiliar or unacceptable to many of his contemporaries. Political and religious sympathies divided his readership. The lines were not so clearly drawn as they would later be, but one finds evidence of vigorous debates during Elizabeth's reign over the value, to a good Protestant, of secular learning in general, and of an artistic and philosophical culture derived from Renaissance Italy and Catholic France. On these points and others in dispute, Spenser's poetry indicates that he sometimes held definite opinions and sometimes maintained a non-committal awareness of conflicting views. As the next two chapters will show in some detail, when Spenser and Gabriel Harvey published their exchange of letters in 1580, as a pendant to *The Shepheardes Calender* and a not-so-modest drumbeat announcing that Spenser had in hand a poem that would 'overgo' Ariosto, both men ingeniously opposed themselves to a form of faith that tended toward superstition, lacking an understanding of *natura naturans* and *natura naturata*.

It is still not adequately recognized that Spenser's enterprise as a poet, beginning with *The Shepheardes Calender* and magnified many times over in *The Faerie Queene*, required acute self-consciousness and constructive thought, devoted not only to making the right career moves but to what some philosophers today call 'worldmaking.' It was once widely believed that just as Shakespeare was an untutored and 'natural' poet, so Spenser, more learnedly but also more naively, made fluent verses by selecting, to suit his needs, from the components of a world picture that was already available to his readers. There is some truth in the myth that during the Renaissance, unlike the crisis-ridden modern age, a poet was not expected to think for himself, since thinking was done for him, inherent in the worn but durable fabric of his culture. For Spenser and other Elizabethans, poetic invention involved the arrangement of pre-existing ideas; they were not supposed to be original with the author. But the Sidneian 'right poet,' a 'maker' whose ideas are 'eikastic' and '*architectonike*,' had to begin with a purposeful design, establishing a foundation beneath the textual surface.[8] We now see that when verbal artifice consists of 'arguments,' this promotes rather than dampens an awareness of alternatives. If arguments consist of manipulated commonplaces, an intelligent poet and his reader are apt to recognize the commonplaces as convenient fictions, with only potential or provisional validity. In a rhetorical culture caught up as Elizabethan England was in change, experiment, and reaction, the meaning of things and the value of opinions would remain somewhat indeterminate, lacking '*termes positifs*' just as language does in post-Saussurean usage.

Spenser's mind and his intentions as a poet will, I expect, always be enigmatic to readers who are not content with simplifications. Perhaps no other English poet, unless it is Chaucer, gives us such contradictory impressions. Spenser is naive and careless; he is also a consummate craftsman and not only wise but devious. His learning is obvious, but sometimes his art makes it seem lightweight. Usually, meaning in *The Faerie Queene* agrees at least superficially with popular opinion, the mental baggage of the ordinary literate Elizabethan reader, but anyone who has exercised much curiosity in following the traces of Spenser's imagination begins at some point to stand in awe of the reach of his mind, the sureness of his grasp, and the depth of his understanding of 'culture' as a profoundly erudite man would define and inhabit it.

T.S. Eliot, who renewed for our time (or yesterday's) the idea that poets must be scholars, emphasized the importance of participation in 'the mind of Europe.' In his examination and development of Eliot's idea of the 'classic,' Frank Kermode observes in passing, 'Perhaps the great English poets must always be at some remove from the central Latin tradition; it is a consequence of our inhabiting, willy-nilly, a province, and one which embodies a culture historically anti-Romanist and much given to Dissent' (*The Classic* 66). Although he was a Londoner with a thorough university education, Spenser's persona is that of a rustic, and when he makes Colin Clout at home in Ireland he appears to be assuming a second level of provinciality. With his penchant for disguise as in his use of the allegorical mode, Spenser negotiated conflicts in the culture of his time. He was the first major English poet to be 'anti-Romanist and much given to Dissent,' but as Kermode observes, 'to be at a remove from is not the same as being at odds with something' (66–7), and Spenser's 'remove' was that of an observer, not an outsider. I imagine Colin on Mount Acidale to be enjoying access to 'the mind of Europe,' and more than willing after a moment's discomposure to share its gifts, even with common readers such as Calidore.

I have arrived at this conception of Spenser's mind: his studies, and his imaginative assimilation of those studies, brought him at an early stage in his career to what would be a constantly deepening understanding of the cultural history of Europe, and of England as a part of Europe but also, potentially, the capital of a new empire. His appreciation for Chaucer is obvious, and his appreciation for Chaucer's age (for Dante, Petrarch, and Boccaccio as well as the *romanciers*, Langland, and other English allegorists) only a little less so. In his formative years he became conversant with the classics, in the terms in which humanist editors and translators had interpreted them: this meant familiarity with Virgil, Ovid, Horace, and other poets together with the commentaries that surrounded their texts in Renaissance editions. Recent scholarship has discovered within the pattern of Spenser's poetic career not only a commitment to the Virgilian *cursus* from pastoral to epic, but complications understandable with reference to the different careers of Ovid, Chaucer, and Ariosto.

Spenser's early poetry and other testimony from the 1570s and 1580s confirm what we would expect, an interest in the French and Italian literature of his century, with that of the most recent years overshadowed by earlier writings that had become canonical. If he read Montaigne's *Essais* upon their publication (two Books in 1580, revised and completed by a third Book in 1588), he does not echo them; I may be eccentric in finding, within the obvious differences, profound resemblances between Spenser and Montaigne. Among the poets, Tasso was a close contemporary; Spenser seems to have read *Gerusalemme Liberata* as soon as it was published in 1581. Sidney's interest in the continental Renaissance set an important precedent with a bearing on the style and subject matter of *The Faerie Queene* and later poems, but in a part of his mind Spenser remained attached to mid-Tudor poetry, at home in the native fields and forests of

Churchyard and Gascoigne. But he was 'myriad-minded,' as Coleridge said of Shakespeare. It is a subjective judgment, but I would say that among the authors of the continental Renaissance, Spenser's deepest affinities are with certain Catholic authors from the period preceding the Reformation. Ariosto was one of these, and the Platonist Ficino was another. It is a measure of Spenser's singularity that one can, in all seriousness, name two such different formative influences as fundamental.

Formally and stylistically, Spenser's poetry exhibits some characteristics of mannerism, but in passages such as the description of the Bower of Bliss he makes a mannerist excess tempting, then ensnares his readers in the unpleasant consequences of an excessive response. The net effect of the episode is disagreeable and instructive. A reader of *The Faerie Queene* must be patient with its interminable artifices and committed to uneasy, off-balance negotiation. While Spenser held mannerism at arm's length in his consistent subordination of art to nature, he was himself clearly a mannerist in his representation of nature. His poem is a fiction: not only an ordering of words into a 'continued Allegory, or darke conceit,' but a contrived world for which the basis is a Faerie land that is uniquely 'Spenserian,' rooted though it may be in literary and popular traditions. The poem refers beyond itself to natural, historical, cultural phenomena and ideals, but it can also be said to contain those phenomena in its world-making.

Spenser's philosophically coherent inclusion of the natural order within his poetic fiction was promoted by two considerations. First, to approach the natural world as the Book of Creation, linked by intricate analogies and a providential design to the Book of God's Word and the course of human destiny, is to perceive all that surrounds humanity as a kind of fiction. Reality, viewed ontologically or historically, had been for several centuries in Christianity a vast text, God's poem: like *The Faerie Queene*, to an educated eye the world yields truth rather than shadows only when the signatures impressed on all things by their Maker are included in the interpretation. Second, if absolute truth has been given to mankind only through revelation and only in those matters essential to salvation, the various forms of humane or secular learning may be best accommodated to the Book of God's Word if they are treated as fictive. Philosophy, then, in the traditions important to Spenser, is best understood as an ordering of fictive discourses, not as a self-sufficient alternative to them. This understanding provides the basis for my interpretation of *The Faerie Queene* as an allegory grounded in philosophy.

PART ONE

The Maker's Mind

chapter one

The Author in 1580 and 1590

The interpretation of *The Faerie Queene* to be advanced in this book is author-centred, rather than reader- or character- or genre-centred. My author is imaginary, accessible only through his writings and other texts around and about him: as I construe him, in keeping with Foucault's view of the 'author-function,'[1] Spenser is inseparable from the genres and the allegorical mode of discourse in which he worked, in which generations of readers have worked in turn. I have learned from interpreters of *The Faerie Queene* who have attended primarily to the internal dynamics of allegorical discourse and the principles and problems inscribed in the history of the heroic poem.[2] Where I depart from a genre-centred approach to Spenser, I do so because his poem exceeds the hybridity built into the heroic genre; my argument seeks to accommodate not only affinities with Hesiod, Lucretius, Virgil in the *Georgics*, Ovid, Dante, Petrarch, and Chaucer, but debts to Plato, Boethius, Ficino, and a host of other imaginative writers often pushed to the margins of 'context' in literary interpretation. I will have the most to say about the 1590 *Faerie Queene*, where the world of the poem and the poet's relation to it are fully established; the three Books added in 1596 and the posthumous *Two Cantos of Mutabilitie* 'play off,' as Barthes would say, codes established in 1590. In the present chapter, I also want to give some attention to the poem's long gestation, interpreting a Latin poem by Spenser and what we can gather from its context, the *Letters* exchanged with Gabriel Harvey, that were published in 1580, a few months after the appearance of *The Shepheardes Calender*.

It is quite remarkable, considering the care and the grand ambition with which Spenser pursued his aims in a laureate poet's career, how self-effacing and modest his figure is as a narrator. Boldly stepping forward to announce, 'Lo I the man,' in his poem's opening gambit, he soon becomes a courtly dissembler. Subsequently, in a climactic moment late in the poem, he appears as a character rather than an observer and gatherer of lore; he is 'Poore *Colin Clout* (who knowes not *Colin Clout?*)' (VI x 16.4). The question alludes to some degree of fame, but it also refers playfully to the enigmatic character of the man behind the borrowed mask of Colin. What *do* we know of Colin Clout? And what do we know of the man who is *not* Colin? (I take it that the narrative's parenthesis pertains in part to 'not *Colin Clout*,' suggesting a figure/ground interplay of Edmund Spenser with his persona.)

Spenser, like nature in the philosopher's proverb, 'loves to hide.' Why? This may be an imponderable question, but 'How?' is worth considering. Allegory gives a poet space in which to hide, even from himself, and space in which meaning, with the self to which it pertains, can take shape over the course of time. In the episode on Mount Acidale, the author presents himself in the guise of Colin as a shepherd who has left his sheep in someone else's care, to be alone with a mysterious 'troupe of Ladies dauncing' (10.7): 'that iolly Shepheards lasse' is at the centre, as we learn eventually, surrounded by the three Graces named in mythology as 'Handmaides of *Venus*,' and in an outer ring, 'An hundred naked maidens lilly white' (see stanzas 10–16). This vibrant apparition frightens Calidore, and when it vanishes, 'All saue the shepheard,' Colin's 'fell despight' leaves him mourning, unconsoled by Calidore's cheery greeting. Before long, however, he makes several stanzas of instruction out of his loss (21–8), and after Calidore apologizes for his interruption, the two men spend 'Long time, as fit occasion forth them led' (30.2), in agreeable conversation.

One lesson of this episode is that Calidore needs Colin as much as Colin needs his Graces. The conversation on Mt Acidale adds flourishes to a theme played, with many variations, throughout *The Faerie Queene*: it is clear that Spenser was proud of his calling as a public poet working in the genre of heroic romance, offering edification even to readers dubious about the value of aesthetic education.[3] The sensuous pleasures and spontaneous creativity Colin enjoys for as long as he is alone with the Graces are directly related, he says, to 'all the complements of curtesie' and the 'skill men call Ciuility' (23.6, 9). In the absence of the Graces, Calidore is so 'rauished' by Colin's words and the pleasures of his *locus amoenus* 'That thence, he had no will away to fare, / But wisht, that with that shepheard he mote dwelling share' (30.8–9). Only when his love for Pastorella 'gan afresh to rancle sore' (31.3) is Calidore moved to leave Colin alone.

'Poore *Colin*' is not nothing when he is left alone with Calidore, but he could not be a poet without private communion with the Graces, so he is bound to accept a vulnerable subjectivity: 'For being gone, none can them bring in place, / But whom they of them selues list so to grace' (20.4–5). By this point in the poem, and with some feeling for Spenser's life-experience, we should understand that the poet's vulnerability mirrors a courtier's dependent status, while the courtier's social obligations run counter to a poet's need for privacy. By Colin's account, his grasp of the 'skill men call Ciuility' (shown in his generous response to Calidore's smooth stupidity) depends on the Graces and on the spacious cosmos from which they descend, having nothing directly to do with experience in the making and execution of policies as a man among men.

Colin's version of courtesy may not be strange coming from a man in Spenser's station, but it runs counter to the standard Elizabethan image of masculinity. This discrepancy deserves more attention than it has received. Spenserians are so familiar with Colin on Mount Acidale, so fond of the poetry in which the episode is couched, and always already so convinced that Spenser was right about life and the supreme importance of beauty within it, that they may never pause to wonder at the implications of this lyrical fable. Don't we see Colin 'fondly overcome by female charm' until he is brought back to his senses by Calidore? The younger Colin Clout of *The Shepheardes Calender*, unhappy in his love of Rosalind, had been a cautionary example, something of a *poète maudit*. His predicament conformed more closely to that of the conventional poet/lover than the picture provided late in Book VI, where he is an ecstatic piper so blessed by intimacy with Venus's handmaidens that even after his vision has been dispersed he is prepared to carry on a civil conversation. Having Queen Elizabeth on the throne and at the forefront in the poem's imagined audience partially explains the ascendancy of sovereign women in Spenser's poetry, but Venus and the Virgin Queen are not that much alike. There is much to be interpreted here.

The great difference between Spenser and most other poets, before his time and until the advent of aestheticism within the Romantic movement, is that in his poetry Venus and her avatars are portrayed as civilizing rather than dangerous influences.[4] This is evident not only in the pastoral enclave within the rarefied romance world of Book VI, but in each of the other Books and the *Cantos*. It is astonishing how important Venus, and the nurturing femininity for which she stands, are to the inspiration on which the poem depends, the authority it claims, and the edifying pleasure it offers.

The Proem to Book I is precedent setting in its emphasis on feminine sources of inspiration and blessing, beginning with the Muse and ending with Queen Elizabeth, with 'milde' Venus keeping Cupid under control and Mars 'In loues and gentle iollities arrayd' (I Proem 3). This Proem prepares us for the active roles played by Una, Gloriana, and the matrons of the House of Holinesse in the Legend we are about to read. The malignant agency of Errour and Duessa can be understood in the light of the misogyny ingrained in Elizabethan culture; that attitude and a countervailing idealization, both characteristic of masculinist discourse, are subjected to reflection in the poem's hall of mirrors. Spenser's sensitivity to women's experience and his blazons of their beauty and virtues have been extensively discussed, but the extent to which the entire poem's narrative voice is feminized has not been recognized. I will argue in subsequent chapters that the pervasive and positive influence of Venus in the world of his poem is best understood with reference to ideas from Plato's *Symposium* and Renaissance commentaries on its myths. Spenser's reading in that literature would not have been decisive, however, without other predisposing factors. To understand them, it will be necessary to reflect upon gender and femininity, ranging widely before returning to Spenser's poetry.

The Subject of Gender

Our own experience of gender and its bearing upon writing and reading continues to open new perspectives on the past. Having naively assumed for a long time that the views of men could and should be normative for mankind, because they could rise to the challenge of accurately mirroring nature (a nature that would be the same for both men and women), we have learned to suspect the biases inherent in this vaunted objectivity, and to see gender as a distorting factor in perceptions of fact and value.[5] There are now so many viewpoints on gender and the interests, both practical and ideological, that go along with any gendered subjectivity, that a smart participant in discussion of the issues cannot settle comfortably in a single position.

In literary studies, the argument that men are inevitably the tools of patriarchy and women are simply the victims has had its day. Notwithstanding the perpetuation of patriarchal institutions in language and the persistence of polarization in ordinary experience, current conceptions of writing and textuality confer upon writers and readers room to manoeuver and uncouple the simple oppositions of 'male' and 'female.' The representations of women in texts written by and for men remain problematic, as before, but they have been opened to interpretations more subtle than allegations of bias or blindness to the possibilities of authentic subjectivity in the Other.

Fresh insights into the functions of gender within discourse, and of discourse in the construction of gender, contain rich potential for revising our understanding of canonical texts. A few examples must suffice as illustration. Petrarch, in his sequence of poems devoted to Laura, stands near the head of a line of poets that includes Spenser. The notion that he wronged Laura by his obsessive attention rests, I believe, on simplistic assumptions about the relationship of poetry to real life, and also on an understanding of gender that is naively dichotomous. Recent scholarship opens those boxes, and like Pandora, we can find hope at the bottom of them.[6] Barbara Estrin's reading of the *Rime* and later poetry in the tradition does not hold Petrarch and his successors responsible for misrepresentation of the woman's part in courtship, but credits them with imaginative responses to the conditions imposed on desire and poetic subjectivity by a working assumption that the woman will always be inaccessible.[7] According to Petrarch (in the words of his belated follower Marvell), the definition of love is 'begotten by Despair / Upon Impossibility.' With reciprocity denied, dialogue with Laura became imaginary, and a new kind of poetry came into being. Thrown back upon his image of Laura, an image he was unable to master, the poet became Love's subject; in subjection, his own voice could be said to have taken on feminine characteristics. Those characteristics of his own narcissistic consciousness are mirrored (though it would be no less true to say that his was the mirror image) in Laura's otherness.

Laura is as much a part of Petrarch's subjectivity as the St Augustine of his *Secretum*. Laura is also substantially independent of Petrarch, in the same way that St Augustine is independent of his interlocutor, although she is accessible to us only through the textual account of his devotion. Both the lady and the saint are cast, opposite one another, as significant Others in Petrarch's subjective and writerly life. The differences between Laura and Augustine – one a quiet enigma overlaid with symbolic extensions of her name and nature, the other a formidable authority figure well known to history and to libraries – are not unrelated to their gendered positions in Petrarch's autobiographical consciousness, differently related to his desire for immortality.

As Petrarch was in love with Laura (i.e., with his allegorical imagining of her elusive essence), Astrophil is represented as in love with Stella. Laura and Stella and all that they represent are objects of desire, but if the poet's real desire is poetry, his frustration amounts to satisfaction, albeit in a minor key. In the lady's absence, where may she be found if not within the poet's textual account of his subjectivity? But to think of her as the poet's property would be to falsify her unattainability. The poet's consciousness contains something other than itself; his gendered language addresses its feminine source, the ground for its figure (cf. Estrin 17–18).

Why is the unattainable Other female? The myth of the androgyne, Aristophanes' contribution to the discussion of love in *The Symposium*, offers an answer to this question that entered the mythology of love during the sixteenth century. This is not the place for a full account of Aristophanes' myth as interpreted in the Renaissance and its implications within the myth-laden narrative of *The Faerie Queene* (see chapter 7), but a few things should be said here, pertinent to the poet's persona, the ground for his subjectivity, and his perspective on gender in the social order. First, it should be noted that although in our time androgyny has been idealized and explicated primarily within feminism, until recently the androgyne or hermaphrodite appeared only within a masculinist discourse. The union or coincidence of male and female traits was not consistently idealized, and 'androgyny has often functioned as a conservative, if not a misogynistic, ideal.'[8] If loss of masculine traits is to be feared, representing androgyny as a gaining of feminine traits may only displace that anxiety. Later discussion will show how Spenser's idealization of androgyny serves several purposes at different points in his poem.

If language itself is not gendered in the Petrarchan poetic tradition, it is definitely an instrument of gender formation. Perhaps *de*formation is more like it: Love's war and idolatry involve blurring distinctions, bending the straight lines separating masculine from feminine behaviour, suggesting that such strict norms may produce deformities. Some of the time, the beloved is in a sovereign or dominant position, the poet is her subject, and his subjectivity, to the extent that it is determined by desire, could be termed effeminate.[9] To the extent that a man's will and wit cleave to his beloved, they will be, according to epistemological assumptions of the time, shaped to her form. Whether the poet-lover's state is perfected or debased by this obsessive attention is open to interpretation. Petrarch's own interpretation is contradictory, fluctuating in some poems from moment to moment, and distributed across a spectrum, since in some poems Laura and the desire she excites are earth-bound and transitory, while in others her semi-divine qualities engage the poet in something more valuable than nostalgia and wishful thinking. This self-division can be understood as a gendered state, participating in both genders. Perhaps the same could be said of all accounts of self-division when the occasion is love:

Ovid's, Chrétien's, Shakespeare's in the *Sonnets*, Sidney's in his lovers' complaints, and much of Spenser's work, beginning with the predicament of Colin in *The Shepheardes Calender*.

Renaissance discourse did not observe a clear distinction between sex and gender, although some distinctions between biology and culture are clear enough, aligned by differences between the body and the soul. A tendency to regard cultural norms as if they were determined by God's will and the nature of things may account for the lumping together of sex and gender. Thomas Laqueur's evidence suggests that gender difference was the primary or more significant factor; he shows how biological discourse prior to the eighteenth century participated in a cultural system of hierarchically ordered correspondences.[10] Bodies were seen as problematic, more apt to confuse than to define individual identities, which were composed for the most part of moral habits (the soul's more than the body's business) and social roles. Although the norms defining what is proper and perfect in human nature were all based on the male anatomy and attributes, in Renaissance culture men were made, not born: becoming masculine took years of 'fashioning ... in virtuous and gentle discipline.' 'We all begin as female, and masculinity is a development out of and away from femininity'; a man's identity and integrity are 'perilously achieved' (Orgel 20, 26). The power and privilege enjoyed by men and denied to women were real enough in early modern culture, but not entirely what literature in the Petrarchan tradition, and in the allied narrative tradition of romance, is about.

For self-aware Elizabethans, gender was an acutely important part of individual identity, fundamental to a person's style or *maniera*, somewhat independent of moral norms and pre-determined social roles. The instability of gender, especially for anxious males, made it all the more significant. The markers of gender were on a par with other hierarchical distinctions, such as noble/base, beautiful/ugly, active/passive, wise/foolish, mature/youthful, steadfast/unstable. Being hierarchically arranged and value-laden, such distinctions function as moral absolutes but sit on the shifting sands of difference, always available for signifying – and challenging – unequal power relationships. Any of these determinants of a moral and social identity could be used to destabilize other terms. The most rational distribution of qualities would place all the best together, but such stereotypes are rarely experienced and inherently uninteresting; a sophisticated sense of style mandates a critique of stereotypes. Narrative depends on conflict and change, and involves departures from the norm even when its purpose is ratification of normative values. When a writer's mind or cultural matrix is cluttered with stereotypes and one aim of writing is to achieve verisimilitude in an individual character, the best way to do so would be to mix together characteristics from both sides of the ledger: to describe, for example, a woman who is beautiful but not nobly born, young and wiser than her elders, apt to guard her integrity fiercely, and steadfast once she has made a decision. Boccaccio's story of Gilette of Narbonne (*Decameron* III ix) presents us with such a character, who is used in a satiric exposé of male privilege and prejudice. In this instance, and in many others readily apparent in Renaissance literature, femininity is overruled by other characteristics but not negated as an identity-defining factor; it becomes a significant attribute in an exceptional character. As modern feminists have noticed, somehow a multitude of exceptional instances never leads to modification of the stereotypes.

An essay by Margreta de Grazia, 'The Scandal of Shakespeare's Sonnets,' shows how excessive attention in modern criticism to the gender differences between the poet's two loves has obscured other more significant differences, between such categories as fair and foul, flourishing and decay, culture and anarchy. In de Grazia's view, the sameness of the young man's sex is less significant than his difference in station from the poet, and the poet's lust-compelled liaison with the 'dark lady' is to be read as an anarchic obliteration of gender and other distinctions. Far from being a normal affirmation of masculinity, heterosexual desire is represented in the *Sonnets* – after the opening sequence persuading the young man to marry – as an urge contrary to order and identity, while the poet's other love is expressed, in all but a few sonnets, without reference to the gender of either person. Although the explicit genital terms in sonnet 20 cast a long shadow across the sequence, so should the young man's androgynous attractiveness and, in the same sonnet, the distinction between 'my passion' and 'thy love' – a moral distinction between appetite and generous devotion. While de Grazia's argument does not disperse all the strangeness of the *Sonnets*, it enables us to read them within an understanding of gender as one element in a system of hierarchical distinctions.

Belief that the perfect form of humanity is to be found in the male of the species obviously discriminates against women. This discrimination can take many forms subtler than Shakespeare's characterization of the dark lady. However, an assertion of masculine perfection involves no assumption that man alone is self-sufficient. Masculinity is incomplete, as Adam found out quite early in Eden. The claim to perfection, therefore, can only be tentative and wishful thinking against the backdrop of fallenness and contingency. Monological masculinity always has to cope with dyadic experience, and with hierarchical arrangements that can never be stable enough. Again, Shakespeare's *Sonnets* illustrate this; so does *Astrophil and Stella* in a different way, and so do each of the erotically motivated quests in *The Faerie Queene*.

The complementarity of masculine and feminine is not a dialectic involving equal terms; in some respects they are not even similar. Jacques Derrida has commented on this difference in a way that is pertinent to Spenser's fiction:

> In our language, when one says 'Man' with a capital M and 'Woman' with a capital W ... it's not at all the same, not at all, because 'man' with a capital M means 'mankind.' Woman with a capital W means ... 'Truth' or things like that, but doesn't mean mankind or womankind.[11]

For Spenser the authorial point of view is, naturally, masculine, and so is that of his Christian Everyman, Redcrosse; his beloved Una is not an Everywoman, but Truth *for him*, the embodiment of an ideal that will eventually, in the life to come, complete him.

According to Aristotelian biology, accentuated by many other considerations in the classical and Christian legacy, masculinity retains within itself a feminine potential, which will be experienced as subversive if it is not acknowledged and controlled. If masculinity is polyvalent, femininity must be even more polyvalent, by definition less stable and organized. Masculinity requires the feminine in its own self-defining project, which involves both exclusion and appropriation of feminine traits (see Breitenberg, *Anxious Masculinity* 5–27). Responding to the threat of slippage into an effeminate position, the masculine construction of femininity takes two forms, both designed to organize by externalization the potential that remains latent within human nature.

One attitude toward the feminine involves a kind of exorcism, a strategy that has come to be called 'abjection.'[12] Whatever is undesirable in human nature as a whole, specifically attributed to women as the source of the undesirable, gets stigmatized, even demonized, as inimical to mankind's health. Like repression, abjection never achieves its declared objective of purification: the undesirable remains desirable to the extent that it still exists, and abjection may render it more powerful as an exotic beauty, alluring and secretly nasty. The process of abjection sets lively confusion over against a purity that can never be more than hypothetical, and experience continually undermines an expectation that the problem has been solved. In a poem firmly committed to problem solving with reference to austere ideals, Spenser's use of the strategy of abjection is distinctive: where another poet would more anxiously hide what he hates, he includes everything that has been marked for exclusion.

Running counter to the strategy of abjection is another construct, an ideal form of femininity, blessed and a source of blessings. The two imaginary processes are complementary (see R. Howard Bloch, *Medieval Misogyny and the Invention of Western Romantic Love*). Wishful thinking of this kind may not disturb belief in male centrality, but it introduces a decentring orientation, involving humility and aspiration. Where abjection expresses fear and guilty desire, the summoning of an angelic femininity enacts a different erotic rationale. The aim of love may be to control or conquer, and it may take more constructive forms, to the extent that the ideal orients activity and is subject to appropriation. Under the discipline of idealization, eros submits to an indefinitely prolonged frustration, oriented toward eventual union with its ideal.

Una allegorized as Truth is one instance of idealization at work. The narrative of Book I leads from Redcrosse's encounter with Errour (the first of the poem's many abject feminine figures) through several errors and rescues by agents of grace to his 'betrouthal' to Una; this ending is complicated by a separation, accepted as temporary, when Redcrosse recalls his obligation to Gloriana (xii 41; cf. 18–19). The ideal or angelic stereotype is multiform and susceptible to misunderstanding; this is illustrated by Spenser's playing Una off against Gloriana as well as Duessa, and by Redcrosse's tendency to veer from one extreme to another, full of courage but confused by the fervour of his desire. Latent desire explains his susceptibility to jealous rage (I ii 5) and his dalliances with Duessa, but Redcrosse confesses his love only after Una has led Prince Arthur to his rescue, Arthur has modeled heroic eros for him by explaining his dream of Gloriana, and Una has approved of the Prince's chivalry (I ix 16–17).

Reading literature of the Renaissance, we should expect to see women always in relation to men, and to regard feminine behaviour and feminine entities (the moon, for example, and other gendered phenomena) within a system of interdependent terms. If masculinity claims to be absolute, femininity is relative, but that relativity has the power to call the masculine absolute – even the law and logic of patriarchy – into question. Such questioning may activate a repressive reassertion of absolute centrality. The feminine persists, over against masculinity as its projected Other, and the external Other corresponds to something within the male's always unfinished project of perfection. For Spenser, the male-centred drama is not all there is: he allows a remarkable number of female characters (Una,

Gloriana, Belphoebe, Britomart, Diana, Venus, Amoret, Florimell, Cambina, and Mercilla; Mutabilitie and Nature could also be mentioned) their own projects of perfection.

From a point of view fully committed to our own culture, based on a desire for freedoms rooted in equality and an assumption of incommensurable differences between the sexes, the pursuit of perfection that animated Renaissance culture may seem absurd at best, tragic at worst in its misrepresentations of the real potential of both sexes. But how real, even in modern culture, are both sexes? Are there only two? Can the ideals of equality and difference be reconciled, with all their implications? If equality is the rule or the goal of the game, shouldn't difference be set aside, reduced to a suit of clothes, traits of character to be assumed in a lifetime of performance? Feminist theory, supplemented by gender theory differently conceived by gay and lesbian writers, has been pondering these questions (see Tina Chanter, *Ethics of Eros*). It seems a good idea, especially for those of us with a stake in cultures constituted differently from our own, not to be fully committed to one culture and the future of its mainstream.

The Faerie Queene is a man's text, but in it masculinity is put in play, put on trial, more often subjected to than dominant over a feminine Other. Artegall's submission to Radigund is only one instance of masculinity occluded; many male characters betray themselves in ways that are legible as effeminacy. Locating *The Faerie Queene* decisively within the traditions of post-Petrarchan narrative, Dorothy Stephens has illuminated the narrator's 'flirtation' with ideas, characters, and his readers (*Limits of Eroticism* 14–22, 102–40). 'While Spenser often expresses anxiety over the feminine imagination for its inconsistency or disapproval of it for its waywardness ... he also invests in this imagination by making his own creative work contingent upon it' (19). Throughout the poem, Spenser refers to his *poesis* and his occult presence in the text with the word 'maske' used as a verb,[13] and as on the Elizabethan stage, this masquerade compromises the ideal of a secure identity, gendered male.

Recall the opening line of *The Faerie Queene*: 'Lo I the man, whose Muse whilome did maske.' The poet, no longer the 'Shepeheards boye' responsible (but unwilling to claim credit) for the *Calender*, is now a man like Virgil. His poetic voice, on the other hand, is that of a masked feminine figure, a quasi-angelic interpreter of 'Knights and Ladies gentle deeds' that have 'slept in silence long.' Spenser is one of those poets for whom 'I' is an Other – a face seen in a mirror, or a painted face. The complicated gender transactions in his poem's first stanza establish a voice, not an identity, and the gender of the poem's voice shifts, as it were, from one iambic foot to another. The man stepping forward with this poem is taking a mysterious Muse in hand, and 'all too meane,' older and more ambitious but still a shepherd, he receives her instruction and prays for her help. 'I' is a man made up to look like Virgil, and more than a little like his rival, Ariosto. The poem is to be imagined as an attempt to 'performe' in accordance with the Muse's 'will' (I Proem 2.2), which at the Proem's end is made dependent upon favourable influence from his 'dearest dred,' the Queen.

Spenser seems to be staging, on the threshold of his poem, the form of subjectivity that was marked in his culture as most threatening to masculine identity. Over and over, a subjectivity of self-assertion and mastery gives way in *The Faerie Queene* to an attitude of patient subjection. The discourse of courtliness, negotiating differences in rank and status, becomes in Spenser's hands a lover's discourse in which gender is a crucial variable. The first invocation begins a discursive process of form-giving and 'making,' conceived as the making of distinctions and a privileging of mind over matter, in recognition of the source of mind and meaning in its opposite number, the world, which is multiform, transformative, elusive – legible, in other words, as feminine.

It should be noted that 'the man' of the first Proem and his 'Muse' are not equally real; the Muse is imaginary, representative of a power not under the poet's control but essential to his being as a poet. This is consistent with Derrida's observation on the difference between Man and Woman in discourse. The Muse is external to the poet's person, but within the range of his imagination; Sidney would locate her within 'the zodiac of his own wit.' Though not of the poet's own making, she is a fiction. I would also identify her as Spenser's 'author-function,' entitling him to echo Virgil and Ariosto. Through the Muse's agency Spenser is also able, without effrontery, to idealize his sovereign and at the same time subject her to his own grand design. Language (in the mother tongue, at least) seems to be feminine for Spenser, as in French (both *la langue* and *la parole*). This fiction and the power granted to it within the fabric of the poem has the effect, I believe, of un-substantiating the gender and identity of 'the man' who draws attention to himself, like Braggadochio, in the first Proem.

The self-consciousness that is enacted through the narrative, its characters, and its spatio-temporal world is unstable, yet enormously resourceful and capacious. The poem's open form has much to do, I believe, with an unusually relaxed, uncommitted, basically playful view of gender as a factor determining identity. For insight into the ways in which Spenser *performs* in his poem, I have turned to Judith Butler's account of gender;

her ideas are uncannily resonant with Spenser's practice. This may be because Spenser was present at the creation of self-consciousness about gender in the formation of both political and intimate identities; he seems unconstrained by the rules that his generation helped to write for English culture. Those rules codified much that we now know as 'compulsory heterosexuality,' but they did not at the same time proscribe affective bonds between men or sexually segregate masculine and feminine traits. The inherited ideals of manly virtue, contemplative retirement, and maidenly obedience were under review in Spenser's time, and the emergent new ideals – for men more than for women – combined traits associated with both genders.

Spenser's character as a poet is remarkably consistent and restrained, but those traits seem to depend on his management of a persona, not on guileless sincerity. He never permits us to see through the mask. I have observed that Spenser was one of those poets for whom 'I' is an Other. Though not stated as such, this principle is the starting point of Judith Butler's account of gender and identity.[14] 'I am skeptical about how the "I" is determined as it operates under the title of the lesbian sign' ('Imitation and Gender Insubordination' 14). Butler's most basic question may be especially pertinent to lesbian and gay experience, but it has a bearing on all our understanding of gender and sexuality: 'What remains permanently concealed by the very linguistic act that offers up the promise of a transparent revelation of sexuality?' (15). In the process of 'coming out,' she explains, something important is *left out* of the declared identity. Identification with a specific sexuality requires an anxious 'redoubling,' an ironic commitment to both a show and an enigma. 'To say that I "play" at being one is not to say that I am not one "really"; ... this is deep-seated play, psychically entrenched play' (18). Butler's solution to the problems posed by pre-existing gender categories and prejudicial distinctions between 'true' heterosexual and 'imitative' homosexual identities involves acceptance (with a difference) of the notion 'that "being" lesbian is always a kind of miming' (20). The transvestite performance of gender provides a basis for claiming that 'drag enacts the very structure of impersonation by which *any gender* is assumed,' and Butler goes on to say that 'heterosexuality is always in the process of imitating and approximating its own phantasmatic idealization of itself – *and failing*' (21).

Two features of this argument deserve further consideration with reference to Spenser: Butler's account of the necessity of imitation and its imperfect efficacy in the construction of gender, and her appropriation of the mime's performance to represent a way of being, with a gender and without being fully defined by it. She also takes from psychoanalytic theory the idea that 'identification and, in particular, identificatory mimetism, *precedes* "identity" and constitutes identity as that which is fundamentally "other to itself." The notion of this Other *in* the self, as it were, implies that the self/Other distinction is *not* primarily external (a powerful critique of ego psychology follows from this); the self is from the start radically implicated in the "Other"' (26). Drawing out the implications of the Other's presence within the self, Butler claims that no one can be 'self-identical'; this is why reiterated attempts to be simply and fully either masculine or feminine are 'bound to fail.' 'The disruption of the Other at the heart of the self is the very condition of that self's possibility' (27).[15]

I take Spenser's Muse, as represented in the first Proem and elsewhere, to be one form that this Other takes; Gloriana, as she appears in Arthur's haunted recollection of his dream, is another, as Artegall is for Britomart and Marinell is for Florimell. On her wedding night, Amoret sees her idealized Other, an anxious servant of Cupid, replaced by his rival, a cruel maestro empowered by Cupid's dark side. The Other is disruptive because its full presence is withheld, but the desire characteristic of melancholia responds with 'incorporation – a kind of psychic miming' (26) – which makes an imaginary substitute for the lost object (see Enterline, *Tears of Narcissus* 21–5, 32–3). Butler's account of the dialogical structure of subjectivity corresponds with what goes on in Spenser's allegory, 'otherspeaking' in which Truth is both veiled and acted out. Allegory provides a mode of articulation for the dynamic of Self and Other in the absence of a self-identical subject.[16] It seems that with its critique of the binarisms that for some centuries supported the norms of bourgeois egotism and compulsory heterosexuality, post-structuralist theory points back to where we started in the Renaissance.

The masking involved in Spenser's narrative can be compared loosely to Butler's 'miming' of a gendered identity. The kind of masque known to Spenser (represented best by Busirane's two-faced 'mask of loue' for the wedding of Amoret and Scudamour – III xii 7–25 and IV i 3) was apt to be a pantomime with few words sung or spoken. Busirane is the poet's demonic Other, and Spenser's verbose narration, tracing Britomart's brave curiosity and Amoret's example of 'wauering wemens wit' (xii 26.4), performs the obverse of Busirane's cruel pantomime; a masque's conventional bodily movements are upstaged in Spenser's text by a sequence of musical words. Spenser's poem is detached from speech to such an extent that Ben Jonson, committed to another kind of masque and fond of identifying language with the body rather than subjectivity, could claim that Spenser 'writ no language.' He wrote, of course, in a tradition that Jonson continued, grounded in imitation, always in a mediated relationship to the mythic original poet, Orpheus, and the singing antiquity from which all stories have descended. It should also be noted that Spenser wrote for the printing press, and he was the first English poet to do so with a large ambition. Some concern about his relationship to this new technology and trade would be understandable. It shows in his nostalgic image of the Muse: she is not the singer who inspired Homer, but the records on which his poem is to be based are kept in an 'euerlasting scryne,' a *scrinium* or box for papers; Spenser's sources are described not as printed books but as 'antique rolles' (I Proem 2.3–4). If these old manuscripts are recognized as also 'antic roles,' we can see the poet presenting himself as a courtly master of ceremonies, for an audience like his master Chaucer's.

Spenser risked inauthenticity and failure when he undertook to 'overgo' Ariosto, to become the English Virgil and (for good measure) the English Ovid, while simultaneously placing himself in the vernacular tradition as a successor to Chaucer, Skelton, and a host of others. The place of imitation in Butler's account of gender insubordination can be compared to the place of imitation in Renaissance poetics and courtly ambition.[17] Spenser was an erudite poet without Ariosto's gifts as an entertainer, and a courtier ambivalent about courtliness; in both parts of his life doubleness is inescapable, and analogous to the 'redoubling' fundamental to Butler's account of gender.[18] Spenser understood how identity is engendered in language. In his experience, this process occurred in several stages: first with the acquisition of language and basic vernacular literacy in early childhood; differently in puberty and adolescence, through the inculcation of manliness with the Latin tongue and its literature; and differently again, in a more anxious relationship to authority, in a profession devoted to writing and publishing, typically in the vernacular. Courtiers in the Elizabethan era were apt to be amateur poets, and a professional writer's career might begin in the amateur's genre of lyric (pastoral poems and Petrarchan sonnets) before reaching for maturity in narrative and discursive forms. The lyric poetry of adolescence and young manhood takes gender and identity formation as its central concerns, flirting with immaturity and effeminacy as it does so. As several critics have noted, the poetry of Spenser's maturity is remarkable for its inclusion of lyric subjectivity within narrative and discursive structures centrally concerned with self-control and masculine agency.[19]

'You will take especial note of the marvellous independence and true imaginative absence of all particular space or time in the Faery Queene. It is in the domains neither of history or geography; it is ignorant of all artificial boundary, all material obstacles; it is truly in land of Faery, that is, of mental space.'[20] Coleridge's observation bears comparison with more recent descriptions of space as it appears in women's self-expression, and textual space that is gendered as feminine. Space suggestive of maternal fertility and *jouissance* is obviously gendered, whether in a man's or a woman's text. Such a space is opened up at the very beginning of *The Faerie Queene* when the 'plaine' across which Redcrosse and his companions move becomes, to 'angry *Ioue*,' 'his Lemans lap,' and the travelers are forced to seek what seems to be 'Faire harbour' in 'A shadie groue' (I i 6–7). The cosmogonic coupling of the Sky God and Mother Earth produces a defensive movement toward another feminine space, turned inward away from 'heauens light' (7.5), a 'labyrinth' (11.4) belonging to Errour. This episode is paradigmatic: delight leads to curiosity and confusion, an impulsive attempt to resolve the confusion leads to the brink of catastrophe, and a gracious rescue is followed by edifying discourse. A similar pattern can be seen in Calidore's experience on Mount Acidale, where Colin with his broken pipe is easier to deal with than Errour and her 'endlesse traine' (I i 18.9).

We should recognize in Errour an antithesis to the poet's Truth, but see in the poem's technique some complicity with the monster:[21] with 'Her vomit full of bookes and papers' (20.6), her spawn of 'Deformed monsters, fowle, and blacke as inke' 22.7), and her 'cole black bloud' (24.9), Errour allegorizes the printing press. Abjection doesn't fully conceal Spenser's necessary engagement with something he has several reasons to fear. When, at the end of his Proem, he seeks the ear of his 'dearest dred,' he makes his ability to imagine Gloriana, 'that true glorious type' of her sovereignty, dependent on her favour (I Proem 4.7–9). Errour is Gloriana's antitype, but when reduced to Spenser's text, the *idea* of Queen Elizabeth is at risk of degradation in the medium of printer's type, with the consequent loss of 'aura' described by Walter Benjamin ('Work of Art in the Age of Mechanical Reproduction' 221–4). Only by keeping Gloriana invisible, off the poem's map, can Spenser preserve her aura, and this strategy carries risks of its own: is the Queen's 'true glorious type' a transcendental signifier, or only ink on a page? In the first Proem and elsewhere in his poem, Spenser goes a long way toward reducing the Queen's 'type' to an imaginary ideal. He makes a risky claim that, with the Queen's favour, he will be able to validate her connection with an ideal sovereignty. Perhaps he recognized, anticipating Stephen Greenblatt, that in the cultural circumstances of the

Reformation, the 'abstractness' of the printed book was peculiarly suited to making public, on an epic scale, 'aspects of the inner life, awkward and eloquent, half-formed, coming into existence.'[22]

The Poet's Career in 1580 and 1590

By 1590, with William Ponsonby as his printer, Spenser could afford to imagine himself on high ground, outside of Errour's den. In its typography and heft, *The Faerie Queene* in three Books closely resembles *The Countesse of Pembrokes Arcadia*, published by Ponsonby that same year in the three-Book revision left incomplete at the time of Sidney's death.[23] After a ten-year interval, the real potential of 'the new Poete' was manifest. The relationship of this achievement to earlier manifestos is worth examining in the light of the preceding discussion of gender and identity. Back in 1580, when Spenser's poem was first mentioned in print, he was following up the solid merit, high seriousness, and ingenious promises of *The Shepheardes Calender* with further advertisements for himself, offered to 'courteous buyers' in a slim pamphlet of letters, without the benefit of a patron's name.[24] The two men of this publication's title page were out to attract the notice of literati like themselves, and perhaps the favourable attention of a patron or two. *Three proper, and wittie, familiar letters: lately passed betwene two Vniuersitie men: touching the Earthquake in Aprill last, and our English refourmed Versifying*: this advertising responded to a sensational event that had already received considerable attention in the popular press, adding, for good measure, obscure references to recherché literary matters, of interest to the coterie that included Philip Sidney.

Although the earliest of Spenser's letters was subscribed 'Leycester House. This .5. of *October .1579.*' (*Prose* 12), by the time the collection was published Spenser had married and was no longer part of the Earl of Leicester's household. He would soon be in Ireland with Arthur, Lord Grey, having shown in print, as well as by his prior service, his readiness for a secretary's career. With the wisdom of hindsight, we can see several things in the *Letters* pertinent to Spenser's future as the poet of *The Faerie Queene*. In addition to what Harvey says about his friend's professed desire 'to emulate, and hope to ouergo' Ariosto (*Prose* 471), the *Letters* show that a similar emulation characterized his intimate friendship with Harvey. Both men discuss the principles involved in writing quantitative verse in English, and offer examples of their own experiments. As if they were gossiping privately rather than writing for publication, both of them claim familiarity with 'the twoo worthy Gentlemen, Master *Sidney*, and Master *Dyer*,' and Spenser expresses some concern that their plans for 'a generall surceasing and silence of balde Rymers, and also of the verie best,' might render inappropriate his desire to dedicate more English poems to Sidney (*Prose* 6). Both of them have other projects in hand, and Spenser's *Dreames* are mentioned as ready for publication, woodcuts included, with a commentary by E.K. (*Prose* 18, 471). Some of this work, imitative of Chaucer and Petrarch rather than Virgil's progress toward the epic, appeared eventually in the *Complaints* volume, published by Ponsonby as a pendant to *The Faerie Queene* (see Loewenstein, 'Spenser's Retrography' 117–28), but other titles sometimes listed as 'lost' may never have been more than dreams.

Spenser's most substantial contribution to the *Letters* is a Latin poem of 114 lines, '*Ad Ornatissimum virum, multis iamdiu nominibus clarissimum, G. H.*,' ostensibly written shortly before his departure for the continent in the service of the Earl of Leicester. When Spenser says, 'I goe thither, as sent by him, and maintained most what of him: and there am to employ my time, my body, my minde, to his Honours seruice' (*Prose* 12), the boast is best understood in the light of Harvey's earlier disappointed hopes for a European errand on Leicester's behalf.[25] Spenser's travel fantasy and the valedictory advice linked with it amount to more than rivalry, however; the poem involves several anticipations of the quests and edifying discourse in *The Faerie Queene*. Spenser testifies to Harvey's importance in his life and to the difficulties attending his transition from a bachelor's status in the Earl of Leicester's household to that of a young married man about to leave London. Discussion of '*Ad Ornatissimum virum*' will prepare for an interpretation of Harvey's contribution to his friend's emergence as 'the new Poete.'

Spenser's verse letter is an exercise in imitation and elaborate disguise; it is also uncommonly self-revealing, closer in spirit to such later poems as *Colin Clouts Come Home Againe* and the *Amoretti* than to *The Shepheardes Calender*. Writing sub rosa in Latin, no doubt with Sidney's erudite coterie in mind at the centre of his intended audience, Spenser displays more ingenuity than genius, but he also registers complex emotions arising from his friendship with Harvey, his commitment to marriage, and his desire for duties worthy of his talents; he marks what I take to be the end of the beginning of his poetic career. He imagines the future in quest romance (and family romance) terms, and he alludes to readings in the Latin poets and moralists that pertain to several episodes in *The Faerie Queene*.

Ambidextrously opportunistic and generous, Spenser uses Harvey as

his foil: sometimes his mentor, sometimes an *alter ego*, sometimes a recipi-
ent of extravagant praise and unnecessary advice. The mirroring function
that has been studied as a feature of Spenser's mature poetics[26] is already
operative here: Harvey figures as the poet Spenser wishes to be, yet the
poem invites him, and the reader over his shoulder, to behold his faults in
the light of its idealizations. With mixed emotions, Spenser anticipates a
long-term separation from his friend. In a seventeen-line passage at the
outset, he complains of being unprepared to set out.[27] Conditions are right
for his departure, but he is 'unfit' (*ineptus*), being tossed by Love on a
metaphorical sea (11–17). Running counter to this variation on his pose as
'Immerito' are signs that Spenser is exercising a good sailor's skills, tacking
across a wind that can't take him directly where he wants to go. Harvey is
praised as a *contemptor Amoris* (18), and as a *magnus Apollo* (20) he
provides examples of lofty aspirations, freed from the bonds of love.
Magnificentia moves his friend to ridicule even Ulysses, whom the poet
admires as a model of conjugal fidelity, an example of the power of Love
(34–41). Having said that 'old Stoic wisdom' would approve of his friend's
opinion (32–3), the poet mildly begs to differ. He admires, and recommends to his sage and serious friend, the wise man who strikes a balance
between behaviour either too sage or too foolish; such a man is capable of
enjoying himself and entertaining others. A poet who would succeed at
court 'learns to play the fool,' following the example of Aristippus, for 'the
world is so full of fools' (47–65). He should not scorn pleasures in abundance, 'Nor a wife brought at last to the altar,' nor money when it is offered
(70–2).

In offering Harvey this jocose advice, Spenser is taking a leaf from his
friend's own book: his ultimate source for much of the poem is one of
Horace's *Epistles* (I xvii), from which Harvey had borrowed in a Latin
poem, *Aulicus*, addressed to Sidney and published in 1578. Within the
Letters, Harvey's serio-comic account of the effects and causes of earthquakes, together with his satiric account of the lapse of learning at Cambridge,[28] show that until Thomas Nashe came along and stole his thunder,
Harvey was quite adept at playing the fool. (He may well have been prone
to *affetazione*, a flaw fatal to would-be courtiers, and Harvey's career after
1580 did not live up to his earlier promise as a scholar, but we should not
take at face value anything that Nashe, after 1592, reported about his
adversary's faux pas in polite company.)

Spenser aspires to a way of life informed by the happy Horatian ideal,
mingling the sweet with the useful (80). He gradually moves away from
offering advice to his friend; his own misgivings and hopes for the future

take over the poem, with Harvey simply complimented for his good fortune (86–7). 'The gods long ago gave me sweetness, but never anything useful' (81). He imagines a life in the great world poetically, not practically. Ambitious and malcontent, he sees himself on a quest 'through the unwelcoming Caucasus, / And through the Pyrenees and the corruption of Babylon' (88–9). Spenser's geography here mixes literary with polemical allusions; 'Babylon' refers to Luther's Rome more than Petrarch's Avignon, and the *inhospita Caucasa* come from Horace (*Odes* I xxii), as McCabe notes (*Shorter Poems* 579).

Spenser's dream of a continental errand on behalf of the Earl of Leicester is the vehicle for a purely literary quest. If his 'endless wanderings' (*inexhaustis ... erroribus*, 91) are unsatisfied, he will join Ulysses at sea. Ulysses, eloquent son and faithful husband, had been mentioned earlier as a model to be imitated; to a quest in his company the poet now adds another, more surprising. He imagines himself accompanying the 'grieving goddess' Ceres as she seeks that 'noble theft' (*Deam ... aegram / Nobile ... furtum*) that the earth has hidden from her (93–4). That Spenser associates himself here with Ceres in her search for Proserpina is an augury of his fascination with the elusive figure of Florimell, whose character may hark back to the beginnings of a concerted effort to assimilate Ariosto. As with his image of Ulysses, he probably has Ovid's *Metamorphoses* on his mind (for Ceres' story, see V 341–486), but Ariosto's allusion to Ceres' search, dramatizing Orlando's desperate hunt for the fugitive Angelica (*OF* XII 1–4), is the more significant precedent. Ovid and Ariosto together have much to do with the extent to which Spenser's narrative persona is androgynous. As we will see, Harvey's response to this poem includes a warning against effeminacy. This difference between the two men seems amicable, but it is not trivial; the erotic tensions between the *Calender*'s Colin and Hobbinol are played out further here.

The figures of resolute Ulysses and desolate Ceres/Orlando (with the secondary figures of Penelope and Proserpina/Angelica) offer divergent rationales for the poet's passionate quest. What is compressed if not confused here will be elaborated throughout the six Books of *The Faerie Queene*, where love in various forms will be an inescapable predicament but also a form of knowledge and a spur to virtue. In this poem, the heroic potential of love remains inchoate. There is trouble at the source of Spenser's desire for a career in the larger world – both the public world and that of his imagination. He is 'ashamed at heart' to be wasting his time at home. Lines 95–8 deserve close reading, and I will quote Spenser's Latin along with my translation:

Namque sinu pudet in patrio, tenebrisque pudendis
   For one feels ashamed at heart, at home in shameful obscurity,
Non nimis ingenio Iuuenem infoelice, virentes,
   An unhappy youth not without talents,
Officijs frustra deperdere vilibus Annos,
   To be wasting the green years in unworthy duties,
Frugibus et vacuas speratis cernere spicas.
   Picking empty ears out of the hoped-for crops.

In the first of these lines, overtones of the phrase *tenebris pudendis* are lost in the translation, 'shameful obscurity'; privacy is troped in terms of pastoral 'shade,' a gendered space, and otium is associated with shameful sexuality.

Although earlier in the poem he had spoken on behalf of pleasure and domesticity, it appears that Spenser has not adjusted to the fact that to be 'in patrio,' at home in his father's place, takes a wife and can be a source of pleasure. Staying at home, he has harvested nothing, as if stuck with the consequences of Ceres' grief, which in Ovid's account caused Sicily's crops to fail. His predicament echoes that of Colin in 'December,' complaining of love 'in secreate shade alone' (5) and lamenting, 'The eare that budded faire, is burnt and blasted' (99). Read with reference to the date Spenser has attached to this part of his correspondence (5 October 1579), the last part of the verse letter to Harvey not only harks back to the *Calender*, but casts a shadow on the near future, the poet's marriage on 27 October 1579 to Machabyas Chylde. The marriage, in turn, should be seen in the context of cultural stereotypes that promoted the unreflective public life while according poetry and privacy only a transitory value.[29] Spenser seems ill at ease with pleasure, yet guiltily susceptible to its appeal. These lines not only relate poignantly to a transitional phase in his personal life and his career, they anticipate the representation of crises in the careers of his heroes, which typically involve temptation to a regressive eroticism. '*Ad Ornatissimum virum*' helps us to identify, in their germinal stage, basic issues in Elizabethan culture that concerned Spenser throughout his career. Can the pleasures to be found in private life, in domestic intimacy and courting the muses, be coordinated with an ambitious and virtuous life in the public eye? Doubts on this point are as persistent in Spenser's poetry as worries about mutability, and the two sorts of problems, cultural and natural, are often linked together.

'I'll go, then, at once' (99), he announces, as if through teeth still clenched in shame and frustration: *Ibimus ergo statim*. The adverb *statim*, meaning 'steadfastly' as well as 'at once,' with its roots in the verb from which 'stasis' is also derived, conveys the tension of a wished-for readiness. But as Harvey reminds him in response to this poem, Spenser is going nowhere fast. The make-believe character of the poem's ambitions and effusive farewells turns them back upon themselves. In time, of course, Spenser will be steadfast: all of his heroic poem, not just the great coda in his *Cantos*, is a tribute to the virtue of 'Constancie.' Yet Spenser's version of constancy, like the Queen's guise as Cynthia and her motto *Semper eadem*, allows for flux. His contribution to the evolving genre of the heroic poem shifts on many occasions from a nuanced understanding of life's complexity to follow a heroic character's loss of nerve or impulsive action. Such disparate elements are already present, presumptively, in this poem. After his declaration and a moment of self-consciousness ('Who calls for blessings on my departure?'), the resolved poet turns quickly to a fantasy of mutual longing. He sees himself singing alone, far from Britain, while Harvey, surrounded by friends, wishes for letters from him and prays for his return (101–14). In these last lines, just the length of a sonnet, the poet puts into the mouth of his friend, 'Angel and Gabriel' (108), an identification of himself in his absence: 'If only my *Edmund* were here' (111). The identity of Immerito had not been disclosed in *The Shepheardes Calender*, nor does it appear elsewhere in the *Letters*. This turn as a ventriloquist is a modest anticipation of the poet's declaration of his personal interest in dedicating *The Faerie Queene* to Queen Elizabeth: 'HER MOST HVMBLE SERVAVNT EDMVND SPENSER DOTH IN ALL HVMILITIE DEDICATE, PRESENT AND CONSECRATE THESE HIS LAB-OVRS TO LIVE VVITH THE ETERNITIE OF HER FAME.'

The letters I have been examining exhibit an immature but far from juvenile talent. In them, Spenser announces that he has begun *The Faerie Queene*, offers hints at his aims in the next phase of his career, and suggests how he will project himself imaginatively in the actions and sufferings he narrates.[30] Some basic principles remain unarticulated, and perhaps unimagined: in *The Faerie Queene* love is bitter but it is also, in noble natures, a spur to virtue rather than an obstacle, because its object has been redefined. Perhaps Spenser was capable of that redefinition in 1580; the sonnet that became *Amoretti* 8 suggests as much, and it dates from his association with the Sidney circle before his departure for Ireland.[31] Already in that poem, he has imagined an ideal woman, to whom he says, 'You frame my thoughts and fashion me within.' The similarity of many phrases in this sonnet to most of the stanza devoted to Belphoebe's eyes when she startles Trompart and Braggadocchio (II iii 23) suggests that that episode, topically related to Alençon's courtship of the Queen, was part of the poem that Spenser shared with Harvey, and perhaps with Sidney and other interested parties. But the impression that comes across most strongly from the correspondence with Harvey is that Spenser had yet to discover, even in his imagination, most of the possibilities to which a heroic poem might correspond. A public poetry, or a poetry that places private experience in the public sphere, requires a sounder footing than Spenser has found in his *Letters*: such a poetry must embody a fictive world that offers some bearing on the reader's as well as the writer's experience. In 1580 Spenser still needed experience and ideals in which to ground his poem, even though *The Faerie Queene* would eventually be, among other things, a critique of the appetite for earthly glory and the possibilities for heroic action available to the subjects of Queen Elizabeth.

The *Letters* offer us longings, pretence, subterfuge or suspect references, words referring to words. They are 'hermetic' in the loose modern sense of that term: elaborately self-referential, and designed both to attract and to mislead readers who look to the printed word for gossip and 'intelligence.' They also establish that Harvey and Spenser are educated, talented, ambitious; their claim to status is as 'University men.' It is unclear what that distinction was worth, in practical terms, to a would-be courtier, but in the ideology of Reformation humanism it mattered a great deal,[32] and extensive learning worn lightly informs Spenser's poetic character from the beginning to the end of his career. Spenser was, in the eyes of his contemporaries, more effectively educated and sophisticated than Harvey, better suited for courtly company and responsibilities, but his troubles with Burghley and others suggest that he was apt to be, like Harvey, impractically outspoken in pursuit of his interests. Pedantry was not the only vice one could pick up at the university. Although he is usually portrayed as unreasonably loyal to Harvey, distance and differences are apparent in the *Letters* along with an erotically charged intimacy. In *The Faerie Queene*, Harvey is replaced by Sir Walter Raleigh, a man of more impressive virtues and faults with whom, again, Spenser would assert friendship and imply differences.

Dialogical Relations between Gabriel Harvey and Edmund Spenser

Earlier in this chapter I drew attention to the ways in which the narrator's voice in *The Faerie Queene* depends upon his muse's masked example and her promptings, along with encouragement from Venus, Cupid, and his

Queen. Spenser often represents his persona as solitary, but never as committed to self-reliance. He is always looking beyond himself for help, often articulating his subjectivity as dependent on external sources of energy and coherence. So in '*Ad Ornatissimum virum*,' after imagining himself in the company of Ulysses and Ceres, the poet is alone, far from home, in the company of a mournful muse, and he evokes the absent presence of his friend back in England to declare that *Edmundus* is still beloved. I have discussed elsewhere the intimacy established between Spenser and Harvey in these letters, touching on the ways in which love presents the poet with inescapable difficulties ('Questionable Evidence in the *Letters* of 1580' 91–8). The path Spenser has chosen leads away from Harvey, and he does not embark on it with confidence. His Latin letter ends, '*Vale, Vale plurimum, Mi amabilissime Harueie, meo cordi, meorum omnium longè charissime*' (Farewell, farewell over and over, my most lovable Harvey, dearer to my heart by far than any other); the close of the letter, in English, contains more words to the same effect (*Prose* 12). We encounter such sentiments, date-lined prior to his marriage, in the context of later dated texts which undo in advance the finality of his farewells, and we also have several responses by Harvey to his friend's sentimental commitments. Since both writers seem to be participating in a staged competition for the public's benefit, it is appropriate to bring Harvey more into the picture. Attention to his criticism of Spenser for becoming too 'woomanish' will open the way to some other themes in Harvey's part of the *Letters*; for all their differences, these two university men seem to have been as interdependent as Pyrocles and Musidorus, or Philip Sidney and Fulke Greville.

The letter from Immerito that begins the two men's exchange closes with a note in Latin; the Variorum editors translate, 'But, as I love you, my sweetheart sincerely commends herself to you, wondering that you have made no reply to her letter. Beware, I beg, lest this be fatal to you. Fatal to me it certainly will be, nor will you go unpunished, I imagine' (*Prose* 267; cf. 17). Once the more serious business of the first set of letters has been dealt with, Harvey responds to this, again using Latin as the medium for intimate jocularity: 'But as I love you, I shall reply to your sweetheart's most delicate letter as soon as I can do so with care, conveying meanwhile as many exquisite greetings and salutations as she has hairs on her head, half-gold, half-silver, half-gemmy. What do you want? By your own Venus, she is another Rosalind; and not another but the same Hobbinol (with your good will as before) loves her very much. O my Mistress Immerito, my prettiest Collina Clout, many more greetings, and farewell'

(*Prose* 476, my translation). These facetious compliments, addressed to Spenser after his marriage, should be compared with the misogynistic tenor of Harvey's response to his friend's valedictory verses. There, warning against 'one of the *praedominant humors* that raigne in our common Youths,' he calls Spenser a '*magne muliercularum amator, egregie Pamphile*' and bids him, '*Respice finem.*' After a patch of moralizing in Latin and Greek, he sums up: 'Credite me, I will neuer linne baityng at you, til I haue rid you quite of this yonkerly, and [woomanish] humor.'[33] There is more: his own and his friend's 'learned experience' must confirm the truth of familiar moral tags. 'Love is bitterness [*Amare amarum*]: Nor is Love a god, as they say, but bitterness and error,' and Agrippa was right to call Ovid's *de Arte Amandi* rather *de Arte Meretricandi*, 'The Art of Harlotry.' Lovers should be compared to alchemists, who dream of mountains of gold and silver 'but meanwhile are almost blinded and even suffocated by the frightful fumes of the charcoal.' Harvey contrasts to Adam's paradise another, for fools and lovers: one is for those truly blessed, but in the other, bliss is 'fantastic and fanatic' (*Prose* 444).

What should we make of Harvey's frantic riposte to Spenser's serious and only partially articulated rationale for love and marriage? He may be responding to what he has seen of *The Faerie Queene*, as well as to the Latin poem. Like Hobbinol, Harvey was apt to find himself on the losing end of a contest to be the apple of Immerito's eye. The loser's predicament in pastoral is comical, but also pathetic in a genre that exists to make pathos manageable. Spenser's rhetorical tactics in '*Ad Ornatissimum virum*' put Harvey in a bind: although Edmundus claims to be embarking on a great adventure, he plays the troubled youth, the loser going into exile, while representing his friend as happy and secure at home. Like Guyon placing himself in jeopardy, Edmundus invites his mentoring friend's concern. Harvey's rhetoric, in turn, has limited his options: he cannot put aside his satirist's mask to be a *magnus Apollo*, but can only 'play the fool.' His exorbitant style creates a travesty of the celibate moralist's position, reflecting favourably on Spenser's account of his choices. It is my guess that the two men planned their dialogue at cross purposes to have this effect, resembling that of the debate between Musidorus and Pyrocles in the *Arcadia*. Remembering, however, the impatience with which Spenser had reflected on being stuck 'at home in shameful obscurity,' we can acknowledge that when Harvey urged his friend 'to abandon all other fooleries, and honour Vertue, the onely immortall and suruiuing Accident amongst so manye mortall, and euer-perishing Substaunces' (*Prose* 442), they were in agreement, and if Harvey ever delivered his promised 'Lecture in *Homers*

Odysses, and *Virgils Æneads*,' Spenser probably sat still for it – even the part about Circe's 'potions, and charms, and drugs, and diseases' (*Prose* 444–5).

Harvey's reference to the opinion of Heinrich Cornelius Agrippa von Nettesheim provides an opening for further interpretation. His allusion to Agrippa's opinion of Ovid's *Art of Love* is not the only reference in the *Letters* to *Of the Vanitie and Vncertaintie of the Artes and Sciences*, a treatise well known among university men in Tudor England, which Philip Sidney may also have been reading at this time in connection with his work on *The Defence of Poesy*.[34] Agrippa's *De Vanitate* participates, willy-nilly, in the vanity and uncertainty of which it complains, but its argument also appeals seriously to the will to believe and the introspective individualism characteristic of Reformation-era piety. In the passage already cited, Harvey alludes to the criticism of Ovid in Agrippa's chapter 63, 'Of the whoorishe Arte,' which mingles pedantry with prurience in a misogynistic catalogue of famous and obscure courtesans. Such testimony against women and the love of women as Harvey offers, echoing Agrippa, is at bottom mischievous: it plays to prejudice, yet it adds no legitimacy to misogyny.

Harvey's other references to Agrippa reveal ambivalence. To the extent that *De Vanitate* can be enlisted in Harvey's own critique of shallow or useless learning, it is commended. In one of his exercises in the new versification, he praises Agrippa for dispraising learning that does not lead to virtue, fame, and wealth:

A thousand good leaues be for euer graunted *Agrippa*.
For squibbing and declayming against many fruitlesse
Artes, and Craftes, deuisde by the *Diuls and Sprites*, for a torment,
And for a plague to the world: as both *Pandora, Prometheus*,
And that cursed *good bad Tree*, can testifie at all times.   (*Prose* 465)

The doubleness of Harvey's mind is evident from one of the manifestos preserved in his personal 'letter-book,' where he praises learning and *dis*praises Agrippa: 'O that I were a compounde of all the sciences as well speculative as active and specially those that consist in a certayne practicall discourse ether of speach or reason (notwithstanding ther excessive vanitye) that the ilfavorid coniurer Agrippa so furiously and outragiously cryeth oute uppon' (*Letter-Book* 71). To this, we can compare one of the best known of Harvey's notations in his extensive library: 'It is not sufficient for poets, to be superficial humanists: but they must be exquisite artists, & curious vniuersal schollers.'[35] One of my aims in this study is to show that ambitions such as these figure in the poetic cosmos of *The Faerie Queene*, and that when he chose secular poetry as his medium, Spenser found a way to answer Agrippa's charge that all secular learning is fatally infected with poetry.

Approached with the interests of a curious universal scholar in mind, there are several things to admire in the persona that Gabriel Harvey establishes, with a little help from his friend, in the bulk of his contributions to the *Letters*. By 1579 Harvey had, like his older and more exotically learned contemporary John Dee, begun to establish himself as a researcher and advisor to members of the aristocracy (see Jardine and Grafton, '"Studied for Action"'), and the *Letters* advertise his credentials. In the first of his letters, Spenser salutes his friend with speculation about 'some great important matter in hande,' then supposes, 'happly you dwell altogither in *Iustinians* Courte, and giue your selfe to be deuoured of secreate Studies' (*Prose* 15). We have evidence that in April of 1580 he acquired a textbook in civil law,[36] but this serious undertaking remains under wraps. In keeping with the precepts of *The Courtier*, a book that he had digested several years earlier,[37] Harvey practices *sprezzatura*, striving with indifferent success to display a few amusing samples of his protean abilities.

The spate of tracts and ballads interpreting the alarming earthquake that was felt in London and elsewhere in southern England on April 6th of 1580 gave Harvey a chance to show off his superior wit and erudition, and his response to Spenser's inquiry[38] includes contrasting accounts of the earthquake and its causes, both opposed to the crude moralizing responses that were still appearing when the *Letters* were published (see *Prose* 477–9). Harvey's ideas will help us to understand how Spenser regarded the order of nature and its relation to supernatural causes, and how art, as a rhetorical repertoire and a mode of inquiry, may be used to interpret the interplay of human and natural events. Spenser has been shown to have employed Harvey's understanding of earthquakes in his description of Orgoglio,[39] and my discussion will eventually come around to *The Faerie Queene* and its handling of what has been called 'the problem of nature.'[40]

In the first part of his letter, Harvey recounts how he entertained his companions with a droll explanation, rife with grotesque anthropomorphisms and the pseudoscience that was part of Renaissance medicine: '*The Earth* you knowe, is a mightie great huge body,' full of 'substantiall matter, and sundry Accidentall humours, and fumes, and spirites, either good, or bad, or mixte.' Naturally, from time to time the mixture becomes intemperate, evil predominates, and the 'abundaunce of corrupt putrified Humors, and ylfauoured grosse infected matter' leads to a disease. Figuratively speaking, the earthquake was 'a violent chill shiuering shaking Ague.' Humorously and verbosely, Harvey offers some alternative explanations, attributed to 'some againe, of our finest conceited heades,' the 'very deepest Secretaries of Nature,' but he is interrupted (*Prose* 451–3). His parody of a lecture gives way to a more serious account, requested by his host, who says, 'I would gladly heare your Iudgement, and resolution, whether you counte of Earthquakes, as Naturall, or Supernaturall motions.' Harvey's answer comes quickly – 'The Earthquakes themselues I would saye are Naturall' – but his Ramistic analysis of their causes requires more than 'a little leaue to laye open the matter' (*Prose* 453). He responds to his absent adversaries, most of them ministers or ballad-mongers, with well-tempered philosophical discourse, drawing on both Aristotle and his Renaissance critics; in so doing, he provides an index of the opinions on nature and Providence available to Spenser.

The earthquake's natural or 'Internall Causes' are 'the Materiall, and the Formall'; 'the Externall Causes, which are the Efficient and Finall, I take ... to be supernaturall.' Harvey follows Aristotle in understanding the material cause to be 'no doubt great aboundance of wynde, or stoare of grosse and drye vapors, and spirites ... emprysoned in the Caues, and Dungeons of the Earth'; an earthquake occurs when this excess seeks its natural place by a 'forcible Eruption.' God is not uninvolved; 'The first immediate Efficient, out of all Question, is God himselfe, the Creatour, and Continuer, and Corrector of Nature, and therefore Supernaturall,' but there is 'a secondarie Instrumentall Efficient of such motions' in celestial influences and the heat of the sun. It is by these instrumental causes, and not by God, that the vapours are drawn back to their natural place; this recovery of its equilibrium is a final cause within nature (*Prose* 453–4). Another kind of final cause, 'depending vppon a supernaturall Efficient Cause,' operates 'sometime also, I graunt, to testifie and denounce the secrete wrathe, and indignation of God, or his sensible punishment vppon notorious malefactours, or, a threatning Caueat, and forewarning for the inhabitantes, or the like' (*Prose* 454). The number of possible interpretations offered for a hypothetical 'supernaturall Morall End' partially prepares the reader for Harvey's sceptical attitude toward any man's presuming 'to reueale hys [God's] incomprehensible mysteries, and definitiuely to giue sentence of his Maiesties secret and inscrutable purposes'; he doubts that any man possesses 'so great authoritie, and so familiar acquaintance with God in Heauen, (vnlesse haply for the nonce he hath lately intertained some few choice singular ones of his priuie Counsell)' (*Prose* 455).

Harvey has argued that God's purposes are 'commonly performed, by the qualifying, and conforming of Nature, and Naturall things, to the accomplishment of his Diuine and incomprehensible determination.' He goes so far as to call God 'very Nature selfe ... *Natura Naturans*,' the world of *natura naturata* being 'the workmanship of his owne hands, and ... euer pliable and flexible Instrumentes at his Commaundement' (*Prose* 454). The world Harvey interprets is grounded in nature, informed by grace; it is open to rational inquiry, but neither reason nor faith possesses 'a key for all the lockes in Heauen' (*Prose* 455). The kind of authority that Harvey claims involves mastery of logic and rhetoric, showing respect for the world's complexity and the limitations of secular learning.

The difference between Harvey's way of thinking about nature and the attitudes of most other interpreters of the earthquake may be seen in a passage from Abraham Fleming's tract, *A Bright Burning Beacon*, which used the earthquake as an occasion to anticipate the biblical apocalypse. Fleming adds to the work he is translating an 'admonition vpon these coniecturall reasons': he resists 'referring that to the course of naturall causes, which come to passe by the prouidence of his [God's] iudgement,' because a slippery slope leads the worldly wise from security to incredulity, then to atheism, and finally 'into open blasphemie,' which invites divine indignation. 'The next way to breede in the mindes of men a deniall of Gods deitie, is to derogate and take from him the propertie of his workes.'[41] Fleming responds to the problem of nature by making natural causes insignificant; it is even dangerous to interpret them. Harvey, on the other hand, sees 'a very presumptuous Errour,' based only in 'Credulitie and Ignoraunce,' in refusals to allow the course of nature its due (*Prose* 455–6). In the absence of evidence 'that Earthquakes, *sine omni exceptione*, are ominous, and significatiue Effectes,' he is unwilling to draw conclusions concerning the designs of Providence (*Prose* 457–8). Subsequent quotations from a treatise by Gianfrancesco Pico della Mirandola[42] provide a rationale for Harvey's cautious approach to the interpretation of causes and effects; the younger Pico had developed in several treatises the austere inductive principle 'that general laws are invalid unless they are true of all of the instances which they claim to cover.'[43] Harvey's argument on behalf of the prudent use of reason in both science and religion makes use of opinions that were in the vanguard for their time.

Spenser may have shared his friend's familiarity with and enthusiasm for one of the more serious and original of the Italian philosophers, although I expect that the elder Pico's writings were of greater interest to him. Spenser and Harvey differed in many ways, and their aims and opportunities called for different uses of their learning: in Harvey's marginalia and other writings we see him eagerly embracing the latest fashions and the most useful knowledge, while Spenser's tastes were, I find, more conservative, less egocentric and worldly. The literary implications of Harvey's interpretation of the earthquake are anti-allegorical, whereas Spenser's poetry encourages belief that there is a spiritual dimension to every event in nature and in human experience, and that immaterial essences can be known through their physical manifestations. I would suggest, however, that Harvey's mindset – an interest in nature *per se*, coupled with a conviction that God is unfathomable – made a fundamental contribution to Spenser's thinking in *The Faerie Queene.*

Some passages from Harvey's marginalia will illustrate further what he had to offer to Spenser. 'Art, little worth, vnles it be transformed into Nature.' Harvey brings several impulses into focus in this comment. On the same page he wrote, 'Aretines glory, to be himself: to speak, & write like himself: to imitate none, but him selfe & euer to maintaine his owne singularity' (*Marginalia* 156). Elsewhere, in his copy of Erasmus's *Parabolae*, questioning the common humanist bias favouring guidance from art rather than nature, he noted, 'Ars, certior dux quam Natura. A disputable Question' (*Marginalia* 140). Everything in the domains of art and nature might be – ought to be, perhaps – disputed. In a book acquired and copiously annotated in 1582, Harvey observed, 'The rational animal ought to say and do nothing without reason, except in those things which exceed human reason, and contain mysteries of the divine reason. Otherwise, nothing without Why; to all things, Why.'[44]

Several lessons applicable to Spenser's poetry can be taken from Harvey's comments. First, the cultural moment in which both men participated can be seen to include already some of the 'naturalism' that only a little later informed the prose of Nashe and the poetry of Donne. Harvey admired Aretino, Machiavelli, and Ariosto for their 'singularity' and irreverent attitudes toward conventions; similar turns toward nature can be found in such French writers as Rabelais, Ronsard, and Montaigne, and perhaps all of these authors contributed to the formation of Spenser's singularity. He registered much that was contemporary and emergent in his culture at the same time that he recalled the past with bookish nostalgia. The relationship of art to nature in his poetry is thoroughly dialectical. Second, and in line with the attitude, 'to all things, Why,' Spenser's poetry does not foreground this questioning as later literature does, but we no longer regard *The Faerie Queene* as a repository of ready-made answers to familiar questions. The genius of his allegory may be that it promotes, by its overdetermined texture, a way of reading that is always putting the question, 'Why?'

The answers Spenser's poetry authorizes aren't always of the sort Harvey would provide; a few glances at the Redcrosse Knight's meeting with Orgoglio will illustrate this. Orgoglio appears like the earth in the leg-pulling part of Harvey's discourse, 'a mightie great huge body' set in motion by 'sundry Accidentall humours, and fumes, and spirites, either good, or bad, or mixte,' and the giant is also open to interpretation as a sign of God's wrath, a judgment earned by Redcrosse's sensuality. Since Book I is full of images from biblical and latter-day apocalyptic literature, it is appropriate to regard Orgoglio's wake-up call in that light. Such a programmatic reading would be incomplete, however, especially if it is undertaken solemnly in search of a univocal and divinely ordained meaning. The guilty attitude toward sexuality that we noted in '*Ad Ornatissimum virum*' comes into play when we see Redcrosse, reunited with Duessa, 'bathe in plesaunce of the ioyous shade' (I vii 4.2); he is soon 'Pourd out in loosnesse on the grassy grownd' (7.2), 'Disarmd, disgrast, and inwardly dismayde' (11.6). While it had been necessary to risk effeminacy for the sake of inspiration, fear of being 'unfit' is at work – and being analysed – here, as in the verse letter to Harvey, on an intimate scale.[45] Within the fiction of *The Faerie Queene*, among what Harvey would call the 'internal' causes of Orgoglio's appearance, the 'material' cause is Redcrosse's sensual fault; both nature and art abhor a vacuum, and the moralized landscape rushes to fill the knight's emptiness.

This meeting had been predicted, and Redcrosse should have been on his guard: when, flushed with his naive triumph over Error, he had asked Archimago 'if he did know / Of straunge adventures, which abroad did pas' (I i 30.3–4), the old man all but gave him Orgoglio's name. Hypocritically denying knowledge 'of warre and worldly trouble' (30.8), he had added slyly,

> But if of daunger which hereby doth dwell,
>   And homebred euill ye desire to heare,
>   Of a straunge man I can you tidings tell,
>   That wasteth all this countrey farre and neare.   (31.1–4)

Even more than the institutional evils of the House of Pride, and on a different plane from the dragon and his minions Archimago and Duessa, this 'homebred euill,' this 'straunge man,' is a shadow of the would-be hero and saint who is also a 'man of earth,' still far from knowing his true nature and destiny.[46] At this point his all-important 'spirit,' from which deeds surpassing ordinary human capacity should spring with the aid of grace, issues only in sexual waste, against which Orgoglio's tumescent pneuma rises as the fundamentally virtuous man's nightmare fantasy.[47] Like Harvey, Spenser is more interested in articulating the natural or internal basis for human actions than in stipulating the external and supernatural causes of events; the apocalyptic dimensions of this episode are anagogical additions to an encounter with 'homebred euill.'

Although Spenser puts images from the Bible and Reformation-era apocalyptic literature to serious use in Book I, in his reluctance to predict the future and read God's will into the present he is just as tough-minded as Harvey.[48] When he ventures to interpret the course of history, he takes advantage of his poem's nostalgic time frame, only predicting what has already happened. Several passages in the poem resemble the procession of heroes interpreted by Anchises for the benefit of Virgil's Augustan audience. The one most pertinent to the present when the 1590 *Faerie Queene* was published was Merlin's explanation of 'the streight course of heauenly destiny' (III iii 24.3), which links Britomart's first unwary glimpse of Artegall in her father's mirror with the eventual reign of 'a royall virgin' (49.6), the Queen, to whom Britomart presents a distant mirror image. But this prophetic moment is not so bright as it is often taken to be.[49]

> But yet the end is not. There *Merlin* stayd,
>   As ouercomen of the spirites powre,
>   Or other ghastly spectacle dismayd,
>   That secretly he saw, yet note discoure: (50.1–4)

Hamilton cites Matt. 24:6, 'but the end is not yet,' a transitional moment in Christ's prophecy of his own end and the end of the world. Spenser's reordering of the words does more than pull them into an iambic rhythm; he *dis*locates the meaning of both 'yet' and 'not,' adding an interpretation of Merlin's stopped speech that makes it impossible to say what he knows. Merlin's speech and silence regarding 'heauenly destiny' may be grounded in principles like Harvey's, but his abruptness is subtly expressive as well. The primary meaning of 'But yet the end is not' remains the same as 'but the end is not yet': England's future will extend beyond Elizabeth, just as Jerusalem's future extended beyond the death of Christ. In Spenser's phrasing, however, 'not' receives an extra stress. The word promises no ending, yet it opens to reveal a closure, unspeakable in 1590: in Elizabeth the Tudor line will end in *naught*, because her virgin *knot* remains inviolate. Some part of the awe-inspiring potential of apocalyptic expectation is turned back upon the present, on the Queen as a mortal person and on the uncertain future of her sovereignty. (Sovereignty may be perpetual in the *aevum*, but it is also subject to unpredictable political processes: see McCabe, *Pillars of Eternity* 127–38.) Spenser represents Merlin as gifted with the supernatural power of prophecy, but he also seems cursed, 'ouercomen' and 'dismayd' as Redcrosse had been by Duessa and Orgoglio (I vii 11.6). The combination of visionary power with extreme vulnerability is also characteristic of the poem's narrator, as we have seen. The next chapter will explore further the paradoxes inherent in his narrative.

chapter two

The World and the Book

I began by considering such indications as we have of Spenser's frame of mind circa 1580, and applying what we can gather from the *Letters* to an illustrative episode in the 1590 *Faerie Queene*. This chapter and the next will present some coordinated ideas about poetry, individual consciousness, and the natural order that constitute a foundation for the kind of poem that *The Faerie Queene* came to be, substantially by 1590, more fully in the 1596 edition of six Books, and definitively with the addition of *Two Cantos of Mutabilitie* in the 1609 folio.

If the conflicts that we witness in Spenser's fictive characters were rooted in his own subjectivity as well as in the culture he was interpreting, we can more readily account for the subtlety with which he portrays moral dilemmas and psychological predicaments, and for the absence of a distinct authorial viewpoint. Some indeterminacy in his own gendered identity is implied in his expressions of sympathy toward feminine as well as masculine characters, and this may account for his readiness to discover sexual politics, or an 'erotic drama,' in topics that another author (Virgil, for example) would regard as asexual (i.e., exclusively male). For Spenser, the order of things seems to be gendered throughout, yet his subjectivity is not rooted in self-assertive masculinity.

Regarded in this light, what Paul Alpers has described as 'the vagueness of the poet's self-definition' gains a new significance, while 'Spenser's failure to maintain a dramatic identity in relation to his poem' seems less a failure than the basis for a unique achievement. Strange as it seems in a poem that proclaims its concern with moral virtues and the active life, 'the condition of [Spenser's] poetry is the abeyance of will' (*Poetry of* The Faerie Queene 332). This paradox remains insufficiently understood. I believe it can be accounted for once *The Faerie Queene* is seen in the light of a concept of the self and its relation to the world that originated with Plato and was elaborately articulated in the Renaissance.

In his progress from 1580 to the 1590 *Faerie Queene*, Spenser moved from self-absorption to an expansive social and political vision, and he composed his narratives of human experience within a cosmological frame of reference. Obedient to the requirements of genre, he shifted from the ab ovo projections of his verse letter to externally oriented in medias res narratives of deeds accomplished. (Embedded within the narrative, however, are several characters' stories which are ab ovo accounts of love and loss: I am thinking primarily of Arthur's and Scudamour's accounts of falling in love.)[1] In the process of developing his theme-centred 'Legendes,' Spenser turned from inner uncertainties to external principles of vitality and order, against which the stories of his characters are played out episodically. His interpretation of the principles governing human life involves the delineation of several myths of origin. A subjective element remains, of course, and it is emphatically voiced by the narrator at many points, usually to stress that although his characters belong to antiquity, their stories are still unfolding. So, however, are history and nature, his great coordinates, so the poem's open-endedness isn't simply an index of the poet's subjectivity.

At the end of the previous chapter, reflecting on the evidence that Orgoglio represents simultaneously an aspect of Redcrosse's decadent inner nature and a frightening, obscurely admonitory event in the elemental world that fell with Adam, I proposed that Spenser's narrative should be understood as an anatomy of the instrumental causes that account for morally significant behaviour. Threats and temptations, features of the moralized landscape placed in the way of Spenser's characters, figure in an interpretive dialogue which is sometimes reducible to that of the mind (or, in Spenser's usage, the 'spright') with itself. In other situations, he shows us what happens when an individual encounters the limitations placed upon consciousness by the external world. Part of my agenda in this chapter and the next will be to account for the ideology and habits of mind that enabled Spenser to conceive the individual's inner nature and the natural world so subtly and systematically in terms of one another.

One essential characteristic of Spenser's fiction is that the boundaries distinguishing external reality from fantasies projected by fear and desire are permeable, just as the differences between nature and culture are indistinct. Sidney's distinction between the 'brazen' world (fallen nature and history) and the 'golden' realm accessible to the poet was useful to Spenser. The fictive world of *The Faerie Queene* is not wholly 'golden,' but what it tells us of the fallen world – which remains the actual subject of poetry for both Sidney and Spenser – is provided under the aegis of 'what may be and should be.' Sidney's conception of fiction as a 'second' nature, and of the process by which the poet brings it into being, illustrates how nature and culture are dynamically related: his 'right poet' is the re-creator of the best that culture has to offer because he is less confined than the exponents of other arts to what nature has given, 'when with the force of a divine breath he bringeth things forth far surpassing her doings' (*AP* 101.19–21), drawing upon Ideas that he regards as superior to the phenomenal world.

To the extent that the poet's images are '*eikastike*, which some learned have defined, "figuring forth good things,"' they manifest the ideal order of nature as the basis of culture. In an important concession, however, Sidney admits 'that man's wit may make Poesy ... to be *phantastike*, which doth contrariwise infect the fancy with unworthy objects' (*AP* 125.24–7), and in this case we are caught up in the brazen world of nature, debased rather than perfected by culture. Sidney's theory finesses the fact that in practice he was as much involved in representing the folly and the tragic potential of fancies infected with unworthy objects as he was in figuring forth good things. Both *Astrophil and Stella* and the *Arcadia* show how difficult it is to distinguish between truly 'good things' and those that only seem so under the influence of an 'infected will.' The fabric of Spenser's fiction is as labyrinthine as Sidney's, and his mixture of fantastic with eikastic images isn't self-explanatory, even though readers are usually given an edge over his characters.

More than Sidney had allowed, Spenser's fundamentally secular discourse intrudes upon the sacred domain of religious authorities; similarly, he makes more than Sidney had of the ancient image of the poet as *vates*, an inspired visionary in the line descending from Orpheus. I regard this as a move to ground his ambitious enterprise in something more reliable than fiction, but he only looks in the direction that Milton took, offering a faith in the harmony of secular and sacred domains that Milton in his maturity tended to discredit.

Recognizing Spenser as more sage and serious than Sidney, we should nonetheless remember from his verse letter to Harvey his endorsement of folly and his confusion in the domain of Love. The Erasmian motto *Serio ludere* describes a commitment to discourse that is a tissue of contradictions, suited to the conditions found by humanists in courtly society. Seriousness is apparent enough on the surface of Spenser's poem, but it is not unalloyed, and the poet seldom seems to be taking *himself* too seriously. Relying extensively on myth and other matter derived from the classical tradition, and mixing classical lore freely with an artificially medieval Christianity, Spenser took risks and incurred disfavour in a court that rewarded insincerity but had not learned to distinguish fiction from lying. In Spenser's allegory, didactic as it is, a ludic impulse complicates the 'darke conceit,' extending the range of Truth's implications. The poet's inventive hand is to be seen in all that has 'chanced' and 'fortuned,' but nothing is entirely 'authorized.'[2]

Does *The Faerie Queene* refer, then, to nothing definite beyond itself? I approach the 1580 *Letters* as a 'hermetic' text, marked by the kind of rhetoric Jonathan Crewe has termed 'unredeemed.' Spenser's progress with his heroic poem required a firmer grip, experientially and conceptually, on a stable order of things beyond the self and its discourse. It seems that the social order didn't provide this stability: Spenser's position within society was marginal and vulnerable, and in the years between 1580 and 1588, critical to the development of his poem, most of the leaders in the courtly faction that had gathered around Leicester and Sidney died unexpectedly, dashing most of the poet's political hopes. I also believe that the extent to which Spenser worshipped power has been exaggerated: he stood in awe of the Queen's sovereignty, and at times he was a cheerleader for the use of force, but even the early years of his experience in Ireland gave him lessons in the powerlessness of some claims to sovereignty. To the extent that power was, under Queen Elizabeth, always already aestheticized and naturalized, it was presumably appealing to Spenser, but he also saw that it was not being translated faithfully into just and effective policies – nor is his poem coherent in its political dimension.

I think that Spenser found the rationale – the 'supreme fiction' of my title – that he needed for his poem's structure in Sidney's teaching that the 'right poet' possesses and communicates access to 'another nature,' because 'he goeth hand in hand with Nature, not enclosed within the narrow warrant of her gifts, but freely ranging only within the zodiac of his own wit' (*AP* 100.21–8). Arguably, this poetical zodiac reconstitutes the one that the soul tours, according to Plato's myth in the *Phaedrus* (247B-8C), before being plunged into forgetfulness and mortality. Sidney's allusive language is appropriate to the subjective source and the cosmic scope of Spenser's poem, and his emphasis on the poet's command of 'that *Idea* or fore-conceit of the work' (*AP* 101.4) finds a basis for fiction in the Platonists' epistemology and logic.[3]

Spenser's meditations on the interplay of nature and art (the Renaissance term) or culture (our rough equivalent) are not confined to the hall of mirrors suggested by Harry Berger's comment on 'the pastoral paradox that *nature* is really a synonym for *art*' (*Revisionary Play* 325). His basic distinctions between one term and the other are not those that come readily to us. We tend to think of nature as everything outside of culture; we have watched the accelerating assault on nature by technology, accomplishing some things on purpose and others by accident, and we have also seen nature consumed as art assimilates 'non-art.' The more reasons we find to distrust human nature and the capacity of culture to protect us from ourselves, the more we value nature as something Other, but anything we value cannot remain Other very long. Our art, meanwhile, in its flight from the familiar, often mimes an Otherness we do not find in nature. Nature, therefore, seems on its way to becoming an empty set within our culture, and such preconceptions don't help us to read Spenser.

We can proceed by way of analogies, which I take to have been the basis for all of Spenser's habits of mind. Something like our disillusioned understanding of the dynamics of culture and nature was available to him in an understanding of 'fallenness.' The effects of original sin upon human nature and its environment were construed variously, as were the possibilities for restoring order and harmony through the agencies of reason and divine grace. The grosser manifestations of fallen nature were regarded as 'unnatural,' and much of culture was suspect because of the pervasive effects of original sin upon human behaviour, influenced both by what St Paul had termed the 'law in our members' and by the dominion of St Augustine's 'earthly city,' the dwelling place of suffering humanity throughout history. Orgoglio and his castle represent this syndicate of natural and cultural evils, as do other characters and places.[4]

Nature and Myth

The many large issues that the concepts of nature, art, and grace have been deployed to interpret will come up at several points in subsequent chapters, and I will have occasion to flesh out, from Spenser's poem and texts pertinent to it, a range of meanings for these and other problematic terms. Here it will suffice to illustrate some of the ways in which the poem's action is grounded in nature. The moralized landscape out of which Orgoglio emerges is a testing ground for the rational will and intellect, for potentialities of which poet, characters, and readers 'partake' (to use a word of which Spenser is fond). Orgoglio is a figure for man's primal sin and its consequences in body and spirit, but he is also represented as a product of the world that fell into disorder with Adam, a world that remained menacing and mysterious, a ghastly scene in which natural events and supernatural warning signs could not be readily distinguished. The inner human world, another aspect of nature, could be equally frightening, equally closed to conclusive rational inquiry and control. Perhaps it was the otherness of this interior that gave rise, at an early stage of the inward turn that Western culture took during the Renaissance, to pervasive and various ways of situating the individual before a mirror. The mirror could be an emblem of prudence as well as vanity; in prudent use, providing consoling companionship in solitude, the mirror might be constituted by scripture, nature, a friend or beloved conceived as a better or a complementary self, or some text interpreting the negotiations of an incomplete identity with these mirroring entities.[5] *The Faerie Queene* is such a text. It submits fears and their mysterious sources, resident or vagrant in Elizabethan culture, to management by reason and imagination, without evading the fact that reason and imagination themselves may be driven by fears.

The Faerie Queene borrows some of its authority from religion, and by using religious discourse metaphorically it tends to confer on secular matters the kind of sanctity that had been at the disposal of religious authorities. Some Renaissance princes – Henry VIII and his daughter Elizabeth among them – claimed prerogatives that blurred the distinction between secular and sacred forms of authority, and Spenser voices support for such claims to sovereignty, but he also asserts his own claims as a presumptive 'prince of poets.' To the categories of mystery and miracle, he prefers a domain that was still emerging during his century as specifically poetic or aesthetic, 'the marvellous.' This is Sidney's 'golden' world, where the poet 'goeth hand in hand with Nature' (*AP* 100.26–7). It only verges upon the heavenly matters in which revelation and its ordained interpreters are our only reliable guides, and for this reason, I think, Spenser is as reticent as Harvey had been, 'definitiuely to giue sentence of his Maiesties secret and inscrutable purposes.' The poet may go hand in hand with *natura naturans*, but his God is characteristically the 'Workmaister' whose purposes are 'commonly performed,' as Harvey had put it, 'by the qualifying, and conforming of Nature, and Naturall things, to the accomplishment of his Diuine and incomprehensible determination' (*Prose* 454). Understood in these terms, God is not a jealous figure whose wrath or glory is always being manifested, but the ultimate ground for meaning that remains 'clowdily enwrapped.' Accordingly, Spenser refers the course of many events in his poem to fate and even more to fortune, and he rarely invokes Providence.

Similarly, and for similar reasons, Spenser is reticent with regard to the representation of secular authority. He avoids overt competition with sovereign power, but compliments it and puts its language to his own uses, just as he uses the language of religious devotion metaphorically. The supreme and central figure for political sovereignty, Gloriana, is made conspicuous by her absence from the poem, although she is, in her symbolic person and her sovereignty, ever-present as the poem's all-implying 'final cause,' and therefore its ultimate subject. Spenser's own subject position, with little status outside his poem, shows in the tissue of fictions and feints through which Gloriana is represented as the manifestation of Elizabeth's public person, while her presence is kept private; she is known through the desire of various knights to see her and be worthy of her grace. Spenser aspired to be a public poet as well as a civil servant, and with *The Faerie Queene* in 1590 he became the first of his kind in the eyes of such readers as he found. Paradoxically, however, in spite of his accomplishments he was neither in nor of the court, and it is not clear that he ever wished to be anything but the visitor he represents in *Colin Clouts Come Home Againe.* He had reason to fear hypocrisy, hostility, and misprision in the upper reaches of the society he sought to enter, to praise, and ultimately to judge.

On what grounds, by what standards, could he offer judgment? For a man of his Protestant convictions, considering the interests of the audience he sought, religious traditions and the moral philosophy of the humanists offered grounds for criticism of power and political expediency, but we don't think of Spenser only as 'a better teacher than either Scotus or Aquinas,' and he took from ancient literature more than its moral messages. He continued to present himself as Colin Clout, and the pastoral domain where he had first organized his reforming and recreative impulses remained his imaginary home. In his heroic poem he had scope for representing much more of the natural order than would fit in his *Calender*; the Orphic matters he found in Virgil's *Georgics* could be incorporated, along with the still greater philosophical themes of the *Aeneid*. For a pastoral poet, and a poet of Spenser's erudition, nature stands over against the city and the court. I will be arguing that his vision of the natural order as more fundamental and stable than the Tudor political regime provided grounds for claims to poetic sovereignty in a poem that makes Elizabeth's rule his subject. Spenser's allegory often constructs the Queen as a sovereign to whom the poet is beholden for such limited authority as he enjoys, but on many occasions he looks above and beyond the Queen for aid. He finds it in Nature personified, most often in the figure of *alma Venus*, to whom he gives a character with political significance chiefly because, unlike Virgil's Venus, she lacks political interests. In the Garden of Adonis canto and related passages elsewhere, Spenser puts the figure of Venus forward not to mimic the Queen's sovereignty, as Susanne Wofford has said,[6] but to rise above political claims, presiding over 'all things, that are borne to liue and die' (III vi 30.5) with a more generous sovereignty than either Elizabeth Tudor or Gloriana could display.

When he reaches to include in his poem a cosmos larger than Elizabeth's *imperium*, Spenser remains committed to a political agenda, but he shows his allegiance to intellectual traditions much older than the forms of nationhood and autocratic rule that took shape during the sixteenth century. In medieval religious tradition, nature was taken to be a book corroborating the biblical revelation of God's goodness. The manifold cultural changes accompanying the emergence of a more scientific attitude had not, by Spenser's day, discredited this attitude, but they had revealed its fictive character, rendering it hypothetical and hence more useful to poets. By the later sixteenth century it was evident to most learned men that, if God had written upon the world, His language could be deciphered only by conjecture. Not that that stopped men from talking: there was so much to comment upon, and the more books there were, the less sacred they became. Depending on one's viewpoint (Agrippa's, say, or Sidney's), their interpretations either turned what had been truth into fictions, or demonstrated the power of fictions to imply the truth.

Spenser is one of the great myth-makers among English poets, and not only one of them, but almost the first.[7] He had to be, in order to write a poem with the scope he set for himself on a level above that of *The Pastime of Pleasure* and similar didactic books. His cultural circumstances favoured myth-making, although they didn't render it as natural as breathing. Spenser's importance in the tradition that includes Milton, Blake, Keats, Shelley, Tennyson, and Yeats rests as much on his daring mythopoesis as on his mastery of poetic language and forms. The fertility of his narrative inventions is informed by fundamental mythic patterns; such patterns also shape his presentation of ideas derived from such philosophers as Plato and Ficino.

It is remarkable that this should be so. Of course, Spenser would not have been participating in Renaissance culture, nor would he have been a worthy successor to Dante and Chaucer, if he had not made himself capable of wielding effectively the mythological lore that is evident in the classical canon. But Homer, Virgil, and Ovid could be his models only in limited ways.[8] In form and manner he did not imitate the ancients to the extent that Milton did, and to the extent that he patterned his poetry after medieval allegory and Ariostan romance, mythology would seem appropriate only as decoration. Apart from such decorative uses, both mythological lore and the more serious matter of 'myth'[9] would seem to have been shut away from Spenser's imagination behind two screens. The first, for him, was Protestant Christianity, which held pagan traditions at arm's length; the second was the classical tradition itself. As Brooks Otis has shown, the epic had been obsolete for some time when Virgil began to write, largely because the mythical subject matter which, since Homer, had been considered the defining characteristic of the epic was no longer accessible on Homer's terms, or even on Hesiod's.[10] D.C. Allen's aperçu describes a process that began within Hellenic culture and was completed by the triumph of Christianity: 'Actually, the gods were turning into metaphors' (*Mysteriously Meant* 1). As W.R. Johnson reads the *Aeneid*, Virgil's revitalization of the Homeric epic involved creation of a kind of allegory to accommodate his ambivalence toward the stuff of myths (*Darkness Visible* 16–22).

As the heir to these developments, how did Spenser get below the surface of mythology to the mythic matter? The manner of the gods' demise, as Allen's and other studies have helped us to see,[11] made it possible for them to be reborn in new forms, but it did not guarantee that they would regain any of their archaic power. More often than not, both in allegorizations of classical texts and handbook interpretations of their divinities' significance, and also in later poets' use of the allegorical tradition, metaphors remained flowers of rhetoric, with little poetic vitality and no claim to a bearing on reality beyond the immediate poetic context. Mythology is decorative in *The Faerie Queene*, but decorative details in the poem often pertain to large patterns and deep structures: Spenser understood the derivation of 'cosmetic' from 'cosmic.'[12] As noted in my Introduction, there is an important truth in Alastair Fowler's reference to 'the strain of cosmogonic myth running through the poem,' which he finds linked with 'a metaphysic of love' (*Spenser and the Numbers of Time* 213). Perhaps the interest Spenser shows in Ceres, 'the grieving goddess,' in his verse letter to Harvey, hints at this: Demeter/Ceres and Persephone/Proserpina, central figures in the Eleusinian mysteries, provide the theme for one type of cosmogonic myth, and appear in various guises throughout *The Faerie Queene*.[13]

The example of Virgil helped Spenser to see how myth and the heroic poem might together be revitalized, although only he would have undertaken to rebuild Virgilian epic within Ariostan romance, the very form that had brilliantly called the serious tradition into question. Ovid's example helped too; it is clear that for Spenser, Ovid's poetry was more than a trove of classical poet-lore and an example of the 'conceited' style. But the tertium quid for Spenser, I believe, was an interpretive tradition within which the stories of the pagan gods contained not only useful morals and obscure renderings of great deeds done in the distant past, but an ancient wisdom regarding the origins, structure, and destiny of the cosmos and humanity, with the inner world of passions and mental faculties understood analogically as a microcosm. The fact that this wisdom had been expressed figuratively must have rendered it more accessible to a poet predisposed to allegory. In many ancient and later texts, some of which we recognize as literary, some as philosophical, Spenser found figurative discourse he could appropriate to his own uses.

'The whole circle or compasse of Learning'

Even in its incomplete state, *The Faerie Queene* is an encyclopedic poem that enfolds in its capacious fiction not only the great and varied repertoire of literary materials and ornaments we would expect from the 'poet's poet,' but symbols and discourse in which lore of all the other arts pertinent to 'self-fashioning' is reduced to poetic form. I will argue that the encyclopedic character of *The Faerie Queene* is not an accidental property of its scope and variety as a narrative, but fundamental to the poet's program: its content and design declare the Renaissance ideal of an *enkyklios paideia* or *orbis doctrinae*, that ordering of the arts described by Quintilian and developed by Renaissance men of letters into an educational program embracing all the arts and sciences.[14] The encyclopedic character of *The Faerie Queene* is nowhere more obvious than in the various set pieces that are concerned with the order of nature; they provide the reader with both a cosmos and a cosmology. In the Garden of Adonis canto (*FQ* III vi), the three cantos at the end of Book IV, and the *Two Cantos of Mutabilitie*, and in related threads of narrative and imagery dispersed throughout the poem, Spenser evokes the diversity of the created world; represents the relationship of human nature, moral virtue, and poetic imagination to the natural order; and reveals the means by which everything in nature is endowed with form and vitality.

We expect some of this material in a Renaissance epic, but it is remarkable that a poem which is not hexameral but heroic deals so extensively and profoundly with the dynamics of creation and the occult source and destiny 'Of all things, that are borne to liue and die' (III vi 30.5). It is not immediately clear how this kind of knowledge is related to 'virtuous and gentle discipline' of the rational will. I will argue that Spenser sought, through his representation of the order and processes of nature, to engender an awareness that, ideally considered, God's creation and mankind's culture are harmonious, and any disunity or fragmentation that we experience constitutes a departure from origins and ends that remain meaningful.[15] This design, which contributes to education of the will through appeals to the imagination and affections, enfolds and complements Spenser's more explicit and practical attention to the moral virtues in narratives of chivalric action.

If *The Faerie Queene* is not only an allegorical heroic poem but a fictive representation of the *enkyklios paideia*, and if as I have suggested the comprehensiveness of Spenser's subject matter is keyed to his representation of the cosmos with humanity at its centre, we are encouraged if not obliged to treat the poem in its entirety as a 'heterocosm,' a 'second nature' whose creator resembles the God of Genesis or the Demiurge of the *Timaeus*.[16] Such a position requires some defence and clarification. Many years ago, Paul Alpers argued strenuously that we should view the poem 'as a continual address to the reader rather than as a fictional world,'[17] and some of the best criticism published since Alpers's book has followed his example, bringing to light small-scale subtleties and large-scale complexities in *The Faerie Queene* which tend to invalidate a view of it as a heterocosm, structurally sound and referentially serious.

Spenser's poem will resemble the kind of heterocosm familiar to us from modern imaginative literature and poetics only to the extent that his world view and poetics happen to resemble modern attitudes. While there are some salient similarities,[18] not to recognize and interpret fundamental differences is as reductive as isolating Spenser in an imaginary time frame labelled 'Elizabethan.' Any Renaissance creator of a fictive 'second world' would be wary of rivalling God, and if he offered in his fiction an escape from or triumph over the world, such a manoeuver served as the means to a moral end outside the poem, not as access to an ivory tower that is modelled within the text. Unlike more modern poems ('Kubla Khan' and 'Sailing to Byzantium,' for example), Spenser's fiction is neither radically subjective nor endowed with a closed structure. It is a book that embraces the world; it is open, indefinite, and mediatory, pointing toward experience and action, and also toward normative ideas, known and examined through the fiction but not themselves felt to be fictitious.

In the introduction I quoted C.S. Lewis's observation that *The Faerie Queene* is 'like life itself, not like the products of life.' If we regard

Spenser's poem as *natura naturans* artfully interpreted, at its most basic level it is like life itself as the Elizabethans most valued it, for what was their culture but a tissue of fictions? Whether we view that culture nostalgically or in recognition of its falsifications and evasions, it responds to all that we know about the importance of the play impulse and the cultural utility of large-scale fictions.[19] The more sensitive we become to the sophisticated, detached, playful side of Spenser's genius, the more likely it seems that he was alert to the fictions pervading Elizabethan courtly culture. Both his life and his poems tell us that Spenser participated in that culture so far as his opportunities allowed, and he was capable of wholehearted devotion to its ideals. When he felt disillusionment or disgust he did not trace it, as a modern would, to the collapse of such inventions as Elizabethan chivalry, the Imperial Virgin, the Muses of poetry and the other arts, or the Platonic/Ptolemaic cosmology, but to the predictable failures of fallen men in a fallen world.

I have suggested that for Spenser the world and his book were both mirrors. A number of principles made possible the acts of faith and imagination by which the world and a secular fiction could be conceived as analogous in this way.[20] First, if the natural world is regarded as the Book of Creation, linked by obscure analogies and a providential design to the Book of God's Word and the course of human destiny, then everything participates in both fiction and truth. The signatures impressed upon all things by their Maker could be said to resemble the meanings given to words in an allegorical poem; even though God's language was lost to mankind after Babel, its meaning was not entirely lost in translation, however much it might be complicated in the divagations of learned commentaries. Efforts to recover the magically powerful language spoken in the world's making flourished during the sixteenth century with Christian interest in kabbalism; the industry of John Dee brought this lore and its promises of adept insight into the cosmos to circles with which Spenser was familiar.[21] An intelligent reader of the world will be curious and critical; if the latent content of creation is unregarded or misunderstood, it is not a book but a false paradise or a prison house where one is held by sinister spells, sentenced to a living death. Many episodes in *The Faerie Queene*, beginning with the experience of Redcrosse and his companions in the Wandering Wood, teach this lesson; they instruct us simultaneously in reading a poem and living in the world.[22]

In the course of the Renaissance, thoughtful people witnessed both the advancement of all forms of learning and a simultaneous increase in uncertainty; the more people learned, the more reason they had to treat human knowledge as 'artificial,' dependent on conventions rather than reality. Impatience with an imprecise, analogical knowledge of nature and the secular aspect of life was not common until the seventeenth century. From Petrarch to Casaubon, humanists were much concerned to root out vanity, deception, error, misplaced certainty, and superstition from the fields of the arts and sciences, but they were not dedicated to the ideals of certainty and uniformity except in matters touching religion, and even there many were tolerant or non-committal. They were moved as much by the play impulse as by a desire to separate truth from falsehood: for an idea or a system to be worth entertaining, its plausibility, internal consistency, and claim to antiquity would be evidence of its truth value. Serious, silly, dubious, even dangerous ideas might all be held together in suspension, in a hypothetical or conjectural argument, open to doubt but not to disproof.

Within the limits of Spenser's lifetime, then, unless religious doctrine or discipline was at issue it mattered to very few that the facts of life as they were generally understood were permeated with fictions. Philosophy and scientific thought had, therefore, much in common with poetry. (As we saw in the previous chapter, Agrippa had noted this; it remains unclear whether his alarm was genuine or rhetorical.) Logic and method appear to have dominated intellectual life in the Renaissance, but it is now clear that their operations were governed by aesthetic considerations and other anthropocentric factors, identified by Sir Francis Bacon as 'Idols' only at the end of the Elizabethan era. The world of the humanists was word-centred, and even though an order made of words could only approximate the order of the world, to be *dulce et utile* sufficed for most purposes, independent of criteria for truth. The nature of this world view may be clarified by comparison to that of the new science which emerged in the seventeenth century. For Galileo the world is still a book, but it 'is written in a mathematical language, and the characters are triangles, circles, and other geometrical figures,' which only the scientist trained in mathematics can comprehend.[23]

Historians of science, philosophy, and political institutions may deplore the prevalence of fictions in the culture of the later sixteenth century, but a literary historian may regard the Elizabethans' counter-factual constructs as characteristics of a culture responding to changes in the dimensions of experience with extraordinary creative energy. Perhaps the strongest motive of the Renaissance mind was a rage for order, a love of complex structures. In all the arts and sciences this impulse was manifest not only in the assumption that reality must in itself be structured, but in incessant attempts to depict both the structures of reality and the mind's intellectual mastery of them, in their full extent from the throne of God to the depths of Chaos. The impulse itself was not new, but I think it will be granted that a widespread disinclination to accept inherited structures on faith was new in the Renaissance, and that no earlier period had been more productive of different structures, sometimes competing with and sometimes completing one another.[24]

Did this structuring make for life, by encouraging the mind to play freely over a mapped terrain, already claimed as an extension of human nature and evidence of its centrality? Or did it tend to overdetermine experience, by ignoring much of its unruly potentiality or introducing a spurious complexity? *The Faerie Queene*, both elaborately organized and an open form, 'vnperfite' by design, suggests that Spenser's answer to this brace of loaded questions would be a twofold 'Yes.' His poem contains – to borrow a metaphor from modern cosmologists – both 'strong' and 'weak' forces, signs of dynamic vitality and of entropic stasis.

Spenser brought a deep and abiding interest, but no naive or pedantic attachment, to several of the kinds of learning by which the Renaissance world was structured: dialogues and other loose-knit discourse, systematic theology and philosophy, cosmology, astrology, mythology, numerology, analyses of human nature into faculties and humours, moral philosophy in the traditions stemming from Aristotle and the schemes of virtues, and history considered both in narrative terms (as by Livy and Holinshed) and theoretically (as by Machiavelli and Bodin). As I read it his poem offers abundant evidence of different kinds of structure, and it is also responsive to the complexities and spontaneous life that render structures only provisionally useful. In all of this, the poem is a mirror of its author's mind and its furniture, so the terms in which we describe Spenser's learning and intelligence and what we find in the text have much to do with one another: he is masked within his work rather than presiding mightily over it.

The Poem as Heterocosm

Paul Alpers has remarked that as we read *The Faerie Queene* we accept as compatible what in the abstract seem conflicting aspects of the poet's mind, 'because of the wholehearted and untroubled way in which Spenser treats truths as having an existence external to him.'[25] But the various truths Spenser invokes and portrays, with an ease that looks at times like carelessness, sometimes are at odds with one another. In the light of today's scholarship, can we maintain that Spenser (as he presents himself in *The Faerie Queene*) was consistently, or even typically, 'wholehearted and untroubled'? Perhaps the fabric of his fiction is such that it partially conceals problems in its subject matter, using the veils of allegory and romance as a panoply of defences against disorder and anxiety, and seldom trying to transcend 'this state of life so tickle' (*Cantos* viii 1.6).

We shouldn't expect *The Faerie Queene* to be the free-standing product of an Olympian intellect; our emphasis should fall on the poet's 'making' as a process, and on passages in the poem which exhibit and explain that process. Such an approach requires doubling back upon Alpers's argument that we should regard the poem 'as a continual address to the reader rather than as a fictional world.' This rhetorical model allows for changes and inconsistencies from moment to moment, but it is apt to trade complexities of depth and design for the immediate appeal of brilliant local effects. In my view, Alpers's argument is founded on a false dichotomy. I have been arguing that Spenser experienced the world around him 'as a continual address to the reader.' Thanks to Alpers and the critics who have learned from him, we can stand at some distance from the formalist and theme-ridden criticism to which his close reading was an appropriate response, but we can also step back from some of his critiques: they now appear implicated in a reductive attitude resembling what he targets for criticism. Alpers rightly objects to readings that construe *The Faerie Queene* as a world with a definitive structure which all readings should aspire to comprehend, but any argument that promulgates 'rules for reading' may be counterproductive.

The notion that works of art constitute figurative worlds has now been freed from formalist assumptions and put on a better philosophical foundation.[26] It may be useful to regard Spenser's fiction as 'worldmaking' rather than a 'world,' if the latter term still implies a finished cosmos that is mapped for us in the poet's articulate design. I agree with Alpers that 'the most serious limitation of *The Faerie Queene* when we compare it to the *Divine Comedy* or *Paradise Lost* is the absence of the deep organizing structures that arise from and in turn give life to individual parts' (*Poetry of* The Faerie Queene 332). Organizing structures are important and elaborate in Spenser's poem, but they are less explicit, and the ground traversed by the narrative is flatter, than what Dante and Milton provide in their differently organized accounts of creation, damnation, and redemption. 'Worldmaking' is the term used by Nelson Goodman in his account of ancient and modern attempts, in various disciplines and through figurative as well as literal means, to create satisfactory versions of experience in some 'actual' world. In his way of thinking, 'many different world-versions are of independent interest and importance, without any requirement or presumption of reducibility to a single base' (*Ways of Worldmaking* 4).

Since 'knowing cannot be exclusively or even primarily a matter of determining what is true' (*Ways of Worldmaking* 21), Goodman argues that 'a statement is true, and a description or representation right, for a world it fits. And a fictional version, verbal or pictorial, may if metaphorically construed fit and be right for a world.' He proposes that 'truth' should be subsumed 'under the general notion of rightness of fit' (132). Goodman's principle is applicable to less than the full extent of Spenser's poem: it sorts awkwardly with the figure of Una, but would make sense in a commentary on the way out of the Wandering Wood. 'That path ... which beaten was most plaine' (*FQ* I i 28.3) can be construed variously, to fit different responses to the poem, as tradition, orthodoxy, the way of Truth (though the erroneous way *into* the Wood seems to be the same path), the 'Elizabethan settlement' in ecclesiastical polity, the Anglican via media, righteousness, or (in Hamilton's note on this stanza, citing Deut. 5.32–3) 'all the wayes which the Lord your God hath commanded you.' Spenser personifies in Una a transcendental and ineffable Truth, and other characters are similarly ineffable at times. I believe it would be an error to reduce the meaning of such figures to fit the poem's world of becoming and the paths on which its quests and errors slowly take shape, but other readers may find such a belief unwarranted. A critical commentary on 'the truth about Una' would be something of indeterminate length and contents, and it could never account definitively for all the ways in which Una's various appearances fit both the poem and the contexts from which it takes its meaning.[27] Regarded in retrospect, Una appears to be more than the sum of her partial revelations, but as we read, Truth is inseparable from the paths she travels; we are given clues to her mysterious nature only gradually. The world of the poem contains, then, phenomena that resist the ways of reading in which it instructs us.

Ways of Worldmaking explores the extent to which we still depend on a kind of mythology, and on deductive rather than inductive reasoning, shaping facts and what we call truth to fit the world, or the plurality of worlds for different parts of our lives, to which self-interest and habit direct our attention. We have seen how useful, but how limited in its scope, inductive reasoning is: it can never take us to things in themselves, unshaped by any theory. 'We are confined to ways of describing whatever is described. Our universe, so to speak, consists of these ways rather than of a world or of worlds ... Worldmaking as we know it always starts from worlds already on hand; the making is a remaking' (*Ways of Worldmaking*

3, 6). Such insights may establish for us a distant kinship with Spenser, who was innocent of Bacon's schemes for an eventual mastery of reality through inductive reasoning, and who had a humanist's tentative faith in the efficacy of worlds that could be constructed out of authorities and experience.

The scope of Spenser's poem is such that readers will always be discovering new ways to claim that it is basically unified, that it lacks unity, or that its essence is a tolerance for differences irreducible to any totalizing form. *The Faerie Queene* is a matrix within which many aesthetic principles can be tested and many tastes can be satisfied. To say that it lacks the structure we find in *Paradise Lost* is not to show that it lacks a structure appropriate to the poet's agenda. Recognizing that at the end of the sixteenth century the world's boundaries were in flux – with many changes being suggested and not yet completed by exploration, cosmological speculation, political conflict, commerce, and colonization – we shouldn't expect any extensive fictional world to possess a readily perceptible structure, or a clearly defined relationship to the actual world.[28] But *something*, we would have to agree, resulted from the formal possibilities and problems inherent in the romance tradition, and in the other discourses that Spenser combined with Ariostan romance in his generic hybrid. If what we have of his poem is, as a narrative, less complete than *Orlando Furioso*, it is in other respects more rationally organized and finely articulated.

In both what he preserved of Ariostan romance and what he added to it, Spenser was a man of his time. The structural principles and weaknesses of *The Faerie Queene* can be understood in terms of principles developed to explain mannerism. John Shearman has written brilliantly on the formal consequences of 'the exaggerated pursuit of variety (prompted, no doubt, by the exceptional opportunities for boredom in the courtier's life) that is so essential a feature in the cultural background of mannerism.'[29] In the decorative arts, painting, sculpture, architecture and the planning of gardens, and in poems such as *Orlando Furioso* (whose greatest popularity coincided precisely with mannerism), interest in variety sometimes involved the sacrifice of unity, but in the most successful works in this style, the consequence is not confusion, but unity 'of a special kind compatible with variety and its consequences, *meraviglie* and elaborate detail' (*Mannerism* 149).

Spenser rejects the excesses inherent in mannerism when he describes the Bower of Bliss, but first he exploits the aesthetic possibilities of that style to the fullest, and Guyon's mixture of curiosity and fury invites a detached, recursive reading consistent with mannerist aesthetics. The structural patterns that emerge from *The Faerie Queene* are analogous in effect to some of the architectural designs discussed by Shearman. Shearman says, for instance, of Giulio Romano's Palazzo del Te, that 'the variety in Giulio's *meraviglie* is cumulative, quantitative, and to be appreciated in the act of perambulation; the building has no structural unity, and it can never in fact be seen as a whole' (145). He draws a distinction between the mannerist and the baroque garden in these terms: 'The former is not usually to be grasped as a unity, nothing predominates, and there is no dramatic focus ... The successive, cumulative impression is more important than the immediate – the grand vista' (125).

These statements harmonize well with the ways of reading Spenser we have learned from Alpers and Berger. If mannerist works of art generally do not attempt to promote a sense of each part's relation to a larger unity, they do not lack devices which relate parts to one another. Shearman provides a perfect architectural analogy for Spenser's kind of structure: 'Vignola ... showed a splendid sense of theatre when he aligned the steps and grottoes of the Farnese Gardens on the Palatine with the great arches of the Basilica of Maxentius across the Forum; but it is a relationship that is appreciable only on an intellectual level, for he did not give us any point from which the elements may be seen in this dramatic conjunction, as a Baroque artist would have done. It is no more than an ingenious "point" that one notices in a succession of ingenuities.'[30] Intellectual appreciation – detached interest in the intricacies and the basic intelligibility of life – is the attitude Spenser's poetry most encourages.

The career of Torquato Tasso began in the heyday of Italian mannerism and extended across years in which tastes changed; fashions in painting, sculpture, and architecture turned to what would be called 'baroque,' and in poetry, Tasso's *Gerusalemme Liberata* led the way in this direction. His *Discorsi del Poema Eroico*, first published in 1594, would not have come into Spenser's hands opportunely, as Tasso's heroic poem apparently did soon after its publication, with a decisive effect on the organization of *The Faerie Queene*, but much of Tasso's amalgam of Italian and ancient ideas about poetry must have been known to Spenser independently. A well-known passage in the *Discorsi* calls for brief discussion, because it is an eloquent statement of ideas that I believe were important to Spenser.

In the course of comments on variety and unity, two coordinate characteristics of the heroic poem, Tasso develops an elaborate analogy between 'this marvellous domain of God called the world' and the fictive world which the poet creates in imitation of God. God's creation is full of variety, 'yet for all this, the world that contains in its womb [*grembo*] so many diverse things is one, its form and essence one, and one the bond [*nodo*] that links its many parts and ties them together in discordant concord.' The poet can be called 'divine' because, 'as he resembles the supreme Artificer in his workings he comes to participate in his divinity,' when he reflects in his poem the variety and the balance of opposing forces, contrasting emotions, and changing fortunes which we see in the world. Having glorified variety, Tasso ends by asserting that a poem, like the world, must be unified: 'Yet the poem that contains so great a variety of matters none the less should be one, one in form and soul.'[31]

It is not surprising that Tasso affirms the unity of creation, but the metaphors he uses are noteworthy: the world extending to the stars has a 'womb,' a single generative centre, and its parts are joined in a single 'bond.' These terms can be paralleled in Spenser's reference to 'the wide wombe of the world' (FQ III vi 36.6), and in Ficino's frequent use of the term 'vinculum,' referring sometimes to the anima mundi, sometimes to Amor, sometimes to human nature as the epitome of creation. As we will see more clearly through Ficino's exposition of ideas from the Timaeus and The Symposium, a figurative affirmation of unity was the consequence of accepting the world's variety: discordia must be closed by concors. The unity of a properly constructed poem, being artificial, is less a matter of faith than the world's order, and the poet is more apt than God to order things as we would like to see them turn out. Affirmations of order in either the world or a poem may be rooted in anxiety and wishful thinking: the course of Tasso's poetic career and his decline into madness should be remembered as a backdrop for his neoclassicism in the Discorsi. Influenced by Aristotle's emphasis in the Poetics on 'fable' or 'plot,' Tasso embraces the principle of 'unity of action,' which obscures the possibility of unity based on a different 'Idea or fore-conceit of the work,' more directly related to the order and vitality that natural philosophers attributed to the macrocosm.

We do not find in the grand design of The Faerie Queene any thread corresponding to the plot of Gerusalemme Liberata; considered as a narrative, Spenser's poem is even less unified than Ariosto's. Gloriana unifies the action more vaguely than God's unsearchable good will as it unifies history. Arthur promises another kind of unity, that of a virtuoso moral example, but he hardly provides the 'single knot' that Tasso requires: his quest for Gloriana and the various services he performs from Book to Book, driven by heroic love of beauty and desire for honour, are neither at odds nor quite at one with each other. Desire for illusory or otherwise unattainable love objects has been aptly identified as the mainspring driving Ariosto's multifarious actions,[32] but Spenser treats the various forms of love and beauty from so many points of view that unless we settle for a reductive idealization of the 'kindly flame,' no general description of this central subject matter could be a satisfactory 'knot.'

David Lee Miller opens his study of Books I–III with this explanation of the poem's form: 'I take the allegory of *The Faerie Queene* to be organized with reference to the anticipated-but-deferred wholeness of an ideal body' (*Poem's Two Bodies* 4). He associates this imaginary body both with the androgynous figure of a 'perfect' individual and, in the poem's political dimension, with the secularized *corpus mysticum* of the Queen's sovereignty (68–76). For Miller the poem is 'organized,' not unified, although he claims that his ideal body 'serves to structure the reading of the text in a manner comparable to the use of a vanishing point to organize spatial perspective in drawing' (4). I would concede that a meaningful claim of 'unity' cannot be sustained, especially when we get beyond the poem published in 1590, but I share with Miller and other critics an interest in describing the continuities and the cumulative effect that *The Faerie Queene* offers to readers. My argument in the course of this book will go beyond Miller's scope to take in Spenser's revisions and additions, and I will also attempt to situate the poem's private and public bodies in its larger textual cosmos.

Louis Adrian Montrose has shown how we can usefully consider Spenser (both the would-be English laureate and an author-function within his text) as simultaneously sovereign and a propertied subject in his poetry.[33] This paradox suits Spenser's political circumstances and the political transactions involved in authorship; the poet's temperament is similarly paradoxical, moving between the poles of Promethean ambition and self-abasing humility.[34] In the course of his correspondence with Harvey, Spenser had exclaimed, 'For, why a Gods name may not we, as else the Greekes, haue the kingdome of oure owne Language?'[35] Spenser's desire for a kind of sovereign authority matured as he reached beyond the scope of his publications in 1579 and 1580; finding his voice as the English Virgil and Chaucer's successor, he claimed a poetic kingdom in his epic. (It is worth remembering that this enterprise paralleled, in the late 1580s and beyond, his difficult, dangerous, and ultimately futile effort to gain a title to estates in Ireland.) His dismay at the ability of the Blatant Beast to ruin 'the gentle Poets rime' (*FQ* VI xii 40.8) is only the last of many indications in *The Faerie Queene* that he was anxious to control the misconstruing of his intellectual property: readers may enjoy access to his lands only if they stay on the paths. Subject to 'a mighty Peres displeasure,' he is reduced to sardonic instructions: 'Therfore do you my rimes keep better measure, /

And seeke to please' (41.6–9). The effect of this tactic is to subject displeasure – and the great man whom he fought across the years with the persistence of an Irish rebel – to his good will.

Although Spenser gave his poem no structural centre, I will argue that he does lead us to a cumulative understanding of the principles unifying the world of its action, and a simultaneous understanding of the dynamics through which the individual 'little world of man' is linked to the macrocosm. Without itself being a unified text, the poem holds out the possibility of unity, and a wish for 'stedfast rest of all things firmly stayd' (*Cantos* viii 2.3) is expressed by characters and the narrator time after time. Throughout the poem, our principle of continuity is the poet's unconstraining voice, which is often conspicuously self-aware and aware of its audience, always aware of the things it is conjuring and interpreting: the script being recited is, after all, already written. (Where Milton in his invocations takes us into a compositional process that is visionary and oral, Spenser is silent about his passage from reading his sources to having his written text to read; his is perhaps the first poem that we can only *re*read.) To say that *The Faerie Queene* is conspicuously a book is not to imply, however, that it rises above its writing: ten years in the making before any part was published, and a serial publication labelled 'vnperfite' at the end of its posthumously published coda, the poem places narrative and narrator in history even if they are not ruled by Mutabilitie. Although he has attracted the attention of experts, the narrator of *The Faerie Queene* remains an enigma.[36] His character hasn't been adequately described, and this may be because Spenser gave him an ever-present mask and an elusive muse. Montrose's description of a Foucaultian 'author-function' is useful ('Elizabethan Subject' 318–20), if it is understood that the author in his book is a function both of Edmund Spenser's imagination, and of all that he narrates.

The author's function, then, is to *mediate*, as (within the mind) imagination mediates between reason and the senses, or as (within the state) a Lord Deputy and his Secretary mediate between the sovereign and her subjects. Tasso's unifying *nodo* and the several *vincula* described by Ficino provide other metaphors for mediation. In my view, Spenser's poem never even pretends to offer an unmediated access to reality or truth; the artificiality of its language reinforces what is writ large in the allegorical narrative: 'This is not a pipe.' I do not, however, take from Spenser the modern or postmodern message that reality and truth are inaccessible, but instead the Reformation message that matters of such moment are private, contingent upon divine grace and a receptive will, and beyond representation in language. In the one moment that represents the poet in communion with the source of his inspiration, Colin Clout is piping wordlessly, not singing (VI x 10–16), and in the course of his partial revelation of a greater source, Dame Nature, Spenser reminds us that the disciples who saw Christ 'in strange disguise / Transfigur'd' on Mount Tabor, 'though else most wise, / ... quite their wits forgat' (*Cantos* vii 7).

With what we know of the circumstances in which it took shape, we should expect both constancy and mutability as we move through *The Faerie Queene*. Mediated though reality is in the semblances, transformations, and mere words of the poem, it is never unintelligible; there are precious few moments of *aporia*. The poet's work of mediation involves an assumption that analogies are fundamental to reality, and it emphasizes likeness in the midst of unlikenesses. To discover discontinuities in so ample a poem is not to show that the author was unconcerned, as he proceeded, to make cumulative sense of his experience and his unfolding narrative, nor does stop-and-go narration dismantle the mental theatre and the interrrelated scenes we constitute through memory, with the author's help, in the course of reading.

For some readers today, the subsequent Books dissipate the coherence achieved by the end of Book III as published in 1590, despite all kinds of evidence (echoes of images, variations on characters and themes, structural parallels, narratological threads and motifs) that the second trilogy was written with elements of the first vividly in mind. The text of Books IV–VI and the *Cantos* is solid and broad enough to support both those who emphasize continuity and the opposing camp, for whom Spenser's vision of things had changed fundamentally by the time he completed Books V and VI, to such an extent that the poem will not hang together. I will argue that as his awareness of political impasses deepened, Spenser's sense of himself and the integrity of his personal vision grew both clearer and more distinct from circumstantial reality, but sharp distinctions between ideals and actualities can be traced through the poem from beginning to end.

In the Proems to each Book, Spenser theorizes his practice as a 'maker' and his position in triangular relationships with his poem and his audience. The Proems of Books II and VI will provide reference points for the terms in which Spenser conceived his relationship to the world of his book. In the first of these, he seeks to manage the attitudes of his readers toward 'that happy land of Faery, / Which I so much do vaunt, yet no where show' (1.7–8); subsequently, in the Proem to his last completed Book, the poet testifies to his own extensive experience of 'this delightfull land of Faery' (1.2), and he seems indifferent to his distance from an audience that doesn't enjoy his privileged access to 'these strange waies,' granted by the muses when they infuse 'learnings threasures, / ... And goodly fury' (2.3–8). In the course of successive Books, then, Spenser moves from '*that* happy land' to '*this* delightfull' one. In almost all the Proems (that for Book III is the exception, which is odd, because no part of the poem is more crowded with antique persons and concepts), the reality to which his poem testifies lies primarily in 'antiquities, which no body can know' (II Pr. 1.9), but what he finds in the past bears a typological relationship to his sovereign the Queen, and Faerie land is both a tribute to her sovereignty and another place by which the present can be judged.

The value of Faerie land as a place substantially like the Queen's 'owne realmes' is stressed appropriately in Book II (Proem 4.8); the parallel will be carried further in the chronicle histories of canto x. In his Proem, Spenser is more playful with facts and fictions than a historian could afford to be. Comparing his antique utopia, which he admits no living person has visited, to golden lands recently discovered, he recommends humility and asks for a willing suspension of disbelief, not because he is a poet but because he resembles the explorers through whose 'hardy enterprize, / Many great Regions are discouered' (2.3–4). Though he describes events in the past, they belong in a continuum which includes 'th'Indian *Peru*,' 'The *Amazons* huge river now found trew,' 'fruitfullest *Virginia*' (2.6–9), and 'things more vnknowne' which 'later times ... shall show,' even a world in the moon or 'in euery other starre vnseene' (3). Exotic but well-attested facts shade over into wondrous possibilities: 'yet such to some appeare' (3.9).

Spenser makes a stronger demand than Ariosto, in stanzas which Alpers quotes in his discussion of this passage,[37] that we allow his fiction an imagined reality. Ariosto says, 'Pretend that fiction is fact, or you will resemble the ignorant stay-at-homes who refuse to believe a traveller's tale of wonders,' while Spenser says, with none of Ariosto's irony, 'Consider that the boundaries of the known world have recently changed, and are still changing.' He does not confuse fiction and fact, nor does he, like most poets for whom the poem is a heterocosm, offer his fiction as either a retreat from or a triumph over circumstantial reality.[38] As Plato and his interpreters sought to do by their dialectical use of myth, *The Faerie Queene* invites us to redefine 'reality' and raises questions about the validity of conventional knowledge. Stanza 4 advises the common reader and the queen that to read this poem rightly is to know the 'fairest Princesse vnder sky' and her 'realmes' in a new light. Spenser is engaged here, of course, in underwriting the Tudor myth, transforming the realities of 'here' and 'now' by unfolding their implications in another order of reality, 'there' and 'then.' Faerie land is both distant and present, and this doubleness is supposed to work like a charm to overcome uncertainties about things unknown and exotic.[39]

'Deepe within the mynd'

The Proem to Book VI also invites us to redefine reality and question what we know through the 'outward shows' of fashion, 'that glasse so gay, that it can blynd / The wisest sight, to thinke gold that is bras' (5). Moving with 'weary steps' in his first line, the poet mimes the state of Artegall at the end of Book V: pursued, scolded, and stoned by Detraction, 'yet he for nought would swerue / From his right course, but still the way did hold / To Faery Court' (xii 43.7–9). Artegall returns a victor, but one imagines Detraction following him all the way home. Understandably, then, Spenser detaches himself from the court and turns for solace to a world diametrically opposed to the rocky landscapes and chilly castles of Book V, finding 'such sweet variety, / Of all that pleasant is to eare or eye' that his 'tedious trauell' is forgotten (1). The continuum of his earlier Proem has broken down into divided and distinguished worlds; the analogical relationship of present to past, Britain to Faerie land, history to fiction, has become suspiciously asymmetrical.

Artegall's story advises us that in the brazen world not even a virtuous man can master his circumstances. The Proem to Book VI reflects upon two defensive responses to such a fallen state: the false civility of the present age, which is really no more than 'fayned showes' and 'forgerie' (4.8, 5.3), is contrasted to the true poet's alternative, a virtue that retreats in order to triumph over the world, for 'vertues seat is deepe within the mynd, / And not in outward shows, but inward thoughts defynd' (5.8–9).[40] In this most Sidneian of all the Books in *The Faerie Queene*, Spenser appeals more conspicuously than elsewhere to Sidney's distinction between the 'right' poet and those who, abusing the art, 'infect the fancy with unworthy objects' (*AP* 125.27). He adds a twist, however, and Book VI will be haunted by it: the art of those other courtiers and poets, which is 'Fashion'd to please the eies of them, that pas,' distorts things as they are, 'Yet is that glasse so gay, that it can blynd / The wisest sight, to thinke gold that is bras' (5.4–7). Here is a critique of all those (including the poet himself, in his weaker moments) who, disappointed by the world's limitations, call it 'brazen' and 'deliver a golden' that is more responsive to their hearts' desires – or to the interests of those they seek to please.

Spenser seems aware that his own pastoral romance is open to criticism

as escapist thinking. Turned to catch the light of a self-reflexive consciousness, pastoral discourse can become the vehicle of satire in which its
own conventions and the tastes they gratify are held up for scrutiny:
Is the golden world a vision, or a waking dream? The uneasiness betrayed
in this Proem will be played out in equivocations throughout the narrative of Book VI, where circumstances, words, and actions are oddly un-
suited to one another, with moments of harmony arising out of irreconcil-
able differences.

Was Spenser finally at odds with his own idealism, or just conscious, as
he was earlier in 'A Letter of the Authors,' 'how doubtfully all Allegories
may be construed'? Even then he was troubled by 'the vse of these dayes,
seeing ... nothing esteemed of, that is not delightfull and pleasing to
commune sence.' Perhaps art is at fault only when it offers brass as if it
were gold, or takes the brazen world and tricks it out with 'colours faire,
that feeble eies misdeeme' (4.9). If beauty and the pleasure it offers are apt
to distract a man from virtuous action, they should be condemned, but
there may be another beauty, and a distinctive pleasure associated with it,
reconcilable to virtue. Though the difference between eikastic and fantastic
images is difficult to maintain, that between 'this delightfull land of Faery'
and the 'present age' is validated by a move 'deepe within the mynd,'
beyond the reach of 'fayned showes.'

Spenser's aesthetic principles require that the seat of virtue in the mind
corresponds to something ideal but substantive, independent of anyone's
imaginings. In this Proem, the mental space evoked at the end of stanza 5
corresponds to 'the sacred noursery / Of vertue' in stanza 3, the hidden
'siluer bowre' maintained in perpetuity by the muses; the virtuous man's
'inward thoughts' (5.9) correspond to the 'heauenly seedes' (3.7) planted
first in that Parnassian nursery, which eventually 'forth to honour burst'
(3.9) in virtuous deeds, just as the poet's 'rare thoughts delight' (1.6) has
issued in the poem to which these lines are a prologue. Echoes of his earlier
description of the Garden of Adonis are unmistakable here; this Proem's
evocation of harmony between heavenly gods and pastoral plenty, its
passage from thoughts to growing things to 'all ciuilitie,' and its assimilation of life forms to a single process of growth from seeds to parturition
and nursing, all take us back through 'this delightfull land of Faery' to its
source in the Garden. The creation myth contained within the 1590 *Faerie
Queene*, reiterated in 1596, provides Spenser with objective correlatives
for his 'inward thoughts' and his continuing 'carefull labour' as a poet.

Tasso had proposed that the ideal heroic poem would be a world by
virtue of its comprehensiveness, and an order reducible to a single soul or

form. Spenser was less anxious than Tasso to affirm that all apparent variety or duality is in fact unified. In the absence of originating or culminating events on which the action of the entire poem depends, however, he has given us elaborately coordinated parts and several places for reflection, offering perspective views of the poem. The Proems we have been examining are two such places, and there are others throughout the six Books and the *Cantos*. None offers a view of the whole poem, but the unfolding and infolded structures of *The Faerie Queene* are such that any intelligible part is consistent with the whole. Such passages as the Proem to Book VI and the source of its images in the Garden of Adonis tell us that unity is not a characteristic of things in this world; it is an appropriate goal, but it may be known in this life only in foretastes (I use the plural deliberately), in a perpetual expectation that contradicts the nullity represented by Sansjoy, Malbecco, and Amoret enthralled – to mention only a few of the poem's haunting instances of radical dejection. We are learning to appreciate allegory *because* of its dualistic nature, not in spite of it. If, as I have argued, the controlling purpose of Spenser's allegory is mediation, it may have a soul – as hard to grasp as Proteus but partially satisfying Tasso's criteria for a fictive world – that is twofold, like the world soul described by Plato and Ficino that will concern me in the next chapter and subsequently.

chapter three

The Poet as *Magus* and *Viator*

'The generall end therefore of all the booke is to fashion a gentleman or noble person in vertuous and gentle discipline.' In this familiar statement and throughout 'A Letter of the Authors,' the poet emphasizes that his subject matter embraces the 'priuate morall vertues,' considered as objects of knowledge and as motives shaping the examined lives of individuals in society. To tell an inward-looking story of instructive encounters with virtues and vices, Spenser departed somewhat from the characteristics of the Renaissance heroic poem, both harking back to older discursive forms and moving boldly into unexplored territory. Modern criticism has shown us what a profound and subtle understanding Spenser possessed of the inner world, the soul's faculties and affections, especially all the mental acts of reflection and projection which for us are comprehended in the term 'imagination.' Given this concern with individual human nature and experience, it is significant that subjectivity and dialogical encounters are often staged against a backdrop established by cosmic forces, while the fabric of social life is represented as rather threadbare.

An interest in the ways in which the cosmos can be made to mirror the mind and contribute to self-realization antedates by many centuries the modern consciousness that human minds have always been responsible for making the world – making, that is, everything they are capable of experiencing. That consciousness is not wholly modern; in earlier centuries too there were ways of recognizing that the mind's dialogue with the world is something of a dialogue with itself. The self may realize its nature not by pure introspection, but by contemplation of the mirror presented by the external world. Such mental activity can be truly creative when it is checked by a reality principle and involved in self-knowledge as well as projection.[1] This kind of consciousness was the motive force behind

Spenser's allegory, which is both analytical in its reflection upon the mind's busy activity and synthetic or creative in its representation of conditions contributing to the soul's health.[2]

Poets and literary theorists of the Renaissance for whom God was a poet and the poet a man remarkably like God were wary of the impiety latent in their analogy. For them the imagination had not been given full freedom, and the world's being and value, as perceived and represented, were contingent on God's *fiat* rather than the poet's. It should also be remembered that in the Renaissance a poem – most of all a heroic poem – was considered a social instrument which proved its worth by its impact on conduct, and only incidentally as a mirror in which the poet regarded himself. However, if the poet was a man speaking to men, he might among other things encourage in his readers a self-awareness and an imaginative comprehension of the world similar to his own.

Isomorphism of the Soul and the World

Many years ago Harry Berger brought to the attention of Spenserians the principle, 'first elaborated by Plato in the middle and later dialogues, that the structure of the world is isomorphic with the structure of the soul – a notion found in various forms in the work of Aristotle, Virgil, Augustine, and in the general assumptions of classical and Christian cosmology' (*Revisionary Play* 28). Like many of Berger's seminal insights, this 'notion' is enunciated breezily, and its applicability to Spenser's poetry is only intimated. Placed in the context of his articles describing 'the ecology of the mind' as it pertains to the Renaissance, Berger's principle of isomorphism offers a useful key to understanding Spenser's imagination and his position in the spectrum of Elizabethan culture.[3] To the old principle that the world and the soul are isomorphic, and to the modern emphasis that the source of all our values and perceptions of structure in the world is within us, Berger adds 'the Axiom of Self-Limitation, which states that human power, the possibility of creative and significant action, is open to the self only insofar as the mind commits the reality of world order to forces greater than self and over against self, forces whose limiting otherness will test, judge, restrain, answer and reward the self' (*Second World and Green World* 45). He undertakes to show how the 'ecological system' has changed from one cultural period to another. Sometimes he succeeds brilliantly, as in his analysis of two images typical of medieval and Renaissance culture – a medieval diagram of the human body and the zodiacal influences on its several parts, and Leonardo da Vinci's image of Vitruvian man (*Second World and Green World* 46–50). Some of his extrapolations from particular examples to general characteristics are no less stimulating. What follows is an attempt to carry further the 'particular interpretations' that Berger has described as the most important phase of ecological theory.

We began by seeking a way of understanding the connection that seems to have existed for Spenser between the moral virtues and the human sphere of action and emotions, on the one hand, and the cosmos and cosmology on the other. Our understanding of the relationship between the world and the self will be enhanced by an awareness of the context of ideas in which he worked. An isomorphic relationship between the cosmos and the soul in search of its own perfection, resembling one of the deep structures of *The Faerie Queene*, is suggestively stated by Marsilio Ficino in 'Five Questions Concerning the Mind,' one of the short treatises published in his *Epistolae*. 'The intellect is prompted by nature,' he says, 'to comprehend the whole breadth of being; in its notion it perceives all, and, in the notion of all, it contemplates itself; under the concept of truth it knows all, and under the concept of the good it desires all' (*RPM* 199). This treatise offers a convenient formulation of an idea, probably known to Spenser from several sources, which forms the basis for his habit of representing individual lives in the context of 'the whole breadth of being.'

Ficino elaborates in these terms his idea of the nexus uniting human nature and the totality of being:

> What, then, does the intellect seek if not to transform all things into itself by depicting all things in the intellect according to the nature of the intellect? And what does the will strive to do if not to transform itself into all things by enjoying all things according to the nature of each? The former strives to bring it about that the universe, in a certain manner, should become intellect; the latter, that the will should become the universe. (*RPM* 200–1)

According to Ficino, 'a natural instinct' makes the soul strive 'in a continuous effort both to know all truths by the intellect and to enjoy all good things by the will.' The hypothetical end of all this striving is 'that the soul in its own way will become the whole universe' (*RPM* 201).[4] Ficino takes the distinctly human categories of truth and goodness to be identical with external reality as mirrored in the soul.

The treatise from which I have quoted is characteristic of Ficino's thought and of Florentine Platonism in general. These ideas may seem exotic as well as formidably abstract, but upon reflection it is clear that

they are latent in the commonplace belief that occult analogies link together the cosmos and the microcosm that is human nature. The fact that
that idea was both popular and of interest to the best minds in the Renaissance owes something to the influence, both direct and indirect, of Ficino's
mode of thought.[5] His ideas may seem to us more preposterous than
wonderful: our conception of the mind in its relationship to the world has
been unalterably affected by the development of empiricism and rational-
ism. Prior to the development of empirical, scientific attitudes toward the
external world and the mechanisms of perception, however, it was assumed that perception and thought depended upon a fundamental similarity between the mind and its object, and that the mind changes to
accommodate what it knows. According to this view of consciousness, to
entertain the thought of infinity is to 'participate' in infinity, or even in
some sense to become infinite. Recognition that while containing or striving for this thought the mind remains in a finite body only offered a second
source of wonder.

Some examples of the bearings of such a way of thinking on literature
and the arts may be useful. Close to Ficino in time, Leonardo da Vinci
wrote of the human eye, 'Who would believe that so small a space could
contain the images of all the universe? ... Here the forms, here the colours,
here all the images of every part of the universe are contracted to a point.'[6]
The idea remained arcane, but its persistence is illustrated by Donne's
reference to lovers' eyes 'So made such mirrors, and such spies, / That they
did all to you epitomize.'[7] By the time of Donne, and of Hamlet's fantasy
of being a king of infinite space, the idea that the self is so unbounded and
the world so suited to its sovereignty was best entertained hypothetically
and ironically. As Berger observes acutely, 'The mind cannot validly count
itself king of infinite space unless it feels itself bounded in a nutshell.'[8] By
our standards, Ficino was inadequately aware of this truth: he seems to
some critics more imaginative than a medieval thinker, and more adept at
making models of reality out of his own projections, but insufficiently
alert to their status as imaginary and contrary to fact.[9] Many readers of
Spenser have thought, similarly, that there are such discrepancies between
his fiction and the actualities to which it is supposed to pertain that either
he cannot be taken seriously at all, or his ideas cannot be taken straight.
Doubts about the plausibility of Ficino's and Spenser's world views are
troublesome and I will return to them, after considering more thoroughly
the ways in which men of the Renaissance construed the relation of the self
to the world.

Socratic and Esoteric Humanism

It is possible to distinguish in erudite culture of the Renaissance two ways of thinking about the paths individuals should follow toward self-knowledge and knowledge of God. One, the central tradition of humanism, stressed retirement into the self as a source of stability; among the intellectual virtues, practice of prudence leads to the perfection of wisdom, and both are consistent with exercise of the moral virtues in an active life. The other tradition, with roots in medieval scholasticism and branches in several esoteric arts, is typified in the thought of Ficino and Pico della Mirandola. As we have begun to see, this esoteric or hermetic tradition stressed an intellectual engagement with the world beyond the self for the sake of what it can reveal about the full potential of human nature and its place in the order of creatures.

The central humanist tradition tended to emphasize that given the fallen nature of the self, human knowledge is limited and desires for knowledge and power should be limited accordingly; the other tended to emphasize that given the nature of the world and our place at its centre, the desire for knowledge is practically limitless and so are the dimensions of the self as it seeks knowledge and power. In the first tradition, whether the soul is seen as corrupt and desperate for salvation or as a lesser paradise, God is to be encountered on the rebound, as it were, from the depths of human nature. In the other, the way to paradise and knowledge of God lies through the world, considered metaphysically and aesthetically; neither the limited self nor the cosmos can be transcended, if that is one's goal, until they have both been encompassed systematically.

These two currents in Renaissance thought correspond to two aspects of ancient philosophy. Emile Bréhier has observed that 'the ideal of knowledge in Greek thought is definitely twofold.' From Hesiod to the time of Socrates, philosophy was 'an endeavor to classify the forms of reality and to discover the rational order according to which they are subordinated to one another,' and wisdom was to be understood as comprehension of man's place in that order. With Socrates 'a new ideal appeared. Wisdom is first of all knowledge of the self and of its own powers. The object of knowledge is not distinct from the subject which knows.' With reference to this new ideal of wisdom, it became possible to distinguish between two types of knowledge, one humane or subjective, and the other technical, with an object different in kind from the mind that knows it. Bréhier observes that 'in Greek philosophy these two types of knowledge did not remain distinct and did not give birth to two distinct groups of sciences, such as the moral and the physical sciences. Mind was not declared to be separate from nature, any more than mind affirmed nature to be separate from itself. Ever since Plato, there has been a continual compromise between these two tendencies,' with the Socratic redefinition of wisdom only lending new depth to engagements with the world beyond the self. 'Not only are the physical sciences permeated with human values, the idea of harmony and of purposiveness, but the first principle of nature is, at the same time, the being in which the self-knowledge laid down by Socrates as the ideal of human wisdom is realized perfectly' (*Philosophy of Plotinus* 97–8).

The compromise Bréhier describes as the legacy of Plato was transmitted through the Middle Ages to the Renaissance; it was also complicated by reformulation during the fifteenth and sixteenth centuries, as a result of the recovery of much more of ancient philosophy – in the Platonic tradition, especially – than had been available earlier. At the same time we find among the humanists, beginning with Petrarch, something resembling Socrates' turning away from nature toward an exclusive concern with man and his relationship to transcendental moral and aesthetic norms, and this turn threatened the compromise on which systematic philosophy had been based. Petrarch imitated Socrates' response to the Sophists in his rejection of a large part of philosophy, though in so doing he was reviving sophistic rhetoric. In the letter describing his ascent of Mount Ventoux, Petrarch gives a personal form to the conception of wisdom typical of the humanists, for whom moral philosophy is superior to all other forms of secular knowledge. Having admired the landscape spread below him as he stood at the summit, and 'lifting up [his] mind to higher things after the example of [his] body,' Petrarch opened his copy of Augustine's *Confessions* and his eyes came to rest upon this sentence: 'And men go to admire the high mountains, the vast floods of the sea, the huge streams of the rivers, the circumference of the ocean, and the revolutions of the stars – and desert themselves' (*RPM* 44). The counsel of his spiritual mentor, in a text which calls upon him to turn away from his physical surroundings, leads Petrarch to regret his admiration of earthly things, and to recall a sentence from Seneca, 'Nothing is admirable besides the mind; compared to its greatness nothing is great.' He then reflects on the folly of men who 'look without for what can be found within' (*RPM* 45).

The inwardness and intertextuality of Petrarch's path to an understanding of human nature is stressed both by precepts and by the autobiographical (yet substantially fictitious) narrative in which he has placed them. He has transposed elements from the allegorical itinerary of the mind to God into a richly circumstantial account of a personal crisis, which has symbolic power because it convinces us of its authenticity.[10] Petrarch's attitude toward experience and the form of his literary response both exemplify fully, at the beginning of the Renaissance, the tenets typical of humanism. Although it may be enclosed in myths and conventions, subjective experience will be central to humanistic culture, and other forms of knowledge will be problematic. According to the humanists, moral philosophy and religious devotion together provide the forms to be followed in cultivation of the self; the purposes served by literature are derived from these sources of guidance. Admiration of the world may figure in this process of self-cultivation, but it is represented as a curiosity from which the mind must be recalled.

A different path to the same goal of self-knowledge is described by Pico della Mirandola in his 'Oration on the Dignity of Man.' Pico's thought is typical of a movement with some claim to the term 'humanism,' although it is significantly different in its ideals and procedures from that exemplified by Petrarch.[11] In both, the nature of humanity and the fullest possible development of the individual's latent potential are central concerns; in both, the ancient world and the traditions by which its wisdom has been transmitted to us provide the field in which individuals can best discover their potential. I will call Petrarch's humanism 'Socratic,' because of its similarity to Socrates' reorientation of philosophy, and Pico's 'esoteric' (the term 'hermetic' could also be used), because of his interest in various forms of magic and his appeals to hermetic and kabbalistic texts.

I don't intend to imply the existence of distinct traditions, but only to identify two frames of reference, one of which is apt to be dominant in the work of an individual writer.[12] Socratic and esoteric humanism arose from different contexts and were adaptable to different purposes as institutions and discourse communities changed. Esoteric humanism developed on a foundation in scholastic philosophy, stimulated by the rediscovery of Platonic and hermetic texts during the fifteenth century; Petrarch's humanism, despite the Greek patron I have found for it, was most concerned with recovering the civic and private culture of ancient Rome, and it was more literary than philosophical. Differences between the interests of Petrarch and Pico are readily apparent, but the combination of their two perspectives in the work of later writers is predictable. Despite the fact that the *studia humanitatis* included only ethics among the traditional 'parts of philosophy,' humanism exercised an immeasurable influence on the development of philosophy in the Renaissance,[13] while Pico's type of philosophy influenced literature and the other arts to a similar degree. Such boundary crossings were crucial to Spenser's formation, and at work in the ambitions animating his epic project.

In his 'Oration,' Pico outlines and elaborates an educational program which begins with moral philosophy, the queen of the disciplines included in the *studia humanitatis*, and then proceeds through the mastery of dialectic to natural philosophy. Study of the cosmos, rather than the rejection of the world and direct consideration of the solitary self that Petrarch had recommended, prepares the mind for the perfection of human nature which is to be found through theology in Pico's scheme.[14] Pico even applies the Delphic precept, 'Know thyself,' to the study of nature: it 'urges and encourages us to the investigation of all nature, of which the nature of man is both the connecting link and, so to speak, the "mixed bowl." For he who knows himself knows all things, as Zoroaster first wrote, and then Plato in his *Alcibiades*' (*RPM* 235). Investigation of nature provides a context for self-discovery, and activity in the macrocosm involves the fashioning of a greater microcosm. Pico praises spiritual magic as 'nothing else than the utter perfection of natural philosophy,' and 'a higher and more holy philosophy.' 'As the farmer weds his elms to vines, even so does the *magus* wed earth to heaven, that is, he weds lower things to the endowments and powers of higher things,' and his art 'rouses him to the admiration of God's works which is the most certain condition of a willing faith, hope, and love. For nothing moves one to religion and to the worship of God more than the diligent contemplation of the wonders of God' (*RPM* 247, 249).[15]

Learned culture of the Renaissance produced an ideal not to be found in the Middle Ages: the 'homo literatus, dedicated neither to an active life nor to religious contemplation, but to the "vita speculativa."'[16] Pico's conception of the *magus* contributed as much to this prototype as Petrarch's type of introspective *viator*. In Pico's ambitious program for unifying the intellectual disciplines and perfecting the human soul, we can see an attempt to accomplish Ficino's project, 'to bring it about that the universe, in a certain manner, should become intellect' (*RPM* 201). For Ficino this had been the object of a 'striving' that is natural to man; success in such an endeavour might be imagined or represented symbolically, but it is attained only in immortality. As a program, a scenario, Pico's 'Oration' provides a form and content proper to the striving consciousness, just as Petrarch's letter provides a form and content proper to consciousness in crisis. The 'Oration' and Pico's other writings are less satisfactory as a body of doctrine than as a program for inquiry and reform. It is improper to treat such texts as edifices, or as arguments designed to separate truths from error. As

Berger observes, 'The central image which emerges from Pico's *opera* - with the possible exception of the *In astrologiam* - is not the world view which Pico sets forth but rather Pico setting forth his world view' (*Second World and Green World* 227).

The subjective element is less apparent in esoteric than in Socratic humanism; its procedures seek to circumvent the dangers posed by subjectivity in its extreme form, accidia or melancholia. The interests of an individual consciousness are central, however, in esoteric as in Socratic humanism. Ficino, Pico, and their followers were creators of encyclopedic fictions – self-validating hypotheses that tend to displace reality and substitute interpretation – to the same degree that the literary humanists cultivated personae, and for similar reasons. It is appropriate to treat Pico's stated aims as within the grasp of the Renaissance *magus* or polymath only if we recognize that, like any culture hero, that figure belonged more to legend and propaganda than to anyone's actual experience or expectations. We should also recognize that the *magus* figure, like the politician, grew complicated within the economy of Renaissance culture through the addition of an evil twin, and men reputed to possess esoteric powers (Ficino, Pico, Leonardo, Trithemius, Agrippa, Bruno, John Dee, Thomas Harriot) gained their reputations partly through the suspicions they aroused.

Petrarch's attitude and assumptions may seem to us more sound and useful than Pico's; it was through following out the implications of what I have called Socratic humanism that Erasmus, Calvin, Montaigne, and a host of others, in their different ways, made their lasting contributions. In the process, and not incidentally, esoteric humanism was largely discredited. However, in our time historians of art, of science, and of literary culture in the Renaissance have shown that whatever we may think about the soundness of Ficino and Pico as philosophers, the world view I have sketched and many of the ideas with which it was filled out were immensely useful to a number of creative thinkers, artists in verbal and visual media, and scientists, throughout a period stretching from the fifteenth century to late in the seventeenth. Their vision of human nature and the universe was subject not only to popularization and some ridiculous applications, but to criticism, to varying degrees of conditional assent, and to combination with other assumptions and ideas. In France, the influence of Ficino and Pico was felt early in the sixteenth century, and what I have called esoteric humanism was an important element in French literary culture from the middle of the century to its end.[17] In the years of Spenser's maturity, cultural conditions in England were such as to make possible a synthesis of Socratic and esoteric humanism, combining a critical scrutiny

of human nature in its fallen separateness from the world with an imaginative vision of the human potential for a return to harmony and fullness of
being in the world. I will argue that, in the ways proper to poetic discourse,
Spenser achieved just such a synthesis.

Poetic and Philosophical Discourses

An attempt to describe the interplay of philosophical and poetic traditions
in Renaissance culture, and to analyse the philosophical content of a poetic
text, raises questions that are not often addressed in criticism. Given the
difference between poetry and other types of discourse, what kind of light
can a nonpoetic text shed upon the ideas embodied in a poem? If the poet is
truly a 'maker' and the meaning he makes differs from the historian's and
the philosopher's, it will be found neither in facts nor ideas. If, as I argued
in the preceding chapter, the poem initiates a worldmaking process, interpretation which traces its meaning to an extrinsic source may involve
substituting a false meaning for the poem's distinctive texture. To leave the
terms of a fiction for some other text, even one from the poet's library, may
involve something worse than the heresy of paraphrase.

I do not, however, consider the world of *The Faerie Queene* autonomous or hermetic. People in the Renaissance attributed an intrinsic order
and vitality to their world, but they also thought of all that they knew as
contingent and ordained to serve purposes beyond their own. A work of
art should, then, be no less open to use and no less connected with a higher
authority than the work of nature. If the poet is both an imitator of God
and a man aware of his status as a creature, his poem will imitate the order
of creation, but not from an Olympian perspective; like the external world,
it will be open to a search for purpose, significance, and relationships
between manifest and latent significance. Just as it does when faced with
chaotic experience and evidence of order in the world, the mind involved
in reading will discover intrinsic significance and account for it by appeals
to absent causes.

The primary absent cause of significance in a poem, controlling others
that may be identifiable or may remain conjectural, must be the poet. We
may wish to gather from the poem and from other sources some understanding of its author's intentions and creative process. The author may
encourage or limit this inquiry. The purely personal elements of the poet's
experience and intentions are, in the absence of authorial working papers
or commentary, inaccessible, but we may be able to learn something about
his opinions and beliefs that will serve as a frame of reference for interpre-

tation. What the poet was and what he intended should matter to us even though these are not discernible as matters of fact; I don't think we can avoid making assumptions about such things unless we are content with mechanically 'objective' or self-centred readings.

The aesthetics of self-expression involve the artist's projecting himself, confessionally or symbolically, into his work. The result is the kind of heterocosm with which we are most familiar. When the author's inner world is more real and valuable than his circumstances, he is apt to confer upon his poem an order and value independent of the external world, keyed instead to his inner landscape. In the previous chapter we saw Spenser's steps moving in this direction in the Proem to Book VI, while the Proem to Book II, tentative in its own way about fiction and facts, set up different referential relationships between Faerie land and historical actuality, less tinged with subjectivity. But even in Book VI the poet's obligations, like his hero's, are defined at court, and he could not have written the shorter and more personal poems published after 1594, in respite from his unfinished epic, without concern for their reception in the great world. Authoritative communication, therefore, rather than self-expression, was the definitive motive throughout Spenser's laureate career. This being the case, his work may be more artificial and therefore superficially more complete than fragments of a great confession, but it is, paradoxically, more legitimate to look beyond the text to other texts in search of his poem's significance. If we are right to see *The Faerie Queene* as an encyclopedic poem, and not incidentally but by design a celebration of the Renaissance ideal of an *enkyklios paideia*, we should regard poetry as one among several allied arts.

In a well-known passage of his *Apology for Poetry*, Sidney distinguishes between 'the mistress-knowledge, by the Greeks called *architectonike*,' and other arts such as astronomy, music, and mathematics: these are 'but serving sciences' which it is absurd to cultivate alone, although they have 'this scope – to know, and by knowledge to lift up the mind from the dungeon of the body to the enjoying his own divine essence' (*AP* 104.10– 37). When, in his definition of *architectonike*, Sidney stresses 'the knowledge of a man's self, in the ethic and politic consideration, with the end of well-doing and not of well-knowing only,' he associates himself with what I have called the Socratic tendency in humanism, and he also pokes fun at those who lose themselves in esoteric knowledge: 'by the balance of experience it was found that the astronomer looking to the stars might fall into a ditch.' These remarks illustrate stresses that could be observed within the family of the arts and sciences, and Sidney was not above fomenting quarrels among its members, advancing 'the poet's nobleness, by setting him before his other competitors' (*AP* 104.38–9) for recognition by 'the mistress-knowledge.' Sidney imagines his rivals, the moral philosopher and the historian, as participants in an academic disputation, the first pacing 'with a sullen gravity, as though they could not abide vice by daylight' (*AP* 105.2–3), and the second 'loaden with old mouse-eaten records, authorising himself (for the most part) upon other histories' (*AP* 105.21–2). Having stooped to conquer by an *ad hominem* argument, he advances 'the peerless poet' as a 'moderator' who can bridge the distance between precept and example that his sophistry has just created (*AP* 107.9, 106.11)!

It suits Sidney's purpose to emphasize the difference between fictive discourse and other forms (he would have the poet be 'peerless'), but a different strategy, recognizing difference but emphasizing similarities, makes more sense of Spenser's practice and its relation to the kind of philosophical discourse that interested him. The philosopher and the poet share a concern with normative ideas and with the relation of ideas to acts. Poetry is more useful than philosophy, according to Sidney, because the poet is more charming in society, and his meaning is both more accessible and more effective, since it moves by delighting. In his verse letter to Harvey, written within or at least on the periphery of the Sidney circle shortly before the *Apology* took shape, Spenser developed his own version of these maxims from Horace. But Spenser also sought for himself the authority over ideas possessed by philosophers; hence his praise of Harvey as a high-minded moralist and his appeal to 'Aristotle and the rest' in his letter to Ralegh. We saw with reference to the Proem of Book VI how the poet's position can be compromised in society, and his interest in normative ideas can be alienating. Comparing *The Faerie Queene* to Sidney's *Arcadia*, one sees readily that Spenser had many uses for the moral philosopher's knowledge, despite what Sidney had termed its 'abstract and general' character (*AP* 107.2). Philosophical discourse figures in the fabric of *The Faerie Queene* right on the surface, in the definition and presentation of its 'Legendes,' and I will be concerned to show how it also supports Spenser's conception of Faerie land as a scene for self-fashioning, in keeping with the tenets of the esoteric tradition within Renaissance thought.

The places where philosophical and poetic discourse can be compared, and where philosophers and literary critics can meet to discuss the theory and practice of interpretation, are nowadays the most crowded intersections on the map of humanistic studies. Scholars with several disciplinary backgrounds and agendas have been studying what was already in Plato's time 'an ancient quarrel' (*Republic* 607B). There are differences today between those who argue that philosophical discourse is ineradicably poetic and those who seek in fictive discourse some of the challenges and satisfactions traditionally associated with philosophy, but while the discourse communities remain distinct it is much easier now than it was twenty years ago to see what philosophers and poets have in common. Unfortunately, most of the excellent work in this interdisciplinary field is irrelevant to my purposes or difficult to apply; it has arisen from the conditions obtaining in modern and postmodern culture, and does not address, even in theoretical terms, the interrelations of poetry and philosophy in the Renaissance. We will take a step toward understanding those issues if we set aside as a modern prejudice (the legacy of Romanticism, the symbolists and aesthetes, and Modernism) the notion that poetry is inherently superior to philosophy *as a mode of knowledge*, because poetic or imaginative cognition and expression are best suited to the paradoxical, irrational nature of life.[18] There may be some validity to this notion, but Sidney, followed by Spenser in 'A Letter of the Authors,' bases his comparison of poetry to philosophy entirely on the grounds that poetry is rhetorically more *effective* with its audience in attaining goals shared with moral philosophy. Sidney's poet 'is indeed the right popular philosopher, whereof Aesop's tales give good proof' (*AP* 109.15–16), and in another place, giving his maker a higher aim, 'that the poet hath that *Idea*' (*AP* 101.5) must depend upon his mastery of the philosopher's subject matter, which implies a command of dialectical reasoning from effects to causes, from *species* to *genera*. We have no evidence that either Sidney or Spenser disagreed with Aristotle's ranking of the disciplines as forms of knowledge, according to which poetry is subordinate to philosophy and 'more philosophical' than history (see *AP* 109.11–34).

One difference between *The Faerie Queene* and a logical argument is that the latter deals rigorously with concepts, while for Spenser concepts are only a part of the whole cloth, and the tenor of his argument is often something much less definite: a sharply defined or ambivalent emotional state, an evocative traditional image, an exemplary action, a category of experience such as Time or Mutability. To these constituents of consciousness, ideas are loosely attached by affective as well as intellectual bonds. In the figure of Una, Truth becomes not a body of doctrine but a way of being in the world. Discursive language remains, and in some places it alludes to doctrines by means of a philosopher's terms of art, but concepts are worked into the fabric of the poem's narrative and its imagery so deeply that they almost lose their identity as concepts. Should they, then, be dug out of their poetic context? Although this type of interpretation can be no more conclusive than any other, I believe it is worth undertaking. Given the differences between Spenser's culture and our own, we cannot expect even to approximate his meaning without making explicit much that to his contemporaries was implicit, often unavailable to consciousness. Equally important, to the extent that we now wish to criticize Elizabethan culture as well as to comprehend it in its own terms, we need to understand the genealogies of its animating ideas.

A partial explanation of the forms given to philosophical thought in Spenser's poetry may be found in his conception of his principal poetic models, and in the nature of allegorical narrative. 'All the antique Poets historicall' and their modern successors should be seen as Spenser's predecessors in the art of allegory, and his own contribution was better grounded in philosophical traditions than most heroic poems. Learned men of the Renaissance saw in ancient allegory and myth a body of knowledge that preceded the development of philosophy, but in their understanding of Homer, Hesiod, and the so-called *prisca theologia* they could not escape participation in a world philosophers and theologians had made. As Roger Hinks observed years ago, the very idea of allegory is 'the product of philosophical reflexion,' and as such it is distinct from myth, although it provided a way of preserving myth in a culture that had discovered poetry and philosophy as different forms of discourse. The dependence of allegory on philosophical thought is evident, according to Hinks, in the fact that *allegoria* referred, in antiquity, both to a process of narration, in which metaphors are used to make abstractions accessible to the imagination, and to a process of interpretation, 'the technique of extracting the metaphysical notions implicit in a complex of imagery.'[19] While instances of 'imposed' allegory occur throughout the history of *allegoresis* and have been used to stigmatize such discourse as a form of bad faith, it can be said that in the main, allegorical invention and interpretation have proceeded simultaneously, offering complex rather than reductive responses to cultural pressures.

In Renaissance editions of the ancient and modern classics, both forms of *allegoria* are found, one putatively in the text and the other emphatically in the surrounding sea of commentary. The shape that this twofold tradition takes in Spenser's poetry may be unique. His allegory absorbs interpretive commentary, with all of its unfolding of 'metaphysical notions,' into the poetic text, thereby making the reflexive act of interpretation – the process of referring images to their animating ideas – explicit and inseparable from the experience of reading.[20] Spenser mimes this experience in the silent voice of his narrator, who is a reader pondering many texts and comments; his characters too are readers, caught in what Harry Berger has nicely called the 'great perhapsing machine' of the allegory ('Kidnapped Romance' 213).

It is sometimes said that abstract language, discursive statements, noncolloquial diction and syntax, and ideas not embodied in things are alien to poetry. Spenser's reputation, like the shield of Redcrosse, shows 'old dints' and 'cruell markes' sustained in the ancient and modern quarrels over poetic language. He was present at the creation of vast new resources for poetry, but his verse preserves features of the older style (variously called drab, plain, and native), enclosing them as if in amber in the 'golden' manner, heightened above speech by elaborate artifice. As a result his fictive Faerie land contains, bathed in exotic atmosphere, relics of workaday life and thought. The kind of reasoning we find within the narrative is consistent with this mixture of the exotic and the ordinary. Except in the *Fowre Hymnes* (and even there he is more like himself than like Chapman or Donne), Spenser avoids logical and systematic exposition of doctrines. His poetry presents us with the preliminary stages and the results of thinking, and involves us in the emotionally coloured accompaniments of reflection and conviction, but subtle thought processes seldom constitute the line-by-line texture of *The Faerie Queene*; thinking is writ large in the various quests and digressions, where it is represented by physical encounters with embodied abstractions, and by the speeches or reflective monologues arising from them. There are, however, descriptive passages in which the narrator is at pains to establish logical connections between phenomena.

Of all the ground that might be held in common by poetry and philosophy, Spenser's share includes only rudiments of the modern philosopher's methods of critique and proof. A poet might share with philosophers certain ideas and assumptions about the world and human nature – the elements or even the totality of a world view. In *The Faerie Queene*, however, we should not expect to find these elements assembled with a philosopher's style and purposes, unless the philosopher in our scenario is one whose methods are substantially those of a poet. Spenser's ideas are represented imaginatively, not proposed and defended with evidence independent of his assumptions. It is not always possible to say what he considers a self-evident truth, and what is a mere opinion or a hypothesis to be entertained. Errour is significantly the first casualty in the poem's 'fierce warres,' yet her offspring remain to be encountered all over Faery land.[21] This kind of paradox would be inadmissible in some forms of discourse, but in a narrative it only keeps us questing, and questioning. (It is noteworthy that in one of the more sustained and subtle argumentative passages in *The Faerie Queene*, the dialogue between Redcrosse and Despair in I ix 37–47, much of it takes the form of questions, as does Una's intervention in stanzas 52–3.)

Paul Alpers states a belief that is common among Spenser's critics when he observes that 'the advantage and importance of poetry in general, and of Spenser's kind of poetry in particular, is that it can coherently express attitudes that prove contradictory when worked out philosophically.'[22] We expect a different kind of coherence from a poem than from a philosophical argument, and we expect it to be achieved by different means. It is also true that the poet is licensed to use both opinions and firm doctrines inconclusively. I believe, however, that when poetry makes serious use of philosophical concepts, its coherence or incoherence at the conceptual level matters significantly. In other words, the poem's meaning – or the part of its meaning that is susceptible to such analysis – should not 'prove contradictory when worked out philosophically.'

Such contradictions as are present in the poet's thinking should not be ignored: unless the critic has introduced or exaggerated the contradictions (as often happens), they are part of the poem's meaning, and it is a matter of aesthetic judgment whether they are strengths or weaknesses in its fabric.[23] Ambivalence and contradiction may appear in a philosopher's discourse as well as in poetry. One more reference to Alpers will clarify this point. Discussing the vexed question of the presence of Time in the Garden of Adonis, he says that 'in order to make us aware of earthly mutability, Spenser is willing to neglect both his fable and its philosophic coherence' (6). Alpers could be right, but if so, shouldn't we admit that the poem is flawed? (Of course, readings of the Garden as a timeless realm might be all wrong.) I submit that an interpretation of the fable and its philosophic coherence which 'saves' Time and the other phenomena in the Garden would be superior to Alpers's way of reading it, and more likely to conform to the poet's programmatic intention. The Garden of Adonis passage is a tissue of paradoxes, but there may be a philosophical frame of reference that can accommodate without incoherence much, if not all, of its phenomenal complexity.

Spenser's Poetry and Ficinian Platonism

We tend to think of philosophy as a discipline dedicated to the discovery of contradictions, but in connection with Spenser's poetry we will be concerned with a way of doing philosophy that is devoted to accommodating potentially contradictory attitudes. The arguments of the philosophers who seem to have been of the greatest interest to Spenser are open to question: their premises were rooted in belief and desire rather than in empirical facts and impregnable principles. The study of philosophy in Spenser's day was not so rigorous as it had been and would soon become,[24] and one salutary result of humanism in the sixteenth century was the production of many handbooks, treatises, and dialogues on natural and moral philosophy, addressed to lay audiences and similar in some respects to conduct books. The plethora of opinions in circulation during the later sixteenth century encouraged, among those who took philosophy seriously, a connoisseur's attitude toward the array of alternative and competing truths. Spenser's stance seems to have been a syncretic habit of mind in which full assent was withheld from all but the most generous and inclusive of propositions.

If *The Faerie Queene* is open to, and in fact in need of, illumination from philosophical sources, how can we choose the most appropriate? Our knowledge of Spenser and his readers, and respect for the principle that poetry is conditioned by the capacities of its audience, combine to establish some practical limits. Spenser's own acquaintance with philosophy was limited, one imagines, by considerations of its utility; at any rate, only that part of his learning which was adaptable to imaginative uses is of much interest to us. Since he wrote to be understood by the literate and serious but not highly educated men and women of his day, what they could be expected to comprehend and accept must matter to us. For several reasons, then, the more recondite philosophical texts will be the least useful.

To be useful, a text would need to achieve some circulation in Elizabethan England, and some currency in the European literary culture to which Spenser saw himself contributing. On the other hand, a book that we can identify as no more than popular might mislead us into a poor understanding of what he thought and what he created. The ideas with which the poet began may not be simpler than the imaginative structures in which they are eventually embodied, but this often seems to be the case, if only because most serious readers of literature are better equipped to perceive complexities of an imaginative nature than those inherent in concepts and a discursive argument. This situation seems to be changing, as criticism deals more subtly with contexts, and with transactions between texts such as Spenser's and the cultural institutions within which the significance of *The Faerie Queene* was constituted; the planes on which we place his texts and what used to be regarded simply as sources are shifting, no longer hierarchical. Viewed in the light of current historicist scholarship, which probes the reasons for simplifications and silences as well as the implications of articulate artifice, even the cruder and more popular texts may gain resonance.

It is one of the peculiarities of Spenser's 'darke conceit' that its exceptional and esoteric contents are covered by a veil of commonplaces. Interpretation is not entitled to ignore the received opinions that pervaded Elizabethan culture, but we should not be content with them, and they should be seen in relation to more arcane and complicated ideas, whether the relation is agreement or discord. That Spenser accepted and manipulated the commonplaces of his age is easy enough to demonstrate, but difficult to manage well. It is even more difficult and more open to question, but also more important, to show how Spenser responded to the exceptional art and thought of his own and earlier times. 'It seems to be a lesson of history,' as Edgar Wind observes wisely at the end of *Pagan Mysteries in the Renaissance*, 'that the commonplace may be understood as a reduction of the exceptional, but that the exceptional cannot be understood by amplifying the commonplace' (238; cf. 13–16, 26–7).

As an example of Spenser's imaginative response to a philosophical concept, I will touch lightly here upon a topic that will come up several times in later chapters. I intend to show that the conceptual basis for several features – mythical figures and the places they preside over – in the fictional world of *The Faerie Queene* is to be found in the doctrine of a world soul. Some of the reasons for Spenser's appropriation of this doctrine, and his transformation of it almost beyond recognition in his own mixture of narrative and worldmaking description, may be brought out by a comparison of passages from Ficino's commentary on Plato's *Symposium*, *On Love*, and Spenser's description of the Garden of Adonis, one of several places in *The Faerie Queene* where the intangible forces at work throughout the physical and biological world are symbolically represented.

I will be focusing on a passage in Speech VI of Ficino's commentary. Of the seven Speeches comprising the text, this is the climactic one, devoted as it is to interpretation of 'the divine mysteries revealed to Socrates by Diotima' (VI i 108).[25] Readers of *The Symposium* will recall that Socrates disagreed with the earlier speakers who had praised Love as a god. Taking his cue from the fact that 'Socrates and Diotima ... place love midway between the beautiful and the ugly, the good and the bad, the blessed and the wretched, god and man,' Ficino develops an argument which reconciles these 'divine mysteries' with the view that love is 'beautiful, good, blessed, and a god' (108). To explain Socrates' opinion that Love is a *daemon* rather than a god, Ficino is obliged to describe the place and function of daemons in the cosmic hierarchy he had set forth in earlier Speeches. In one place this hierarchy consists of God, the Mind, the Soul, Nature, and Matter or Body (II iii-v 47–52). The level of Mind or *mens* is also referred to variously as *angelus*, *angeli*, and *mens angelica*, and the level designated as *anima* or *anima mundi* usually absorbs the function assigned to *natura*. ('When we say Soul, we mean, following the custom of the ancient theologians, the power placed in the Soul's reason and sensation; when we say Nature, we mean the power placed in the Soul's faculty of procreation,' II iii 48–9.) In Ficino's ontology everything created is regarded in relation to God or 'the One.' Everything except undifferentiated Matter or Body serves, in relation to higher and lower entities, a mediating function, making possible a unifying circulation of vitality and intelligibility among the forms of being, which are linked by manifestations of the Ideas that originate with God. Everything is hierarchically and concentrically ordered. Lower forms are physically included (i.e., logically implied) in higher forms, and *species* are included or implied in *genera*.

To explain 'how the daemons inhabit the middle region between heaven and earth' (VI iii 109), Ficino starts at the level of the hierarchy which includes daemons, that of the Soul. He works not from experience but from the views of Plato, which he supports by deductive reasoning.

> Plato thinks that the whole machine of this world is ruled and moved by a single soul, because the whole body of the world is a single body (composed of all of the four elements) of which the parts are the bodies of all living things ... Therefore to the same extent that a whole is more perfect than a part, the World Body is more perfect than the body of any individual living thing. (*On Love* 109–10)

This world body is not the sum of individual things, but something ontologically prior to all *species*. This body must have a soul: 'Certainly it would be an absurdity if an imperfect body could possess a soul but a perfect body could neither possess a soul nor be alive' (110). The reasoning is Plato's: Jayne cites *Laws* 886A in support of this statement. There are twelve spheres in the universe (again 'according to Plato ... eight heavens and the four elements below the heavens'), but its matter and structure are single. 'Therefore the soul of the one prime Matter must be single, but the souls of the twelve spheres must be twelve.' Such souls 'the Platonists call *gods* because they are very close to the Angelic Mind and the Supreme God'; the rational creatures who inhabit the regions of fire and air 'the Platonists call *daemons*' (110).

Secured at one end by a demonstration that the world is one body and its soul is single, the argument of Speech VI iii moves far from its foundation in Plato's *Timaeus* to embrace the description of daemons developed by Neoplatonists in late antiquity, with Socrates' description of Love as a daemon for their starting point.[26] Earlier, Love had been praised as a unifying energy, 'the eternal knot and link of the world' (III iii 68), present at every level of the creation. By the end of this chapter, Love retains its original scope and significance, but it has been embodied in plural forms devoted to the care of individual human lives. Platonic daemons are identified with Christian guardian angels: 'The good daemons, who are our guardians, Dionysius the Areopagite usually calls by the proper name *angels, rulers of the lower world*; this differs very little from the opinion of Plato' (111).

The bearing of Ficino's themes in Speech VI iii on several places in *The Faerie Queene* will call for more extensive discussion in later chapters. At some risk of obscurity here, I have undertaken to place the argument for the world's possession of a body and a unifying soul in its context, because Spenser was, I believe, responsive to more than bits and pieces of this system, although some of it seems to have been either uncongenial or simply irrelevant to his purposes. (Ficino's thought makes no sense except as a *way* of thinking, but no one interested in his ideas on love or on the *anima mundi* is obliged to accept his whole system.) There are notable differences between Ficino's mode of discourse and Spenser's. The coupling terms and conclusions of logic (therefore; because; if ... then ...; must be) aren't necessarily alien to poetry, but in general Spenser has little use for them. When one thing depends upon or follows from another in Spenser's conceptual economy, he demonstrates this by narrative rather than logical means, creating labyrinths that contain conceptual clues and working toward rather than reasoning from general principles. (It is reasonable to suppose, however, that in his '*Idea* or fore-conceit' general principles were often uppermost, creating the structure within which images and events would take shape.) For the reader of his text as for characters within it, existence precedes essence.[27]

In their dependence on traditions, religiously motivated but not based on appeals to Christian revelation, Ficino and Spenser had much in common, but their appeals to authorities were profoundly different, as befits their genres. Each offers an intertextual discourse, entitled to respect and yet not beyond question. Ficino makes a show of reasoning from first principles, but they are conspicuously derived from 'Plato,' 'the Platonists,' spokesmen for the *prisca theologia*, and the patristic authorities he finds congenial; his debt to Aquinas's systematic theology is extensive, as modern scholarship has shown,[28] but hidden. Spenser's borrowings are similarly extensive, but not so programmatic and not nearly so conspicuous, except where the poetry of his predecessors is concerned; his indebtedness to philosophers is *sub rosa*, veiled by his vague reference to 'Aristotle and the rest.' The description of the Garden of Adonis, for example, features the most esoteric learning, the subtlest allusions, and the most inventive adaptations of its sources to be found in *The Faerie Queene*, yet Spenser's references to his authorities are slight, playful, even devious.

In the stanza introducing us to Venus's 'ioyous Paradize,' after alluding to pleasant places traditionally associated with Venus he professes ignorance of this garden's location, although he knows 'by tryall' that it surpasses others; then he closes by calling it 'The *Gardin* of *Adonis*, farre renowmd by fame' (III vi 29). Spenser hints at his membership in a community which his poem, in effect, discovers: whatever the fame of Adonis in 1590, no such garden named for him had been described before. This analogue of Eden alludes to the little 'gardens of Adonis' mentioned derisively in Plato's *Phaedrus* 276B; Spenser has taken an emblem of the ephemeral and created its opposite, perpetuity on a cosmic scale.[29] Similarly, when he comes to the 'gloomy groue of mirtle trees' on top of Venus's 'stately Mount' (43.1–3), Spenser transforms the ending of Adonis's story, which in Ovid and various adaptations is a mawkish tragedy of unrequited love, reckless youth, and violent death, into a transfiguration: 'There wont faire *Venus* often to enioy / Her deare *Adonis* ioyous company' (46.1–2). Rather than the 'lost louers name' of the introductory stanza (29.8) we have in stanza 46 the 'secret' presence of a 'wanton boy' whose 'sweetnesse' Venus can reap 'when euer that she will.' So, according to the poet, 'some say' (46.4), 'And sooth it seemes they say' (47.1), but these conspicuous references to other voices (with still others at 47.8 and 48.8) diffuse the originality of stanzas 47–9. Spenser is his own soothsayer, with a message from beyond the grave that obscurely echoes the mythographers' association of Adonis with the sun.[30] Spenser says nothing to encourage an identification of Adonis with the sun, but his cult figure may be taken as a mysterious manifestation of much that the sun means when we read nature as an allegorical text, a story about mortality and the cyclical continuity of life. Spenser's myth-making may make more sense if we regard Adonis as, like the sun, a manifestation of the world soul's creative agency.

Some lines from stanza 47 will take us back to Ficino's mode of discourse and his conception of the world as unified by a single soul. To an
unusual degree, Spenser's justification of what 'they say' about Adonis is
shaped by the logical connectives and the appeals to necessity we found
Ficino using: the hearsay seems true '*for* he *may not* / For euer die, and
euer buried bee / In baleful night.' (Here and in what follows, I have added
italics for emphasis.) Why may not Adonis die? Because he '*is eterne* in
mutabilitie, / And by succession made perpetuall,' and the reason for this
lies in the identity 'they' have discovered for Adonis: '*For* him the Father
of all formes they call; / *Therefore needs mote* he liue, that liuing giues to
all.' Adonis's apotheosis is of the sort familiar from pastoral elegy, and
Spenser invites us to see him alongside Amintas, 'To whom sweet Poets
verse hath giuen endlesse date' (45.9), but Adonis is supposed to enjoy an
eternity in the realm of nature, not art. While practising an art that hides art
and includes nature, supplementing his description of Acrasia's artificial
bower, Spenser doesn't entirely conceal the fact that this Adonis, for all the
roots that connect him with primitive vegetation rites and the no less
primitive dynamics of love and loss, is substantially the new poet's own
creation, an original myth of origins.

A deductive logic applies here that resembles Ficino's, accounting for
order and vitality in the world by a series of causes. From the way both
writers employ deductive logic, we can see that it arises not from the
nature of things, but from a human reluctance to accept mortality, which
Spenser understood to be the basis for both poetry and philosophy. The
poet has more freedom to confess his vulnerability than most philosophers
would use, and in his text the trappings of logic are conspicuously the
means to a foregone conclusion.[31] Like a philosopher who gives all mortal
life a single source, Spenser represents in this garden 'the first seminarie /
Of all things, that are borne to liue and die' (30.4–5), placing its progeny in
the hands of 'Old *Genius*' (31.8–9), whom we can now recognize, by
contrast to the young Genius of that other bower of bliss, as 'that celestiall
powre, to whom the care / Of life, and generation of all / That liues,
pertaines in charge particulare' (II xii 47.2–4). While the image of Genius in
the Garden was derived from other sources, his function is consistent with
the mediating role Ficino assigned to daemons in the commentary *On
Love* (VI iii–iv 110–12). As we have seen, Spenser elaborates his myth of
generation further when Adonis is represented as 'the Father of all formes,'
paired with Venus, 'their great mother' (40.3). Together, Venus and Adonis
represent the occult energy that unifies and renews all of life that is subject
to time and death, and the Garden as a whole is a poetic analogue to
Ficino's doctrine of the world soul and its daemons.

Like the several concentric spheres with their upward- and downward-tending inhabitants in Ficino's hierarchical universe, much of what Spenser says to account for the generation of life may now seem redundant rather than necessary. Living as we do in the shadow of a 'less is more' aesthetic, we comprehend with difficulty what Lovejoy called the 'principle of plenitude,' which made elaboration a necessity for centuries of thinking about the world as a system.[32] Some Elizabethans accounted for the generation of mortal creatures simply, appealing directly to the will of God that sustains their existence by a continuous *fiat*, but even for them God's goodness guaranteed a complex hierarchy of creatures. Spenser honours this world view when he cites the originating word of 'th'Almightie lord, / That bad them to increase and multiply' (34.5–6); he surrounds it, however, with references to the creatures' growth 'of their owne accord' because they 'remember well' the words of Genesis 1:22, and because they contain 'in themselues eternall moisture' (34.2, 4, 9). Without entering further into the thick of things in the Garden, we can see that Spenser's account of generation is richly over-determined. It is quite possible that the several agents and contributing factors so far identified could be analysed into a series of causes, such as Harvey mentioned half-seriously in his explanation of the earthquake in 1580; in any case, they serve to demonstrate what Ficino had said, 'that love may rightly be called the eternal knot and link of the world' (*On Love* III iii 68), a principle that unifies but is manifested through proliferation.

Spenser has, then, much in common with Ficino and other philosophers in the Platonic tradition. I have cited passages from the commentary *On Love* not as sources with a unique importance, but as instances of a way of reasoning and a repertoire of concepts that were available to Spenser and the more literate members of his audience from many authors. Especially in such texts as *On Love*, the mode of argument is more fictive than philosophical. Everything depends upon our perception of mortal creatures as participants in the immortal life surrounding them, our respect for the authority of Plato and his interpreters, and our willingness to grant a priori that what 'is proper' or 'must be' is in fact the case,[33] rather than anything that 'would be an absurdity.'[34] As George Boas has observed, 'The Florentine Neo-Platonist ... took as his fundamental premise the incorporation in all experience of the moral and aesthetic values' ('Philosophies of Science in Florentine Platonism' 250).

Sidney's 'right poet' was expected to proceed similarly from this fundamental premise in devising his images of what might be or should be. The difference between Ficino's 'must' or 'ought' and Sidney's 'may' or 'should' brings out the poet's concern with possibilities rather than imperatives, and with phenomena in a fictive world that is tenuously related to both actual circumstances and theoretical premises. Generally speaking, philosophers claim to be telling a kind of truth that is beyond the reach of poets, but if Ficino, having claimed to describe reality, doesn't meet the burden of proof, does he forfeit respect for his unwillingness to separate 'is' from 'ought'? Is he not involved in constructing a model, a hypothetical world as ideal and in its way as tenuously related to ordinary reality as Faerie land or Arcadia? One misses in Ficino the irony and diffidence with which Plato encloses the most memorable of his teachings in myths, calling his account of the world's order in the *Timaeus* no more than a 'likely story,' but Ficino's own discourse is rich with metaphors and allegorical myths. We mistake its spirit if we take his system-building literally, just as we mistake the spirit of Spenser's work when we look for simple correspondences between details in *The Faerie Queene* and events in England or doctrines in a schematic account of the moral life.

Classical lore and the conventions of romance freed Spenser from obligations to represent either facts or beliefs literally, which was convenient because both were recognized as being disputable and variable. Ficino had gained a similar freedom by assuming an interpreter's role on behalf of the Platonic tradition. In a sense, he is never more than a translator, obliged to make sense of his texts and not to criticize their departures from the truth if any were to be found. Where Plato's teachings were at odds with revelation and Christian tradition, Ficino and his followers could withhold full assent while continuing to entertain ideas despite their heterodox potential.

In relation to the discourse of philosophers, Spenser's position combined responsibility and freedom. His prototypical poet, Orpheus, was both a mythic figure and a supposed founder of the *prisca theologia*, the tradition in which Ficino placed Plato, claiming for that theology an obscure but supportive relationship to Judaeo-Christian revelation and church doctrines. An Orphic poet might gain through his muse a privileged access to knowledge older than philosophy, but who had granted the muse such power? Who but Ficino and his followers, on the basis of their reading of Plato's *Ion* and the Neoplatonists' understanding of ecstatic knowledge? Spenser's poetry offers such knowledge in belated and mediated form, and his mediation depends upon the philosophers' interpretation of mediation in the cosmos. Further discussion of his poetry and philosophical texts on which it draws will show that in both modes of discourse, the relation of concepts to their phenomenal manifestations involves a two-way movement between interdependent levels of a hierarchy. For both Ficino and Spenser, it is as true to say that the fiction validates the '*Idea*' as vice versa.

chapter four

Platonic Natural Philosophy in the *Aeneid*

This chapter will broaden the base of the argument offered in the previous chapter, adding weight to my claims that *The Faerie Queene* deals extensively with the subject matter of natural philosophy, in a discursive mode that closely resembles the way of thinking found in expositions of Plato's legacy, especially in what I have termed 'esoteric' humanism. The content of nature as a category varies with the context in which the term is used and the purposes to be served by an account of the natural order. Usually human nature is included in the category, but only that part of it understood to be mortal. Often one is asked to ponder some discord: birth inserts a human being into both nature and history, but whether fallen or redeemed, humanity is not entirely at home in recurrent cycles. With this in mind, Platonically oriented natural philosophers imposed upon the open-ended temporal sequence of natural events a goal consistent with Christian ideas about the end of time. Also, in the here and now, they tended to regard nature as a category open at the top, informed from a transcendental source and designed to permit some creatures a return to that source. More than in the Aristotelian tradition and the new science that succeeded it, writers in the Platonic tradition distinguished between the Creator and his creatures but (as we saw at the end of the previous chapter in Ficino's account of Love as a daemon) conferred shaping and motivating agency in the sublunary world upon the higher orders of creatures.

Is nature spiritual or physical? It is both, a *discordia concors*; but the two terms are seldom mixed equally. Louis Dupré opens his history of nature understood as form with Leslie Stephen's observation that the term had been 'contrived to introduce the maximum number of equivocations into any theory it enters.'[1] Such equivocations are grist for the mill of allegory, and the alignment of nature with form – regarding all things not as a chaotic system but as the successor to chaos in a triumph of reason – provided underwriting for allegory. Dupré offers this account of the foundation for Western metaphysics and natural philosophy: 'If there is one belief Greek thinkers shared, it must be the conviction that both the essence of the real and our knowledge of it consists ultimately of *form*. Basically this means that it belongs to the essence of the real to *appear*, rather than to hide, and to appear in an orderly way' (*Passage to Modernity* 18): hence, as we have seen, the world is a book open to allegorical interpretation.

Nature extends from the sublunary world of four elements to include the planetary spheres and the fixed stars. It is not limited to the physical or material aspect of that universe, but includes presences bridging the difference between immaterial essences and physical phenomena: the souls and spirits, daemons, or intelligences that account for form, motion, and all degrees of sense and life within the cosmos. Typically in the sixteenth century, and contrary to our own habits of mind, *natura* is distinguished from *materia* and refers to the formative, vivifying, and regenerative principles in physical phenomena. A French treatise on 'the occult marvels and secrets of nature' provides a series of definitions that circumscribe the term's meaning adequately for my purposes:

> Nature is a quality infused in things from their beginning and birth.
> Nature is temperature and mixing of the four elements.
> Nature is the instinct and inclination of the spirit of each thing.
> To philosophers, Nature is the beginning of movement and rest.
> Nature is that which gives form to each thing according to its special quality [*selon sa speciale difference*].
> Nature is the virtue and efficient cause and preserver [*conservatrice*] of all things, infused [*inserée*] in all the world.
> Nature – to define it more appropriately – is the order and continuation of the divine works, which obeys God's power and his words and commandments, and borrows its powers [*ses forces*] from him.[2]

In these definitions, nature is more than a class concept, an *omnium gatherum* like Wittgenstein's 'everything that is the case.' It is hardly an ontological or epistemological domain at all, but something both ordinary and ineffable within the phenomenal world: 'a quality infused in things,' the 'temperature' that establishes order, an 'inclination of the spirit of each thing,' 'powers' derived from God and accomplishing God's will. Like

God, nature is a unitary concept, but its function is to serve as the principle of individuation, the *natura naturans* through which all *naturata* are constituted and united, 'from their beginning and birth.'

Lemnius's principles are obviously relevant to natural phenomena as we have seen them interpreted by Gabriel Harvey, and as the concept was personified later in Spenser's *Cantos of Mutabilitie*. They can be related to other passages in *The Faerie Queene* as well, but they were not commonplace and uncontroversial. Anything like God would seem to be good, but the likeness was open to challenge in the sixteenth century if it lacked a basis in Scripture and might intrude upon either the authority of God's anointed deputy or an individual's unmediated relationship to God. As Dupré demonstrates magisterially, the Judaeo-Christian tradition of belief in a transcendent God and creation *ex nihilo* introduced lasting tensions into Western thought about nature, and the slow passage to modernity that Dupré traces back to the fourteenth century involved occasional breaks with the assumptions that justified allegorical representation of the natural order. Calvin and some English Protestants were reluctant to allow for any unifying spiritual agency in the world other than God. Spenser was also exposed to ideas about nature as an autonomous domain whose materiality and particularity called for a new logic and a new language,[3] and we have seen how Gabriel Harvey, having partially assimilated the new natural philosophy, used allegory to ironic and comic effect. During the 1590s if not earlier, Spenser probably became familiar with some of Giordano Bruno's heterodox writings, which redefine the relationship of nature to God. His own more traditional views, and his use of the old-fashioned mode of allegory, should not be regarded as naive, but as artful archaism consistent with a critical stance toward differing conceptions of the natural order.

The Organic Soul or *Spiritus*

The legacy of Plato was central to the new conceptions of the natural order and the position of humanity within it that developed during the Renaissance, emerging late in the fifteenth century and flourishing over the course of the sixteenth. Philosophers as different as Ficino and Pomponazzi agreed in giving human nature a central place in the cosmos, and in making the soul and its faculties central to their philosophical investigations. For Ficino, a Platonist well grounded in scholasticism, the soul must be shown to be immortal but this involved conceding that the rational soul is separable from its lesser faculties; for Pomponazzi, an Aristotelian who assimilated many ideas from the Platonists, the rational soul's need for embodiment in order to enjoy its faculties made its separable immortality a matter of faith, not susceptible to proof. The Platonic and Aristotelian traditions both contained well-articulated accounts of the soul's different parts, and both could be drawn upon to develop a twofold understanding of the soul. Its rational or intellectual part is immaterial, immortal, and supernatural in both its origin and destiny; its lower parts or faculties, often described as properties of the sensitive and vegetative souls, are material though made of finer stuff than the body on which they confer form, vitality, a sensory apparatus, and all the mental functions that rely on the five senses.

The Cambridge History of Renaissance Philosophy, noting that the term *psychologia* was coined late in the sixteenth century ('apparently by the German humanist Joannes Thomas Freigius in 1575'), begins a comprehensive account of the subject by observing that it was a sub-division of natural philosophy (*CHRP* 455). This account is twofold, as the subject was during the Renaissance: the 'organic' soul was described within the context of natural philosophy, while the 'intellective' soul, different in its nature and its immortal destiny, was a matter of concern to theologians. Only the 'organic' soul concerns us here; it will become apparent in the next section that Platonic doctrines related to that part of human nature were important in Cristoforo Landino's interpretation of Virgil, and subsequent chapters will examine how this part of human nature, distinguishable in its origin, functions, and destiny from the immortal soul or mind, is represented in *The Faerie Queene*.

When the organic functions of the soul – those that begin with its embodiment and direct all the body's functions – are described in Renaissance texts, the term *anima* is often supplemented or replaced by *spiritus*, a slippery term with a currency outside the discourse of faculty psychology. *Spiritus* appears in many sixteenth-century contributions to natural philosophy and its subtopics (e.g., astrology, alchemy, magic, horticulture), and to related fields such as medicine and music. In the macrocosm and in human nature, 'spirit' acts – mysteriously in some accounts, mechanically in others – to create an interface, as today's jargon would have it, between an immaterial mind or soul and the physical body. When Lemnius described nature as 'the instinct and inclination of the spirit of each thing,' and as 'the virtue and efficient cause and preserver of all things, infused in all the world,' he was appealing, first in particular and then in general terms, to a doctrine familiar from many sources and significant in several aspects of life. It was generally agreed that without the spirit contained in seeds they could not germinate; without the spirit descending on them from the heavens when they were planted at the proper time, they could not be expected to thrive. The concerns of farmers were echoed, metaphorically, in scholars' studies, where the language of pastoral and georgic culture was used to describe introspective and speculative labour, and ways were sought to draw down beneficial spirits from the heavens, improve health, and lift the soul's higher faculties above its bodily confinement.

Within the human body, all vital functions and the organs providing for them (vegetative powers seated in the liver, emotive functions of the sensitive soul centred in the heart, faculties of cognition and will directed by the brain through the nervous system) 'relied for their operations on a substance called *spiritus* – a subtle vapour or exhalation produced from blood and disseminated throughout the body by the arteries and nerves, which were assumed to be hollow. The source of all activity in the living body, *spiritus* was often referred to by Renaissance philosophers as the "first instrument" of the soul.'[4] A number of sixteenth-century authorities, beginning with Melanchthon in his *Liber de anima* (1555), found it plausible to regard this *spiritus* as not the instrument but the corporeal essence of the organic soul, linked with an incorporeal and immortal soul that is infused by God.[5] This way of thinking, which found favour with Sir Francis Bacon, disposed of the tripartite soul that ancient opinion had devised, replacing it with an innate spirit and an infused soul, the one corporeal and natural and the other with a higher origin and destiny.

According to both tradition-oriented and innovative authorities, the organic soul or spirit was in charge not only of involuntary and 'lower' bodily functions, but of all sense perception and some cognitive activity, including imagination, the *sensus communis*, and memory associated with sensory experience. In the summary of the tripartite soul's functions found in Gregor Reisch's encyclopedic *Margarita philosophica*, a comprehensive index to received opinions, the intellective soul presides over the functions of the lower souls but its own faculties are limited to 'the three rational powers of intellect, intellective memory (memory of concepts, as opposed to sense images) and will' (*CHRP* 465–7); all other functions involve bodily organs and the flow of *spiritus*, and even rationality must deal with the conditions of embodiment. This schema, or something like it, provided the grounds for Renaissance attacks upon poetry and the other arts as pandering to the unruly lower parts of human nature, and it also informs some of the distinctions made by poetry's defenders, such as Sidney's between *eikastic* and *fantastic* images.

Landino's Commentary on the *Aeneid*

The Florentine humanist Cristoforo Landino (1425–98) is known for his commentary on Dante's *Commedia* in a fine edition (1481) to which Sandro Botticelli contributed illustrations; the defence of poetry as divinely inspired, which forms part of this book's apparatus, has been mentioned by Geoffrey Shepherd and others as the basis for Sidney's mention of him near the end of *An Apology for Poetry* (see *AP* 142.5 with Shepherd's note, 236). Landino is equally well known for the *Camaldolese Disputations* (1472), a dialogue modelled on Cicero's *Tusculan Disputations*, in which the merits of active and contemplative ways of life are debated, then the nature of the highest good, followed by an allegorical reading of the first six Books of the *Aeneid*. Readers familiar with Ficino's commentary on Plato's *Symposium* may recall that in Speech IV of that dialogue Landino is called upon to interpret Aristophanes' myth of mankind's original form and the splitting by which its pride was punished. For Ficino, eight years younger, Landino was in some respects a mentor, although as the careers of both men developed Ficino became more deeply learned in philosophy and theology; Landino devoted himself to applying ideas from the Platonists to literary interpretation, relying heavily on Ficino's work. Beginning in 1456 and for forty years thereafter, Landino lectured on poetry and moral philosophy in the Florentine Studio, interpreting Dante and Petrarch as well as the classical poets before large audiences of the city's well-born and ambitious young men. 'He lectured on philosophers as if they were poets and on poets as if they were philosophers,' as Arthur Field puts it.[6]

Landino's views on the *Aeneid* are best known today from Books III and IV of the *Camaldolese Disputations*, but out of his teaching, beginning with a course of lectures in 1462–3 on the first seven Books (Field 246), Landino developed an elaborate commentary on the *Aeneid* and the *Georgics* that undoubtedly reached a larger audience, within Florence and beyond, than did his dialogues staged at Camaldoli. Virgil's poems with Landino's commentary were first published in Florence in 1487, and the commentary was reprinted many times, often in combination with those of Servius, Donatus, Antonio Mancinelli, and Domizio Calderini as *Virgilius cum commentariis quinque*.[7] For the *Georgics* and the *Aeneid*, *Virgil with Five Commentaries* reproduced Landino's 1487 edition, in which his commentary follows the notes of Servius and Donatus. Until about 1520, when it was eclipsed by editions including the commentary of Jodocus Badius Ascensius (less imaginative and more precise in its scholarship), this was the standard scholar's edition of Virgil's *Opera*, published by competing presses throughout Europe.[8] At the end of his *Prooemium* to the *Aeneid*, Landino says that, having given a philosopher's interpretation of the poem in his *Disputationes*, in his commentary he does the work of a grammarian and rhetorician, focusing on the poem's literal sense. This misleading generalization has been repeated many times, most recently by Field.[9] In fact, the *Prooemium* includes a justification of his approach to the poem as a Platonic allegory, and the commentary that follows, surrounding small segments of Virgil's poem with a sea of fine print, omits few details of the interpretation developed in his *Disputationes*. In some important respects it augments and otherwise modifies that account of the poet's place in a philosophical and theological tradition. In addition to brief comments elucidating details in Virgil's text, the commentary contains many excursuses of a sort that probably originated in Landino's lectures on the poem.

In his view of the *Aeneid* as a Platonic allegory, Landino was heir to a tradition reaching from Servius and Macrobius to Dante and beyond. Unlike medieval and trecento allegorists, he was familiar with the *Odyssey* and the ancient Neoplatonists' interpretations of it.[10] He had access to Ficino's translations and commentaries prior to their publication. A passage from Ficino's Preface to his translation of Dante's *De Monarchia* (1468) presents ideas that Landino would later elaborate: Plato, he says, described three kingdoms, 'one of the blessed, the other of the damned, and a third of pilgrims ... Virgil was the first to follow this Platonic schema, which Dante followed afterwards, drinking with Virgil's vessel at the Platonic sources.'[11] Although Landino's criticism pays little attention to the characteristics of the epic genre that would concern later critics, his understanding of intertextuality and latent content in post-Homeric poetry is profound. The inward turn that Spenserian romance gives to the matter of epic is also underwritten by Landino's reading of Virgil in the light of Dante and Plato.

Landino treats the geography and scenery of the *Aeneid* as consistently and schematically allegorical, all pertinent to an educative itinerary. At the beginning of Book VI in his edition, he sums up the allegory in these terms:

It was proper that, kept on the move by several errors, he came to know what he sought: that the highest good consists of nothing other than the knowledge of divine things. Thus he left Troy (i.e., corporeal pleasure), which Venus ... true love of divine things, showed was pleasing to no god ... He left Crete ... when he understood that our origin is not from the body, which is fleeting and temporary, but from the mind ... Nor was it unsuitable that, when he sought Italy, Juno (signifying ambition) thrust him back to Carthage (signifying civil life). Now truly, when he finally sailed away from Sicily, a place very near to Italy, he was not able to reach port until Neptune, whom we understand to be the superior reason, had entirely placated the seas (i.e., the concupiscible part of the mind). And Palinurus (appetite resisting reason) was removed from the helm (administration of life) and Aeneas himself (the intellect) took control. For we will never be able to come into a tranquil port, in which we are intent upon knowledge, until the sea is first cleared of tempests (i.e., the appetite is free of all perturbations).[12]

The forest where Aeneas meets Venus in Book I and the dark grove where he finds the golden bough are *sylva* or *hyle* as understood by philosophers: prime matter and the circumstances of earthly life, which threaten to degrade the soul but can also be the medium through which higher things are made known to it. 'Plato calls God father, since he begets all, and *Sylva* mother, because she supplies matter, [and] the world soul, seed; [and] the forms that are produced, offspring.'[13]

Landino fully shared Ficino's commitment to a revived understanding of the *prisca theologia*, the age-old theology of the Gentiles, and in his commentary, more emphatically than in the *Disputationes*, he argues that Virgil, imitating Homer and instructed by Plato, veiled the wisdom of the *prisca theologia* in his poetry. Like Ficino, Landino had to relate what he found in this tradition to Christian faith and doctrine. As an interpreter of Virgil, however, and neither a theologian nor the maker of a philosophical system, he was not so deeply obliged as Ficino to reconcile the different traditions. With a scholar's neutrality and a rhetorician's delight in plenitude, he could present Platonic doctrines not because he himself thought them true, but because Virgil did. Although it is clear that he warmly endorsed most of what he found in Hermes Trismegistus, Plato, and Virgil, he did not have to make Christians of them, and in fact much of the appeal of their writings lay in truths that were independent of Christianity, and only *similar* to revelation and the dogmatic system of the church.

Landino's *Prooemium* to the *Aeneid* contains a justification of his image of Virgil, and his most succinct statement of the relationship of pagan theology to Christian doctrine. After discussing the implications of the Greek and Latin terms for 'poet,' he states that God has given poets access to 'his mystery.' Pagan as well as Christian poets may be theologians: 'For theology is twofold [*duplex*]. There is one they call *prisca*, whose fountain that divine man Mercurius Trismegistus first opened. The other is ours, which is not only shown to be more true, but so much the truest that nothing can be added to or subtracted from it.' From this statement he goes directly to a summary of the theology contained in the writings of the archetypal poet: 'Was not Orpheus, therefore, versed in the *prisca theologia* when he wrote much about God, angels, incorporeal minds, and human souls? ... That Linus and Musaeus sang almost the same, I think we must believe from what we see written by others about both of them. Also Homer, if we read with some care those hymns written by him. If we also consider in this way what is fabled of Ulysses, so that we bring to light what lies beneath the fiction [*sub figmentis*], will we not wonder at the theology in that poem?' He speaks of the *Aeneid* in the same terms, summarizing the action of the poem and asking, 'Who, I say, does not understand that with admirable and almost divine artifice he shows us that man's highest good consists of inquiry into divine things, and that that pathway is most difficult?'[14]

Virgil, then, inherited a theological tradition begun by the ancient Egyptian Mercurius Trismegistus,[15] sung by Orpheus, and continued by Homer. By Landino's account, the theology of Orpheus appears consistent with Christianity, and there is nothing dubious in his summary of theology in the *Aeneid*. But if, as he says, Christian theology is truer than the pagan tradition, and 'so much the truest that nothing can be added to or subtracted from it,' what of lasting value can be gained from studying the *prisca theologia*? The question is pertinent to the labours of Ficino, Pico della Mirandola, and a host of other Renaissance thinkers, and to Spenser's extensive appeals to motifs and doctrines of pagan provenance with a bearing on religious issues.

The august antiquity of the *Corpus Hermeticum* was exposed as a pious fraud early in the seventeenth century. Most of the texts associated with the name of thrice-great Hermes can be traced to a time no earlier than the Alexandrian milieu of fading and emerging cults (Jewish, Christian, Mithraic, Pythagorean, Gnostic, native Egyptian) and the first centuries of the Roman empire. Other texts later made out to be testimony to the *prisca theologia* and an allied *philosophia perennis* (Orphic hymns, neo-Pythagorean texts, the *Chaldaean Oracles*, and *Sybilline Oracles*) come from the same era, claiming similar origins in the storied past. And many of these writings – the *Hermetica* most of all – bear traces of Plato's influence, directly from the dialogues and indirectly through Alexandrian Neoplatonism.[16] When these texts, part of the Hellenistic legacy that had been preserved in Byzantium, came to light in the West during the fifteenth century, it was all too convenient to believe the fictions that nostalgia had woven around the names of Hermes Trismegistus and Orpheus. They provided for several satisfying responses to the problems posed by polytheism in ancient literature, and new information about the pagan mysteries could be brought under control by the syncretizing principles they contained. When the late classical theosophy of the *Hermetica* was taken to be the oldest and most authoritative statement of a Gentile theology, the polytheism of Homer and Ovid could be regarded as metaphorical, refractions of a monotheistic truth and interpretations of a cosmos that is full of changes but ultimately ordered by fatal laws. Equally important, perhaps, the athletic spirituality to which adepts are urged in the hermetic texts, seeking transcendence in a world that declares its creator's greatness but offers no home for an immortal soul, was consonant with much of the content of late medieval piety, especially that found in circles of studious laymen (Field, *Origins of the Platonic Academy* 134–7).

Many humanists of Ficino's time and later (down to Philippe Duplessis de Mornay, whose *Woorke concerning the trewnesse of the Christian Religion* was studied and partially translated by Sidney, translated in its entirety by Arthur Golding, published in 1587) finessed the question I have raised by treating the *prisca theologia* as a preparation for the gospel and a useful prop for Christian orthodoxy. Landino's strategy is different, and more prudent, although in providing for a 'twofold' theology he risks comparison with the late medieval Nominalists' doctrine of a 'double truth,' one according to reason and another taken on faith – the bogey that Ficino had undertaken to dispel with his appeals to the Platonists. Prudence with a tincture of insincerity shows in the superlatives with which Landino characterizes 'our' theology, the 'more true' of the two. He is clearly more interested in the less true tradition, and his fascination is a consequence, I believe, of the proposition 'that nothing can be added to or subtracted from' Christian doctrine. At the end of the passage I have quoted, he defines the highest good as consisting '*in diuinarum rerum speculatione.*' To devout humanists of the fifteenth century, the edifice of Christian theology must have seemed closed to speculation. In the obscure and still exotic texts attributed to Hermes Trismegistus, Orpheus, and other contributors to the *prisca theologia*, and even more in poetry such as Homer's and Virgil's that could be said to perpetuate it in veiled form, Landino and readers willing to follow his lead found a field in which discovery and interpretation were called for, where one could be not only devout but imaginative. The Reformation changed perspectives on the edifice of Christian theology radically for both Catholics and Protestants, but when controversial items of doctrine had divided nations and become inextricable from politics, and after Calvin and other Protestant scholastics had done their work, men like Philippe de Mornay, and Sidney and Spenser in England, may have felt again the need to move from the province of doctrine to that of imagination in support of 'speculation on divine things.'

Where non-Christian testimony confirmed Christianity, Landino could cite it and marvel, valuing it all the more for its independence from revelation. The idea that theology is *duplex*, neither unanimous nor divided against itself, permitted an ambivalent attitude toward ideas divergent from Christian orthodoxy. In one of the few passages I have seen in his commentary that reflect critically on either Plato or Virgil, at the end of his comments on Anchises' explanation of the pre-existence and transmigration of souls (*Aeneid* VI 724–51), Landino concludes: 'This kind of reasoning, then, I have pursued to interpret these verses, not because I believed them or approved of them. For regarding our soul I think without hesitation wholly what the Christian religion asserts: that they are created by God out of nothing, at the same time created and infused into bodies, and many other things of which we have written at some length in our dialogue, *De anima*. But since our Plato was ignorant of our religion, and he [Virgil] was wholly Platonic, I decided to interpret his statements in accordance with Platonic doctrine.'[17] A mind committed to both 'our religion' and 'our Plato' (not to mention 'our Ficino') may have much to teach us about 'our sage and serious poet.' We should entertain the possibility that Spenser, similarly tolerant of ideas in Virgil that are errors in the light of Christian doctrine, followed him even along some theologically dubious paths, on the principle that an epic poem, constituted in the first place by intertextual echoes, may best include revealed truths in enigmas and similitudes.

Landino read the *Aeneid* with reference to a metaphysical framework and a cosmology derived from the *prisci theologi*, informed also by Ficino's new learning. Müller-Bochat observes that the *Disputationes* articulate a 'poetic theology' similar to that proposed by Pico della Mirandola years later in his commentary on Benivieni's *Canzone*.[18] For the ontological basis of this theology Landino glosses Homer's golden chain let down from heaven, presenting his schema as a doctrine shared by Hermes Trismegistus, Homer, and Plato. The chain originates in the *essentia Dei*, and in the second place comes *potentia*, then *sapientia*, then *uoluntas* (all within God, I take it, and obviously analogous to the three Persons). Next comes *fatum*, then the *anima mundi*, then a series of celestial *daemones* (aetherial, aerial, watery, and earthy). Last and lowest is *hyle* or *sylva*, matter, the mother of all forms. God is the father, by means of the seminal power of the world soul, breathed into the womb of matter (*Disputationes* 177–9).

So far as I know, this account of the golden chain allegory is not repeated in Landino's edition of Virgil. He does not find the highest members of the chain personified in the *Aeneid*, but Fate and Jove are of course prominent in the poem, and require interpretation. *Aeneid* VI 376, '*desine fata deum flecti sperare precando*,' the Sibyl's advice to Palinurus that he should not hope to change the gods' decrees by prayer, provides the occasion for an excursus on Fate and Providence. He quotes two passages from *The City of God* (V viii 1–18; V ix 83–94) in which Augustine interprets the Stoics' conception of Fate as 'the connection and sequence of all causes,' subject to God's will and power. Most of the excursus, however, interprets Plato's and Hermes' teachings. 'Plato writes that Fate is the divine law by which the inevitable thoughts of God, once begun, are completed.' What is termed Providence in the mind of God is Fate in the course of its execution, in which God is not directly involved. 'For the soul [*animus*] of the world is God's minister; it executes diligently what Providence ordains and knows. It both completes, and entrusts execution to its ministers, the stars and daemons ... Among the Platonists *fatum* signifies four things: the mind of heaven [*Mentem ipsam caeli*], the law engendered in it, the law bestowed upon other gods, and finally, the execution ordained by the first God and administered by the second gods.' Quoting a long exposition of this schema from Hermes Trismegistus, who first defined it, he says that besides Plato, later philosophers did not receive Hermes' doctrine of the three Fates in its entirety (*Virgilius* fol. 228v).[19]

Much of the hierarchy derived from the *Hermetica* is irrelevant to the *Aeneid* and Landino's commentary, where various divinities are usually glossed in moral and psychological terms, but it provides a rationale within which Jove can be understood. Landino did not identify him with the Christian God, yet he recognized that in Virgil's eyes Jove was the sovereign deity, not merely the first among equals in a disorderly pantheon. A Platonic cosmology is also appropriate to an interpretation of Book VI, the core of the poem, where Jove's management of the world and the destiny of Rome within it receive a philosophical rationale. For Landino, the first part of Anchises' speech (724–51) is the inner core, and in his edition it is given an especially detailed commentary (fols. 237v-9r). The lines regarding the *Spiritus intus* and the 'mind that agitates the mass, and mingles with the great body of the world,' declare Virgil's belief in the *anima mundi* that figures prominently in the cosmologies of both Platonists and Stoics, and so on this score Landino is not unjustified in considering Virgil a philosophical poet.

Landino consistently identifies Jove with the world soul as described by Plato in the *Timaeus*. In both the *Disputationes* and his edition, he quotes from the Orphic *Hymn to Jove* ('*Iupiter primogenitus est, Iupiter nouissimus, Iupiter caput, Iupiter medium. Vniuersa autem è Ioue nata sunt*'), comparing the message in *Eclogues* III 60.[20] Here he follows Macrobius, who also cites '*Iovis omnia plena.*'[21] If Jove represents the world soul and its power, dispersing life and purpose throughout the body of the world, Anchises' famous lines about the *Spiritus intus* explain the workings of that power and its involvement in the births and destinies of men: Anchises speaking to Aeneas resembles Hermes instructing his son Tat in the *Corpus Hermeticum*. In the *Disputationes*, Virgil's version of the world soul is traced to Stoic sources, but by the time he completed his commentary on Book VI Landino had worked out an ingenious Platonic interpretation, in which Anchises is found referring to both a transcendent divine mind (in '*mens agitat molem*,' VI 727), 'the divine daughter of the Good itself, removed from the world,' and 'to an immanent world soul, the *Spiritus intus*. 'For Plato thought that when God had decided to perform this most beautiful work, and to restore to order the parts and commotions of matter, he devised the soul as a rational and wise mind, to which as a deputy he gave the care of the material world [*cui ut vicario sylvestris prouinciae curam mandaret*]; the soul curbed its malignity with a bridle, reduced everything to order and put it at rest.' The phrases coming before and after Anchises' reference to the divine *mens* moving the world's mass ('*totamque infusa per artus ... et magno se corpore miscet*') refer to 'another mind, given to the world soul by the divine mind as a mover connected to it' (*Virgilius* fol. 238v). This forced interpretation of Virgil's slippery language shows how anxious Landino was to make Virgil a Platonist and to make his Platonism consistent with a Christian rejection of pantheism.[22] Like Plato in the *Timaeus*, Anchises passes from the universe, and the vitality and purpose that all things within it derive from the world soul, to the processes by which human souls are created and enclosed in bodies. The occasion for his explanation was his son's curiosity about the River Lethe and the crowd of men at its banks: Aeneas is bewildered by their desire to return to 'sluggish bodies' (VI 710–21). Anchises explains that souls are seeds with a fiery vigour and a celestial origin, as long as harmful bodies do not slow them, nor dying members dull them. The soul's fears and desires, griefs and joys, and its ignorance of heaven all arise from its union with the body, a dark dungeon (VI 728–34).

Landino explains the descent of souls into bodies and their susceptibility to vice even more elaborately in his edition of Virgil than in the *Disputationes*, and in both this topic is linked with that of purgation and a return to knowledge of divine things. The creation of the soul and its union with the body is discussed not only with reference to Anchises' speech, but also in the course of explaining Aeneas's descent to the underworld. Such a descent can mean five different things, 'first, according to the Platonists, when the soul [*animus*] descends into the body; this is termed the soul's death (its separation from the body is termed the animal's death).' He adds, 'On this descent you will find many fine things in Macrobius the Platonist.'[23] The other senses of 'descent' may pertain as much to episodes in Spenser's romance as to Virgil's poem. The second applies to souls condemned to damnation, and the third to 'when we call forth souls with certain rites and necromancy.'[24] The fourth and fifth descents are metaphorical, and paired instructively: 'when we slip into vices' and 'when we descend to contemplation of vices, in order to abstain from them, knowing their dangers.' Landino understands both Aeneas's and Dante's descents primarily in terms of the fifth sense, Virgil treating the subject of purgation and ascent to contemplation of divine things 'for the same purpose' as Dante, 'as far as one may who is not imbued with Christian truth' (*Virgilius* fol. 220v). We might see Guyon's descent with Mammon in these terms, noting Spenser's allusions to *Aeneid* VI in that episode.

In one of the most famous passages in the *Aeneid* (VI 125–31), the Sibyl tells Aeneas that it is easy to descend to Avernus, 'but to recall a step and come forth to the upper air [*auras*, used in the sense of 'heaven' or 'light' in l. 733, with reference to what incarnate souls have forgotten], *hoc opus, hic labor est.* A few have succeeded, whom friendly Jupiter has loved or radiant virtue raised to heaven.' Landino applies these words not narrowly to the physical and spiritual trials that Aeneas faces in his adventure with the Sibyl, but to the difficulty of regaining the purity enjoyed before life on earth. Of the phrase '*pauci, quos aequus amavit / Iuppiter*' he says, 'These are from profound knowledge of Plato. For Plato says that while they remain in heaven, our souls are fed ambrosia and nectar (i.e., enjoy God), and know the highest joy. Still when man is put in the confines of a rational creature, he can rise above himself by virtue, with God's favor, or tumble below himself to hell through vices.' (Here the distinction between the fourth and fifth senses of 'descent' is relevant.) He adds that 'we cannot return to the upper regions unless we regain the two wings' of the soul, which he glosses as Justice and Religion, the moral and intellectual virtues. Jupiter's love is necessary, he says, 'because although God alone was the creator of our souls, and therefore they are subject to no stars, yet from the contagion of the bodies in which they are enclosed, which are subject to the stars, they draw concupiscible and irascible power and irrational appetite, and from thence, various dispositions toward virtue and inclinations toward vice' (*Virgilius* fol. 221r). He goes on to explain the importance of natal influences and the nature of Jupiter's benign effect.

In his edition of Virgil, Landino's fullest statement regarding the creation of the soul is his comment upon ll. 730–1 of Anchises' discourse, '*igneus est ollis vigor et caelestis origo / seminibus* [fiery is the vigour and celestial the source of those seeds].' 'Corporeal life,' he explains, 'belongs to all living things by virtue of celestial life, and the natural heat of this life takes food from celestial heat. This much is said of all living things [see ll. 728–9], of which he now states that they possess a fiery vigour.' The phrase '*caelestis origo*' applies, however, only to human souls: 'Then he separates our souls from those of the remaining brutes, and says that while a fiery vigour is theirs, yet celestial is the origin of the seeds, i.e., our souls.' His subsequent explanation is based upon a careful reading of the *Timaeus*, and no doubt of Ficino's *Compendium in Timaeum* as well. 'Quite rightly, as a follower of Plato, the poet calls our souls seeds. For he had read in the *Timaeus* that rational souls [were] formed [*concreatas*] by the divine mind in the superior world out of the seeds of all things, mixed in a bowl in accordance with a musical rationale. Further, he says that God, maker of the world, sent rational souls below the moon as the seeds of men, and subordinated to celestial gods the irrational life common to all' (*Virgilius* fol. 238v).

Both Ficino and Landino identify the rational soul as the essence of human nature, immortal and endowed, before being joined with the body and its own irrational faculties, with a knowledge of those divine things that, according to its nature, it should contemplate. In explanation of Plato's statement (*Timaeus* 41E) that souls are placed in *vehicula* before being shown the nature of the universe and told the laws of fate, Ficino says that these are 'etherial bodies.'[25] Landino appeals to this Neoplatonic doctrine in explanation of ll. 745–7 in Anchises' discourse, where the 'pure etherial sense and flame of unmixed upper air [*purum ... aetherium sensum atque aurai simplicis ignem*]' are said to be recovered at the end of the soul's purgation. 'Ether, fire, and air,' Landino says, 'are the three refined bodies, wrapped in which the soul falls into an earthly body. Nor must the soul alone be purged of corporeal blemish before it returns to heaven, but these three veils must be purged of the fog caused by grosser bodies.'[26]

Anchises' account of the soul's pre-existence is introduced, of course, to explain what Aeneas has seen of the afterlife and of souls awaiting reincarnation. Landino was as shy of the doctrine of transmigration that he found in *Aeneid* VI as Ficino had been of similar ideas in Plato. Virgil's references to punishment and purgation required little explanation. When Anchises says (ll. 743–4) that the souls are sent through wide Elysium, Landino glosses Elysium as 'the celestial region. Different souls [are sent] to different spheres and stars after purgation.' One can see from this statement that he did not think it proper to make Virgil's meaning Christian, but he minimized his departures from the truth: Elysium stands allegorically for the heaven of Christian faith. In l. 744, 'a few abide in the joyous fields' not, he says, 'because few are returned to heaven, but either because few are returned to the firmament, or because few when they have left the body are immediately advanced to heaven.' The thousand years through which returned souls roll the wheel (l. 748) are spent in Elysium, not in an underworld, and their afterlife resembles the pre-existence described in the *Timaeus* and the *Phaedrus. Mille,* Landino says, 'is an indefinite number; therefore, many ages. For blessed souls lead a much longer life in heaven than the unhappy, whether sinning on earth or being purged in the aerial body.' They are said to roll the wheel because 'in heaven they agreed with the world soul in the celestial motions, and in contemplation went in turn from forms to forms.' Neptune is responsible for calling them back to earthly life: 'promoting the generation of things, he entices them to conception [*genitura*] at certain times' (*Virgilius* fol. 239r). Without entirely obscuring the idea of cycles of earthly and heavenly life, Landino explains it in terms of the Platonic dichotomy of contemplation and generation, pertaining to moral choices within a single human life.

Contemplation and generation, considered as contrary impulses of the soul, are prominent among the subjects discussed in the *Disputationes.* To explain the significance of Venus and the favour she shows her son Aeneas, Landino adapts Ficino's account, in *On Love,* of the two Venuses described by Pausanias, Venus Urania and Venus Pandemos, glossed as '*coelestis*' and '*vulgaris.*' The heavenly Venus is 'placed in the angelic mind, transported by inborn love to the knowledge of God's beauty,' while the vulgar Venus is 'assigned to the world soul ... for she proceeds from that power which is in the world soul, and creates the power which produces all these inferior things and comes to rest in the matter [*sylvam*] of the world.' Like Ficino, Landino also understands the two Venuses, and the Cupids associated with them, as potentialities within the human soul. The impulses toward contemplation and generation are 'both necessary to human nature,' but the latter is apt to be abused.[27]

Somewhat to my surprise, I do not find a distinction between Ficino's two Venuses in Landino's edition of the *Aeneid.* He does not use the obvious opportunities (Aeneas's meeting with his mother in the wood outside Carthage, I 314–409; his vision of her in the ruins of Troy, II 589–

621) to identify the hero's guide as the heavenly Venus. Glossing VI 190, he explains that twin doves led Aeneas to the golden bough 'because according to Euripides there are two Venuses, heavenly and humane, i.e., love of heavenly things which constitutes the contemplative life, and of human, which constitutes the active; hence wisdom is rightly termed the knowledge of divine and human things' (*Virgilius* fol. 223v). In the only other passage I have found that distinguishes between several Venuses, Aeneas is said to be the son of the third, the daughter of Jove and Dione (*Virgilius* fol. 127v). When, in II 591, Aeneas terms Venus '*alma parens*,' Landino comments that *alma* is 'a most fitting epithet for Venus. For creating every living thing, she nourishes all kinds'; he quotes Lucretius's apostrophe to the 'mother of Aeneas' race, joy of men and gods, life-giving Venus' (*Virgilius* fol. 160r).

In place of a discourse on the two Venuses and the corresponding Cupids, Landino includes in his edition, at the beginning of Book IV, an essay on the varieties of love. Venus is not mentioned, but Ficino's influence is otherwise evident. 'Among mortals there is,' he says, 'nothing greater and more excellent than love; on the other hand, nothing more wretched and unhappy can be imagined.' In explanation of this paradox, he defines 'true' and 'corrupt [*adulterinus*]' love. All love is desire for the beautiful. 'Beauty is threefold: that in the soul, which arises from the harmony of virtues; that in the body, from the consonance of many colors and lines; likewise, with great pleasure, that in sounds, from the consonance of diverse voices.' Only the mind, eye, and ear can perceive beauty; 'the appetite of the other senses is not love, but is called furious desire and madness [*rabies*].' Landino goes on to describe the three forms of love, divine, human, and bestial: the first, 'raising us above man, joins us with God'; the second 'keeps us among men, so that we do not slip into worse forms'; the third, of course, 'makes men into beasts' (*Virgilius* fol. 183r–v).

Commenting on *Aeneid* IV 3, where Virgil says that Aeneas's virtue rushes back many times to Dido's heart (*multa viri virtus animo ... recursat*), Landino says that Dido is portrayed as 'most chaste, and temperate in every respect,' so it is proper that she should be 'moved to love only by the weightiest cause.' Her love is human, founded from the beginning upon virtue, not looks. Allegorically, Dido represents the active or civic life, and 'indeed, in the beginning the civic life is so instituted that it is directed to a virtuous end,' but earthly things are prone to corruption. Dido begins in exemplary temperance, but her love for Aeneas draws her to mere continence, then to incontinence, and finally into intemperance. Landino suggests that the civic virtues are not sufficient in themselves to control the destructive appetites; Aeneas will need the purgatory virtues and those of a soul already purged.[28]

I have expounded Landino's interpretation of the *Aeneid* at length because I think that it probably shaped Spenser's understanding of Virgil and his assimilation of Ficinian Platonism. It is important that we recognize how many of Ficino's interests and ideas were applied to the exegesis of literary texts and thus became accessible and attractive to many humanistically educated men in the course of the sixteenth century. Landino's interpretation of Virgil is only one example, but perhaps the best, of the assimilation that quickly made many features of Florentine Platonism a living and lasting, though not always recognizable, part of European literary culture. Unlike some of the Platonizing literati of the sixteenth century, Landino was fired with a scholarly enthusiasm like Ficino's, and neither vulgarized what he found in Plato and the *prisci theologi* nor lost himself in fantastic and heterodox ideas.

English Protestant Responses to Platonic Natural Philosophy

Was the achievement of Ficino and his fellow Platonic syncretists a 'seething mass of confused thinking,' or 'a triumph of "decompartmentalization"'?[29] Readers will respond variously to the ideas I am tracing back to Plato and the revival of Platonism. While not blind to the errors and excesses of Renaissance Platonism, I choose to admire the daring and the broad scope of that endeavour, in which Ficino and Landino were followed by many others. I join Erwin Panofsky and E.H. Gombrich in admiring a philosophy that succeeded in 'the opening up, to secular art, of emotional spheres which had hitherto been the preserve of religious worship.'[30] In Robert Ellrodt's study of Neoplatonism in Spenser's poetry, the continuity and complexity of developments from the Middle Ages to the later Renaissance are recognized, but insufficiently so. Ellrodt's attempt 'to make out whether Spenser was more deeply influenced by the new trends displayed in the works of the Italian Neoplatonists or by an older tradition inherited from the Middle Ages' (11) is skewed by a partiality for the older tradition, and by preconceptions regarding Spenser's poetry and Elizabethan culture in general. Having sided with Brents Stirling in his old difference with Josephine Waters Bennett over the character and provenance of Spenser's Platonism, Ellrodt adds, 'Whereas Stirling laid emphasis on the popular character of Spenser's notions, I mean to stress their *mediaeval* character: a change in perspective rather than substance, since the mediaeval had become the popular in Spenser's age' (70–1). When scholars today attempt to describe the 'notions' at play in the minds of Sidney, Spenser, and their peers, the components of popular or middle-class culture, as codified in such books as *Shakespeare's England* and *The Elizabethan World Picture*, no longer seem so monolithic as they did in the 1940s and 1950s, when the learned and courtly culture of the 1570s and 1580s was rather shallowly understood. It now seems valid to stress not the *persistence* of medieval attitudes but their *revitalization* during the last quarter of the sixteenth century, as part of the 'refeudalization' that helped make early modernity a patchwork of uneven development.[31]

'I do not think that it is sufficiently realized how very peculiar the Elizabethan Renaissance was, both socially and intellectually,' Frances Yates wrote in 1969 (*Theatre of the World* 19). A good deal of subsequent scholarship substantiates Yates's observation. We know, for example, that John Dee and others were committed, on the one hand, to public, practical enterprises, benefitting artisan and entrepreneurial groups, and they were involved at the same time in inner circles devoted to cultivating 'secret arts' and 'intelligence,' much of it derived from foreign sources. Although Spenser, cut off from the capital and the great houses of England for much of his working life, could never have been a participant in this twofold culture in the way that John Dee, Philip Sidney, and Walter Ralegh were, I imagine that he compensated intellectually for his lack of social opportunities. I believe that his poetry reveals him to have been, as Yates said of Dee, 'both extremely exoteric and practical, and at the same time esoteric among some vaguely defined inner circle' (18).

Pursuing this train of thought, and giving it a specific application to Platonic natural philosophy as it was known in England, I will examine an instance of the way in which the older tradition, considered by Ellrodt to have been more popular, was sometimes conflated with esoteric ideas derived from Florentine Platonism. The case in point is an important vernacular compendium, *Batman vppon Bartholome*, Stephen Batman's edition of a thirteenth-century encyclopedia, *De Proprietatibus rerum* by Bartholomaeus Anglicus. Batman (or Bateman, as the name is sometimes spelled) did more than modernize John Trevisa's translation, which dates from the end of the fourteenth century. His title page advertised the book as 'Newly corrected, enlarged and amended: with such Additions as are requisite, vnto euery seuerall Booke.'[32] Bartholomaeus's erudition is systematically augmented and brought up to date with chapters from various Renaissance books. At the end of Book XI, which concludes a discussion of the celestial spheres and the properties of the four elements, Batman placed his translation of several chapters from Heinrich Cornelius Agrippa's controversial treatise, *De Occulta philosophia*.[33] With this redaction, a medieval encyclopedia became a conduit for ideas representative of esoteric humanism. On close inspection, parts of these chapters from Agrippa turn out to be heavy with borrowings from Ficino's *De Vita coelitùs comparanda*, a treatise on magic, astrology, and the improvement of both spiritual and physical health.[34]

Several passages in the chapters from Agrippa explain how the soul of the world, as an 'intelligible' part of the created order, mediates between God and specific material things, both animate and inanimate. The soul is midway between Ideas that are 'in God, by the manner of the cause,' and their effects in the physical world, 'as shadowes.' According to Agrippa, 'there are so many seminall reasons of things in the world, as there bee *Idees* or conceites in the diuine mind' (*Batman vppon Bartholome* fol. 170r; *De Occulta phil.* I xi). Agrippa explains the function of these 'seminall reasons' by quoting Anchises: '*Igneus est ollis vigor, & coelestis origo: / Seminibus ...*' (*Aeneid* VI 730–1); a Spenserian is bound to think of the seed-beds in the Garden of Adonis. With these 'reasons,' separate from its own indivisible Ideas, 'the diuine minde ... hath builded it selfe in the heuens, beyond the starres euen shapes, and hath imprinted properties in them all' (fol. 170r).

For Ficino, and subsequently for Agrippa, the soul of the world does not suffice as a mediating entity. In addition, a 'spirite of the world' mediates between the otherwise incompatible soul and body of the world, just as a vaporous spirit created by the heart and distributed by blood vessels and nerves unites the human soul and body. Thus 'spiritual' magic works its wonders:

> By this spirit then, all hidden propertye is spread abroade, vpon hearbes, stones, and mettalls, and vppon liuing creatures: by the Sunne, by the Moone, by the Planets, and by the Starres, higher then the planets: And this spirit maye the more profite vs, if a man knowe how to seuer him most of all from other Elements, or at least very much to vse those things which most of all abound of this spirit: for those things in the which that spirit is lesse plunged in the bodie, and matter is lesse ministred, do work more might[i]ly and perfectly, and also doe sooner ingender and beget a thing lyke vnto them. For all vertue generatiue and of seede is in it, wherefore the Alcumists indeauour to seperate that spirite from golde and siluer, which beeing well seuered and drawen out, if afterwarde they applye him to any matter of the same kind, that is, to any of the mettalls, they shall immediatly make golde or siluer. (*Batman vppon Bartholome* fol. 173r; *De Occulta phil.* I xiv)

This remarkable chapter, '*Of the Spirit of the world, what he is, and that he is the bonde of hidden vertues*,' offers a brief rationale for various forms of natural magic, including alchemy. Agrippa aligns his terms with elements of the traditional Aristotelian cosmology: the soul is the *primum mobile* and the spirit *quinta essentia*, understood as a characteristic of the heavens above the moon that is present, as a 'hidden propertye' that can be 'seuered' by art, in the finer things found below the moon. When he discovers the 'hidden vertues' implanted in things by celestial influences, the occult philosopher has turned from the 'shadowes' of forms found in matter to the seeds or 'seminall reasons' from the world soul, the pure forms constituting all natural things ('According to their kindes,' as Spenser would say, *FQ* III vi 30.6). According to Ficino and Agrippa, 'euery kinde, hath a celestiall figure agreeing vnto him: from whence also, proceedeth vnto him, a meruailous power in working, which proper endowment, it receiveth from his *Idea*, by the seminall reasons of the soule of the world' (fol. 170r).

When Stephen Batman chose several chapters from Agrippa to complete Bartholomaeus's account of the spheres and the four elements, he inserted two from Book III of the *De Occulta philosophia* between the eleventh and twelfth chapters of Book I. The second of these insertions (III xxii in Agrippa's treatise) explains '*That euery man hath 3. keepers, and from whence each of them proceedeth*':

> Euery man hath a three-fold good *Demon* for his keeper, the one holy, the other of his begetting, the thirde of his profession. The holy *Demon* according to the learning of the *Aegyptians*, is assigned to the reasonable soule, descending not from the stars nor planets, but from the supernall cause (euen from God, the very ruler of the *Demones* or Angels[)]; & is vniuersall aboue nature. (*Batman vppon Bartholome* fol. 171r)

This 'holy *Demon*' resembles, in his source and function, the guardian angel who watches over the insensible Guyon after his return from Mammon's underworld (II viii 1–8); he seems a conspicuous irrelevance in this part of *Batman vppon Bartholome*, indicating by his presence the the permeability of the boundary between immortal and mortal creatures.

The second of the 'keepers' pertains to mortal life, but is another immortal:

> The *Demon* of begetting, which also is called *Genius*, doth descend from the disposition of the world, & from the starry circuits, which are occupied in generation ... This *Demon* being the executor & keeper of life, doth win life

vnto the body, & when it is in the body, hath a care of it, & helpeth man for the very same office, to the which, the heuenly bodies haue appointed him in his birth. (*Batman vppon Bartholome*, fol. 171r)

Here, I would suggest, is a description of the 'Old *Genius*' who presides over the letting in and letting out at the gates of the Garden of Adonis (III vi 31–2). This passage appears in close proximity to an account of 'seminall reasons' and their place first in the process of creation, and then in the arts by which nature can be manipulated and improved upon. Such ideas would have been available to Spenser and his readers from many sources, some of them without the Platonic inflections transmitted through Ficino and Agrippa to readers of *Batman vppon Bartholome*. Very little in Spenser's poetry came into it for only one reason, or from a single source,[35] but the relevance of Plato and other contributors to the *prisca theologia* is not to be denied when we are dealing with mediating terms in a hierarchical system. Ficino's revival of Platonism removed from its bottle a genie that medieval culture had hardly been able to keep under control.

Stephen Batman's appropriation of ideas from Agrippa of Nettesheim, and indirectly from Ficino, provides one instance of the English Protestant response to the new learning in natural philosophy. It is compatible with Gabriel Harvey's distinction between *natura naturans* and *naturata*, except that Harvey identifies the former with God. As we saw in chapter 1, in his focus upon instrumental causes Harvey was at odds with other interpreters of the prodigious earthquake, most of whom preferred to see providential justice rather than 'the course of naturall causes' in such events. Spenser took the more superstitious attitude seriously, but his poetry is full of characters and incidents showing how the world is constituted and salvation is accomplished by mediation, with the hand of God hidden or only hypothetically present: grace completes a natural order that is already committed to accomplishing God's will. I will close this chapter by returning to Virgil's lines about the *Spiritus intus*, to sample other responses that were in the air along with Landino's thoroughgoing Platonism and Agrippa's rationale for magic.

Adverse reactions to Virgil's lines, or rather to ideas with which they could be polemically linked, were inevitable in the context of the Reformation and Counter-Reformation, when Christian theology was no longer the complete edifice that inspired Landino's tribute and his curiosity about an alternative ancient tradition. For example, Book I of Calvin's *Institution of Christian Religion* is concerned with our knowledge of God as the creator. No knowledge of God as father or saviour is available except through Christ, but we can know our complete dependence upon God through reflection upon his works in heaven and earth.[36] God 'hath in al his works grauen certain marks of his glory' (*Institution* I v, fol. 5v). The glory is more important to Calvin than the works, and the glory is God's, not nature's. The great powers of the human soul are impressive only as evidence of God's nature, and it is an error to think that man himself deserves credit for the invention 'of so many artes & profitable thinges'; similarly, it is God and not a 'secret inspiration that geueth liuelines to the world.' Virgil's *Aeneid* (VI 724–31) and *Georgics* (IV 219–27) are quoted in this context to illustrate an opinion that 'is not onely weak, but also vngodly.' Calvin finds the same principle at work in 'the blasphemous sayings of the filthy dogge *Lucretius*,' the principle being 'to make a shadowish God, to dryue farre away the true God whom we ought to feare and worship.' He allows 'that this may be godlily sayd ... that Nature is God,' but to do so is to use 'an vnproper maner of spech, forasmuch as Nature is rather an order prescribed by God ... it is hurtful to wrap vp God confusedly with the inferior course of his works' (*Institution* I v, fol. 7r–v). Natural religion is an inadequate basis for faith; the many opinions that Renaissance syncretists sought out as evidence that religion is universal are to Calvin 'the dotages or erronious inuentions of our fleshe,' by which 'we corrupt the pure veritye of God' (*Institution* I v, fol. 9r). Faith must be based on the Bible, not on the sacred books of any other tradition. He concludes: 'And therefore the Scripture, to make place for the true and only God, condemneth of falshod & lieng whatsoeuer Godhead in old tyme was celebrate among the Gentiles, & leaueth no God at all, but in the mount Sion, wher florished the peculiar knowledge of God.'[37]

From our perspective it appears that Calvin was in some respects right: the syncretists were confused, some may have been *pro forma* Christians, and their approach to the formulation of a universal truth did not answer to the need felt by many for certainty in matters of faith. Further, we can agree with Calvin that the Creator and creation, as interpreted by syncretists and literati of Ficino's persuasion, were coloured by the 'inuentions of our fleshe.' However, we may not believe that such inventions were any more erroneous than those that Calvin failed to recognize in his own theology. They may, in fact, have been less pernicious, when recognized for what they were – more akin to the figurative language and 'inventions' of poetry than to the 'peculiar knowledge' that theology and science are expected to offer. As noted in the previous chapter, poets and some philosophers of the Renaissance shared and enjoyed this recognition, but they were apt to suffer from the misinterpretations of the literal-minded.

'Literal-minded' would describe the man whose opinions I will consider next. Calvin had called for a knowledge of nature, and of God as revealed in his creation, that was responsive to Scripture and careful to maintain distinctions between God and his works. Lambert Daneau (1530–95), a professor of theology in Geneva, provided Protestants with an appropriate philosophy of nature; translated by Thomas Twyne, his book appeared in England as *The Wonderfvll Woorkmanship of the World: wherin is conteined an excellent discourse of Christian naturall philosophie, concerning the fourme, knowledge, and vse of all thinges created: specially gathered out of the fountaines of holy scripture* (London: for Andrew Maunsell, 1578). Daneau's attitude toward Virgil's *Spiritus* doctrine resembles Calvin's; his argument enables us to understand more fully the objections to Platonic (indeed, all classical) natural philosophy that developed among Protestants during the sixteenth century.

I will go directly to the chapter in which Daneau discusses Anchises' lines, and then give an account of the principles and attitudes at stake. In chapter 14, 'Whether the worlde haue one onely soule,' without attribution he translates *Aeneid* VI 724–7 as a testimony to the opinion of '*Aristotle*, & certayne other,' claiming 'That this whole world hath a soule, and that one onely.' After the quotation he remarks, 'But this is not so much a solemne sentence or saying, as it is a great errour' (fol. 29v). The idea is rejected not on the grounds that it is pantheistic, or confuses God with his works, but because 'verely this worlde is not a liuyng creature. For the members thereof are disioyned, and separate.' In its time this was a unusual observation. For Daneau the metaphors, honoured by centuries of use, according to which the physical universe is not only 'one' but a complete 'body' in need of a soul, have lost their value; what was 'fitting' and an alternative to absurdity for Ficino has itself become a gross error that marks hitherto authoritative voices as erroneous. Daneau concludes the chapter by rejecting 'the opinion of the *Stoikes*, *Platonikes*, and of certeine other Philosophers,' nor will he allow the doubt expressed by St Augustine, 'whether this worlde were a liuyng creature or not' (fol. 31r; cf. fol. 57r–v).

Daneau himself expresses some doubt whether the study of nature is proper for a Christian. Some 'now a daies,' he says, have neglected the study of the gospel's 'veritie' and 'simple stile,' and 'conuert themselues wholy vnto these swellyng and puffed Artes of Naturall Philosophie, addictyng them selues vnto them, and openly preferryng the ambicious name of a naturall Philosopher, before Christian godliness, and Diuinitie' (fol. 4v). One wonders how Daneau and his translator would have regarded *Batman vppon Bartholome*. A true art, according to Daneau, is composed of knowledge, purged of vanity and uncertainty. 'Whenas the Historie of the creation of the worlde is set forth by art, when the vertues whiche God hath giuen vnto things are declared Gods: Miracle is not diminished, but augmented' (fol. 5v). To declare God's those 'vertues whiche God hath giuen vnto thinges' seems to be his main concern; this, and not the possibility of natural magic, is the 'vse of all thinges created' mentioned on the book's title page. He goes on: 'Neither do wee set doune these things, as though wee did professe that we would alledge any other causes of these naturall thynges, besides the will and wisedome of GOD onely' (fols. 5v–6r). Chapter 4, 'The difference between Christian and heathen Naturall Philosophie' (fols. 10v–13r), fully establishes his position. '*Aristotle* and the Heathen Naturall Philosophers' (fol. 10v)[38] are at fault because they confine natural philosophy to study of the phenomenal world, and 'place seconde and onely instrumentall causes, in steede of true and first causes,' neglecting to ascend, 'as it were by a Ladder, vnto GOD the Creatour of them' (fol. 11r). With so little attention paid to intermediary entities spanning the distance between God and the physical universe, it is not clear how Daneau's ladder reaches from here to there. He has, in effect, stripped the ladder metaphor of its traditional association with contemplative discipline in a hierarchically ordered universe.

A reader familiar with Ficino's antagonistic attitude toward the natural philosophy associated with Padua may smile with a sense of dejà vu. Daneau might have respected the aim though not the content of Ficino's natural philosophy, but he seems entirely unaware of that school of thought. Among the ancient philosophers, he admits respect for the earliest, especially for Pythagoras and his school, because they did not divorce philosophy from theology (fol. 11r–v). He has several reasons for rejecting Plato: he objects to idealism on common-sense and religious grounds, and lumps Plato with the gnostic heretics (fol. 23r–v). Further, 'as touching *Plato*, let vs bid hym farewell, for that hee is not onely an *Academike*, and doubtfull of minde, and vncertein in euery thing: but also an Ethnike, and nothing beelonging vnto vs Christians' (fol. 24r). His opinion of Plato seems to have been formed at second hand, from Cicero's *Academica* and perhaps from Augustine's *Contra Academicos*, in the context of the scepticism flourishing in France at the time.[39] Daneau's way of thinking anticipates early modern empiricism, and helps us to understand the connections between earnest Protestantism and the new science that would develop during the seventeenth century. Daneau regards the physical universe as itself a world of wonders, not a prison for the soul or a shadow-box where evidence of a mysterious *Spiritus* is fitfully apparent.

While Spenser probably felt obliged to respect the views of such authorities as Calvin and Daneau, who had a considerable following in England, it is clear that he was deeply committed to intellectual traditions and a view of the world toward which Daneau, for one, appears prejudiced and largely ignorant. With Gabriel Harvey, Philip Sidney, Walter Ralegh, and others of his generation, Spenser combined Protestant convictions with an interest in secular learning across the whole spectrum of the arts and sciences. As the next chapter will show in some detail, his representation of the natural world is not without its own kind of empiricism (though 'phenomenology' might be a more accurate term), but he habitually regards the soul's embodiment in 'sinfull mire' as problematic, and nature in his account contains within itself both the 'mortall state' and a spiritual dimension.

I will end this chapter with a brief discussion of ideas found in an author who was not, in conventional terms, a Protestant, who nevertheless, during an important part of his career, enjoyed hospitality within the Protestant intellectual elite in England: Giordano Bruno.[40] While I do not believe that many intellectual affinities drew Spenser to Bruno's flamboyant and radical ideas, they claimed a prominent place in the tableau of conflicting opinions to which he responded as an erudite poet. I will confine my attention here to Bruno's appropriation of Virgil's lines about the *Spiritus intus*, and it will become clear that in many respects Bruno's thinking about nature resembles Ficino's and Landino's.

The most important of several appeals to Virgil's authority in Bruno's writings are found in the dialogue *De la Causa, principio et uno*, first published in London in 1584, and it is likely that Spenser was familiar with this major statement of Bruno's philosophy.[41] Teofilo, Bruno's spokesman in the dialogue, introduces the lines '*totamque infusa per artus / Mens agitat molem, et toto se corpore miscet*' to explain the nature of the '*intelletto universale.*' He defines this entity as follows: 'The universal intellect is the intimate, most real and proper faculty and potential part of the world soul. It is the same which fills all, illuminates the universe, and directs nature to produce its species as is proper.'[42] Teofilo quotes Virgil as a spokesman for the Pythagoreans, the first of several representatives of the *prisca theologia* (followed by Platonists, the '*Maghi*' or Zoroastrians, Orpheus, Empedocles, and Plotinus) by whom, in similar terms, something resembling Bruno's 'universal intellect' is described (*Dialoghi* 232–3). Teofilo adds, 'We call it the internal artificer, because it forms matter and shapes it from within, as from within the seed or root it sends forth and unfolds the stem, from within the stem it shoots the branches,' and so on (*Dialoghi* 233). Bruno's description of the '*artefice interno*' agrees with Virgil's of a '*Spiritus intus ... infusa*' that works through seeds drawn from heaven, and several other opinions lend support: the Platonists' '*fabro del mondo*,' the '*seminatore*' of the Zoroastrians, and Plotinus's '*padre e progenitore*' who 'distributes the seeds throughout the field of nature, and among the dispensers of forms, is the one nearest to us.'

Among the problems addressed in *De la Causa*, the thorniest involve distinctions between God and the world. The world soul and the universal intellect figure in those distinctions. God is, first of all, a Unity and a cause of being extrinsic to the created order. Bruno also speaks of God as the 'first principle,' but with regard to nature, he uses the terms 'cause' and 'principle' to mean different things. A principle is 'that which intrinsically contributes to the constitution of a thing and remains in the effect.' Matter and form are principles. A cause is 'that which contributes to the production of things from without, and has its being outside of the composite' (*Dialoghi* 230–1). Through the world soul and the universal intellect, which together are both cause and principle, forming things from within and bringing them to perfection, the extrinsic Unity and other attributes of God become intrinsic characteristics of the natural order.

Teofilo calls the world '*questo grande animale e simulacro del primo principio*,' and says that not to affirm 'that the world with all its members is animate' is to detract from God's goodness and the excellence of his creation (*Dialoghi* 238). He goes on to argue that all individual things are animate by virtue of a world soul, 'the constitutive formal principle of the universe and of everything contained in it.' In this context Teofilo's disciple, Dicson, cites *Aeneid* VI again, quoting 724–7 in full and finding Anchises in agreement with 'the sense of the theologian [Solomon, in Wisdom 1:7], who says, "The spirit fills and completes the earth, and is that which contains all."'[43] The differences between Bruno and Daneau could hardly be more marked, and Spenser's way of thinking is much closer to Bruno's than to Daneau's.

Here at the end of Part One in this study, before shifting the focus from contexts to readings of Spenser's text, it is worth considering for a moment how the ideas of Plato and his interpreters can be expected to be present in the poem. I will be arguing that in some passages Spenser's 'fore-conceit' involved motifs – images and implied doctrines – derived from Plato and his interpreters; I also think that some ideas and assumptions of Platonic provenance were so much a part of his intellectual and social milieu as to be inescapable, although some genius shows in his handling of ideas that were 'in the air.' And the range of meanings and implications that a curious reader finds in any passage of *The Faerie Queene* may, quite properly, extend beyond the author's conscious intentions. C.S. Lewis, in a review of Ellrodt's study of Spenser and Neoplatonism, wrote tellingly of the 'iconographical ambiguity' basic to Spenser's poetry. 'If more, and more erudite, symbolism than the poet had consciously intended were read into any image, he would not be displeased.' Lewis concludes, 'To show that many passages do not, as some thought, demand a Neoplatonic interpretation is not the same as showing that they do not admit it.'[44]

The original audience for *The Faerie Queene* was variously educated and prejudiced. It included women as well as men, and it was divided by different political interests and religious commitments. Spenser himself, I believe, was given to ambivalence on the most important issues of his day. He was also committed to the continuation, in his own language, of an encyclopedic kind of poetic narrative, a tradition traceable through several languages back to the origins of poetry and the legendary founding figures, Orpheus and Homer. As part and parcel of that tradition, according to Landino and other critics, there was a *philosophia perennis* to be translated into terms that would suit an Elizabethan audience and its posterity. And the vehicle of poetic narrative, like the fine-textured *vehicula* clothing the soul for its descent into a mortal body, communicates its spiritual messages through veils that are suited to several recipients.

Allegory and allegorical interpretation, taken together, have been aptly described by Gordon Teskey as semantic violence, a 'capture' of meaning in which its original vitality, akin to chaos, is dispelled, while the other part of allegory, personification, reifies noumenal abstractions within the phenomenal world. Although some of the terms in Teskey's post-Hegelian, post-Nietzschean, post-Derridean argument would mystify Spenser, the gendered terms in which Teskey presents the relationship of matter to form (see *Allegory and Violence* 15–21) might intrigue him, and this summary statement may serve as a preface to my argument in the next chapter: 'The figure of personification directs our attention beyond it to allegory's positive other in absolute meaning, on which a cosmos depends. The figure of capture directs our attention to the region of struggle and growth, the forest of life, which the cosmos is always attempting to enclose' (29–30).

'Within this wide great *Vniuerse*'

chapter five

Nature in *The Faerie Queene*:
Concepts and Phenomena

Part One has established an elaborate frame of reference for Spenser as an author and for his poem's representation of the natural order; now I can proceed to fill in the frame. This chapter will not, as a rule, develop its readings in the light of sources or backgrounds;[1] I am interested, rather, in the texture and plain sense of the poem, bearing in mind Paul Alpers's observation that the depths of *The Faerie Queene* are on its surface. The intellectual tradition that I have termed esoteric humanism, and within that tradition the example set by Landino's interpretation of the *Aeneid*, will inform my reading. It would be inconsistent with Landino's own principles, however, to look for obvious correspondences, and we should also take account of Spenser's different circumstances: in England and Ireland late in the reign of Queen Elizabeth, his temperament and the culture he shared with his audience mandated a program very different from that of the quattrocento revival of Platonism or Landino's Platonizing interpretation of Virgil. In the two chapters that follow this one, devoted to the 'Garden of Adonis canto,' I will argue that Spenser composed that subtle and mysterious passage in accordance with a specifically Platonic program, but in this chapter, dealing more generally with the poem as a heterocosm, I will locate significant passages from the six Books and the *Cantos* within a broad landscape, where concepts grounded in history and sensitive to Elizabethan cultural politics stand out within the unfolding narrative.

Hierarchical and Dynamic Principles

One of the obvious features of Spenser's world view, composed partly of unexamined assumptions, partly of fervent beliefs, partly of convenient tropes, is its hierarchical ordering of things. For Spenser and his contemporaries, according to the dominant ideology the orders of angels, the heavenly spheres and sublunary elements, the infernal regions and demonic forces, all species in the physical world, the microcosm of human nature, society and its governing officers, the family and household as a social unit, all were supposed to conform to a schema that distributed interdependent degrees of being and goodness, giving to each a proper place, linked not only from top to bottom but by interlacing analogies between cosmic and microcosmic categories. Elizabethans may have needed reminding of these traditional truths, but few were inclined to challenge hierarchical arrangements as artificial, not natural. Hierarchy was implied in the very idea of creation, and departures from the norms defining order were felt to imply a turning toward chaos. Such schemas provided a way of organizing the plenitude and mutability of things that both delighted and threatened thoughtful people. They also served to discipline superabundant energy, or at least to affirm that energy should be disciplined: rebellion, ambition, and fantasy had to be controlled. Discipline was rationalized by value-laden distinctions, using such terms as 'noble' and 'base,' 'golden' and 'brazen,' 'heavenly' and 'earthly.'

In our culture, although hierarchical arrangements are pervasive, they no longer enjoy their traditional status as virtually inescapable sources of meaning and value; more often they are sites of stress. For this reason we may be inclined to exaggerate the significance of Renaissance hierarchies. As we saw in the previous chapter, several authorities within the intellectual culture of the sixteenth century differed over the terms in which the top-to-bottom order of things should be understood: even the original divine *fiat* was parsed in various ways, with more or less room provided for complexity in intermediate levels of the system. Spenser found openings for his imagination in the various opinions available in his culture.

I intend to show – borrowing Yeats's formula for Platonism – how Spenser represents nature as both 'the spume that plays' and 'a ghostly paradigm of things.' Terms controlled by hierarchy and analogy form the ghostly paradigm, and dynamic movement produces the spume of phenomena. Hierarchy and analogy are at work both obviously and unobtrusively in *The Faerie Queene*, creating simpler and subtler patterns than one might expect within the unfolding economy of the narrative. Spenser's intricate stanzas involve us constantly, as a couplet form or blank verse would not, in the perception of predetermined patterns and vertically arranged relationships. Played off against these reminders of hierarchical order, however, is the onward and often wayward tendency of the narrative, which emphasizes process and becoming. At intervals we are shown the way up or down, teleologically, or we are taken inward to a source; these rationalizing moments confer some structure on the poem's open-endedness. Good and evil are defined in terms of a schema with specific places for heaven and hell, but their avatars meet one another in dialectical opposition 'on the plaine' designated in the opening line of Book I, a space in two dimensions, flat like the printed page.

Allegory is sometimes, and somewhat appropriately, described as dependent upon a hierarchical model of the cosmos, a theatre of elaborate images that added literal and figurative dimensions to the plain sense of language at the same time that it added immaterial implications to the world presented to our senses. Landino's interpretation of the *Aeneid* certainly supports this belief, and other authorities at least as well known to Spenser and his audience pointed in the same direction. For Spenserians, the classic statement of this proposition is Thomas P. Roche's: 'the basis of allegorical reading is [the] analogical nature of the universe' (*Kindly Flame* 8). Roche refers us to the universe described by Pico della Mirandola in his *Heptaplus*, an ingenious Platonizing commentary on the first chapter of Genesis that was copied and disseminated, in part, by Pierre de la Primaudaye's encyclopedia of received opinions. In the words of *The French Academie*, 'the secret amity and affinitie of all nature' connects phenomena in the sublunary world with causes in the celestial and super-celestial worlds (*Kindly Flame* 7–8), thereby ensuring that things mean something specific beyond themselves and also determining what the allegorical reference should be.

This rationale for allegory hypothesizes 'an hierarchical universe where each thing has a fixed place.'[2] Spenser refers to such a universe in many passages of *The Faerie Queene*, but a full account of his allegory should take note of the fact that however much his characters may long to be at rest in a fixed place, most of the time they are either stuck where they should not be or involved in restless motion toward a distant goal. The scene for human action in the poem's *paysage moralisé* is more stable than the characters, but even there much of the meaning emerges from movement. Furthermore, the cosmos in Spenser's poem and the meanings lodged in its theatre are less schematic than Pico's theory would lead us to expect, and we learn little from Spenser about the 'super-celestial' emanations that Pico, fascinated with Neoplatonism and kabbalistic lore, made fundamental to the structure of the cosmos. Although Roche's rationale for Spenserian allegory has been elaborated by other scholars,[3] the most persuasive recent accounts of the principles animating allegory have regarded the hierarchi-

cal model of the universe deconstructively. My argument, which reintro-
duces and relies upon a cosmological frame of reference, must take some of
those views into account.

The *Cantos of Mutabilitie* have prompted several readings that expatiate
upon its 'affirmatively Neoplatonic' program, and others that look askance
upon Jove's regime, finding subversive undermeanings fundamental to the
allegory. The *Cantos* will figure prominently in my last chapter and this is
not the place for a synoptic commentary, but a few quotations and comments are appropriate here. Sean Kane, in the fine concluding chapter of
Spenser's Moral Allegory, sees 'debate' rather than cosmology as the basis
for Spenser's poem. 'Jove and Mutabilitie act as each other's foils in a futile
debate,' and Jove's defence of the status quo is not a partial version of the
truth so much as it is 'an abstract and paranoid hallucination of order.'[4] To
the extent that Jove stands for the poet's worldly interests and his perception of mutability as a threat to his peace of mind, Spenser's investment in
the traditional cosmos must seem irredeemably retrograde today, and
Gordon Teskey rightly takes the Jovian aspect of Spenser's world view to
task for its negation of history. In Teskey's account, an appreciation for the
genealogy of 'Truth, the daughter of Time,' becomes a part of the allegory
by inference from a conspicuous silence. Must we, however, be historicists
to the extent of invalidating all metaphysical programs? And does Spenser's
poem lend support to this Nietzschean, Derridean project? Teskey's argument suggests as much. Kane, on the other hand, is concerned to show that
while Mutabilitie and Jove are tragicomically at cross purposes, Nature
and the poem concur in representing a hierarchical order to which the
poet's ambivalence is a proper response, amounting to 'a counsel of patience' (*Spenser's Moral Allegory* 221) that must be relevant to 'Constancie,'
the titular virtue of a hypothetical Book VII. Whether Spenser's appeals to
hierarchical principles can be made subtle enough to escape Teskey's
strictures, we shall see. What is called for is an account of nature in *The
Faerie Queene* that somehow includes both Mutabilitie and Jove, explaining why their debate in the *Cantos* is futile and showing how other
oppositions in the poem provide a more satisfying *discordia concors.*

A well-articulated 'vertical axis' in Spenser's representation of the world
has been described by Isabel MacCaffrey (*Spenser's Allegory* 133–52), but
the bearing of that axis on events in the narrative has not been comprehen-
sively examined. What follows, as a part of that analysis, is a close look at
passages that exemplify Spenser's tendency to collapse the hierarchy in
which heavenly and base things are ordinarily kept separate. Narrative in
The Faerie Queene does not violate or disregard the principle of hierarchy,

but it often depicts human experience that conventional schemes do not explain adequately.

The most familiar of my examples will be Una's deliverance from Sansloy by the sudden appearance of 'A troupe of *Faunes* and *Satyres*' (I vi 7.7). Sansloy's transgression and Una's presence in his company involve a conjunction of heavenly goodness and base evil that the narrator is pleased to deplore. Una is a 'rocke of Diamond stedfast euermore' (4.5) in the face of Sansloy's persuasions to sin, and when 'to feed his fyrie lustfull eye' he snatches away her veil, 'Then gan her beautie shine, as brightest skye' (4.7–8), which only encourages him to more 'greedy force' (5.3). The terms describing these antagonists come from worlds usually kept apart, here yoked by violence together. Sansloy's outrage against a 'heauenly virgin' moves the narrator to exclaim, 'Ah heauens, that do this hideous act behold, / ... How can ye vengeance iust so long withhold, / And hurle not flashing flames vpon that Paynim bold?' (5.6–9). But the heavens do not fight fire with fire. In an unusually baroque figure, Spenser says that 'molten starres do drop like weeping eyes' in response to Una's shrieks, and the sun 'hides for shame' (6.5–8), but while the cosmos shudders in response to the heavenly Una's distress, the 'wondrous way' made by 'Eternall prouidence exceeding thought' (7.1–3) is not apocalyptic but pastoral-comical: Sansloy is not frightened off by prodigies in the heavens, but by what Spenser calls 'A rude, misshapen, monstrous rablement' (8.7).

Spenser's main purpose in this episode is to assert the goodness, limited though it may be, of animate nature when it is not, like Sansloy, sophisticated by a devilish appetite and an anti-Christian creed. The 'wyld woodgods' signify that the preparation for the gospel begins in uncivilized nature. Una recognizes that the satyrs' good will toward her is a 'barbarous truth' (12.2), and she cannot dissuade them from idolatry: they lack the human capacity for reason and reverence that, debased in Sansloy, is intact but uninformed in Satyrane. But the satyrs provide more than a light interlude, and more than a dramatic contrast to Una's sublimity and her plight. They illustrate a truth found elsewhere in the poem, that 'wondrous grace' (I vi Argument) will not be revealed by lightning strokes or avenging angels, but will reach as far as possible down the chain of being, entering nature as if by accident.

Una's rescue is replayed, riddlingly, in the story of Florimell, Una's avatar, when in the absence of the appropriate knightly rescuers, who have no idea where she is, Proteus takes her out of the hands of the lustful fisherman. Spenser introduces Proteus in these terms:

See how the heauens of voluntary grace,
And soueraine fauour towards chastity,
Doe succour send to her distressed cace:
So much high God doth innocence embrace.   (III viii 29.2–5)

Does the last line add a grace note, or a false one? Is Proteus heaven-sent, or just another opportunist in the long line attracted by Florimell's beauty? God does not embrace innocence any more than Proteus does in this instance; Florimell is left for a long time to her own devices, avoiding violation by a monstrous antithesis of 'high God.'[5]

High and low, spiritual and material, innocence and appetite, are often found thrown together in *The Faerie Queene*. Such events can be felt as lapses in the hierarchical order that keeps discordant members safe from one another, but in fact, Una and Florimell remain safely separate from their low company. In the woodgods' pity and awe and in Proteus's courtship, desire is bound by certain decorums, and the ideas adumbrated in Una and Florimell are not violated, only temporarily juxtaposed against the world's rough texture. The meeting of extremes affirms the value of hierarchy while showing that it is open to transgression.

The scene in canto v of Book III where Belphoebe discovers the wounded Timias contains similar juxtaposed elements from the sublime and the humble ends of the scale of nature. The episode as a whole shows that commonplace notions of order and degree were only points of departure for Spenser's narrative. From her first appearance in the poem (II iii 21–42), Belphoebe is clothed in an aura that makes her more an embodiment of divine grace than a lowly instrument of higher purposes. Her appearance on the scene of Timias's mortal injury is proof, like the rescue of Una, that 'Prouidence heauenly passeth liuing thought' (III v 27.1; cf. I vi 7.1). The pleasures afforded by a marvellous coincidence of opposites arise in this case from several sources: not only from the difference in degree between the rescued squire and his rescuer, but from tensions between the elements of Belphoebe's complex nature, and from the discrepancy between her sense of herself and Timias's perception of her. With every aspect of the situation, Spenser simultaneously makes much of the distances that are to be bridged and affirms the possibility of a category-stretching *discordia concors*.

The author's point of view throughout this episode is close to that of Timias but never confined to it, and at the canto's end Timias has excluded himself from the happy harmonies that are to be admired in Belphoebe. Deserting his unhappy squire, Spenser turns in stanza 53 to address a virgin posterity that is invited to 'follow her ensample dead' (54.9). The narrative makes the most of the surprises inherent in Timias's epiphany and his subsequent predicament. The wounded squire incongruously sees himself as a base sinner, with 'sinfull wounds' (35.9) and, after these have healed, a 'villeinous' passion that with difficulty he converts to 'service bace' (45.4, 47.1). We are told more than once that Timias thinks of Belphoebe as heaven-sent: upon awakening he looks up 'toward the azure skies, / From whence descend all hopeless remedies'; with no relief in sight he looks to one side, to find there 'The goodly Mayd full of diuinities, / And gifts of heauenly grace' (34). His salutation, 'Angell, or Goddesse do I call thee right?' (35.5), appropriately heightens the language of Trompart at Belphoebe's earlier entry (II iii 33) and its pattern in the *Aeneid* (I 327–8). But Spenser has already prepared a different perspective on Belphoebe. The 'heauenly salues and med'cines sweete' (35.8) for which Timias gives thanks were not that in fact; Belphoebe's 'trew Nobility' (32.5), a lesser thing than divinity, includes to our surprise a mastery of herbal medicine, and it is with such natural means, 'whether it diuine *Tobacco* were, / Or *Panachæa*, or *Polygony*' (32.6–7), expertly administered, that his return to physical health is effected.

If 'trew Nobility' is a condition consisting of many gifts both earthly and heavenly, Belphoebe's definition of herself – 'Nor Goddesse I, nor Angell, but the Mayd, / And daughter of a woody Nymphe' (36.2–3) – opens outward even as it eliminates the upper end of the scale of creatures. Belphoebe conceals from Timias what we will learn in the next canto, that she is a foster daughter of Diana, but she lays claim to the anomalous status that her conception and upbringing have earned. As 'the Mayd' (the definite article is used obtrusively), she seems conscious of herself as an archetype. At the heart of her identity is a simplicity surrounding a mystery, for she is the Virgilian *virgo*, the goddess Venus disguised as a Tyrian maiden, who had seemed to Aeneas to be either Phoebus's sister or 'one of the race of nymphs' (*Aeneid* I 329).[6] Belphoebe's sublime nature, inhabiting the boundary that usually separates divine and human natures, Christian and classical categories, can only be honoured by a careful blurring of distinctions. The last of the possibilities brought into play by the Virgilian allusion coincides with Belphoebe's sense of herself as 'daughter of a woody Nymphe,' but it is hard to know what we are to make of this. We will learn that she was wondrously conceived by Chrysogonee, 'A Faerie ... yborne of high degree' (vi 4.3). The connections between the race of faerie and classical *nymphae* are significant but tenuous, and in the spectrum of immortal and mortal creatures, both nymphs and fairies are hard to place: they are mortal but long-lived, with a beauty that unites physical and spiritual traits (see *SE* under 'faeries').

Belphoebe's character is, then, not quite human – or should we say more than human? Toward the end of the canto and at other points in the poem, Spenser emphasizes her 'heavenly' qualities. Here, in the face of Timias's response to that aspect of her, Belphoebe modestly includes herself among 'mortall wights'; she feels 'bound with commun bond of frailtee' (36.6, 8). Coming upon Timias injured, apparently dead, when she expected to find 'some wild beast, which with her arrowes keene / She wounded had' (28.2–3), she has suffered an epiphany of her own, seeing 'faire eyes' and 'sweete lips' and growing 'Full of soft passion and vnwonted smart' (29.3, 7; 30.8). She discovers an unfamiliar part of her own nature, and when Timias awakens she is still feeling the full force of that discovery. Hamilton's note on stanza 30 is apt: 'In effect, Diana becomes Venus who nurses a dying Adonis.' She also reminds us of the cold but finally vulnerable Angelica, whose infatuation with the lowly Medoro in *Orlando Furioso* XIX gave Spenser his pretext for this episode.

Belphoebe's herbal medicine and a long rest in her 'earthly Paradize' (40.5) heal Timias's thigh wound and Belphoebe recovers from her 'vnwonted smart,' but inadvertently she hurts his heart; he passes from one despair to another. The two wounds may be different in kind, pertaining to physical and spiritual impulses and thus belonging in a neat hierarchy, but Spenser invokes the customary categories only to show that the different manifestations of desire, like the flesh and spirit in human nature, are not easily divided. Timias's first wound, like that of Adonis, was occasioned not by selfish lust but by a reckless high-mindedness, and he recovers from his Pyrrhic victory over the three foresters only to discover in himself a version of the desire that had prompted his vengeful pursuit. While it is founded on appreciation of Belphoebe's 'celestiall' qualities, the squire's love remains a passion that he tries not only to subdue with reason, but to 'dislodge out of his nest' (44.2–3), the nest being 'his will, / ... / His inward parts, and all his entrayles' (48). Spenser suspends his account of this hopeless love with an image of melancholia in its terminal phase: 'neither bloud in face, nor life in hart / It left, but both did quite drye vp, and blast' (48.6–7). This is a lover's malady with religious overtones, and Spenser confronts the difficulties that attend the deifying of a mortal woman with a bifurcated response: after scapegoating Timias, in whom Ralegh's predicament is readily apparent, he offers a hymn to Belphoebe's chastity that registers his own ambivalence toward the conjunction of flesh and spirit. The last lines of the stanzas given to Timias's self-searching introduce two principles on which Spenser's understanding of hierarchy may be based. 'How then? Of all loue taketh equall vew' (47.5): love both levels and ennobles those who experience it. Further, and with a different emphasis, 'And doth not highest God vouchsafe to take / The loue and seruice of the basest crew?' (47.6–7). Both the love associated with Cupid and the more 'kindly' love circulating between creature and creator tend to bring together high and low.

The malady of melancholia offers one kind of evidence that spirit and flesh are fused together in human nature; idealized as it is in Spenser's hymn of praise, the state of virgin chastity demonstrates, with a difference, a similar truth. Stanzas 51 to 55, praising Belphoebe's 'fresh flowring Maidenhead' (54.6), celebrate virtues that are indistinguishable from the maid's physical person, while both virtues and beauties, embodied in a human being (Queen Elizabeth almost entirely displaces the fictional Belphoebe as the referent here), retain the 'heauenly' character of their putative origin. Spenser's poetry here arises from assumptions about the natural order in relation to its creator, and about the social order in relation to its sovereign. In keeping with the two continued metaphors woven together in these stanzas, involving light and a transplanted flower, the meaning grows as a flower does and is gradually revealed like the light of the rising sun.

The poetry I have been discussing could not have been conceived without reference to a hierarchically and analogically ordered model of the universe, but no schematic picture of the Ptolemaic universe could account for what Spenser had to say about human nature and its place in the cosmos. The classical image for a fully articulated world order, the golden chain that Homer describes as held by Zeus (see Ludwig Edelstein, 'The Golden Chain of Homer'), used by Landino and allegorists before him as the occasion for metaphysics, is found in *The Faerie Queene* in the hands of Mammon's daughter Philotime, sitting deep in the underworld:

> There, as in glistring glory she did sit,
>   She held a great gold chaine ylincked well,
>   Whose vpper end to highest heauen was knit,
>   And lower part did reach to lowest Hell.   (II vii 46.1–4)

Philotime's chain is called '*Ambition*, rash desire to sty' (46.8), rather than Order or Science; this line and its context tell us that to conceive of the world between heaven and hell as so organized that it permits men 'To clime aloft, and others to excell' (46.7), is to be captivated by a vain fiction. Spenser says of Philotime, 'Nath'lesse most heauenly faire in deed and vew / She by creation was, till she did fall,' and the chain is one of her 'helps, to cloke her crime withall' (45.7–9). Seated and holding the chain as she does, she can pretend that its orderly ascent depends as much on her as on Jove. It measures the depth of her fall as well as the extent of her 'rash desire,' and it is best understood in the terms supplied by an earlier visit to the underworld: 'the chayne of strong necessitie, / Which fast is tyde to *Ioues* eternall seat' (I v 25.5–6).

Night and Day; Destiny, Necessity, Providence

The passages discussed so far offer several indications that Spenser's intelligence tended to deconstruct the world we used to think of as the common property of Renaissance intellectuals. This is not to say that he distrusted that structure or regarded it as provisional. He obviously feared disorder, and he habitually identifies creation with 'workmanship,' the articulation of parts, not with an effusion of energy.[7] One of the scariest of his demonic characters is Ate or Discord, whose threat to society and all personal relationships is amplified by a metaphysical objection to divine grace and the Concord achieved by it:

> For all this worlds faire workmanship she tride,
> Vnto his last confusion to bring,
> And that great golden chaine quite to diuide,
> With which it blessed Concord hath together tide.   (IV i 30.6–9)

These lines declare that there is truth in Homer's symbol of 'this worlds faire workmanship,' and *The Faerie Queene* is imbued with Spenser's conviction that it is a truth necessary to the survival of the social order. Book IV, the Legend of Friendship and the basis for an emphasis on the social order in the poem's second triad, emphasizes this point obsessively.

Declarations of the world's orderliness often arise as answers to the poem's demons. Spenser seems to enjoy magnifying threats to peace in small human groups into unlimited wishes for apocalyptic disaster. This trait, which may look to us like paranoia, is inseparable from his great architectonic abilities. It is good, according to Spenser, for the separable and potentially antagonistic orders of culture and nature to be 'together tide.' Although division is fundamental to rationality, in the abjected figure of Ate an unreasoning divisiveness is taken to be dedicated to total confusion. Where the poem's many figures representative of discord are concerned, Spenser's own workmanship is open to suspicion: demons lodged in the world's fabric provide easy explanations of flaws in society and frustration with the course of human events.

Sometimes Spenser makes evil account for its own limitations. When Duessa visits Night in search of aid for the wounded Sansjoy, her urgings to 'Go gather vp the reliques of thy race, / Or else goe them auenge' (I v 24.2–3), move Night to 'some compassion' but do not shake her melancholy fatalism:

> But who can turne the streame of destinee,
> Or breake the chayne of strong necessitee,
> Which fast is tyde to *Ioues* eternall seat?
> The sonnes of Day he fauoureth, I see,
> And by my ruines thinkes to make them great. (25.4–8)

In Duessa's descent to the Cave of Night, Spenser created an occasion for his first and most comprehensive account of the roots of good and evil.[8] In doing so he reaches down and backward to the limits of the cosmos, and establishes a conceptual framework within which we still find him working when we come to the *Cantos of Mutabilitie*. By canto v of Book I we are already familiar with his emphatic association of Day and all natural light with good, Night and all darkness with evil. We know Archimago to be an avatar of the Prince of Darkness. The temporal dialectic of Day and Night has been keyed to a cosmic hierarchy defined by Heaven and Hell, and to an allegorical plot in which Truth and Errour are diametrically opposed, the one 'clothed with the sun' and the other dispersed to the poem's persistently menacing shadows.

In none of this is Spenser original; he is using the language of the New Testament, and his conception of Night and her children stems from a mythographic tradition that goes back to Hesiod and the Orphic hymns.[9] The extent to which Night is reflexively demonized shows how devoted Spenser was, in the last analysis, to an Apollonian culture and a biased reading of nature. A modern reader for whom questions of fact and of value are independent of one another may be unhappy to find that all of Spenser's heterocosm – the quotidian succession of day and night as well as the vast expanse from '*Ioues* eternall seat' to '*Dæmogorgons* hall' (22.5) – has been structured superstitiously by a pair of moral absolutes. Regarded genealogically, however, the moral significance of Night becomes imaginary, associated with human need and weakness rather than metaphysical principles.

The mythology Spenser brings into play in Duessa's descent identifies Night as the 'most auncient Grandmother of all,' not unbegotten, but still privy to 'the secrets of the world vnmade,' older than the heavens and the earth (22.2–6). Night herself, 'griesly *Night*, with visage deadly sad' (20.1), is so described as to inspire awe and deepen our understanding of her descendants, Sansjoy and his brothers, 'old *Aveugles* sonnes' (23.7), and Duessa: 'I the mother bee / Of falshood, and root of *Duessaes* race' (27.6–7). The brooding melancholia evident in Night is at the root of Sansjoy's negation of Hope, and evident also in Duessa's more desperate nature. Night herself, from whom the active enemies of Redcrosse and many others ultimately come (according to Hesiod, Ate is another of her offspring), is passive and hopeless, unresponsive to the energetic Duessa's encouragement to 'let be seene, / That dreaded *Night* in brightest day hath place, / And can the children of faire light deface' (24.3–5). Mutabilitie will eventually act out such an imperialist impulse, but in Book I, Night is restrained by her awareness of 'the stream of destinee' and 'strong necessitee' favouring 'The sonnes of Day.'

In Arthur's complaint against Night (III iv 55–60), Spenser relocates his metaphysical bias inside a character, and even though that character is his hero, impatience with Night and all the threats associated with it is opened to examination as special pleading. Arthur's occasion is the frustration of his pursuit of Florimell, whom he, sleepless and tormented by 'sad sorrow ... / And thousand fancies,' mixes with the memory of 'his Faery Queene' (54). The ironies here are delightful: Florimell had first come before his gaze like a comet, 'a blazing starre' (III i 16.5) invisible in daylight, and of course Gloriana is dear to him only because she entered his dream 'all that night' (I ix 14.8), turning his single state as one of the sons of Day into longing for a bride. (Conventional associations of both the fairy queen and Elizabeth Tudor with the moon are relevant here.) Arthur's complaint, in which Night is 'foule Mother of annoyance sad, / Sister of heauie death, and nourse of woe' (55.1–2), useless to 'th'eternall Maker' (56.1–4), is not blessed by the moon, although we are told that the darkness against which he protests 'with thousand starres was decked faire' (52.3). When Arthur makes Truth out to be Day's daughter (59), not the child of Time in all his diurnal rotations, he is resisting the full truth of Gloriana's promise to him, 'For dearely sure her loue was to me bent, / As when iust time expired should appeare' (I ix 14.3–4). Since Night, like Errour, is frightfully feminine, we can see in Arthur's predicament a theme recurrent in the poem and its *poesis*: masculine desire faces endless work in its attempt to achieve wholeness, and is seldom able to embrace its feminine Other.

It will be recalled that in Landino's interpretation of Virgil, Fate and Necessity were important concepts, and they were lodged within the created order ruled by Jove. In her meeting with Duessa, Night accepts this dispensation. Spenser's own thinking was not so bound by 'the chayne of strong necessitee.' The word 'necessity' appears rarely in *The Faerie Queene*, and in only one other place does it carry a meaning like that given by Night to Homer's golden chain. This is in a stanza from Despair's argument with Redcrosse:

> Is not his [i.e., God's] deed, what euer thing is donne,
>   In heauen and earth? did not he all create
>   To die againe? all ends that was begonne.
>   Their times in his eternall booke of fate
>   Are written sure, and haue their certaine date.
>   Who then can striue with strong necessitie,
>   That holds the world in his still chaunging state,
>   Or shunne the death ordayned by destinie?
> When houre of death is come, let none aske whence, nor why.   (I ix 42)

This voice prompting Redcrosse's guilty conscience echoes Night's complaint about necessity and destiny without mentioning that 'The sonnes of Day' are predestined to succeed. It is remarkable that the concept of necessity, so prominent in the legacy of Boethius,[10] is found in bad company in *The Faerie Queene*. Further inquiry into Spenser's use of related terms, 'destiny' and 'fate,' will show that for him, 'what euer thing is donne, / In heauen and earth,' is dependent upon God's will and power but is still not 'his deed.' An image of 'strong necessitie' does not suffice to explain the relationship of the world and its 'still chaunging state' to God.

Redcrosse's encounter with Despair is paramount among the poem's numberless temptations to melancholy passivity. We have seen that 'abeyance of the will' is both a dangerous state and one that the poem cultivates in order to accomplish its worldmaking and its simultaneous fashioning of virtuous self-awareness and purposeful commitment. Individual autonomy is not so much affirmed as it is accepted among the problematic conditions of human life. The burden of responsibility must be assumed along with the possibility of heroism, and beneath that possibility lies an innate instability that makes even heroes and saints prone to error. For this reason, 'destiny' is important in Spenser's vocabulary and 'necessity' is rarely invoked. What is more surprising is the fact that 'Providence' appears only four times in his entire poetic corpus. Two of these instances, accounting for the marvelous rescues of Una and Timias (I vi 7.1 and III v 27.1), have already been discussed. A look at the other two will carry further this inquiry into the relationship of God to the world as the sustainer of the created order and the course of history.

In the absence of many explicit appeals to divine providence, a number of other terms serve to indicate the Christian God's involvement in the course of temporal events. Without a theologian's obligation to define terms, construct arguments, and resolve problems, Spenser did not choose his words with a concern for perfect consistency, but one does discover that, by habit or design, he made some clear distinctions. 'Providence,' for example, is used in its root sense of 'foresight,' with reference to the predestined course of individual lives.[11] The following passage makes this clear, and it also offers an index to other terms used throughout the poem to describe the activity of God in the world in its relationship to individual responsibilities:

> It was not, *Britomart*, thy wandring eye,
>   Glauncing vnwares in charmed looking glas,
>   But the streight course of heauenly destiny,
>   Led with eternall prouidence, that has
>   Guided thy glaunce, to bring his will to pas:
>   Ne is thy fate, ne is thy fortune ill,
>   To loue the prowest knight, that euer was.
>   Therefore submit thy wayes vnto his will,
> And do by all dew meanes thy destiny fulfill.   (III iii 24)

This passage will be recognized as part of Merlin's advice to Britomart, concerning the love she has conceived by means of the abstracted and reflected image of an unknown knight, identified in stanza 26 as Artegall. The first thing to be noticed is the contrast between images of Britomart's 'wandring' and 'Glauncing vnwares' and the path she has been unconsciously tracing, a 'streight course ... / Led with eternall prouidence.' What had seemed to Britomart shameful was predestined; a divine purpose required her vulnerability to the effects of this 'charmed looking glas.' For all the differences between them, divine foresight and this chosen maiden's unwary gaze are interdependent. The poem takes Britomart's search for her husband in and out of the central actions of three Books, but the apparent indeterminacy of her progress is balanced by the fact that her 'wayes' are always a 'streight course.' We are not mistaken if we understand that constancy as expressive of prim self-possession, a character trait that Spenser, anticipating Henry Fielding, manages to make both comic and heroic, but the theological rationale supplied by Merlin helps to account for Britomart's human complexity.

Despair had emphasized that it is pointless to 'striue with strong necessitie,' but while Merlin tells Britomart to 'submit,' he stresses individual responsibility in bringing 'his will' to pass, fulfilling a personal as well as a national destiny. (Between 'his will' in l. 5 and the same phrase in l. 8, the referent changes to include Artegall, but it appears that providence will continue to superintend Britomart's story.) The problematic ending of her quest in Book V is already inherent in the terms used here. Differences between the two founders of the Tudor dynasty are built into the story too, and not limited to sexual stereotypes. Merlin goes on to advise Britomart that although 'the fates are firme, / ... Yet ought mens good endeuours them confirme, / And guide the heauenly causes to their constant terme' (25.6–9). It is advice that would do Artegall good: more burdened than oriented by his awareness of 'heauenly causes,' he tends to vacillate between passive suffering and over-reaction, lacking the self-possession that Britomart can usually muster to mask her inner turmoil.

In one of the emblematic encounters at the beginning of Book V, Artegall lectures the radical reforming Giant, and the terms of his argument are uncannily reminiscent of the counsel of Despair: things are best left alone, for 'All in the powre of their great Maker lie' (V ii 40.8), and 'What euer thing is done, by him is donne, / Ne any may his mighty will withstand' (42.1–2). When Spenser tells us near the end of Book V that 'occasion' called Artegall away from his reformation of Irena's 'ragged commonweale,' and 'of necessity / His course of Iustice he was forst to stay' (xii 26.4, 27.1–4), we find 'necessity' being used in a Machiavellian and bitterly ironic sense, to account for the failure of a policy.[12]

Her submission to superior wills leaves Britomart unfulfilled, and the men around her, similarly chastened by advice and harsh experience, do not fare better. When Britomart meets the desperate Scudamour outside Busirane's castle, she consoles him with a short version of the lesson she received from Merlin: 'submit you to high prouidence' (III xi 14.4). She hopes that 'heauenly grace' will render that submission possible, adding that he should also trust to 'vertues might, and values confidence' (14.3, 7). When she learns more about Scudamour's pain and its occasion in Amoret's captivity, she commits her own virtue and self-confidence to 'Deliuer her fro thence, or with her for you dy' (18.9). As to whether Scudamour ever receives support from heavenly grace, the text is silent.

Beyond those already discussed, *The Faerie Queene* offers only a few clear instances of divine intervention on behalf of individuals. Arthur's defeat of Orgoglio is the most extravagant example of divine grace in action, and even there the narrative is nonchalant in the way it prepares for 'blazing brightnesse' from Arthur's accidentally unveiled shield (I viii 19). Una's need for a miracle is well established prior to Arthur's entry, but from the lines that introduce him we cannot tell what is about to take place: 'At last she chaunced by good hap to meet / A goodly knight, faire marching by the way' (vii 29.1–2). Combining playful reticence with showy rhetoric that makes Arthur at least as frightening as he is a vessel of redemption, Spenser reminds us that we should not be quick to discover the hand of God in human events. When it is introduced and elaborately described (33–5), Arthur's diamond shield suggests vain pride more than a true anathema of evil: our principal reassurance comes with the statement that 'all that was not such, as seemd in sight, / Before that shield did fade, and suddeine fall' (35.3–4).[13]

A somewhat clearer example of divine grace and its presence in the natural order would be the chance – '(eternall God that chaunce did guide),' I xi 45.6 – by which the exhausted Redcrosse Knight is rescued at the end of his second day's combat with the dragon. When he fell backward and slid disgracefully 'in the mire,' the very soil on which he fell had been made into an ointment by 'A trickling streame of Balme' from '*The tree of life*, the crime of our first fathers fall.' Of 'that first tree,' distinguished from the tree of knowledge, we are told, 'Great God it planted in that blessed sted / With his almighty hand' (45–8). Since the tree in Eden can be connected with the cross of Calvary (see Hamilton at 46.9), the balm derived from it brings life out of death. In accordance with a pattern we have seen before, the promise of redemption enters the poem in a coincidence of opposites, a meeting of high and low rather than a relocation of meaning at some higher level of abstraction.

Many fortunate rescues of innocent or hapless victims serve to remind us of the Christian doctrine of particular Providence, and it is sometimes presented with Calvinist inflections.[14] In the poem's longest reflection on this subject, the passage beginning 'And is there care in heauen' (II viii 1.1), Spenser uses the occasion to marry Calvin's conviction of man's wretched helplessness (a note often heard in the poem) to an account of the instruments available for redemption that many Calvinists might not accept. In this episode, where the exhausted Guyon is rescued from Pyrochles and Cymochles, it is worth noting how Spenser brings into play the hierarchy of nature and a cognate hierarchy of virtues. Having begun with anxious rhetorical questions about 'loue / In heauenly spirits to these creatures bace,' the opening stanza ends:

> But O th'exceeding grace
> Of highest God, that loues his creatures so,
> And all his workes with mercy doth embrace,
> That blessed Angels, he sends to and fro,
> To serue to wicked man, to serue his wicked foe.   (II viii 1.5–9)

The activity beginning toward the end of this stanza is intensified in the verbs of the next:

How oft do they, their siluer bowers leaue,
  To come to succour vs, that succour want?
  How oft do they with golden pineons, cleaue
  The flitting skyes, like flying Pursuiuant,
  Against foule feends to aide vs millitant?
  They for vs fight, they watch and dewly ward,
  And their bright Squadrons round about vs plant,
  And all for loue, and nothing for reward:
O why should heauenly God to men haue such regard?   (II viii 2)

The backdrop against which all this militant love is enacted is the vertical axis familiar from Book I. As a synoptic statement about the need for grace and its availability, this lyrical passage adds emphasis to the analogous passage in Book I, introducing the rescue of Redcrosse by Prince Arthur and Una, 'heauenly grace' and 'stedfast truth' (viii 1). Since 'blessed Angels' do not enter the poem after this occasion, and since Guyon has done little to deserve being called God's 'wicked foe,' we may conclude that like Book I's rescue of Redcrosse as 'The righteous man' (I viii 1.2), this is to be a general account of Everyman's situation.

After its lyric beginning in 'siluer bowers' and 'flitting skyes,' the canto locates its narrative in the bleak landscape of mortal conflicts that is characteristic of Book II. In keeping with the opening stanzas, the good grey figure of the Palmer is greeted, 'being on his way,' by an urgent voice and a startling figure: he discovers not only Guyon, 'slumbring fast / In senselesse dreame' (4.8–9), but 'a faire young man, / Of wondrous beautie, and of freshest yeares' (5.1–2). Guyon's guardian angel appears, to the Palmer's slowly comprehending eyes, first as an erotically appealing youth, then more majestically 'Like as *Cupido* on *Idæan* hill' (6.1), then as a 'child' who, when he speaks, becomes an admonitory figure and turns the task of protecting Guyon back to the Palmer: 'watch thou I pray; / For euill is at hand him to offend' (8.6–7). After promising that he will 'euermore him succour, and defend / Against his foe and mine' (8.5–6), Guyon's guardian angel vanishes.

Throughout these opening stanzas, Spenser's focus is not on the way things are, but on subjective apprehensions: first, the narrator's own need to believe that there is 'care in heauen,' then the rational Palmer's emotion-laden attempts to interpret the evidence of his senses. The result is not confusion, but complexity: the supernatural enters the natural human condition in a way that remains uncanny. Spenser's way of honouring that *meraviglia* is a mixed appeal to both erotic interest and religious awe, and both Christian and classical categories. When he describes the angel 'Like as *Cupido*,' he invokes Neoplatonic authorities in the tradition interpreted by Ficino (in *SE*, see 'angel, Guyon's'). The figure of Cupid disarmed had been invoked in the poem's first Proem (3), and the presence of Love in many forms throughout *The Faerie Queene* lends credence to the angel's promise that, although he vanishes, he will 'not forgoe, ne yet forget / The care' of Guyon.

Finding himself alone, 'beguiled' and 'sore affraid' (9.2–3), the poor Palmer is soon faced with Pyrochles and Cymochles. He is aided just in time by Arthur. Grace returns with this 'armed knight, of bold and bounteous grace' (17.5); to the grateful Palmer he is 'hope of helpe, and timely grace' (25.6). As is well known, however, 'grace' here is almost stripped of the theological connotations that the word carried in Book I; in Arthur's actions defeating Guyon's foes, sinister but only human, his shield is kept under wraps. At the critical moment (stanza 40), the Palmer arms Arthur with Guyon's sword, asking God's blessing on a right hand that seems, with this aid, to have more than human but less than supernatural strength ('like as a Lion,' 40.7).

The passages we have just considered reiterate the idea that all things depend upon the will, omniscience, and love of God, but divine purposes are accomplished indirectly, by the free actions of human agents and with the aid of humble instruments. While not impersonal, Spenser's God is remote and provides only a beginning and an end, both unsearchable. The poet's concern is for the most part with the elaborate middle ground of creation; his pen quickens and imagination comes to the aid of faith when he describes the marvelous means by which destiny is accomplished here on earth.

Fate and Fortune

Whether God's agents exercise a delegated power as part of a system, on the model of late Roman polytheism and the philosophical theology of Neoplatonism, or are seen as serving God and man 'all for loue, and nothing for reward' (II viii 2.8) as do the angels, they enjoy a good deal of autonomy, and their autonomy is conferred upon the natural order that they govern. 'Fate' is one of the terms used to interpret events within the natural order, and it is used in various ways. Often, like 'fortune,' 'fate' refers simply to the end of an individual's life, and no personification or abstraction of an overarching principle is involved. Guyon's advice to Tantalus, 'Abide the fortune of thy present fate' (II vii 60.2), is a typical example of this usage, which may imply that fate is indistinguishable from 'character.' At many points, however, giving a metaphysical dimension to his moral teaching, Spenser represents fate or 'fatal purpose' as an order external to the individual. The case of Britomart, already discussed with a different focus, provides a starting point for analysis of Fate in this sense.

The canto containing Merlin's explanation of the destiny that has caused her to fall in love with the as yet unknown Artegall begins with this invocation:

> Most sacred fire, that burnest mightily
> In liuing brests, ykindled first aboue,
> Emongst th'eternall spheres and lamping sky,
> And thence pourd into men, which men call Loue; (III iii 1.1–4)

Such love, derived from heaven and different from the source of 'base affections' and 'filthy lust' (1.5–6), is praised for its power 'ouer mortall minds ... / To order them ... / And all their actions to direct aright' (2.2–4). Love here is mobile, beginning in heaven and then, working from within, exercising a civilizing power. The stanza continues:

> The fatall purpose of diuine foresight,
> Thou doest effect in destined descents,
> Through deepe impression of thy secret might,
> And stirredst vp th'Heroes high intents,
> Which the late world admyres for wondrous moniments. (2.5–9)

Love links the highest principle, 'diuine foresight,' with 'th'Heroes high intents,' so that character not only determines its own fate but achieves a grander 'fatall purpose.' As the narrative resumes the story of Britomart and links it with that of the future Queen Elizabeth, it becomes clear that 'destined descents' extend across time as well as along a vertical axis. Love personified is linked with the concept of fate, and in the process both are reconciled with individual freedom and self-fulfillment.

In canto iii, Spenser confronts the common fear that love is apt to be a fatal affliction. At the end of the previous canto, Britomart was shown suffering 'the furie of her cruell flame' (ii 52.2), rapidly wasting away; she has suffered under the tyrannical power of 'Imperious Loue' (23.2; cf. 40.9). Glauce, whose voice jumbles together superstition, commonplace morality, and sentimental practicality, tends to see 'evil' at work in Britomart's suffering (ii 30.7, 32.4, 46.2; iii 16.4, 18.5 & 9); she fears that it 'Doth course of naturall cause farre exceed' (iii 18.6). And this fear coincides with Britomart's unusual distress: her mind is afflicted because she loves not a man, 'But th'only shade and semblant of a knight' (ii 38.3). She believes that 'wicked fortune' has condemned her to 'feed on shadowes ... / And like a shadow wexe' (44.1–4). As he dramatizes Britomart's distress and disintegration, Spenser is both preparing for the next canto's reassurances and laying the groundwork for his heroine's empathy with Amoret in the house of Busirane. What is at stake throughout the poem, nowhere more vividly than in Book III, is the legitimacy of claims made by ideals upon the lives and the physical health of noble natures. Without fate, such ideals as the dynasty that produced Elizabeth Tudor as its last exemplar would have no rationale; without love of the noble sort that Spenser partially disentangles from its apparent irrationality, there would be no way to connect the heavenly plane of ideals with 'the termes of mortall state, / ... which do play / With double senses, and with false debate, / T'approue the vnknowen purpose of eternall fate' (III iv 28.6–9).

The concept of fate provided Spenser with an instrument for shaping the events of the poem as if from within, but in line with aesthetic principles that impose conspicuous artifice upon characters and events. In his hands fate itself is adaptable to the demands of the narrative, with no fixed place in a hierarchy of forces acting upon human lives. All lives are subject to fate prior to birth: Genius in the Garden of Adonis chooses, from the babes crowding about his gate, to clothe and send forth 'Such as him list, such as eternall fate / Ordained hath' (III vi 32.6–7). All things, according to Nature in the *Cantos*, 'Doe worke their owne perfection so by fate' that they 'raigne ouer change, and doe their states maintain' (vii 58.7–9). But Nature's long view of things, with beginnings and endings neatly connected, is available only in pieces and at moments to the poem's characters and its narrator. The personification of fate, dispersed by nature into the world system, is sometimes a powerful rationale, sometimes an alibi. When an event, present or anticipated, offers an occasion for rejoicing, as does Britomart's predestined love, fate may be traced to the heavens and above, but more often it is embraced with less enthusiasm, as circumstantial inevitability.[15] Characters who are inclined to think the heavens malignant or indifferent will locate a cruel fate in them, as do the false Una in Redcrosse's dream (I i 51) and Amavia when she justifies suicide and takes leave of her helpless infant (II i 36–7).[16]

Agape's errand to the underworld (IV ii 47–53), described by Lotspeich as Spenser's 'fullest picture of the Fates' (*Classical Mythology* 58–9), is in fact the only passage that constitutes a 'picture,' and the only one in which the three classical Fates are named and located 'Downe in the bottome of the deepe *Abysse*,' associated with Demogorgon and 'hideous *Chaos*' (47.6–9). Despite the company they keep (the entire episode is weirdly reminiscent of Duessa's descent to Night on behalf of Sansjoy), these Fates are not regarded by Agape as demonic, and the narrator later refers to their 'diuine decree, / For lifes succession in those brethren three' (iii 21.4–5). The close association of the three Fates with chaos should probably be taken to imply, in keeping with Nature's judgment and the allusion to 'An huge eternall *Chaos*' that supplies the Garden of Adonis (III vi 36), that chaos is under benign control and nothing enters the world of change casually.[17]

Much that happens in *The Faerie Queene* seems casual and unjust. The stoical Guyon falls to 'Accusing fortune, and too cruell fate' after Amavia's death (II i 56.8; cf. 41.9, 44.6). This is not the only place where fate and fortune are coupled, although as we have seen, fate is usually represented as immutable and ultimately rational. In the play he gives to both terms, Spenser is consistent with literary precedents and at odds with the authority of Calvin and other theologians.[18] The rationale for fate provided by Landino and others in the Platonic tradition may have played a role in Spenser's thinking on this matter. In the poet's usage, 'fate' typically refers to forces at work behind events but within the world's order; 'fortune' gives a name to frustrating circumstances.

The most virtuous characters are as likely as not to regard themselves as subject to ill fortune: to Una deserted by Redcrosse fortune is 'tempestuous' (I vii 25.1) and 'wilde' (50.2); toward Arthur seeking Gloriana it is 'fauourlesse' (II ix 7.9). Guyon's response to Arthur's complaint implies that he sees within the nature of things something opposed to human virtue; fortune means much the same thing as Night:

> Fortune, the foe of famous cheuisaunce
>   Seldome (said *Guyon*) yields to vertue aide,
>   But in her way throwes mischiefe and mischaunce,
>   Whereby her course is stopt, and passage staid.   (II ix 8.1–4)

This truth is borne out by Guyon's experience as well as Arthur's, as is the value of Guyon's remedy: 'be not herewith dismaid, / But constant keepe the way, in which ye stand' (8.5–6). In the course of his fight with Maleger, Impotence, and Impatience, Arthur's plight prompts the narrator's wise comment, 'So feeble is mans state, and life vnsound, / That in assurance it may neuer stand, / Till it dissolued be from earthly band' (II xi 30.3–5): Arthur is opposed by 'fierce Fortune,' and only 'grace' preserves him (30.8–9). Usually, however, it would be too much to say that fortune is in league with evil; it is more often simply a mirror in which human wishes are distorted. The proverbial inconstancy of fortune is well illustrated by Arthur's experience in pursuit of Florimell. His is the 'fairest fortune' when he happens to take the path she has followed (III iv 47.6), but in a few stanzas, when darkness stops him, he begins to lament 'His wicked fortune, that had turned aslope' (52.8; cf. v 7.4).

The sea, a powerful presence in several episodes, is an ally of fortune and a symbol of it, as we see in Artegall's encounter with the twin brothers Amidas and Bracidas, whom the sea has variously robbed and enriched (V iv 4–20). They are about to submit their dispute to the 'Fortune' of a trial by combat (6.1–4), but they agree to submit to Artegall's judicial arbitration. The older brother, Bracidas, has lost land but gained a virtuous and fortunate bride; he is content with the status quo and does not need to know who is responsible for it, 'Or God or Fortune' (14.3). Bracidas is confirmed in what he has by Artegall's decision. The patron of Justice omits both God and fortune from his judgment, leaving things as 'the mighty Sea' has settled them 'by his imperiall might' (19). Implicitly, as several scholars have pointed out, this opinion depends on an Elizabethan understanding of natural law – the principle 'that the grosser element must sustain the higher, as here the earth feeds the sea' (Hamilton at V iv 19).

In the episodes set along the shore at the beginning of Book V, Artegall deals with issues spilling over from Book IV. At the end of that Book, tying up narrative strands that originated in Book III, the question of Proteus's claim to Florimell is resolved in a way that sets a precedent for Artegall's justice: 'by fortune' she is his 'propertie,' but Neptune, 'the seas sole Soueraine,' is encouraged by Cymodoce to assert his 'high prerogative' and the selfishness of Proteus is finally defeated by a higher principle, also within the nature of things, that favours love and finally unites Florimell and Marinell (IV xii 30–3).

Earlier in her part of the narrative, Florimell is alternately 'Driuen to great distresse by Fortune straunge, / ... that cruell Queene auengeresse'

(III viii 20.2, 6), and rescued by 'high God,' who ordains the events that we sometimes suppose are in fortune's hands (III vii 27.1, viii 29). Her imprisonment by Proteus is the dark side of one such fortunate rescue. The reversals and dramatic ups and downs traditionally associated with fortune's sway in the world obviously suited Spenser's sense that we are creatures of our circumstances, and the romance genre supported an inclination to represent those circumstances in metaphysical rather than naturalistic terms. To a large extent, however, his metaphysical apparatus is metaphorical: often the words 'fortune' and 'chance,' with the common verbal forms 'chanced' and 'fortuned,' allude ironically to Spenser's way of maintaining authorial control, deferentially imitating his divine Maker. He sometimes shapes the episodic, polyphonic narrative into formal patterns and explicit statements that highlight order in his heterocosm, but he is also apt to leave issues of authorial design up in the air. The famous crux involving Amoret and Scudamour in Book IV provides an example of fortune's sway. We are told that Arthur, seeking Timias, 'chaunst to come where those two Ladies late, / *Æmylia* and *Amoret* abode' (IV viii 19.2–3); that later, returning to 'his former quest,' Arthur bore with him 'Faire *Amoret*, whom Fortune by bequest / Had left in his protection whileare' (ix 17.5–8); and a few stanzas later, that '*Scudamour*, and that same Briton maide, / By fortune in that place did chance to light' (28.2–3). So Amoret is fortunately present when Scudamour begins to complain of his loss of her in stanza 38, and then, responding to Britomart's encouragement, 'To tell through what misfortune he had far'd' when he first gained 'that faire Ladies loue' (41.5, 40.9). What has become of Amoret? We cannot tell whether it was the poet's sly wit or a fortune contrary to his wishes that has denied us the satisfaction of seeing the unfortunate lovers reunited between stanzas 39 and 40.

Strife and Love

Spenser never contradicts a belief that human events are driven toward concord by benevolent agents of a comprehensive providential design, but there is so much scope in the poem for discord and delay that Spenser has been compared to Nietzsche and called 'a quiet apostate' by one of his most penetrating and thoughtful critics (Teskey, *Allegory and Violence* 175). Concord is sometimes defended overzealously; it only manages discord, with no hope of eliminating it. Telling how he won Amoret from the Temple of Venus, Scudamour shares the lesson enacted on the temple porch, a lesson already reiterated many times in the poem, and familiar to Elizabethan readers acquainted with their sovereign's policies.[19] Of the two brothers 'tempred' by Concord,

> *Hate* was the elder, *Loue* the younger brother;
> Yet was the younger stronger in his state
> Then th'elder, and him maystred still in all debate.   (IV x 32.7–9)

The brothers are 'both her twins, both borne of heauenly seed' (34.3), and the fact that the younger is always victorious in debate does not deprive the elder of legitimacy, or of his due by primogeniture. Hate is evident in the natural strife among the elements, while the most basic form of love appears in their tempering throughout the sublunary creation: Concord 'holds them [the four elements, as well as her twin sons] with her blessed hands' (35.7). Spenser's ordering and moralizing of this elemental dialectic resembles his account of Night and Day, but it is less hierarchical, less involved in idealization and abjection.

Temperance is forever meeting a resistance in matter that is apparent in the vulnerability of form to decay: a perfectly equal mixture of the elements cannot be attained, despite the best efforts and promises of the alchemists.[20] Much of Book II's analysis of the passions and the virtue of Temperance is structured by conflicts between innate 'forward' and 'froward' tendencies, as William Nelson showed in his classic study (*Poetry of Edmund Spenser* 180–98). These drives, which Spenser treats as characteristics of moral identities, are linked to the natural enmity between elements – 'froward' water and 'forward' fire, for example. In *Colin Clouts Come Home Againe* (ll. 835–54) and *Fowre Hymnes* (*HL* 59–98) we find creation myths explaining how Love emerged from chaos to subdue Hate and temper the discordant elements; in *The Faerie Queene* this explanation appears in attenuated form, in the passage just examined. The connection between elemental discord and discord among (and within) human beings pervades the poem but remains largely implicit.

One is not surprised to find Spenser valuing harmony and tranquility of mind, but it is somewhat remarkable in a heroic poem, given his admiration for most forms of energy, to discover how little use he has for striving. Like strife and discord, striving carries negative connotations, referring to effort misguided and spent in vain. Despair lists 'Feare, sicknesse, age, losse, labour, sorrow, strife' among the constituents of 'a loathsome life' (I ix 44.6, 9); he reduces the heroic life to 'strife, and bloud-shed, and auengement' (43.4). Despair's perspective calls for correction, but Spenser does not respond by glorifying heroic striving per se; it must be limited and directed by a worthy purpose. Una responds to her knight's quaking on the verge of suicide, 'What meanest thou by this reprochfull strife?' (52.7), and she reminds him of his commitment to 'battell ... / With that fire-mouthed Dragon, horrible and bright' (52.8–9). As that battle looms she encourages Redcrosse to 'striue your excellent selfe to excell' (xi 2.7). An external enemy pacifies internal conflict, as does an externalized ego ideal.

Most striving is self-centred and therefore vain, as when 'The ladies for the girdle striue / of famous Florimell' (IV v Argument). Such vanity is implicitly condemned in Mammon's words about 'all this worldes blis / For which ye men do striue: few get, but many mis' (II vii 48.8–9). All striving, even for honour, is rendered dubious by Mammon's temptations to it. The other terms used to describe heroic activity are similarly questionable. To 'aspire' is to follow a natural and virtuous appetite for life, honour, and fame,[21] but aspirations may surpass the bounds set by nature, as do those of Lucifera, the followers of Philotime, and Mutabilitie.[22] Only Redcrosse, chosen for sainthood and blessed in his adventure by divine grace, is able to surpass the bounds set by nature.

While he devalues strife, Spenser is obliged to admit that it is intrinsic to the dynamics of its antithesis, love. *The Faerie Queene* offers a bifurcated account of love: idealized, love transcends strife more successfully than pure reason can, but the experience of lovers often contradicts idealization. Love is invoked, with Venus and Mars, in the poem's first Proem (3), and the *Cantos* end with the poet acknowledging that 'all that moueth, doth in *Change* delight' (viii 2.6): in some form, love is a factor in everything that happens in *The Faerie Queene*. Cupid, or Love personified, is less of a literal presence than one might expect: among the multitudinous appearances of 'loue' and 'Loue' in the text (5½ columns in Osgood's *Concordance*), the vast majority refer to a human emotion or a love-object, not to Love as a god. However, like fate and fortune, Love personified is often represented as exerting a decisive influence, usually contrary to an individual's will. If Love is not entirely a man-made god, his many forms have always been coloured by the human imagination and its detritus in cultural traditions. Spenser used allegory to register a critical awareness of the fantasies involved in his culture's images of Cupid. He does not discard or explode the received ideas and images, as many poets of the seventeenth century would do after him; he applies his intelligence to conscious manipulations of traditional motifs and mythology.

Mythopoeia is at work in Scudamour's story of his experience at the Temple of Venus, but we cannot doubt that for Spenser the Love whose strength is 'tempred' by Concord is active throughout the cosmos, as well as in all human 'pleasure and delight' (IV x 32–5; cf. 42). Venus too, as the mother of Cupid, often extends her symbolic significance beyond beauty to include a pacifying and ordering influence, fertility, and reproductive energy; the 'hymn' from Lucretius, IV x 44–7, testifies to this. Cupid's power comes from his benign mother, but he is usually portrayed, when ruling, as behaving autocratically: 'he enioyes / The wide kingdome of loue with Lordly sway, / And to his law compels all creatures to obay' (IV x 42.7–9). But if noble and virtuous characters suffer excessively under Cupid's law, it is not supposed to be in vain. Conventionally, the pains of love are wages of sin, but Spenser often makes them out to be the pains of maturation. Arthur interprets his love of Gloriana as the work of 'that proud auenging boy' (I ix 12.3): he must pay for his pride, his condescending attitude toward lovers and 'beauties chaine' (11.7), and his 'libertie' (10.7, 12.4). The 'iollitie / Of looser life, and heat of hardiment' (12.5–6), typical of youth, give way to a sense of mystery inspired by 'that face diuine' (15.5), a deep purpose 'cast in carefull mind' (15.6), and overshadowing all, an awareness that 'Nothing is sure that growes on earthly ground' (11.5).

In the context of Book II, 'loue does raine / In stoutest minds, and maketh monstrous warre' (II ii 26.5–6); it subverts nobility and is the enemy of virtue. As a central feature of his blazon of Belphoebe, Spenser introduces a distinction between 'the blinded god' and 'his wanton darts,' broken by Belphoebe, and on the other hand, the 'loftie triumphes' of Love's 'great godhed' that are engraved upon her forehead and reveal 'All good and honour' (II iii 23–4). A similar lesson in love is conveyed (again outside Sir Guyon's experience) by the guardian angel's appearance 'Like as *Cupido*' (II viii 6). In later Books, Spenser uses both the narrative and his commentary to insist upon the difference between love and lust, 'sweet affections' and 'wanton will.'[23] True nobility is revealed in an ability to bear love's 'goodly fire,' while the same natural impulse stirs 'The baser wit ... / ... to sensuall desire' (III v 1).

The difference between base and noble natures partially explains divergent portrayals of Cupid, who is sometimes irrationally cruel and destructive, sometimes benign. At the head of one canto, for example, the narrator asks Cupid, 'What glorie, or what guerdon hast thou found / In feeble Ladies tyranning so sore?' (IV vii 1.6–7); at the head of another, he addresses 'gentle ladies, in whose soueraine powre / Loue hath the glory of his kingdome left' (VI viii 1.1–2), advising them, 'But cruelty and hardnesse from you chace' (2.4). Elizabethan society bred both Amorets and

Mirabellas, and might instil the emotions of both in a single heart; Spenser's mythology had to be flexible enough to do justice to this experience. The cruelty of Cupid is explained by some of those for whom love is 'wretched anguishe and incessant woe' (IV ix 39.6), but ultimately it remains confused in the interplay of nature and culture. Lust and jealousy are self-centred drives toward possession of an object that is unworthy and unattainable, so it is easy to show why these passions are destructive. Among the nobler of his characters, those who resist the law of nature (as do Marinell, Artegall, Radigund, and Mirabella) are justly punished by a show of force. In his account of Mirabella's discourtesy and the penance imposed upon her, Spenser explains, 'The sonne of *Venus* ... is myld by kynd, / But where he is prouokt with peeuishnesse' (VI vii 37.1–2).

It is not so easy to explain why virtuous lovers should experience Love's law as 'cruell,' as it seems to Britomart (III ii 38.5). The reasons may be as numerous as the lovers. All, however, must complete the pattern described by Glauce: 'louers heauen must passe by sorrowes hell' (IV vi 32.7). Hell is different for each character, and for most of them heaven remains a distant prospect, but Spenser seems committed to taking each of his lovers through something like the axially organized world traversed by Redcrosse in Book I. If a lover's success is an imaginary heaven,[24] no fallen lover can earn entry, and grace, if it comes to the lover, will be accompanied by educative trials.

The cruelty of Cupid is most insistently present in the house of Busirane, where Cupid himself, Busirane, and the emblems of their powerful enchantments (flame, dart, and knife) are termed 'cruell' thirteen times.[25] What is the meaning of this cruelty, and how much does it have to do with the natural order? Eventually we learn by a series of disappearances that everything threatening and fascinating in Busirane's house is insubstantial. Of the masque of Cupid, except for Amoret 'streight were vanisht all and some' (xii 30.4) once Britomart has made her way to the room from which the pageant came. The chain, pillar, 'cruell steele,' and even Amoret's 'wyde wound' are harmless after Busirane has reversed his charms (37–8). Britomart then discovers that the outer rooms, whose rich displays of Cupid's power had caused her almost to lose herself in 'wonder' (xi 49.7, 53.3), have been 'cleane subuerst / ... and all their glory quite decayd' (xii 42.3–4); on 'that perlous Porch, / Those dreadfull flames she also found delayd, / And quenched quite' (42.6–8). Everything that disappears depends, it seems, upon the 'thousand charmes' contained in Busirane's 'wicked bookes' (31.8, 32.2).

In the phantasmagoria that Britomart encounters, only Busirane and the 'murdrous knife' with which he wounds Britomart (32–3) are entirely real; the rest is artifice and susceptibility to its illusions. The 'wicked bookes' can be construed as the library of a grand, deplorable cultural tradition, literary in its inspiration but with sources in religion and social customs, and ramifications in the visual arts, pageantry, and theatre: the Triumph of Cupid.[26] The tradition behind Busirane's art expresses and excuses many dreadful effects of love as faits accomplis, consequences of an irresistible force of nature, as if the maleness of Cupid could be abstracted from the actions of men. The culture for which Spenser was a spokesman was not, of course, entirely captivated with Cupid; his is only the first of the *Trionfi* in which Petrarch provided a popular representation of human life as a predicament controlled by grand and insidious forces. But Spenser knew that Busirane's power was all too pervasive in the outwardly polite and moral world of the Elizabethans.

What is the nature over which Busirane's art triumphs, and what drives his 'cruell' desire for mastery? I will take the second part of this question first. Busirane himself is a grotesque figure, but his desire for Amoret's love is natural enough, as natural as the 'greedy will, and enuious desire,' the 'threatfull pride' and 'mighty rage,' with which Scudamour assaults the fire defending Busirane's porch (xi 26.3–7). Both men not only feel the promptings we have seen in Proteus and other lovers; they are locked in an intense competitive struggle, and Amoret becomes valuable as a prize to be treasured or stolen. The many critics who have analysed this episode have not sufficiently recognized that it is as much about 'Fowle Gealosie' as about 'loue diuine' (xi 1.5) – or perhaps about the consequences, in jealousy, of promoting love as something 'diuine' rather than natural.[27]

Everything represented in Busirane's castle is a mixture of natural and cultural imperatives in which art adulterates what was already fallen. The separation of true substance from false semblance, easy in the bifurcated story of the true and false Florimells, becomes in this episode a task that might defeat Psyche, and Britomart prevails not by understanding what she sees, but by a surveillance that includes her own emotions. She traces Busirane's power to its source in the castle's inner room and his 'wicked bookes' (32.2), but Kenneth Gross rightly observes that 'Spenser in this episode continually problematizes our search for sources – whether it derives from our need for ontological security or the comforts of moral accusation' (*Spenserian Poetics* 163). Busirane's phallic 'wicked weapon,' which wounds 'her snowie chest, / That little drops empurpled her faire brest' (33), derives its point from the dubious imperatives of masculine culture that inform Spenser's own discourse: rationalizing rape, fetishizing women as property, and sentimentalizing the loss of virginity.

Cupid, present in the Garden of Adonis, reunited with Psyche and playfully 'wanton' with Adonis (49–50), is absent from Busirane's castle, but conspicuously represented as a golden statue, raised on an altar to '*the Victor of the Gods*,' where he receives 'fowle Idolatree' (xi 47–9). This image of Cupid tells us nothing reliable about the god himself; it is all about his second-order presence in human culture. In representation, his 'powre and great effort' (46.5) are indistinguishable from the sculptor's power and effort, on the one hand, and the idolatry which it serves. As Isabel MacCaffrey has observed of the tapestries decorating the castle's public space (xi 28–46), Britomart is presented 'with the equivalent of a cosmic vision, a universe enthralled to love' (*Spenser's Allegory* 107), but Busirane's version of the universe and the love that courses through it are, like the promise of peace in Acrasia's bower, unauthorized distortions of the principles animating Spenser's poem.

What is most remarkable, I think, in all that Spenser includes and omits in this episode, is the obliteration of clear distinctions between noble love and common lust: as noted earlier, such distinctions are emphasized elsewhere in the poem, and they have been taken, rightly enough, to be an important part of all that Spenser has to teach us. It can be said that the absence of such distinctions

> Kings Queenes, Lords Ladies, Knights and Damzels gent
>> Were heap'd together with the vulgar sort,
>> And mingled with the raskall rablement,
>> Without respect of person or of port   (xi 46.1–4)

shows plainly how false Busirane's version of love is, but that would not explain his power over Amoret or the importance of this trial in Britomart's development. I think, rather, that when he shows what Busirane's art can make out of love's destructive power, and shows how two women (one enamoured, one in armour) can withstand and finally destroy it, Spenser is considering the possibility that his own art, in its high-minded devotion to a 'goodly fire, / That to all high desert and honour doth aspire' (III v 1.8–9), is valid only if it acknowledges that the noblest and purest of lovers cannot escape the torment of a fire that the baser sort feel only as excitement.

The strife and suffering that persist in love's internal dynamics are rooted in gendered differences that Spenser almost certainly regarded as natural, though to us they look specific to the culture in which he was, like Britomart, an interested party. Except in the privileged moment of their union at the end of the 1590 Book III, Amoret and Scudamour experience love discordantly. For Amoret, it begins in chastity and the company of other women, where she is brought up and presented to the world 'To be th'ensample of true loue alone, / And Lodestarre of all chaste affectione' (III vi 52.4–5). From within this company she is singled out once she has given her love to Scudamour: 'Once to me yold, not to be yold againe' (III xi 17.4), as her lover puts it, or in the narrator's words, 'In faithfull loue, t'abide for euermore' (III vi 53.4). The man to whom she is supposed to yield, who supposes that all the yielding had taken place before the marriage night, has his own desire 't'abide for euermore,' but his emotions and his conduct differ markedly from Amoret's. At the end of canto vi we are told that he is only one of the many admirers who 'found / His feeble hart wide launched with loues cruell wound' (52.8–9), and he is not safe from rivalry even on his marriage night, which causes him far greater pain than he had felt (or said he felt) during courtship. Jealous rivalry – the 'triangular desire' that René Girard has analysed in the novel and Eve K. Sedgwick has examined in turn – corrupts and intensifies Scudamour's love; Busirane has more power over him than over Amoret. When Britomart offers to rescue Amoret she neglects to explain her altruism, and Scudamour is bound to regard this knightly stranger as yet another rival. His generous thanks include a fantasy of betrayal: 'what couldst thou more, / If she were thine, and thou as now am I?' (xi 19.3–4). In his characterization of Britomart and Amoret, Spenser implies that only a woman can escape the anxiety of love as strife, and her alternative is another anxious state, the vulnerability of an 'ensample of true loue alone' who must somehow learn to 'loue the worker of her smart' (xii 31.7). Like Shakespeare in the *Sonnets*, Spenser suggests that something in the dynamic of true love brings its demonic Other into play, in the lover's imagination if not at the heart of desire itself.

The Four Elements

I will turn now to the four elements constituting the world's body and the conditions of the human soul's embodiment. Our understanding of all that Spenser does with the tetrad of the elements is aided considerably by S.K. Heninger's study of Pythagorean cosmology and the many forms of learning that borrowed its structures.[28] Heninger shows how, for centuries of Western culture including the Renaissance, interrelated tetrads of elements and qualities were fundamental to thought and experience, defining the terms by which harmony and conflict, stability and change, were understood. As we have already seen, *discordia concors* was a principle Spenser celebrated in many ways. The phenomena of *The Faerie Queene* that are explicitly associated with one or more of the four elements will flesh out the meaning of *discordia concors* and tell us much about Spenser's habits of mind. Plato explains in the *Timaeus* why four elements are needed to compose a stable three-dimensional universe. The two extreme terms, earth and fire, must be mediated by two other elements, water and air. Relationships between the parts of this tetrad, bound together by *philia*, are characterized by harmony and proportion.[29] My exposition will begin with earth and fire, the extreme terms, then introduce air (for Spenser's purposes the least apparent and significant of the elements) and end with water. Compounds formed of the elements' tempered differences will be discussed at what seem the most appropriate points in this sequence.

We do not think of Spenser as a chthonic poet, but in *The Faerie Queene* earth is unquestionably the most significant of the elements. In such phrases as 'the heavens and the earth' and 'heaven and earth,' it stands for all of the sublunary world.[30] In the Ptolemaic cosmology, 'The earth was in the middle centre pight, / In which it doth immoueable abide' (V ii 35.5–6). Although Faerie land is not synonymous with any earthly realm, the poem's action and its meaning repeatedly bring us down to earth. (This should be emphasized in spite of the impression shared, I suppose, by all readers of Spenser, that with everything 'clowdily enwrapped in Allegorical deuises,' the poem's matter is never quite substantial.) One of Spenser's favourite figures for his labours represents the narrator as a ploughman; in his own mind the matter of Faerie is as earthy as a farmer's field. Once the poet has done his work of cultivation, his hero Calidore is seen 'Reaping eternall glorie of his restlesse paines' (VI ix 1–2; cf. III xii 47 [1590] and V iii 40).

Although the immortal part of humanity is of a different nature, the poem's heroes must come to terms with the fact to which Archimago and Mutabilitie allude, that Earth is the 'great mother of vs all' (II i 10.6; *Cantos* vii 17.6). The villains of several Books explicitly stem from or return to Mother Earth: Sansloy (I ii 19.6), Orgoglio (I vii 9.1), Maleger (II xi 42.9), the giants Argante and Ollyphant (III vii 47–8), Grantorto (V xii 23.7), the giants who rebelled against the Olympians, and Mutabilitie (*Cantos* vi 20–1, 26). The derivation of heroes from the earth is less often insisted upon, but when Redcrosse is addressed as a 'man of earth' (I x 52.2) before being shown his heavenly destiny, we are reminded of his status as Everyman. The name *Georgos* points to the changeling hero's discovery 'in a heaped furrow' and his raising by a ploughman 'in ploughmans state to byde' (66.2, 5); etymologically it refers to his 'tilyenge the erthe / that is his flesshe.'[31] Facing Orgoglio, 'this monstrous masse of earthly slime, / Puft vp with emptie wind, and fild with sinfull crime' (I vii 9.8–9), Redcrosse confronts his own body in a distorting mirror. At the end of his quest, mankind's ultimate enemy is also a chthonic figure: 'like a great hill' when it is first sighted, the Dragon defeated is 'like an heaped mountain' (I xi 4.6, 54.9).

Before he begins the 'chronicle of Briton kings, / from Brute to Vthers rayne' (II x Argument), Spenser celebrates his sovereign's lineage, stretching 'forth to heauens hight' (2.5), but first he must acknowledge that 'from earth it be deriued right' (2.4). Similarly, Britomart anticipates the dynasty that will 'fetch their being from the sacred mould / Of her immortal wombe, to be in heauen enrold' (III iv 11.8–9). The British chronicle begins with several stanzas (II x 5–9) on the land's wild state before its giant inhabitants were subdued by Brutus and his followers. The Castle of Alma, in whose substance and design we are shown the temperate human body, is built 'of thing like to that *Ægyptian* slime, / Whereof king *Nine* whilome built *Babell* towre' (II ix 21.5–6). Although the castle's 'goodly workemanship' is acclaimed as 'worke diuine' (21.8, 22.2), Spenser emphasizes that 'Soone it must turne to earth; no earthly thing is sure' (21.9). In this moral tag, repeated with variations throughout the poem,[32] we have one of Spenser's reasons for emphasizing what human nature owes to the basest of the elements.

A passage from H.C. Agrippa's *De Occulta philosophia*, found in *Batman vppon Bartholome*, will shed some light on Spenser's thinking about earth and its latent potential:

> As for the Earth, it is the Bace, and the Foundation of all the Elementes: for it is the obiect, the subiect, and the receiuer, of all the beames and influences of heauen. It contayneth in it the seedes, and seminall vertues of all things, therefore is she called Animall, Vegetall, and Minerall, which beeing made fruitfull by all the other Elementes and Heauens, is apte to beget all things. Of it selfe, it is receyuer of all fruitfulnesse, and as it were also, the first springing Parent of all things, the Center, foundation, and mother of all things.[33]

In Agrippa's terms, quite consistent with what we find in *The Faerie Queene*, 'the seedes, and seminall vertues of all things' are derived ultimately from heaven but latent in matter. Spenser distinguishes between different offspring of Earth by making one or another of 'all the other Elementes and Heauens' the fructifying agent. Water, fire, and air (this last seen in combination with 'earthly slime' in Orgoglio) each enter into distinctive combinations with 'the first springing Parent of all things.'

Spenser often represents earth and water together as the substratum of animate life; several references to 'slime' illustrate this. According to Hamilton, the 'hideous storme of raine' that Jove pours 'into his Lemans lap' (I i 6.6–7) is not only the genesis of the poem's action, but 'the creation of fairyland' in an oblique reference to the primal springtime union of Heaven and Earth.[34] The slime, mire, and mud produced by spring rains has a fertility sometimes associated with evil, as when the 'fertile slime' and 'heapes of mudd' produced by the overflowing Nile appear in a description of Errour's 'fruitfull cursed spawne of serpents small' (I i 21, 22.6). Spenser uses a similar vocabulary of abjection, again associated with repulsive fertility, to describe Orgoglio: 'Earth his vncouth mother' took three times a woman's term for pregnancy to produce his gargantuan form (I vii 9). Fertility and parturition are evoked when slime and mire are mentioned, usually with repulsive connotations. When Spenser says that Genius, sending 'naked babes' out from the Edenic Garden of Adonis, clothes them with 'sinfull mire' (III vi 32.7), he implies that only by union with bodies do they encounter 'Fleshly corruption' and 'mortall paine' (33.4).

We are told that Belphoebe is free of the 'loathly crime, / That is ingenerate in fleshly slime' (III vi 3.4–5), yet her conception – and Amoret's – is explained by a variant of the analogy used to characterize Errour's offspring: 'So after *Nilus* invndation, / Infinite shapes of creatures men do fynd, / Informed in the mud, on which the Sunne hath shynd' (8.7–9). Spenser's emphasis on the sun makes a crucial difference in this second instance: not only in the line just quoted, but in the entire passage (2.8, 3.1, 6.4–5, 7.5–9, 8.5), 'th'author of life and light' (9.2) replaces 'old father *Nilus*' of the earlier anecdote (I i 21.1) with an instrument of the Apollonian *logos* capable of giving innocent life to Chrysogone's 'matter fit' (9.4). By a more orthodox parthenogenesis, 'th'eternall Lord in fleshly slime / Enwombed was, from wretched *Adams* line / To purge away the guilt of sinfull crime' (II x 50.2–4). The purgation of Adam's line has made the 'mire' into which Redcrosse falls at the end of his second day's fight (I xi 45.7) no longer 'sinfull'; 'A trickling streame of Balme' from the tree of life has 'ouerflowed all the fertill plaine, / As it had deawed bene with timely raine' (48.2–5). Consistent with the Easter holy days, imagery of seasonal renewal here and elsewhere in the episode (xi 51, xii 6–7 and 21–3) revises the first canto's association of fertility with confusion and monstrosity.

An essential evil seems to reside within the element of earth when it symbolizes the mortal body, but the same element properly tempered will be fruitful, and life springing from it can even aim at perfection and redemption if its life is infused from heaven. Book I firmly establishes the sun as a symbol of that source, and later references build on the association. Spenser's imagery tells us in other ways as well that human nature derives its immortal, virtuous, and aspiring character from fire, the element standing furthest from earth in the Pythagorean tetrad. Elemental fire cannot be as obvious in *The Faerie Queene* as earth, but where there is life, some form of fire is at least implicit, and it often enters the poem's language (in *SE*, see the article devoted to fire).

At its most benevolent, fire is insubstantial and mysterious; it is experienced as light rather than heat, but felt as an insurgent energy. (Shade, on the other hand, is associated in many scenes with passivity and moral failure.) 'Fiery is the vigor and celestial the source of those seeds [*igneus est ollis vigor et caelestis origo / seminibus*],' the animating sources of all forms of life. As we saw in chapter 4, these lines from the *Aeneid* figured in many accounts of the occult principles that guarantee the continuity of species. Virgil's imagery informs many of Spenser's references to vitality and virtue derived from heaven. Fire is not all heavenly, however, nor is natural vitality reliably virtuous; the many manifestations of fire in the poem lead us to wonder whether they are all derived from a single source in the most sublime of the elements. When Artegall surveys the parts of the world to show how 'at the first they all created were / In goodly measure' (V ii 35.1–2), he goes from the earth to waters to air, then concludes: 'Al which the heauens containe, and in their courses guide' (35.9). The idea that fire is the heavens' essence is left implicit, and nothing is said of the derivation of earthly fires from the heavens. The high-minded Artegall seems to be evading an instability in human nature that Spenser was at pains to display early in the poem, with Redcrosse facing Errour 'full of fire and greedy hardiment' (I i 14.1; cf. 12.4), and burning 'with gealous fire' when Archimago shows him his false Una in bed with another (ii 5).

Phenomenologically, at least, fire is sometimes heavenly in origin, sometimes infernal. Mutabilitie distinguishes between an everlasting elemental fire and 'his parts' which are self-consuming; she acknowledges Vesta's claim to 'the fire æthereall,' separating it from the lower forms of 'this, with vs so vsuall,' the domain of Vulcan (*Cantos* vii 24, 26.4–5). With most manifestations of fire in the poem it is easy enough to distinguish between the benevolent and the destructive. The 'kindly flame' of love (IV Proem 2.2), however, can have a questionable status in lovers' eyes and in the poet's own account: its power to purify involves destroying, yet some desire is only destructive.[35]

Another passage from Agrippa found in *Batman vppon Bartholome* helps account for the phenomenology of fire in *The Faerie Queene*:

> Fire is one, and pearcing thorough all thinges as sayth the *Pythagorians*, but in heauen stretched abroade and shining ouer all, and in hell straightened, darke and tormenting, in the middle partaking of both. Wherefore the fire is one in it selfe, manifolde in the recipient. (fol. 165v)

According to Agrippa, 'euerye thing that lyueth, lyueth by reason of the included fire.' Having declared that 'Fire is one,' he still distinguishes sharply between its 'supernall' and its 'infernall' forms: 'The properties of the fire supernall, aboue, are heate making all things fruitfull, and lyght, giuing life to all things. The properties of the fire infernall, are a burning, consuming all things: and a darkenesse, making all things barraine.' Infernal fire gives life to 'the *Demones*, or Spirites of darkenesse,' but they are driven away by 'the heauenlye and lyght fire' that originates in God and is communicated 'first to the Sunne, and to other heauenlye bodyes'; ultimately that brightness is poured 'into this our fire' (fol. 166r), with its various household uses. The terms of Agrippa's account, commonplace enough in its distinctions and its rejection of a Manichean dualism, are consistent with Spenser's imagery and the hierarchies in which it is deployed. In this as in other aspects of life, the poem's centre of gravity is 'in the middle partaking of both' the light 'shining ouer all' and fire that is 'darke and tormenting.' Both Agrippa and Spenser seem at times to be affirming, with some effort, the values that Georg Lukács attributes to 'integrated civilisations' and the epic form: 'The world is wide and yet it is like a home, for the fire that burns in the soul is of the same essential nature as the stars; the world and the self, the light and the fire, are sharply distinct, yet they never become permanent strangers to one another' (*Theory of the Novel* 29).

According to the fable told through Guyon's reading of the '*Antiquitie of Faerie* lond' (II ix 60.2), when Prometheus created the first man, he 'stole fire from heauen, to animate / His worke' (x 70.7–8). This fire, like the *igneus ... vigor* in Anchises' discourse, is the masculine counterpart of the 'eternall moisture' that guarantees fertility to the seeds growing in the feminine Garden of Adonis (II x 71; III vi 34.9). The referent for many metaphorical uses of such terms as 'fire,' 'flame,' and 'spark' is moral and spiritual (courage, love, friendship, appetite for fame or glory, desire for knowledge), and through fire's agency some movement takes place between heaven and the human body with its humours and passions.[36] But if this language supports the values of an integrated civilization, Spenser also shows us humanity in disintegration, burning with a fire that is infernal or expressive of the body's ascendancy, in wrath (I v 10.2 and vi 3.3), lust (III i 53.3 and vii 49.8; IV vii 19.8 and viii 48.8; V v 53.7–8), jealousy (I ii 5.6), and greed (II vii 17.9). In the kitchen of Alma's Castle, the heat of the liver and stomach is cooled by the lungs (II ix 29–30): here the element of air tempers fire in a scene of sweaty labour. Other fires are untempered: the dragon's 'blazing eyes' and 'flake of fire' (I xi 14 and 26), the fires of Mammon's forges (II vii 3.6–9, 35–7), the flames that destroyed Troy and consume Malbecco's house (III ix 34 and 39–40; x 12.6–9 and 14–17), and the fire in Busirane's porch (III xi 21 and 25–6).

The meeting of masculine fire with the feminine element of water, or with moist matter, can be a mutually destructive conflict or a vivifying union. The Lucretian hymn heard by Scudamour tells how all animals, when inspired by Venus, 'In generation seeke to quench their inward fire' (IV x 46.9). Image patterns and related episodes in Books I through IV show that desire without a procreative purpose and love without genuine beauty as its object will be unquenchable and barren, but properly tempered, fire and water can be a creative *discordia concors*. Extremes defined by the gendered conflict between fire and water figure significantly in the differences between Books I and II. At the end of Book I, scorched by both the dragon and an 'inward fire,' near death, Redcrosse is revived overnight by 'a springing well, / ... *The well of life*' (I xi 28–9), just as the sun at day's end steeps 'His fierie face in billowes of the west' (31.1–2). Fire and water are combined in the ceremony that unites Redcrosse and Una, when the 'housling' or consecrating fire is sprinkled with 'holy water' and from it both 'the bushy Teade' of the nuptials and a 'sacred lampe' are lit, the latter to burn continually as a symbol of the marriage union and its promise of eternal life (I xii 37). So sanctified, Redcrosse is allowed to enjoy Una's 'ioyous presence and sweet company' for some time, 'Yet swimming in that sèa of blisfull ioy' he still remembers his obligation to return to Gloriana's service (41). The terms describing *discordia concors* in Book I provide reference points for subsequent Books.

In Book II, fire and water are often linked but never productively reconciled. The charm placed by Acrasia upon the linking of '*Bacchus with the Nymph*' (II i 55.6) renders the reconciliation of Mortdant and Amavia impossible. The 'image of mortalitie' presented by the two dead parents and their son Ruddymane (see ii 2) is among the more intricate passages in *The Faerie Queene*, and a full account would be out of place here. Suffice it to say that Acrasia's witchcraft has worked, like Spenser's art, upon antipathies rooted in the nature of things: 'forward' and 'froward' tendencies, male and female, desire and fear, hot and cold, corruption and purity. What distinguishes Spenser's art from Acrasia's is the sympathy, tempered by a detached understanding, that it shows toward the victims of unresolved conflicts.

With their contrary qualities, forward fire and froward water provide the fundamental terms for portraying Pyrochles and Cymochles, whose body-based passions set them against Sir Guyon's practical reason. Their behaviour presents in exaggerated form the different dangers posed by the irascible and concupiscible appetites and the irrational parts of the tripartite soul when it is not governed by reason. These brothers' unbounded elements are infernal in origin, like the characteristics of the Sans brothers, their counterparts in Book I: the intemperance of their father Acrates comes from his parents, the fiery river Phlegeton and '*Iarre*' (II iv 41.7), the Empedoclean principle of Strife. Imagery that brings together fire and water is used to represent the instability of both brothers. Pyrochles first appears as 'One ... / That as the Sunny beames do glaunce and glide / Vpon the trembling waue, so shined bright, / And round about him threw forth sparkling fire' (v 2.3–6); he is later seen, no longer so flashy, striving in vain to drown himself in the Idle Lake, burning with a fire kindled by Furor (vi 41–50). Cymochles tends to the other extreme, and has been one of Acrasia's devotees:

> he, by kind,
> Was given all to lust and loose liuing,
> When euer his fiers hands he free mote find:
> And now he has pourd out his idle mind
> In daintie delices, and lauish ioyes,
> Hauing his warlike weapons cast behind,
> And flowes in pleasures, and vaine pleasing toyes,
> Mingled emongst loose Ladies and lasciuious boyes.   (v 28.2–9)

Cymochles can still feel an angry impulse in the form of flame: when Atin calls him away from Acrasia's bower to rescue Pyrochles, 'As one affright / With hellish feends, or *Furies* mad vprore, / He then vprose, inflam'd with fell despight' (v 37.6–8). He soon yields to Phaedria's charms, however: 'So easie was to quench his flamed mind / With one sweet drop of sensuall delight' (vi 8.6–7). An hour later, he 'Gan him aduize, how ill did him beseeme, / In slouthfull sleepe his molten hart to steme, / And quench the brond of his conceiued ire' (27.4–6). In Pyrochles' irascible temperament, unresolved elemental conflict produces self-destructive aggression; in Cymochles, concupiscence is seen as a feminizing pleasure principle, all too quickly resolving the same conflict.

An artfully contrived harmony of the elements, especially fire and water, is part of the fascination exercised by Acrasia in her Bower of Bliss. The example of Cymochles makes clear the dangerous appeal of such a place to a mind with Spenser's openness to feminine aspects of experience, coupled with a deep appreciation for the stresses involved in moral idealism. The bliss offered by Acrasia must be countered not with Cymochles' attacks of remorse and regressive anger, but with an understanding of the value, within limits, of such an artificial harmony: the relief from discord that it offers is not entirely illusory, but like poisoned wine it can corrupt the whole body.

Threatening and monster-filled seas surround the Bower; pools and fountains are strategically placed within it. To these waters Acrasia brings an art that works its enchantment through the play of light on surfaces and a simultaneous offer of more secret satisfactions. Spenser's own narrative, similarly, combines prolix examination with mysterious hints and silences. In contrast to his handling of Archimago and Duessa, he tells us nothing about the provenance of Acrasia's powers; the 'faire Witch' (72.2; cf. 81.8) is, like Busirane, without parents, which suggests that she and her wicked powers come from literature, not the underworld. The Mediterranean light in which the Bower's delights are bathed must come from the sun, but its light is diffused and implicit[37] ('the Heauens alwayes Iouiall, / Lookt on them louely,' 51.1–2), nor is Acrasia associated, like other witches, with the moon.

As Guyon learns from Amavia (i 54–5) and we are reminded by the 'mighty Mazer bowle of wine' at her gate (49) and the golden cup offered by Excesse (54–7), Acrasia's enchantments use wine, occasionally adulterated with drugs. Fire is hidden within her body (belied by her 'vele of silke and siluer thin, / That hid no whit her alablaster skin,' 77.4–5) as it is in wine and drugs. The Bower's gate depicts Medea with 'Her mighty charmes, her furious louing fit' (II xii 44.5), and 'th'enchaunted flame, which did *Creüsa* wed' (45.9), an instance of Medea's magic, provides an objective correlative for Acrasia's vengeful appetite. The effect of her fire is degenerative, as in venereal disease. She is seen (through the suspicious eyes of Guyon and the Palmer) as capable of sucking Verdant's spirit 'through his humid eyes ..., / Quite molten into lust and pleasure lewd' (73.7–8). Acrasia's own eyes

Moystened their fierie beames, with which she thrild
Fraile harts, yet quenched not; like starry light
Which sparckling on the silent waues, does seeme more bright.   (78.7–9)

If this description of Acrasia is complicit with the prurient interests of the two men spying on her post-coital delight in Verdant, it also adds an artist's detached connoisseurship; Acrasia mirrors the poet's distance from his subject. Intertextual echoes also submit her to judgment: she can be compared to Fidelia, 'able, with her words to kill, / And raise againe to life the hart, that she did thrill' (I x 19.8–9), and to Belphoebe, whose eyes 'darted fyrie beames ... / That quite bereau'd the rash beholders sight: / ... and quenched base desire' (II iii 23). The many instances of *discordia concors* that are displayed in Acrasia and her Bower suggest not only the dangers of concupiscence but the value of art as a sublimation of desire. At the end of the day, however, to the extent that art is enervating it must be left behind.

Of the four elements, air carries the least complex significance, but it is not without symbolic resonance, within the human body and in its ambiance. To be alive is 'to breath out liuing aire' (II i 43.9; cf. II Proem 1.6), and it is the shock of breathing in 'this vitall aire' (II vii 66.6) after three exhausting days in Mammon's claustral kingdom that causes Guyon's swoon. The relationship of elemental air to the biblical 'breath of life,' Greek *pneuma* and Latin *anima*, is left mysterious; air and fire tempered together support, but do not constitute, the 'spright' or 'spirit' that is often mentioned in the poem.

Light breezes are characteristic of the poem's moments of repose, but there is usually something dangerous in the relaxation that they encourage. Duessa overtakes Redcrosse when 'foreby a fountaine side' he 'bayes / His sweatie forehead in the breathing wind, / Which through the trembling leaues full gently playes' (I vii 2.7, 3.1–3). At the same time Una, unable to escape the harshness of reality, is 'Long tost with stormes, and bet with bitter wind' (28.7). In the Bower of Bliss, the 'stedfast state' of the heavens is evident in the weather: 'the milde aire with season moderate / Gently attempred, and disposd so well, / That still it breathed forth sweet spirit and holesome smell' (II xii 51.2, 7–9). 'The gentle warbling wind' is the last element in Spenser's analysis of the 'one harmonee' surrounding Acrasia's bed (70.8, 71.9). This pleasant ambiance, an adjunct to Acrasia's enchantments, also provides a contrast to their illusory character: however unusual and enviable such weather (borrowed from Tasso) was in England, it is clearly an aspect of nature, conducive to seduction but not itself open to criticism. Belphoebe's virginal 'dainty Rose' flourishes in the same Mediterranean weather (adapted this time from Ariosto) as Acrasia's intemperance, although her situation requires that she protect it from 'the Middayes scorching powre' and 'the sharp Northerne wind' (III v 51).

Just as mild weather is emblematic of pastoral relaxation, variously promoting either spiritual tranquility or a regressive passivity, storms and tempests are used to represent passion. Some, such as the 'hideous storme of raine' that descends from 'angry *Ioue*' at the beginning of the poem (I i 6.6), are to be taken as admonitory signs, but winds usually express human emotion. Guyon destroys Acrasia's 'goodly workmanship' with 'the tempest of his wrathfulnesse' (xii 83.3–4). Some metaphorical storms are not internally generated, but visited upon characters: 'An hideous storme of winde' (III xii 2.1; cf. 3.1) is one of the disturbances preceding the masque of Cupid in Busirane's house, and a 'stormy blast' (27.2) drives the door closed at the end. Perhaps Britomart is expected to recall how, early in the throes of her own love, she was made 'to pant and quake, / As it an Earthquake were' (III ii 42.8–9). Earthquakes accompany both the overture to the masque of Cupid (xii 2.3–4) and the reversal of Busirane's spells (37.1–2). Winds are joined with water to express Britomart's 'tempestuous griefe' when she stops by the seashore (III iv 8–10), and in Isis Church her strife of love in a dream takes the form of 'An hideous tempest' that kindles 'outragious flames' (V vii 14). While flames suggest the painful urgency of an active and unsatisfied desire, stormy winds and waters depict another aspect of the lover's predicament, the hysteria accompanying a surrender to passion that is the opposite of *jouissance*.

It should be noted that even though Spenser makes clear early in Book III that Britomart's love is providentially blessed and will be fruitful in marriage, the imagery of elemental strife that is used to dramatize her emotions does not allow her peace of mind. The characters from whom we expect the most are most exposed to conflict and frustration, and recognition of this harsh truth may help us to understand the dialectic of curiosity and rejection with which offers of repose and harmony are greeted. The appeal of a lasting and creative reconciliation of discordant elements is obviously very strong, but in *The Faerie Queene* most peace accords are illusory, or at best temporary.

Of the four elements, Spenser handles water with the most personal feeling. I imagine that he found in himself, and not to his own liking, an affinity with Cymochles' temperament, and sought through moral and aesthetic discipline the self-control that Pyrochles and Cymochles, lacking reason, can only hate. 'Fluidity,' as G. Wilson Knight perceived, is one of the distinctive features of his verse ('The Spenserian Fluidity' 339–40). Beginning in his earliest publication, the translations contributed to van der Noodt's *Theatre* (1569), and extending to the *Prothalamion* (1596), one finds in comparisons of the poet's voice to falling or running water what one critic has called Spenser's 'poetic signature.' Another, writing of the symbolic properties of springs and fountains in his poetry, rightly sees in their 'radical mutability' a 'paradoxical union of flow and form' and a two-fold significance in the water from such sources, 'dissolution or the loss of form' and 'birth or the manifestation of form.'[38] Further discussion of this subset in Spenser's elemental imagery will be found in chapter 8; a few remarks here will bring this segment of the present chapter to an end. The seas and fresh-water springs, streams, and rivers should be seen as parts of a single complex system; I will discuss the larger before the lesser parts.

Spenser was a Londoner for whom the city was closely associated with the Thames, its central avenue for local and sea-borne commerce, travel from one part of the city and its environs to another, and removal of much of the city's filth. His persona Colin Clout, not city-bred, is even more a landsman, for whom the sea between Ireland and England is 'Horrible, hideous, roaring with hoarse crie' in his self-mocking account of a voyage with the Shepherd of the Ocean (*Colin Clout* 199). Britomart, coming from South Wales, must be no stranger to the sea; familiarity with the perils faced by a 'feeble barke' may make it easier for her to project her inner turmoil upon the 'Huge sea of sorrow, and tempestuous griefe' (III iv 7–10). Not only literary conventions but the rocky coastlines of England and Ireland and the nation's involvement in many forms of ocean-going commerce required that the sea's raging disorder be respected. Both the Bible and classical authorities encouraged Spenser to see in the world's seas an undifferentiated matter older than the earth, just as Night is older than Day.[39] The sea and night are associated in many ways throughout *The Faerie Queene*; as threats to life and form and meaning they are frightening, but they are also, as MacCaffrey observes, 'emblems of potentiality' (*Spenser's Allegory* 291–7).

At several points in the poem, most elaborately at the end of Book IV, Spenser brings the ocean's governing principles powerfully into play. In the Proem to Book VI, Spenser alludes to the reciprocity that, having been at work throughout the poem, will be especially important in that Book:

Then pardon me, most dreaded Soueraine,
    That from your selfe I doe this vertue bring,
    And to your selfe doe it returne againe:

So from the Ocean all riuers spring,
And tribute backe repay as to their King.   (VI Proem 7.1–5; cf. IV iii 27)

Ocean, 'father of all things' according to Virgil (*Georgics* IV 382), is the oldest of sovereigns (see IV xi 18.1–4), and a source of power to which Queen Elizabeth herself can be expected to pay tribute. Spenser exerts himself at several points to show that the seas are prolific as well as devouring. Often they are emblematic of fortune, and as we have seen, fortune is one of the masks assumed by the author's deviously rational will. It is quite appropriate, then, to see in 'the seas abundant progeny' an analogue to the 'endlesse worke' of Spenser's worldmaking and meaning-making (see IV xii 1), although as a narrator he typically presents himself as a mariner, claiming nothing like the power of Proteus or Neptune.[40] In the hands of both Ocean and Neptune, patriarchal sovereignty is not auto-cratic but on friendly terms with its partners and successors. If the sea is often averse to life and happiness, it does not, like the earth, breed either evil or ambitious strife. The energy and mere flux of the seas are only apparently purposeless; their fertility serves, with an emphasis on dynamic processes rather than the imposition of order from above, many purposes beyond the limits of the Ocean, since from it come 'the famous riuers ... / Which doe the earth enrich and beautifie' (IV xi 20.1–2).

I will close this segment with a few remarks on themes associated with lesser forms of running and still water. If the seas and their progeny provide a vast analogy to the poem's scope, it should also be recalled that a more down-to-earth self-image appears in several passages where a singing voice is joined in harmony with a passing stream. To this I would add that, just as the sea and night are linked symbolically, the oblivion of sleep is often associated with water. Morpheus's house is inevitably dark; for less obvious reasons (probably dictated by the theory of humours) it is moist with waves, dew, and rain.

> *Tethys* his wet bed
> Doth euer wash, and *Cynthia* still doth steepe
> In siluer deaw his euer-drouping hed,
> ...
> And more, to lulle him in his slumber soft,
> A trickling streame from high rocke tumbling downe
> And euer-drizling raine vpon the loft,
> Mixt with a murmuring winde, much like the sowne
> Of swarming Bees, did cast him in a swowne.   (I i 39.6–8 and 41.1–5)

Archimago's night-time conjuring, a demonic opposite to Spenser's Apollonian art, introduces near the beginning of the poem an instance of the strategy to be followed throughout: artful inclusion of that which is marked for exclusion. It is a strategy for coping with anxieties that cannot be entirely dispelled. The body's temperance cannot be maintained without water and sleep, yet without reason in control, imagination is prone to intemperance. Una and Redcrosse are the first of many characters to be 'all drownd in deadly sleepe' (I i 36.6).[41] In nearly all cases, the oblivion of sleep is dangerous. Even where rest is innocent and well earned, it may have unhappy consequences. While Britomart 'did her passed paines in quiet rest assoyle' (IV vii 3.9), her care for Amoret lapses and, carelessly, the girl walks off to be 'rapt by greedie lust' (vii Argument)

Sleep is associated with drowning in contrast to frantic waking states, as illustrated variously in Mammon's feverish will to power, Phantastes with his 'sharpe foresight, and working wit, / That neuer idle was' (II ix 49.8–9), the 'long anguish, and selfe-murdring thought' of Malbecco (III x 57.1), Amoret's nightly torments, and Florimell's similar imprisonment for seven months in Proteus's undersea dungeon, where she 'thought it all one night, that did no houres diuide' (IV xi 4.9). On the other hand there are two famous instances of beneficial sleep and visionary dreams. Britomart, whose success in rescuing Amoret from Busirane had required extraordinary wakefulness, lies down beside the altar in Isis Church at a later stage in her education:

> Where whilest her earthly parts with soft delight
> In sencelesse sleepe did deeply drowned lie,
> There did appeare vnto her heauenly spright
> A wondrous vision, which did close implie
> The course of all her fortune and posteritie.   (V vii 12.5–9)

This episode recalls Arthur's experience, 'Whiles euery sence the humour sweet embayed, / And slombring soft my hart did steale away' (I ix 13.5–6). The narrator's account of Britomart's dream vision makes clearer than Arthur's confession of love that in a prophetic dream, sleep occupies the body and frees a 'heauenly spright' from promptings by the senses.[42] The 'spright,' as we will see, can rise above the sublunary domain of the four elements.

Drowning and fear of drowning are associated with still water; like the soul, to be on the side of life water must be in motion. The word 'lake' carries negative connotations. Most of the lakes named in *The Faerie*

Queene are infernal: Limbo (I ii 32.5, III x 54.9), Lethe (I iii 36.6), the 'Stygian lake' (I v 10.6, II v 22.7, V xi 32.4), and Lerna (I vii 17.3). Spenser's own invention, Phaedria's Idle Lake, is essentially infernal too, with similarities to Virgil's Cocytus and Dante's Styx. These considerations lend plausibility to Hankins's argument that the 'standing lake' (II xi 46.6) into which Arthur throws Maleger is not an emblem of baptism, but of formlessness and extinction (*Source and Meaning* 80–3). In contrast to such stagnant places, which are not sources but sinks disconnected from the circulating economy of rivers and seas, the poem's many fountains and wells, each with a 'virtue' available to the narrative by an etiological digression, provide occasions for Spenser's favourite pastime, reflection on his sources and the nature of his own poetic invention.[43] Following other poets in the tradition of romance going back to Ovid, he calls upon natural magic to point the moral of a marvellous turn of events.

If it were desirable to make this chapter much longer, it would be appropriate to include a discussion of the whole apparatus of the humoural body, and within it the flow of blood, to which Spenser attaches considerable significance. Like the poem's scenery and topography, however, the physical body and its parts will have to be left to others.

Sprights and Spirits

The Faerie Queene contains no master concept that unifies the phenomenal diversity of the physical forces at work in the world, and within human nature, at the level of the four elements; there is no passage equivalent to Anchises' explanation of the *Spiritus intus* and the *mens* implicit in the world's mass. As we have seen, however, the narrative includes many reminders that nature is a moral order and events transpiring within it are directed toward divinely ordained goals. Subsequent chapters will deal with places and personifications by which the world's *anima* and *spiritus* are brought – *in potentia*, not explicitly – into the text, along lines consistent with the legacy of Plato, Virgil as Landino interpreted him, and such thinkers as Ficino, Agrippa, and Bruno. In this section, building upon the evidence gathered from imagery involving the four elements, I will examine the terms Spenser used to describe the microcosmic equivalent of Virgil's cosmic *Spiritus*: the mediating parts of human nature that link the incorporeal and immortal soul with its corruptible body. It will become apparent that Spenser was well acquainted with sixteenth-century interpretations of the organic *spiritus* as an agent in all of the body's vital functions, including consciousness, moral disposition, and by implication, many of the traits constituting an individual's 'character.'[44]

The terms 'spright' (also 'sprite') and 'spirit' are synonymous; the disyl-labic form, used less frequently, appears where it is metrically convenient and Latinate precision is appropriate. Spenser refers to 'soul' and 'mind' much less often, and those terms carry more specific meanings. 'Spright' means something elusive, and the term's polyvalence suits Spenser's pur-poses: his poetry often interprets the ill-defined boundary zone where inner and outer forces, incorporeal and corporeal entities, take question-able shapes.

The first sprights we learn of are distractions, sowing confusion before we can grasp what the term usually identifies, which is an agent essential to human nature and moral virtue. Archimago conjures, 'out of deepe darknesse' suggestive of the underworld, 'Legions of Sprights,' and they appear 'like little flyes / Fluttring about his euer damned hed' (i 38.1–3). The lord of these flies chooses 'two, the falsest twoo, / And fittest for to forge true-seeming lyes' (38.6–7), sending one to retrieve a dream decep-tive like itself and making the other into an *imago* of Una. Archimago's duplicities, added to the 'dull wearinesse' he feels after his battle with Errour, give Redcrosse himself an 'irkesome spright' (55.4–5), difficult to pacify and easily aroused to jealous rage the next morning. This episode mingles common medical lore with superstitious interest in necromancy and demonic agents; whatever Spenser believed about the operation of spirits in the human body remains veiled, like the false Una 'fram'd of liquid ayre' (45.3), in 'true-seeming lyes.' Redcrosse's next *unheimlich* encounter provides some clarification: when he hears Fradubio's warning voice he suspects it is a 'damned Ghost from *Limbo* lake, / Or guilefull spright wandring in empty aire' (ii 32.5–6). The fiction asks us to believe that part of Fradubio's human essence remains alive in his metamorphosed state, retaining his story and enabling him to tell it with pathetic skill. Subsequent episodes and many casual references imply that an organic and corporeal *spiritus* is instrumental in the preservation of life, memory, emotions – virtually everything that constitutes an individual identity.

Other-worldly sprights are not confined to the shady domains of Archimago and Duessa, and they are not all guileful or otherwise danger-ous. In Book II the 'covetous' and 'cruell' sprights of Mammon's domain (vii 32.1 and 57.4) are contradicted by Guyon's guardian angel, one of the 'heauenly spirits' descending 'all for loue, and nothing for reward' (viii 1–2), and in Alma's castle Guyon reads how Elfe, 'the first authour' of the race of faerie knights, found his mate in the gardens of Adonis after 'wandring through the world with wearie feet'; he is convinced that his Fay is 'no earthly wight, but either Spright, / Or Angell' (x 71).

The magic used in Book III includes, in the making of a false Florimell (viii 4–8), conjuring reminiscent of Archimago's. Wicked male sprights do the witch's bidding and are dressed in Florimell's form and cast-off clothes; this hermaphroditic simulacrum takes the true beauty's place for much of the story that follows. It is hard to say how seriously we are to take the lowly witch's analogue to Archimago's demonic magic; for the poem's romantic lovers, heaven and hell are more make-believe than they are shown to be in Book I. Like the folklore associated with Merlin, which makes him the child of a 'guilefull Spright' (III iii 13.4) who grew up to command 'thousand sprights with long enduring paines' (9.4), the witch's power to command spirits does not invite belief, but parodies the author's art, which remains playful even in its most serious activity, making beauty and allegorical meaning.

The power that makes Merlin 'the Prophet' is to be taken more seriously than the witch's art. Spenser's account of the peace-producing dynasty that will 'descend' from Britomart (III iii 21–49) begins and ends with references to 'his spirite' and 'the spirites powre' (21.5 and 50.2), and this is the same kind of 'spirit' that is called upon in some of the poet's requests for inspiration (see II x 1.6, IV ii 34, VI Proem 1.9, and *Cantos* vii 1.3), a mental power that comes mysteriously from an otherworldly source. Prophecy, poetry, and the higher form of love all, according to Ficino and other followers of Plato, involve allied forms of *furor*, which is made good rather than destructive by the flow of corresponding spirits in the cosmos and microcosm. Inspired *furor* was credited with providing the basis for an understanding of spirits, but that knowledge was carefully elaborated by rational argument and reflection on experience.[45] In the Platonists' scheme of things *spiritus* ranks below *anima*, well below the level of *mens* or *angelus*, but all the entities associated with the *anima* and *spiritus* serve the purpose of mediation, so they are not confined to a niche in the scale of being.

Among Spenser's references to a character's spirit, the most common identify it as the basic principle of vitality and the seat of emotions. Emotions tend to deplete or distort it, and the spirit's vitality is only tenuously linked to the body whose life it sustains. The rational soul imposes a beautiful form and purpose on the body and its actions, but the soul's grip on the body and its irrational imperatives can be no stronger than the spirit, its instrument, which is apt to be weak or, under the pressure of a strong emotion, irresponsible. After Sansfoy's death Duessa calls upon Sansjoy to revenge his brother's 'restlesse spright' (I iv 48.7); in his indecisive battle with Redcrosse, Sansjoy is laid 'In slombring swownd nigh voyd of vitall spright' (v 19.5). At the beginning of his encounter with

Mammon, Guyon attributes to himself a 'high heroicke spright' that delights in chivalric activity (II vii 10), but three days without food and sleep – emblematic, it seems, of the waiting game of chivalry at court, where only ignoble opportunities present themselves – deplete his 'vital powres' and 'his enfeebled spright' encounters 'this vitall aire' as a shock: 'The life did flit away out of her nest, / And all his senses were with deadly fit opprest' (65–6).

As the seat not only of animal vitality but of emotions, the spirit presents a challenge to rational control but is also fundamental to moral action and identity. Virtue is, after all, a matter of habits that enhance innate qualities, rather than precepts learned by rote. Some assembly is required in the artifice that Spenser imposes on nature, and a complex character's spright is often shown being shaped by external stimuli. The next-to-last phase of Redcrosse's development illustrates this. Ending his encounter with De-spair, Una chides her 'fraile, feeble, fleshly wight,' calling upon a 'constant spright' that has been very little in evidence (I ix 53.1–3). She takes him to the House of Holiness, where 'that soule-diseased knight' is persuaded to reveal 'all that noyd his heauie spright' (x 24.1–3). Only after his corrupted body and spirit have been purified 'In that sad house of *Penaunce*, where his spright / Had past the paines of hell,' is Redcrosse ready to be schooled in Charissa's 'vertuous rules' (32.5–9). Further instruction by Contempla-tion requires another season of fasting and prayer, 'Till from her bands the spright assoiled is' (52.8): the vision shown to him on 'the highest Mount' (53.1) is experienced by a spirit unencumbered by the flesh. After this, and after Contemplation has revealed the truth about his lineage and destiny, 'At last whenas himselfe he gan to find' (68.1), Redcrosse is ready for Una's encouragement: 'The sparke of noble courage now awake, / And striue your excellent selfe to excell' (xi 2.6–7).

Britomart's spirit is portrayed at length, and with the greatest sensitivity. Love, of course, confuses her conscious thoughts with fantasies, doubts, and longings; the manner of her falling in love with an imaginary object seems calculated to accentuate the spiritual aspect of sexual desire. Over-stimulated, 'full of fancies fraile' (III ii 27.5), she is unable to sleep, and when 'her wearie spright' manages to find rest, 'Streight way with dreames, and with fantasticke sight / Of dreadfull things the same was put to flight' (29.1–5). Later, on the road and preoccupied with thoughts of Artegall and the destiny Merlin has foretold, when she sees a knight in armour galloping toward her she converts 'Her former sorrow into suddein wrath, / Both coosen passions of distroubled spright' (iv 12.6–7). Just the opposite hap-pens when she finally sees Artegall's 'louely face' during a truce in their hand-to-hand combat: 'Therewith her wrathfull courage gan appall, / And haughtie spirits meekely to adaw, / That her enhaunced hand she downe can soft withdraw' (IV vi 26). Britomart's spirit is active in the whole sequence of changes that transpire in this stanza and the next: in the vision of her 'sharpe auizefull eye,' taking in beauty 'Tempred with sternesse and stout maiestie,' then in the memory and judgment that prove this to be the same face she saw 'Long since' in her father's mirror, then in quieting her wrath and forcing her hand up again 'As fayning choler, which was turn'd to cold,' then when 'She arm'd her tongue, and thought at him to scold' but could produce only 'speeches myld.' The moral of this humorous vignette is that a person's spirit, when it is gentle like Britomart's, knows better than her will, which is ostensibly rational but may be too selfish, trapped in what we have learned to call inauthentic behaviour. And Britomart's character is only the most full-blown instance of a truth that interests Spenser throughout his poem: that in the ensemble of faculties, impulses, and bodily instruments constituting human nature (the 'selfe' that Redcrosse belatedly discovers), the rational or intellectual soul may be sovereign, but it is apt to be little more than a figurehead.

To a remarkable extent, Spenser makes the spirit rather than the soul or mind the primary vehicle of moral character, manifesting innate nobility and often taking the form of an idealized and idealizing desire. After Arthur's rescue of Guyon and the recovery of Guyon's shield, Arthur compliments his new friend on the picture displayed upon it, reminiscent of course of the woman in his dream, related in the corresponding episode of Book I. Guyon obliges with praise uncannily appropriate to his listener's interests, and suggestive of values at odds with the Palmer's version of temperance:

> Faire Sir (said he) if in that picture dead
>   Such life ye read, and vertue in vaine shew,
>   What mote ye weene, if the trew liuely-head
>   Of that most glorious visage ye did vew?
>   But if the beautie of her mind ye knew,
>   That is her bountie, and imperiall powre,
>   Thousand times fairer then her mortall hew,
>   O how great wonder would your thoughts deuoure,
> And infinite desire into your spirite poure!   (II ix 3)

Here the heroic spirit – Arthur's, more authentically than Guyon's – is described as overflowing with a desire spilled into it by a mind overwhelmed. When Arthur meets the personification of his virtue in Alma's castle, the relation of thought to passion is stated differently: Praise-desire appears to Arthur 'somwhat sad, and solemne eke in sight, / As if some pensiue thought constraind her gentle spright' (36.8–9). The difference between masculine 'infinite desire' and feminine 'pensiue thought' is instructive, and illustrative of the poem's commitment to open-ended dialectical processes. An emphasis on 'gentleness of spright' as an innate trait,[46] inherently unstable and open to influence but capable of invigorating and unifying the character it inhabits, is consistent with Spenser's process-oriented design.

Decay

An individual's spirit is essential to his or her earthly identity, the natural counterpart to the proper name that culture supplies, and crucial to the continuity and coherence of a moral life. Its frailty accounts for mortality, but to the extent that it is united with the individual's soul, it also participates in life after death. The theological virtues of faith, hope, and love are devoted to this ultimate destiny, and Spenser's poem also supplies secular analogues to the theological concerns that are emphasized in Book I. Throughout the poem, delight in the perpetuity of natural processes is involved in dialectical tension with desire to escape the decay and death that nature imposes on individual lives.

Scudamour's story of his visit to the Temple of Venus, where he won his shield and met his bride-to-be, includes several stanzas (IV x 21–8) describing the 'second paradise' in which the Temple is set. In this carefully cultivated forest park, Scudamour sees a 'thousand payres of louers' walking, 'Praysing their god, and yeelding him great thankes,' talking of nothing but 'their true loues' (25). In addition to this parade of anonymous lovers, he sees in the next stanza,

> farre away from these, another sort
> Of louers lincked in true harts consent;
> Which loued not as these, for like intent,
> But on chast vertue grounded their desire,
> Farre from all fraud, or fayned blandishment;
> Which in their spirits kindling zealous fire,
> Braue thoughts and noble deeds did euermore aspire.   (IV x 26.3–9)

While he seems intent on making himself and Amoret the only exemplary couple committed to marriage, Scudamour names several of the ideal friends: Hercules and Hylas, Jonathan and David, Theseus and Pirithous, Pylades and Orestes, Titus and Gesippus, Damon and Pythias are mentioned, who 'there did liue for euer, / Whose liues although decay'd, yet loues decayed neuer' (27). The common-sense meaning of the last line is that, for as long as they lived, these friends' loves never decayed. But Scudamour is also speaking on behalf of the poem that he inhabits, implying that the paradise he has been privileged to visit resembles the classical Island of the Blessed, a place where virtuous lovers 'liue for euer' after death. Like the 'infinite desire' that Gloriana's inner beauty inspires in her acolytes, the 'zealous fire' of love in these friends' spirits, devoted not to reciprocal physical pleasures but aspiring toward an idealized 'chast vertue,' is inherently excessive, tending away from worldly prudence, harmony, and temperance.

Such a love is at odds with life on earth, and so, frequently, is *The Faerie Queene*. In a sense, Spenser's poem feeds off the instability and decay that it comments upon repeatedly, with a focus that some readers may experience as obsessional while others welcome it like a musical *leitmotif*. Contrasting perspectives on decay are offered in the first two Books, reconsidered in Book III, and examined further in the broader social contexts of Books IV through VI; in the *Cantos*, the complementarity of desire and decay is foregrounded and inescapable. Discussion here will be preliminary to further exploration of this theme in chapter 8.

In Book I, Caelia welcomes Una, with Redcrosse in 'his late decayed plight' (I x 2.9), to the House of Holiness, wryly commenting that the place receives few visitors. 'O foolish men,' she exclaims, 'why haste ye to your owne decay?' (10.9). In Book II, Guyon finds the roof, floor, and walls of Mammon's Cave 'all of gold, / But ouergrowne with dust and old decay' (vii 29.1–2); as he resists the temptations presented to him as 'the worldes blis' (32.7), the narrator comments, 'Eternall God thee saue from such decay' (34.7). In the Bower of Bliss another form of getting and spending is encouraged in the 'louely lay' chanted as a commentary on Acrasia's pleasure with the passive Verdant: 'So passeth, in the passing of a day, / Of mortall life the leafe, the bud, the flowre, / Ne more doth flourish after first decay' (xii 75.1–3). Caelia's comment on the heedless hurry of most human lives is turned around: 'why haste ye?' becomes 'why not haste?' in a place that promises prolonged lassitude.

Flowers stand for the flesh and its mortal life in both Book I and Book II, but in Book I we find more emphasis on seasonal renewal. (In both, Arthur's virtue is metaphorically floral: Una salutes him first as 'Faire braunch of noblesse, flowre of cheualrie' in I viii 26.7, and the Palmer welcomes him as a 'flowre of grace and nobilesse' in II viii 18.4.) When Redcrosse is recovered from Orgoglio's sunless dungeon, we see 'all his vital powres / Decayd, and all his flesh shronk vp like withered flowres' (I viii 41.8–9). In the House of Holiness, however, human nature is cured by killing and regeneration. In the course of his last ordeal Redcrosse's life is renewed once again by the Well of Life (xi 30); after the dragon is slain it comes as no great surprise that Una is presented to him 'So faire and fresh, as freshest flowre in May' (xii 22.1).

Book III carries the poem's meditations on mortality and immortality into the realm of paradox, again using floral imagery and other references to organic cycles of decay and regeneration. All of this advances the poem's analysis of love as the original destroyer and preserver. Marinell's mother vainly protects him from 'hart-wounding loue,' believing that it would bring him 'vnto his last decay' (iv 28.5); her self-protective maternal interests provide a contrast to the long ordeal of Florimell, whose virginity symbolizes another way of resisting decay. Just as Caelia took seriously the heedlessness of men who hasten to their deaths, avoiding the path leading to rebirth through her strenuous discipline, at the end of Book III we are called upon to join Britomart in 'beholding earnestly' the spectacle decorating Busirane's walls, 'Of mighty Conquerours and Captaines strong, / Which were whilome captiued in their dayes / To cruell loue, and wrought their owne decayes' (xi 52.2–4). The corrective proposed in Book III, responsive to this cruel desire for death, is not the grace available in Book I, but a gracious form of love, personified in Venus, who knows death intimately and brings life out of it. In her Garden, 'called ... by her lost louers name' (vi 29.8–9), 'that faire flowre of beautie fades away' (38.8) just as we were reminded it would in the Bower of Bliss: 'For all that liues, is subiect to that law: / All things decay in time, and to their end do draw' (40.8–9). Death is not the end, however, but the beginning of Venus's fascinating, nurturing power, which will be central to my subjects in the next two chapters.

chapter six

Reading the Garden of Adonis Canto

The sheer volume of criticism devoted to Spenser's description of the Garden of Adonis, and the complexity of the issues addressed in it, may induce a numbed humility in anyone who ventures beyond the *jouissance* offered by that 'ioyous Paradize' toward an educated understanding of its themes. How can that mass of information and disparate opinions be assimilated? It is clear already that interpretation of canto vi in Book III is inescapably central to this book. I must therefore hope to proceed, carrying patient readers along, beyond *tristesse* to a recuperated pleasure in Spenser's description of the Garden. This will require examination of the texts and traditions on which that most dense of all the obscure passages in the poem rests – rather as the 'stately Mount' sheltering the Garden's central mysteries rests upon the 'strong rocky Caue' imprisoning Adonis's nemesis (III vi 43 & 48).

I will try to avoid 'that wilde Bore, the which him once annoyed,' chastened by a recognition that some responses to the Garden have been wild, and others have been – dare I say it? – boring. Taking cues from Spenser's conduct of his narrative, I will model my reading on the hovering attention that Freud recommended to psychoanalysts, also bearing in mind the model of interpretation offered by structuralist and post-structuralist studies of myths. An interpreter is obliged 'to define ... as exhaustively as possible, the framework within which the myth must be set'; interpretation of individual elements 'is only valid in so far as it is carried out within a definite field of enquiry that can adequately ensure on the one hand comprehensiveness and, on the other, internal coherence.'[1]

It is now many years since Thomas Roche, in the study that inaugurated modern interest in the Garden's place within the central Books of *The Faerie Queene*, complained that 'the basic questions of poetic structure and logic have been overlooked in order to plaster the relics of the poem over the walls of the temple of source studies' (*Kindly Flame* 118). From the 1960s to the present, many interpreters of the Garden have followed Roche's precept and example. They have dwelt upon the Garden of Adonis canto as poetry – poetry as marvellous as anything else in *The Faerie Queene*. These interpreters have also shown how the sentiments expressed and the doctrines invoked in those stanzas are related to far-flung incidents and themes in a narrative to which the canto contributes both complications and explanations.

Roche's temple of source studies hasn't lacked for fresh tributes. In part through the narrowness of its emphasis and in part through the intelligence with which it developed new knowledge, Robert Ellrodt's critique of earlier studies provided an impetus for fresh interpretations that brought the Garden's backgrounds in philosophical and theological traditions into the foreground (*Neoplatonism in the Poetry of Spenser* 70–90). Also, while he minimized the relevance of Florentine Neoplatonism to Spenser's poetry apart from the *Fowre Hymnes*, Ellrodt contributed substantially to our understanding of the conduits of translation and adaptation through which ideas articulated in Florence late in the fifteenth century were both simplified and elaborated, suiting the interests of courtly elites and the literati throughout Europe, during the second half of the sixteenth century. Contributions to the study of sources and the explanation of doctrines relevant to Spenser's Garden[2] have not been so numerous as readings that accept the status quo of such knowledge as their point of departure,[3] but they have been resourceful, and they have enlarged the range of references that a curious reader may bring into the Garden.

So many opinions have accumulated around the Garden and matters pertinent to it, both literary and philosophical, that a synthesis is needed. It may provide a basis for fresh insights. I will try to attend with equal sensitivity to Spenser's poetry and to the traditions and specific ideas it invokes. Ideally, it seems to me, textual and contextual interpretations can be checks upon one another, and each can pose questions which the other mode of interpretation can be employed to answer. The poetic text comes first and is worthy of our undivided attention. Not only the stanzas on the Garden but the canto as a whole exhibit Spenser's imagination fully engaged, unfaltering, with articulate energy in every line. The narrative moves along in a coordinated series of surprising effects that is consistently delightful. The canto's poetry offers us immediate, privileged access to an order of things that is rarefied not only by comparison to ordinary experience, but within the exotica of Faerie land. Roche observed that although

Venus and Diana are often invoked in the poem, their appearance in the first half of this canto marks 'the only time that they are part of the narrative action' (*Kindly Flame* 109). That action takes place within the natural order, but it becomes sacred and dangerous ground, and within the Garden's precincts in the second half of the canto, we are in the domain of myth and mystery.

The canto's marvellous discourse is elaborately intertextual at the same time that it offers access to otherworldly primal scenes of being and becoming. At his most daring and magus-like, Spenser is most deeply indebted to his reading, and most involved in his poem's network of images and incidents. More than he does in other core cantos, Spenser alludes in this one to characters and situations encountered elsewhere, and in Books IV–VI and the *Cantos of Mutabilitie* he will hark back repeatedly to motifs developed in the Garden canto. Its imagery and its place within the fictive world of *The Faerie Queene* encourage us to see the Garden as an originating matrix for the poem's proliferating vitality. If our interpretation is to be faithful to the poet's design, it is important that we recognize Spenser's allusions to other source texts in the encyclopedia of Renaissance learning. Rightly understood, those texts offer almost as much to satisfy a modern reader's imagination as does Spenser's poem.

Sources of the Source

It will be useful if I survey at this point the several kinds of lore, with some of the specific texts, that have been claimed as sources for some design or detail in the canto. In the interests of economy I won't offer full documentation at this point, and subsequently in the chapter I will be exploring only a few of the possible intertextual connections that figure in the canto's cultural codes. Chapter 7 will take up those connections more systematically.

Spenser's program for the canto (an '*Idea* or foreconceit' no less specific and recondite than those discovered by historians of art for such paintings as Botticelli's *Primavera*) involved a more pure and thorough-going classicism than was his custom. Classical mythology provides more than decorative details and incidental motifs; it is fundamental and pervasive. Ovid's version of the story of Venus and Adonis (*Metamorphoses* X 503–59, 708–39) was a point of departure rather than a source. Spenser could assume familiarity with Ovid's poem, to which he and some of his readers would add the opinions of Renaissance mythographers, found in various synoptic accounts and in editions with commentaries. The Hesiodic beginning of the *Metamorphoses* and the rationale for mutability provided by Pythagoras in Book XV are also pertinent to Spenser's themes. The philosophical Virgil of Book VI in the *Aeneid* and Book IV of the *Georgics* is similarly an important presence. Virgil's predecessor Lucretius was probably also on Spenser's mind, and the poetry of Claudian, cited extensively by Renaissance mythographers, should also be mentioned. Spenser's treatment of love, loss, and regeneration involves allusive appeals to the pastoral tradition, in both its idyllic and its elegiac strains. The story of Venus's search for runaway Cupid in the first half of the canto echoes an idyll by the Alexandrian poet Moschus that provided material for several Renaissance translations and adaptations. According to E.K.'s comment on 'March' 79, Spenser had translated Poliziano's Latin version; he may also have known Marot's freer and longer version. Tasso's variations on Moschus's theme in his *Aminta* must have been familiar and might have been the foremost of several intertexts, considering the buzz of interest with which Tasso's pastoral drama was received in the Sidney circle.[4]

Our critical tradition is apt to celebrate the indebtedness of Renaissance poetry to generically similar classical antecedents, and in doing so we follow examples set by humanists and the poets themselves, but we have been less alert to allusions involving philosophical texts. If, however, Spenser was involved in imitating some of the more esoteric passages in classical poetry, it is plausible that he followed his predecessors' intentions back to their sources, as identified in the scholarship of his time. A comparison of Spenser's passage on the Garden to Virgil's on the underworld visited by Aeneas in Book VI would show that Spenser's appropriations of philosophical doctrines are more extensive and schematic, even in the absence of a resident explainer like Anchises. The gist of Anchises' message concerning the force of the *Spiritus intus* in nature and history is embodied in the Garden and its inhabitants; it is also turned to serve an anti-Virgilian purpose, glorifying love's pleasures rather than the rigours of duty, and making love rather than heroic self-sacrifice the basis for a claim to immortality.

The philosophical background for the canto resembles what Renaissance readers thought was appropriate to Virgil's Book VI. As we saw in chapter 4, Landino responded somewhat ahistorically to *Aeneid* VI, reading it in the light of a Neoplatonizing tradition of exegesis that began in antiquity and flourished in the twelfth century, subsequently influencing Dante; Landino's contributions to that tradition reinterpreted it in the light of Ficino's scholarship and speculations. As he contemplated the mysteries veiled and revealed in Virgil's underworld, Spenser in his turn was an eclectic witness to many developments in philosophical thought and its literary interpretation.

In this tradition, places of honour were held by the myths in several Platonic dialogues concerning the structure of the cosmos and the soul's itinerary within it before birth and after death. Spenser's associate Abraham Fraunce testifies to serious interest in such lore in England, at least within the Sidney circle, with this comment on the cosmological verses at the beginning of Ovid's *Metamorphoses*:

> Both poetry, a speaking picture, and paynting, a dumbe poetry, were like in this, that the one and the other did vnder an amyable figure and delightsome veyle, as it were, couer the most sacred mysteries of auncient philosophie. Nay, *Pythagoras* himselfe by his symbolicall kinde of teaching, as also *Plato* by his conceited parables and allegoricall discourses in his bookes called, Phoedrus, Timoeus, and Symposium, may make any man beleeue, that as the learned Indians, Æthiopians, and Ægyptians kept their doctrine religiously secret for feare of prophanation, so the Grecians by their example, haue wrapped vp in tales, such sweete inuentions, as of the learned vnfolder may well be deemed vonderfull though to a vulgar conceit, they seeme but friuolus imaginations. (*Third part of ... Yuychurch* fol. 3v)

In his account of the meanings available from myths to readers of various capacities, Fraunce gives a higher place to natural philosophy than some commentators would. The several secrets veiled in myths suit a stratified audience, he says, and beyond those who can appreciate a heroic narrative and its 'morall sence,' 'the rest, that are better borne and of a more noble spirit, shall meete with hidden mysteries of naturall, astrologicall, or diuine and metaphysicall philosophie, to entertaine their heauenly speculation' (fol. 4). Addressing an audience already acquainted with the 1590 *Faerie Queene*, Fraunce testifies to the importance of the tradition I have termed esoteric humanism.

The cosmology and natural philosophy of the Stoics, important to Virgil, was also available to Spenser, but may have been muffled among other influences such as philosophical writings of Cicero (including that medieval classic, *Scipio's Dream*, with Macrobius's commentary), the treatises among Plutarch's *Moralia* that are sometimes termed 'theosophical' (e.g., *On Isis and Osiris* and *On the Face Discovered in the Moon*), and Boethius's *On the Consolation of Philosophy*. Apuleius's *Golden Ass*, the *locus classicus* for the story of Cupid and Psyche and a syncretizing tract disguised as a romance, should also be mentioned in this context, along with another popular book, the *Tablet of Cebes*, an educational allegory containing the image of 'Old *Genius*' as a monitor at the Garden's gate (31.8–9).[5] Porphyry's treatise on the 'cave of the nymphs' in Book XIII of *The Odyssey* should also be mentioned here.[6]

Ancient Neoplatonism, and especially the system of Plotinus, has been regarded by several scholars as a key to Spenser's thinking in the Garden canto. The influence of Plotinus, Proclus, and other Neoplatonists was so extensive in Hellenistic culture and the development of Christian theology, and so important once again in Ficino's revival of Platonism, that it seems impossible to determine the direct pertinence of such texts as the *Enneads*, or of the commentary accompanying Ficino's translation of them. Similarly, we may never know the extent of Spenser's access to the philosophical poetry and scholarship produced during the twelfth and thirteenth centuries by the School of Chartres and other circles devoted to the memory of Plato and the Platonists, at a time when most ancient texts in that tradition were unknown in the West. *The Complaint of Nature* of Alanus de Insulis is pertinent to the Garden as it is to the *Cantos of Mutabilitie*, and Spenser may have been led by his interest in Chaucer's *Parliament of Fowls* to seek out his master's model (in *SE*, see 'Alanus de Insulis').

To the extent that Spenser's account of the Garden resembles a creation myth (and it recalls 'the mightie word, / Which first was spoken by th'Almightie lord,' 34.4–5), it occupies some of the territory interpreted in hexameral commentaries. Beginning in Hellenistic Judaism with Philo of Alexandria and involving the founders of theology in both the Greek and the Latin traditions, interpretation of Genesis provided an occasion for Christian thought to assimilate much that pagan metaphysics and natural philosophy had to offer; basic principles of allegorical interpretation were also worked out in these commentaries.[7] Humanists and reformers revived learning in this genre, and the creation of the world was recognized as a great subject for Christian poetry long before Milton.[8] Ellrodt's stress on the usefulness of Augustine's *De Genesi ad litteram* as a gloss on Spenser's 'first seminarie / Of all things' was crucial to his argument that Platonism in *The Faerie Queene* should be seen as fundamentally patristic and medieval, rather than under the aegis of the Florentine revival (*Neoplatonism in the Poetry of Spenser* 77–81); the case for Augustine's importance has been accepted and elaborated by Nohrnberg (*Analogy* 539–47) despite his belief that the writings of Ficino, Pico, and their followers are also pertinent.

Spenser's themes in the Garden canto can be placed in the context of the discourses sometimes termed 'occult sciences.' An evocation of the purifying energy to be derived from things in their sempiternal original forms, which is one way of stating what the Garden is about, suggests comparison with the ideas and aims of various esoteric arts: with the gnosis and praxis that some found through the *Hermetica*; with the scriptural study and spiritual discipline that Christians and Jews alike pursued through the Kabbalah; with the art of alchemy and other forms of natural magic.[9] Heinrich Cornelius Agrippa, whose ideas in *De Occulta philosophia* came under discussion in chapters 4 and 5, was an important spokesman for this body of beliefs and practices, and John Dee was only the most prominent among Elizabethans with serious interests in the theory and practice of magic. The cultivation of an erudite poetry honouring Orpheus as its inspiration was a related development, important in Italy and later in France, and Spenser presents himself as an Orphic poet on many occasions, from the beginning to the end of his career.[10] As we saw in chapter 4, Orpheus was regarded by Landino as a founder of the Gentile *prisca theologia*. This tradition was the basis for several arcane arts and for esoteric humanism. During his years at Cambridge and afterward, even after his removal to Ireland, Spenser seems to have shared at least as much as Sidney and Ralegh did in the esoteric interests of John Dee, Everard Digby, Thomas Harriot, Giordano Bruno, and others in England.

My survey of intellectual contexts for the Garden canto should begin to explain its function in a poem that I have called encyclopedic. Building on what has been said about esoteric sources of purifying, life-enhancing power, I will develop a theme suggested by Harry Berger and brought into the foreground by some recent criticism.[11] Like Mount Acidale and the scenes of Mutabilitie's challenge to Jove's sovereignty, the Garden is a place to which the poet claims a privileged access, although he represents it as a source without which the whole world, and not just the poet's imagination, would be empty. As all culture is supposed to flow from the Graces' dance, accompanied and subsequently interpreted by the poet, all life in the sublunary world is said to originate in the Garden of Adonis. With this mythology, Spenser grounds his fiction at the unadulterated sources of nature and culture, at a level of abstraction accessible to his 'erected wit.' As Harry Berger put it in his seminal essay, the stanzas on the Garden have the 'virtue not only of exemplifying the poetic process whereby force becomes form but of being *about* that process' (*Revisionary Play* 138). Berger's dialectical pairing of force and form may be un-Spenserian and all too modern, but there is no doubt that the whole canto is concerned with generative and transformative processes. The poet's account of *natura naturans* at work allegorizes his own making of a world of words, but his authorial interests and inventions are occluded: he is revealing the secret source of Amoret's good nature, and he celebrates creativity not in the muses' garden but in a revisionary myth of Adonis's apotheosis.

Reading the Garden as a Woman

The contexts sketched so far may seem massively irrelevant to the question Roche raised so helpfully, 'why Amoret is introduced into the scheme of this miraculous garden' (*Kindly Flame* 118). Clark Hulse may be alone in considering Amoret's upbringing 'the flimsiest of pretexts' for including this visionary passage in Book III (*Metamorphic Verse* 277), but the more we think we know about the Garden, the more problematic its bearing upon Amoret's development becomes. At the end of the canto we are told that Venus committed her foster daughter to Psyche to be nurtured in the company of her daughter, Pleasure, with whom she was 'lessoned / In all the lore of loue, and goodly womanhead' (51.8–9); once her virtues have grown 'to perfect ripenesse' she is introduced at court as an example 'To all faire Ladies, that doe liue on ground' (52.1–6). This passage isn't the only indication that Spenser addressed his poem to ladies at court as well as gentlemen. We should bear in mind that there was a wide discrepancy between the interests of university-educated men (Spenser, Harvey, and Ralegh, for example) and those of women brought up for very different roles in life; we should therefore recognize that, without an imaginative leap across the gender gap, the poet and his exemplary maiden would have enjoyed profoundly different experiences of all that the Garden represents.[12] We have been taught by the poem itself to seek common ground on which differences can be reconciled, and where reconciliation fails we have a problem that is open to interpretation. It is time to ask what contexts for the Garden canto were familiar to the women in Spenser's intended audience, and to consider whether they were also pertinent to the poet's interests in worldmaking and self-fashioning.

The better discussions of Book III, and of the Garden canto in particular, have reminded us that no matter how bookish the discourse of Faerie land may get, Spenser's primary concerns are individual psyches, female as well as male, and their construction by the institutions of society. One set of referents for the Garden canto, then, would be experience of childhood and growth to adulthood, focusing upon the enjoyment of sexuality and appreciation for vitality in the natural order, but allowing for the strictures voiced in the first half of the canto by Diana in her debate with Venus. The primary site for the discipline of developing sexual impulses was the family household. More than elsewhere, in the Garden canto Spenser's authority operates *in loco parentis*: his interests, therefore, closely resemble those of Venus, who is portrayed as a *magna mater* figure, motivated by a matronly solicitude toward her disobedient son in the first instance, and then toward 'her deare brood, her deare delight' (40.4), including Amoret. Even Adonis, her sexual partner, is a 'wanton boy' in contrast to her ageless maturity. If, in line with my discussion of gender in chapter 1, we try to imagine the feminine aspect of Spenser's imagination, the figures of Venus and Amoret may appear in a new light as indicators of the poet's involvement in his fiction.

It is remarkable though not inexplicable that in the whole course of *The Faerie Queene*, Spenser pays scant attention to the dynamics of family life. The cultural norms of his time didn't encourage realism in a romance, of course; nevertheless, one reflects with some surprise that after Una's parents ('that auncient Lord and aged Queene,' I xii 5.1), almost the only married couple seen at home are Malbecco and Hellenore, to whom we are introduced on the eve of their breakup. Their travesty of marriage and sexuality is, of course, childless. Although the union of Mortdant and Amavia produced a child, what we see of their marriage exemplifies tragic dysfunction. The attention given in Books IV to VI to social institutions, beginning with the interlaced bonding of brothers and sisters, husbands and wives, deals elaborately with familial ties and not at all with family life; late in the poem the marginal figures of Matilde and Sir Bruin (VI iv 26–38), the foster parents of Calepine's inconvenient foundling, do not contradict a sense that the poem's primary concerns are at odds with domesticity. We do find within the Garden, however, what Spenser may expect us to regard as the ideal domestic unit, Cupid and Psyche with their daughter Pleasure. Pleasure is Amoret's first playmate and her only peer, apparently, until she has grown to 'perfect ripenesse' as a woman and is prepared to endure 'the worldes vew' in the marriage market at Gloriana's court.[13]

Having emphasized the importance of women among Spenser's readers, and of feminine experience within his subject matter, I will touch here on an issue that prompted my discussion of gender in chapter 1 and will call for further discussion later: the motives, both conscious and unconscious, involved in Spenser's idealization of 'womanhood.' Theodor Adorno addressed the underlying issues in a trenchant and provocative fashion in one of the aphoristic paragraphs of his *Minima Moralia* (1951), a book contemporary with Simone de Beauvoir's *Le deuxième Sexe* and similarly insightful.[14] Adorno observes, 'The feminine character, and the ideal of femininity on which it is modelled, are products of masculine society' (*Minima*

Moralia 95). This was far more true in Spenser's day than in Adorno's. The presence of a queen on the English throne stimulated the production of ideal images for women, but this cultural work remained in the hands of men even more than Elizabeth's government was under their control. And as Adorno observes, 'The image of undistorted nature arises only in distortion,' in a dialectical relationship to masculine society. 'Where it claims to be humane, masculine society imperiously breeds in woman its own corrective, and shows itself through this limitation implacably the master.' While Adorno's association of masculinity with implacable mastery owes much to modern cultural circumstances and to guilty consciences raised on Nietzsche and Freud, his observation that men use women in order to 'breed' what they lack in themselves has a bearing on Elizabethan culture and many passages in Spenser's poetry, with the Garden of Adonis prominent among them. The feminine character is separated from society and associated with nature, Adorno points out, and he demystifies this 'bourgeois delusion': such purity 'is merely the scar of social mutilation,' whereby women are found to lack what men conspicuously possess (95–6).

Then Adorno offers this observation, which pertains, accidentally but powerfully, to Amoret's two states of being in Book III, first in the Garden and then in Busirane's captivity: 'The woman who feels herself a wound when she bleeds knows more about herself than the one who imagines herself a flower because that suits her husband.' And finally: 'Glorification of the feminine character implies the humiliation of all who bear it.' Adorno's indignant pessimism may not be the best frame of mind in which to read Spenser, but if his poetry registers an understanding of sexual politics that is as subtle as Ovid's and at the same time more humane, insights from Adorno and contemporary feminism may help us to articulate a full response to it. Amoret 'ripening' in a prospect of flowers is already a victim, woefully unprepared for the psychosomatic wounding that will place her in Busirane's hands, but the mature women in the Garden, Venus and Psyche, while still figments of a man's imagination, may offer correctives to bourgeois delusions emergent in Elizabethan culture.

Courtly and Erudite *Trattati d'Amore*

My account of contexts informing a reconstructive reading of the Garden canto remains incomplete in an important area. Like the woods in which Belphoebe encounters Timias, the scenes of Chrysogone's childbearing and Venus's 'ioyous Paradize' are supposed to be remote from the court, but the whole poem was composed for a courtly audience, with the culture of that world in mind. Spenser didn't entirely accept its norms (he was, after all, himself remote from the court for most of his working life), but sought to shape the development of a reforming, humanistic, more thoroughly classical and European culture. While much of the learning that has been claimed as pertinent in source studies of the Garden canto cannot have been available to many of Spenser's contemporary readers, the erudite poet should be seen in a mediating role, quite conscious of what was generally accessible to his readers, what he had to explain, and what would be unacceptable to some whose opinions he valued. If my argument toward the end of chapter 5 is plausible, the poem's 'gentle discipline' was addressed to the organic as well as the intellective soul, so Spenser must have believed that his fiction would do much of its cultural work subliminally, in lively images that manifest but do not unveil the ideas motivating them.

When the source studies devoted to various aspects of the Garden canto have been sifted, they yield an impression that Spenser was, like his scholarly interpreters, a library-bound archaeologist, hunting and gathering *arcana* from an archive much larger than the 'euerlasting scryne' of 'antique rolles' managed by his muse (I Proem 2.3–4), but most of this material was unknown or of little interest to Spenser's audience. Some of the poet's work of synthesis had been done for him: much of the lore pertinent to the Garden can be found already loosely organized in a context that is learned and theoretical, yet adapted to the manners and concerns of men and women in courtly society. I am referring to the abundant literature devoted to ideas about love and beauty, which overlaps treatises and dialogues on 'courtliness.' Castiglione's *The Courtier* is the best-known guide to the latter subject, and an indicator of the extent to which – in books if not in real life – philosophical ideas about love and beauty were assimilated in courtly discourse alongside the conventions of behaviour and poetic usage often called Petrarchism. *The Courtier* and similar conduct books found an avid reading public throughout Europe in the course of the sixteenth century, and were instrumental in disseminating what has been called 'Platonism for the ladies.'[15] An interpreter of the Garden canto who could cite only Castiglione would find plenty to say, although many of its mysteries would remain either obscure or unrecognized for what they are. A fuller understanding depends, I believe, on texts that were produced for courtly audiences but pursued their questions

about love and beauty in greater depth and breadth, and with more conspicuous erudition, than Castiglione's form permitted.

Robert Ellrodt surveyed the production and dissemination of *trattati
d'amore* thoroughly, citing from them to good effect in his interpretation
of *Fowre Hymnes* and Spenser's other poetry of the mid-nineties. His
argument that an interest in Ficino's *On Love* and other philosophical
treaties on love cannot be traced in Spenser's earlier poetry has not de-
terred other scholars interested in sources, but even James Nohrnberg,
fascinated with a wide array of possible analogies to Spenser's language in
the Garden, did not make all that he might have out of Ficino's popular
treatise and other texts of a similar nature.

Polite discourses full of fine learning, devoted to 'questions' or 'problems' of love, and often to literary exegesis, constituted an important genre
in the Middle Ages, and Ficino's interpretation of Plato's *Symposium*
inaugurated a new stage in its development. His treatise circulated in
manuscript, both in Latin and in his own Italian translation, before its
publication in 1484 with the complete *Opera Platonis*; in Italian and
French translations it was widely distributed in the sixteenth century,
conveying Ficino's version of Platonism to readers who may not have had
independent knowledge of the *Symposium* or other dialogues of Plato.
Through this and similar treatises, ideas that had been austere and esoteric
became, in the course of the sixteenth century, part of the fabric of intellectual life in the centres of culture throughout Europe.[16] Especially in France,
where translators made the work of their Italian predecessors readily
available in the vernacular, such learning provided substance, style, and
purposes for poetry.

After Ficino's *On Love* the Italian texts which dealt most seriously with
the philosophical aspects of love and beauty, and yet in a way that could
captivate a courtly audience, were Giovanni Pico della Mirandola's
Commento sopra una Canzone di Benivieni, Mario Equicola's *Libro de
natura d'amore*, Leone Ebreo's *Dialoghi d'amore*, Pietro Bembo's *Gli
Asolani*, and Giordano Bruno's *Degli Eroici furori*; all but Bruno's book
were translated into French, and Leone Ebreo's, like Ficino's, was available
in more than one version. In addition, Louis Le Roy produced a series of
translations of Plato, gathering in one book texts that establish the soul's
immortality, translating and commenting at length on the *Symposium*,
translating the *Timaeus* (with less in the way of commentary), and finally
(too late for our purposes) translating the *Republic*. Of these texts, three
have stood out for me as the most pertinent to Spenser's program in the

Garden canto as a whole: Ficino's *On Love*, Leone Ebreo's *Dialoghi d'amore* in Pontus de Tyard's version, and Le Roy's *Le Sympose de Platon*. Each will be discussed with reference to the Garden canto in chapter 7.

Formal Symmetries in the Garden Canto

Canto vi of Book III is one of several that were designed as two equal segments with a two-stanza hinge in the middle. This design is compatible with the canto's content, which consists of many pairings that establish analogies and complementary relationships. Years ago Thomas Roche directed our attention to the hitherto neglected first half of the canto, but several details and overarching relationships seem to have escaped the attention of readers. The canto consists of 54 stanzas, breaking into two segments of 27. Stanza 27 brings Venus and Diana, who had been conducting an unresolved quarrel about love and the joy that accompanies it, to the marvellous sight of Chrysogone with the twin daughters she had conceived and delivered 'vnwares' (27.1): 'They were through wonder nigh of sense bereaued, / And gazing each on other, nought bespake' (27.5–6).

The first segment ends here in a moment of concord, in the silence of ineffable surprise. In their silent 'nought,' the two goddesses bear witness to a full circle. Runaway Cupid is forgotten; their quarrel and their search have ended. Chrysogone's natural childbirth has the effect of reconciling Venus and Diana, and in the stanza on the other side of the hinge at the end of stanza 27, the two babies are named and dedicated, like their foster mothers, to the ideals of 'perfect Maydenhed' and 'goodly womanhed' (28.4, 7). Since the ordering of the narrative here puts some emphasis on 'nought,' and since Diana has discovered the baby who will become Belphoebe, it is possible to correlate this moment, so full of potential, with the earlier one in which Merlin declared to Britomart, 'But yet the end is not' (iii 50.1), bringing his encouraging prophecy abruptly to an end.

The canto's central moment of wonder, followed by action that solves a problem and carries the narrative forward, is a signal instance of a device that Spenser uses elsewhere, probably more often and more meaningfully than we have recognized.[17] Mark Rose, cited by Hamilton in his note on the passage, pointed out that in the first canto of the poem, the central stanza (28) 'divides the canto into two balancing episodes of twenty-seven stanzas each.'[18] The poem's first canto is prototypical, not unique: canto v of Book III also consists of 55 stanzas, and in the central one Belphoebe enters, following 'the chace / Of some wild beast' (28.1–2), only to find Timias bleeding 'in deadly swownd' (29.2). As Spenser comments wryly,

'But ah, her expectation greatly was deceau'd' (28.9). The 27-stanza episode that follows is part of that canto's examination of 'How diuersly loue
doth his pageants play, / And shewes his powre in variable kinds' (v 1.2–3);
it also bears a complex relation to the two halves of canto vi.

The number of stanzas in these narrative segments will not appear
accidental if we recall, with readers of the *Timaeus* and Macrobius's *Dream
of Scipio*, that 27 is a number associated with the fabrication of the *anima
mundi*, and subsequently of the physical cosmos.[19] At the end of chapter 3
I argued that the Garden contains a poetic equivalent of Ficino's account of
the *anima mundi*; in this chapter and the next I will flesh out that idea and
connect it with others, with the place of Venus in the poem prominent
among my themes. The presence of the symbolic number 27 within the
canto's significant patterns is only a beginning. Throughout the poem,
designs featuring either odd or even numbered sets of lines or stanzas
probably illustrate the distinction made by Ficino and other interpreters of
Plato, whereby odd numbers are masculine, even numbers are feminine
(Allen, *Nuptial Arithmetic* 48–9, 52). This principle must have something
to do with the splitting and doubling patterns in which feminine characters
(and male characters who undergo some feminization) are so often found.

The Garden canto as a whole, considered in relation to what precedes
and follows it, displays an extraordinary dynamic range, traceable to the
doubleness of a coincidence of opposites. Spenser's organizing trope is
transformation: conventional thinking or the narrator's own signals lead us
to expect one thing, and we find instead, or in addition, something startling
that corrects expectations. Throughout the canto, however, Spenser's narrator works his spell serenely, with themes in hand that organize the bright
moments into a fluid sequence. Only in retrospect is it clear that a narrative
beginning with Belphoebe, to explain 'how this noble Damozell / So
great perfections did in her compile' (1.2–3), deserts her in the second half to
dwell on Amoret and the setting for her growth 'To be th'ensample of true
loue *alone*' (52.4, my emphasis), casting some doubt on the value of
Belphoebe's 'faire ensample' and 'perfect complement' of virtue and beauty,
promoted as preemininent at the end of canto v (54.1, 55.9).

Just as Belphoebe's 'dew perfection' (3.9), evident at the beginning, is
balanced by Amoret's 'perfect ripenesse' (52.1) at the canto's end, so nature
and grace, reason and revelation are balanced, in the opening stanzas, in an
elaborate equation justifying the canto's golden world. 'The heritage of all
celestiall grace' (4.7) that is divided between the twins seems also to be
doubled, as Christian and classical dispensations are combined. To the
ideal horoscope in stanza 2 Spenser adds, in the next stanza, echoes of a

Psalm associated with the virgin birth of Christ. His 'goodly storie' (5.1) of Chrysogone's conception and childbirth harmonizes dissimilar elements: 'this wild forrest' contrasts to 'the sacred throne / Of her chaste bodie' (5.4, 7–8), but the 'pleasaunce' defined by 'a Sommers shynie day' and 'a fresh fountaine, farre from all mens vew' (6.4, 6), provides the mollifying influences of heat and moisture essential to creation. With the sun for their father, the twins are 'wondrously ... begot' (6.1), but Spenser only allows this to *seem* miraculous; 'reason teacheth that the fruitfull seades / Of all things liuing' are brought to life in just this way (8). Taking his natural history from Ovid's account of mysterious *'fecunda semina'* and the generation of 'Infinite shapes of creatures' from the seasonal overflowing of the Nile, Spenser lets his reason go far afield, and by recalling his own description of Errour's monstrous brood (I i 21.6–9) he injects some irony and indeterminacy.

Uncertainty about the poet's intentions at this moment is appropriate. Chrysogone's happy predicament ('Vnwares she them conceiu'd, vnwares she bore,' 27.1) is a perfect instance of 'the will in abeyance,' the vulnerable condition that precedes a transformative experience. Chrysogone's passive body is played upon by gracious natural influences, personified in the sun ('Great father' and also 'th'author of life and light,' 9.1–2: Apollo's role as leader of the muses is not to be forgotten) and his sister the moon, who presides over creativity in women as Apollo aids it in authors. By transforming this 'straunge accident' (5.2) into an object lesson in the generation of 'all things liuing' (8.4), Spenser says something remarkable about what I take to be, for him, the substratum of human sexuality. He has mythologized a virgin birth that is at once a nonce occurrence and the source of 'ensamples' that all virtuous women – whether destined for virginal single life or faithful love in marriage – are supposed to follow.

The starting point for both Belphoebe and Amoret is a coupling of masculine and feminine that is without sex just as it is without pleasure. As the woman is perfectly receptive, no man is involved other than the omniscient poet, a disembodied voyeur in this place 'farre from all mens vew' (6.6). Similarly, Chrysogone may have been conceived without a father, since none is mentioned and her mother's name, Amphisa, suggests 'both natures,' like the hermaphroditic statue of Venus that eventually presides over Amoret's capture by Scudamore (IV x 39–41).[20] Spenser's myth about the origin of human love writes gender across the skies, finding it also in 'matter fit, which tempred right / With heate and humour, breedes' (9.4–5).

Ordinary fallen sexuality remains peripheral to the action in the next segment of the canto, but it sets things in motion. Runaway Cupid, Venus's 'little sonne, the winged god of loue' (11.2), is sought, not seen, but his effects are evident wherever Venus looks until she comes to 'the saluage woods and forrests wyde, / In which full many louely Nymphes abyde' (16.4–5). Diana and her nymphs have seen nothing like the 'griesly foster' who set upon the runaway Florimell and, in the preceding canto, ambushed Timias in similar woods. Cupid is represented here as a prepubescent boy, resentful of his mother's attempts to civilize him, but we are also warned that he is a master of disguise, apt to appear 'in thousand shapes, that none might him bewray' (11.9). Cupid's artful dodges may be ironically related to the poet's own devious designs in this canto and others linked to it.

Spenser seems to be holding a mirror up to his culture and showing that the common image of Cupid, which represents a powerful natural and cultural force in trivial, sentimental, self-indulgent terms, is responsible for mischief that has run out of control through society. If Cupid, as a representation of male sexuality, were seen by men and women as neither an irresponsible child nor a monstrous rationalization of lust, but as human, all too human, life would be much simpler. It might even approach the paradise regained toward the canto's end – by Cupid, not by the 'many wretches' in whose hearts he triumphs – in Psyche's company, where he has cast off disguises along with his 'sad darts' (49.8), growing into an adult role as a husband and father (49–50). It is significant, however, that Cupid's eventual maturity as a family man is left for us to flesh out from the hints in two stanzas: domestic intimacy seems to have been at once too mundane and too unlikely to be a subject for Spenser's heroic poem.

Anxieties, defences, and aggressions are evident in Spenser's adaptation of the fashionable *Amor fugitivus* material; similar dream work is less directly evident in the representation of Venus and Diana. What Spenser says of them displays, of course, the same idealization and polarization that we see in the characters of their acolytes, Amoret and Belphoebe. There is no telling how aware Spenser was of the angle from which he was viewing women and the sponsors of their virtues. It is clear that in the goddesses' debate and reconciliation he is playing – at Diana's expense – with the stereotypes of Diana and Venus. His Venus is maternal as well as being devoted to 'ioyfulnesse, / In beds, in bowres, in banckets, and in feasts' (22.3–4), and it is she, not Diana, who voices respect for higher authority: 'We both are bound to follow heauens beheasts, / And tend our charges with obeisance meeke' (22.7–8). Addressing Diana as 'Faire sister' (21.7) and 'gentle sister' (22.9), and apologizing after her inquiries have provoked an angry tirade (23–4), she gets her way by yielding. By comparison, Diana appears self-absorbed and rigid, almost hysterical. Although Venus gains the upper hand in this canto, Spenser knew that their rivalry could be resolved only in nonce events like Chrysogone's childbirth. Their difference is only transferred to the twins, separated and destined to meet much later in Book IV, in a moment of misunderstanding that proves almost fatal to Timias. From the start Amoret is identified as 'in the second place' (4.5), and even before we know her origin Belphoebe has been promoted as the embodiment of a higher perfection, but the poem displays Spenser's ambivalence toward all that Belphoebe represents. Between canto vi and the climactic episode of Book III, Amoret's virtue and vulnerability are shown to be more pertinent to Britomart's character.

The charming vulnerability Venus exhibits in the first half of the canto becomes a kind of power in 'her ioyous Paradize' (29.1). Again, she dominates by yielding: the place 'called is by her lost louers name, / The *Gardin* of *Adonis*' (29.8–9), but as everyone knows, the mount at its centre (43–8) belongs to her. So does Adonis: 'she her selfe, when euer that she will, / Possesseth him, and of his sweetnesse takes her fill' (46.8–9). Even more than the presence of Time in the Garden, which was once regarded as a great crux, Venus's domination of Adonis has vexed interpretation. This is a place where contextualization can help us to read the text for its themes, distinguishing between Spenser's preoccupations and our own and trying to establish the principles – philosophical or poetic – being invoked.

The texture of the poetry in stanzas 29–51, describing the Garden, has been determined by an ideological program, so the impressions we form of its meaning develop not in a simple hermeneutic circle, but in a system involving epicycles of allusion. In the rest of this chapter, I will confine myself as much as possible to the text, in order to address four topics, raising questions which will lead, in the next chapter, to the sources informing Spenser's program for the canto: (1) the ontological status of the Garden in relation to our everyday experience; (2) the emotional overtones of the terms in which Spenser imagines the union of Venus and Adonis and the womb-like space where Pleasure and Amoret are nurtured; (3) the dynamics of death and life on earth and in the Garden; and (4) the memorial purpose of poetry, responsive to human mortality. Close reading will show that the patterns apparent in the canto's first half – transformations, reversals, *discordia concors*, marvellous revelations – are complicated and rationalized in the second.

The Ontological Status of the Garden

The Garden serves several purposes that compete for the poet's articulation and a reader's attention. It is a place excelling 'All other pleasant places' (29.7), but it is also crowded with an 'endlesse progenie' (30.7), 'A thousand thousand naked babes' (32.3), 'Infinite shapes of creatures ... / And vncouth formes' (35.1–2) that hardly anyone – certainly not a poet with Spenser's need for order and formal limits – can contemplate with uncomplicated delight. In the course of conjuring the spirit of this place, Spenser locates it in several ways that are potentially confusing, but can be accepted as meaningfully paradoxical. First, it is located 'on earth' (29.2) and in nature; but no, it is 'So faire a place, as Nature can *deuize*' (29.3; emphasis added), and it is identified by comparison to the haunts of Venus familiar from literature, so Nature here is that goddess with whom the poet 'goeth hand in hand,' devising a world of words. It is a flower garden, a source of beauties like Venus's astrological 'house of goodly formes and faire aspects' (12.1–5); it also recalls the heavenly 'Paradize' from which Belphoebe's 'dainty Rose' was derived in the previous canto (v 51–2), and the 'earthly Paradize' to which the wounded Timias was taken (v 39–40).

One formula, however, controls the comparisons Spenser invites us to make (reaching back if we wish to the Eden liberated by Redcrosse from the dragon; remembering the pleasures and lessons of the Bower of Bliss; and looking forward with the whole poem in hand to the Temple of Venus and its environs, the appearance of Venus and the Graces on Mount Acidale, and Nature's court on Arlo hill): 'there is the *first* seminarie / Of all things, that are borne to liue and die, / According to their kindes' (30.4–6; emphasis added). Venus's seminary comes first in the sequence of causes by which life on earth grows from seeds, and it is pre-eminent as the archetype of other paradisal places in the poem. Spenser's reference to 'kindes' is clarifying: in general, the Garden's creatures are exemplars of the species to be found in nature, not individuals.

The seed-beds of 'kindes' provide a backdrop for the naked babes crowding around Genius, and for Amoret, whose name and subsequent place in the plot individualize her, although her character never has much depth. Genius and Psyche preside over processes of individuation in which creatures of the highest form, 'fit for reasonable soules t'indew' (35.5), are distinguished from the lower species. They are not sharply distinguished, however, which has encouraged many readers to seek in the Garden a place for the pre-existence and reincarnation of human souls in their entirety. Doubt that Spenser would entertain such a heterodox notion won't be resolved completely by the text; this is a place where intelligibility depends upon cultural contexts. The Garden's design takes for granted a frame of reference in which the generative and formative functions of the soul – everything that human beings share with other species – can be treated separately from the reasonable part, which comes from elsewhere to 'indue' a mortal body suited to its use.[21]

This Garden is the source of mortal life, then, but not of mortality; within it, life is endlessly renewable. Higher and lower forms are involved together in a single cycle of eternal return. The 'goodly flowres' and 'weedes' are mentioned first and used, as a stock metaphor, to stand for all species of transient vitality and beauty. For three stanzas (31–3) the focus shifts to the 'two walles' and 'double gates' defining the Garden, as the Bower of Bliss had been defined, by differences between life inside and outside, entrances and exits. Within these stanzas, where 'Old *Genius*' presides over the traffic, human beings ('men' in stanza 31, 'naked babes' asking to be clothed 'with fleshly weedes' in the next) are singled out from other life forms when they leave, but 'planted ... againe' to 'grow afresh' when they return (33.1–2).

This stanza's account of what happens to the returning human forms, which mixes categorical with either/or statements, is bound to be confusing. The replanted forms remain 'Some thousand yeares' (33.5), and 'like a wheele around they runne from old to new' (33.9): these lines, the canto's only verbal allusion to *Aeneid* VI, echo l. 748 in Anchises' explanation, '*has omnis, ubi mille rotam volvere per annos*' (all these, when they have rolled the wheel through a thousand years). Spenser puts a positive spin on Virgil's dreary prospect, and he includes two possibilities at the end of the thousand-year term: either they are 'clad with other hew, / Or sent into the chaungefull world againe' (33.6–7). I take this either/or as an admission, like other fabrications of allegory's 'perhapsing machine,' that Spenser isn't sure, beyond being confident of renewal rather than nothingness, what happens to the human body's form after life and death on earth. The 'other hew' would be different from the 'sinfull mire' of another earthly body: it could be resurrected and glorified flesh, or it might be, within the fiction's own terms, an immortal flower like those decorating Venus's arbor, catalogued in stanzas 44–5.

After stanzas that focus, like Virgil, on human lives and their afterlife, we return to a garden plot that separates species but treats them all alike: 'euery sort is in a sundry bed / Set by it selfe' (35.3–4). These vegetating 'shapes' will produce individuals in the various species, animal as well as vegetable. The inclusion in these beds of 'vncouth formes, which none yet euer knew' (35.2), like the slow cycle of return and renewal described in stanza 33, locates its life in the *longue durée* of millennia past and yet to be; it also suggests comparison to the human imagination, famous for its capacity to bring to virtual life things never seen on sea or land. (To the 'infinite shapes' here, compare the 'Infinite shapes of things dispersed thin' in writing on the walls of Phantastes' chamber in II ix 50.) The Garden's topography and climate separate it from our experience on earth, but its processes imitate what we know to be basic to life: individuals die but species continue, thanks to the resources provided by nature. A similar 'endlesse date' is provided by 'sweet Poets verse' for the transformed lives of 'sad louers' (45): art lives by imitating what dies.

If we regard the Garden as a source, what I have called its imitation of life processes is to be regarded as their initiation. But if the Garden shows us the beginnings of all forms of life, where in the world are we? The destructive presence of Time disrupts what some have wished to consider a Platonic 'world of forms,' suggesting that Spenser was either an inconsistent Platonist or no Platonist at all. His Garden is too much like the earth to resemble heaven or any Other World described by Plato; considering this, some have regarded philosophical sources and interpretations of the Garden's doctrines with suspicion, and argued that as poetry, Spenser's discourse obeys other impulses, reflecting on what Wordsworth would call 'nothing more than what we are.'

There is one passage (and only one, I believe) in which Spenser's focus shifts from the Garden as a place set apart from life as we know it in the world: in stanza 37 his mind is on bodies which 'inuade / The state of life, out of the griesly shade' once their matter, which they 'borrow' from Chaos, has caught 'form and feature' – apparently from the Garden's repertoire of shapes. In the next stanza Spenser seems to be describing change and the fading of forms not in the Garden but in 'the state of life,' where what had flourished is soon subject to decay,

> By course of kind, and by occasion;
> And that faire flowre of beautie fades away,
> As doth the lilly fresh before the sunny ray.   (38.7–9)

These lines complicate the poet's earlier recognition of the sun as 'Great father ... of generation / ... th'author of life and light' (9.1–2) and cast a shadow on the Garden, where 'wicked *Time*' is now discovered (39): there, as in our world, 'All things decay in time, and to their end do draw' (40.9).

Almost immediately, Spenser's wheel runs around from old to new and the golden age returns, 'For here all plentie, and all pleasure flowes, / ... Franckly each paramour his leman knowes' (41.5, 7), and Time brings not destruction, but 'continuall spring, and haruest there / Continuall, both meeting at one time' (42.1–2). Yet even in these celebratory stanzas disjunction is evident: 'all plentie, and all pleasure,' which had been flowing '*here*' and 'in *this* delightfull Gardin' in stanza 41, are '*there*' and in '*that* Paradize' in the next and subsequent stanzas (see 42.1, 43.1, 44.1, etc.; emphasis added). The narrative also shadows its descriptions of full and intense pleasure with chiaroscuro effects: 'the middest of that Paradise' contains 'a stately Mount, on whose round top / A gloomy groue of mirtle trees did rise' (43.1–3), and the stanzas that follow promote Adonis, 'hid from the world, and from the skill / Of *Stygian* Gods' (46.6–7), as 'the Father of all formes' (47.8), but they do so with the emotion-driven logic and many of the trappings of pastoral elegy. In a probing, disjointed, lyrical narrative, the poet promotes both participation in the Garden's vitality and detached pondering of its dark paradoxes, anticipating the unresolved tensions of such modern poems as Keats's odes and Yeats's later visionary poems.

What threw Spenser's account of the Garden's prolific production into some confusion, or at least into a digression, was the mention of 'An huge eternall *Chaos*, which supplyes / The substances of natures fruitfull progenyes' (36.8–9). Beginning with Brents Stirling's sensible but sometimes reductive response to Josephine Waters Bennett's Platonizing, and continuing in Harry Berger's brilliant but sometimes wayward interpretations of the Garden, Chaos has loomed large as a topic for interpretation, and a sound account of Spenser's thinking will have to explain the relationship of the Garden and its progeny to Chaos and the 'substances' it supplies.

Spenser does as much to bring out the likeness of the Garden to Chaos as he does to distinguish one place from the other: Chaos is not just aboriginal, but eternal, and it lies 'in the wide wombe of the world,' as horrible as the Garden is delightful, prompting a recognition that the Garden is no less womblike than Chaos, and in its central 'gloomy groue' it may be no less frightening. We are also reminded of Chaos by the explanation that Venus has imprisoned Adonis's nemesis 'In a strong rocky Caue, which is they say, / Hewen vnderneath that Mount' (48.8–9). The difference between Chaos and the boar is that Chaos is prolific, not devouring. The difference between Chaos and the contents of Venus's womb, adumbrated in the Garden, lies in the difference between Chaos's 'substances' (36.9), 'first being' and 'matter' (37.1–2), and the Garden's 'Infinite shapes ... / And vncouth formes' (35.1–2). But is this a distinction without a difference? Some critics have found the progeny of Chaos and the Garden indistinguishable.

Upon close examination, stanza 36 supplies a logic that *includes* Chaos in an account of the Garden but *excludes* it from the Garden's place in an ontology of generation and corruption.

> Daily they grow, and daily forth are sent
>   Into the world, it to replenish more;
>   Yet is the stocke not lessened, nor spent,
>   But still remaines in euerlasting store,
>   As it at first created was of yore.
>   For in the wide wombe of the world there lyes,
>   In hatefull darkenesse and in deepe horrore,
>   An huge eternall *Chaos*, which supplyes
> The substances of natures fruitfull progenyes.

The purpose of the Garden myth is clear in this stanza: it is to account for the replenishing of all species (i.e., the 'shapes,' 'formes,' and 'euery sort' of stanza 35) in a world where everything that lives also dies. If the Garden is the source of life but is in the grip of Time no less than the 'mortall state' to which it sends its progeny, how is its 'stocke not lessened, nor spent'? Earlier stanzas (31–3) explained how human and other forms return from life and death in the world to be planted 'And grow afresh, as they had neuer seene / Fleshly corruption' (33.3–4), running in a cycle like the year, in which movement from youth to age is indivisible from the return journey, 'old to new' (33.9). Subsequent stanzas (37–40) will emphasize, as already noted, that 'formes are variable and decay' (38.6), carrying that message from the world back into the Garden, where contradictory facts come and go as if on a wheel: the effects of 'wicked *Time*' will be answered by the plenty and pleasure flowing from 'sweet loue' in stanza 41 and subsequently.

In this environment of overdetermined flux – decay and renewal in equal measures – stanza 36 introduces another explanation for equilibrium, based on the difference between form and substance, and their different sources in the world's soul and body. The Garden's 'stocke … remaines in euerlasting store' not only because it is a renewable resource, but because Chaos 'supplyes / The substances' from *its* everlasting store, so no matter ever leaves the Garden and needs to be replenished. Despite unimaginably intensive cultivation, the Garden's metaphorical 'fruitfull soyle of old' will never be exhausted. Chaos is also inexhaustible, for a different reason: the 'substances' it supplies are only briefly put into circulation, and do not undergo growth, decay, and renewal as forms do. As the next stanza explains, 'That substance is eterne, and bideth so' (37.6); while life, form, and beauty fade, 'matter' or 'substance' is changed only superficially by the 'forme and feature it does ketch' (37.3). The combination of matter from Chaos and form from the Garden 'Becomes a bodie, and doth then inuade / The state of life, out of the griesly shade' (37.4–5). As wombs, the Garden and Chaos are alike, yet they are distinct just as form and matter are conceptually different.[22] (As complementary terms, form and matter, the Garden and Chaos, are structurally aligned with other pairs, including Adonis and Venus, Belphoebe and Amoret.)

Our experience and capacity for imagination are such that throughout his description of the Garden Spenser has to 'borrow matter' from Chaos, siting its seed-beds 'in fruitfull soyle' (31.1) and attributing 'eternall moisture' to the roots of the plants themselves (34.9). The Garden's creatures seem substantial and self-sufficient – most of all in the stanzas (41–2) describing their innocent and fruitful love-making, and in the subsequent places made for Adonis, Cupid and Psyche, and Amoret – but the picture of paradise is contradicted more than once. The 'thousand thousand naked babes' at the Garden's gate are not ready to leave the nursery, or even to be born; they are ready to be attired 'with fleshly weedes' (32.3, 5), and they leave the cosmic womb to grow as individuals in their mortal mothers' wombs once Genius has blessed their conception. The orderly renewal of life in stanzas 33–5 and the innocent sexuality celebrated from stanza 41 to the end of Amoret's nurturing rely upon the Garden's separation from the 'sinfull mire' with which Genius clothes the babes at his gate. Similarly, creatures within the Garden are spared the 'hatefull darkenesse and ... deepe horrore' associated with Chaos and matter. It seems that in Chaos and in the 'rocky Caue' imprisoning Adonis's boar, Spenser has hollowed out receptacles for the world's anxieties in order to promote a generous response to Venus's 'stately Mount' and 'gloomy groue.'

Gender Roles and Family Life in the Garden

When Spenser describes Adonis as 'Lapped in flowres and pretious spycery, / By her hid from the world' (46.3–6), he seems even more passive, more enthralled by a woman, than Redcrosse in the 'gloomy glade' with Duessa (I vii 4), Verdant with his head drooping in Acrasia's lap, Marinell protected by his mother yet still gored by Britomart, and Timias teased back to miserable health by Belphoebe.[23] But what is the significance of these echoes? Do they undercut the transfiguration of Adonis, or do they provide instances *in malo* against which Adonis's otherworldly liaison with a goddess becomes a more powerful and enigmatic triumph of love over death? And is the life-in-death suspended animation of Adonis, 'eterne in mutabilitie, / And by succession made perpetuall' (47.5–6), communicated only to those forms he is called upon to father, or is this a place where the children are father to the man, and Adonis lives on as the prototype of all the recurrent, fading forms in which Venus, 'their great mother' (40.3), honours the possibilities cut short by his early death?[24] Having mentioned earlier the distorting effect of masculine idealization on the image of Amoret, flower-like in the Garden and an open wound in Busirane's enchanted procession, I would point out here that Adonis is similarly idealized, but with a difference: his 'eternall blis' (48.1) comes after life and death, not before, and the idealization of Adonis, contradicting death itself rather than the *petit mort* of sexuality, is an extreme instance of the fetish formation that we see in Petrarchism and Platonism.

The presence of Cupid and Psyche in the Garden has raised few questions; in this instance, unlike his representation of Adonis, Spenser does not transform the traditional story by his additions to it. Apuleius had supplied him with the happy ending in which Psyche, reconciled to Venus and Cupid 'After long troubles and vnmeet vpbrayes' (50.3), honours the reconciliation with her child, Pleasure. Amoret will eventually be obliged to recapitulate Psyche's sufferings, but while she is in the Garden, 'lessoned / In all the lore of loue, and goodly womanhead' (51.8–9), Pleasure is her playmate. Cupid is present without his 'sad darts,' and plays harmlessly with both Adonis and Psyche; having tired of 'spoiles and cruelty' in the outside world, he has come home to 'true loue' (49.5–50.1). Stanzas 50–2 describe a cozy domestic scene, radiant with nurturing femininity. Although Spenser's entire description of the Garden can be applied to Amoret's education in 'goodly womanhead,' her incorporation in Psyche's household is apt to have meant more than the earlier stanzas 'To all faire Ladies, that doe liue on ground,' for whom she is to serve as 'th'ensample of true loue alone' (52.4, 6).

The assumption governing this part of Spenser's fiction seems to be that one is equipped for the roles of maiden, sister, wife, and mother by having had a happy childhood in a soft pastoral place that promotes innocent pleasures and anticipation of a spontaneous fruitfulness in marriage. Berger and others have argued that the Garden is conspicuously inadequate as a seminary for ladies,[25] and I tend to agree. I do not, however, find any indications in the text that Spenser knew what we know about raising daughters, or that he expected readers, especially women, to see through the veil over his Garden's feminine space to find its pleasures responsible for Amoret's later tears and fears. It is clear that men are given marginal roles in the Garden, but they are not extirpated, as happens in the first half of the canto, where the sun is the most remote of fathers and Cupid leaves only traces of his mischievous passing. Both Adonis and Cupid, together in 'safe felicity' (49.4), lend themselves to erotic play. Eros, so powerful and pervasive elsewhere in Book III, is mysteriously mild at home. This is not the way of the world, but I take it to be Spenser's vision of love at its source in unspoiled nature.

When Venus takes Amoret up 'in her litle loues stead' (28.8), the substitution of a foster daughter for her errant son begins the narrative's shift of focus from Belphoebe to Amoret. The triangular reconciliation of Cupid, Venus, and Psyche in stanza 50 completes this reformation of love. In place of the irrational appetite that a wanton Cupid had visited upon lovers' 'wofull harts' (13.8), we are given the promise of a moral occasion for love, and a vision of sexual pleasure that is consistent with a woman's virtue. Docile 'womanhead' first takes the place of rebellious adolescence, then tames it 'in stedfast loue and happy state' (50.6). The differences between the Garden and the world can be read two ways, then: to the disadvantage of either innocence or experience. As I read him, Spenser promotes the full consciousness of ideals and dangers that Blake called 'organiz'd innocence.'

In the Garden both Adonis and Cupid figure as fathers although they are described as wanton boys, lovable for their immaturity. It is noteworthy, even shocking, that in stanza 49 Cupid 'playes his wanton parts' not with Psyche but 'with faire *Adonis*'; homoerotic pleasure keeps Venus's consort ready for her. In the background, 'Franckly each paramour his leman knowes' (41.7). Although this love's knowledge is underwritten by 'the mightie word, / Which first was spoken by th'Almightie lord' (34.4–5), it seems not to be sanctified by marriage. Two other masculine figures are important, representative of natural imperatives rather than cultural constraints: 'Old *Genius*' at the Garden's double gates and 'wicked *Time*' with his destructive scythe and wings, whose function suggests a return of the repressed '*Stygian* Gods' and their ally, 'that wilde Bore' (48.5). Together, as fair and foul faces of a reality principle that links life and death in a *discordia concors*, they offer endorsement and regulation of sexuality. It is in relation to their aged authority, no less than in the presence of Venus's ageless appetite, that Adonis and Cupid are portrayed as perpetually boyish and reduced to subjects of a feminine pleasure principle.

'Goodly womanhead,' portrayed sympathetically but with the inevitable distortions that accompany gendered discourse, dominates in the Garden canto as much as masculinity dominates in the House of Busirane. The poet's awe or envy of the feminine mysteries of procreation and nurturing may have aroused in him a complex of idealization and exaggeration, in which maternal femininity, abstracted from its cultural roots and grafted into nature, is both spiritualized and eroticized. It would be a misreading of Spenser and the culture he was interpreting to regard relations between a masculine Self and the maternal Other as necessarily antagonistic. If an iconographical program set up the Garden's cosmic womb (displayed, as in an anatomy of Venus) as an image of the poet's imagination, it would be proper to think of the poet's interests in the Garden as androgynous, appropriating figures of speech from the feminine domain to describe creative processes that include a masculine component but are not controlled by it.[26] Katharine Maus has examined, with passing reference to Spenser, the use by men 'of the womb as a figure for the imagination,' and the Garden canto is a perfect case in point for her observation, 'The safe possession of a hidden or unreadable space can ... be extremely agreeable ... to those who want to protect some aspect of themselves from public scrutiny or control.'[27]

In the two climactic episodes of Book III, both of them featuring Amoret in a subject position that seems marginal but turns out to be central, Spenser places Venus and Psyche in charge of a nurturing initiation in one, while in the other a demonic masculinity (represented by Cupid's idol and Busirane, his acolyte) is put in charge of initiation by torture. First nature, love and pleasure; then culture, jealousy and pain. Taking Amoret as a figure for subjectivity in both episodes, joined by the poet as a disembodied presence in the Garden and by Britomart – vulnerable but armed against all occasions – in the House of Busirane, we find subjectivity diversely engaged with its environment. First Amoret experiences love in a harmony that preserves order within uncontested boundaries; in the Garden's economy of abundance, all losses are acknowledged and compensated. Later, in experience anticipated by stanzas 52–3 of the Garden canto, the commitment of 'her louing hart' begins a bitter competition between vengeful masculine will and 'Her former loue, and stedfast loialty.'

Femininity is seen in the first place primarily in its maternal role, with children following their mother's example and propagating her good nature; in the House of Busirane we see patriarchal authority in league with Cupid, imagined as a baleful maestro. As noted in the previous chapter, Scudamour's desire for Amoret's hand and heart in marriage entails anxiety and jealous rivalry, which I take to be central to Spenser's understanding of patriarchal power. Busirane's regime preserves the terrible records of Cupid's rebellion against his mother's kind of 'vertuous and gentle discipline.' Spenser has imagined the feminine and masculine domains so separately that they are hard to read as a system, but in spite of the enigmas and narrative ruptures that obscure Amoret's passage from the Garden gate to captivity with Busirane, the common consent of critics who have studied Books III and IV is that they reflect deeply upon love as it pertains to marriage, providing a rationale for 'stedfast loue and happy state' as well as elaborate attention to dysfunction and unhappiness. The schematic aspect of Spenserian allegoresis is in fruitful though sometimes confusing tension with its prolific and centrifugal tendencies, and it will take more than another chapter to follow the development of this pattern.

The separation of women from men and the creation of dichotomized domains, with different codes for feeling and acting when they meet one another in the clash of nature and culture that we call love, is hardly a healthy state of affairs, yet it is not uncommon, and Spenser's account of these two cultures, separate and unequal, still has much to say to us. In the places he established for Amoret's education in love, Spenser was interpreting with androgynous sympathies the social and psychological experience of his time, giving it a form that enables us to recognize fantasies and rationalizations. He may have seen discord rather than concord as the most likely outcome of Elizabethan family life: women of the upper classes enjoyed considerable authority, but only within the household, especially in the circumscribed area of child rearing and the preparation of daughters for life in some other household. While the Garden's hothouse environment seems to be a preparation for traumas upon coming out, Amoret's patient endurance of Busirane's spells must have something to do with what she learned from Venus and Psyche. Amoret believes in a love that is free from jealousy, she is attuned to a state of nature that is ideal but not illusory, and Psyche's story models for her a life in which faithful suffering in love is rewarded by reconciliation and pleasure. At the end of Book III she lacks Britomart's maturity and boldness, but she knows (as Britomart, still a bewildered observer of courtship rituals and sexual initiation, does not) that Busirane's death would doom her too. She does not become in Book IV what modern readers wish for, a sensible and passionate .woman who has worked through an association of *jouissance* with fear of loss, but our own loss of satisfaction in a return to the loving union symbolized in 1590 by 'that faire *Hermaphrodite*' might be instructive: perhaps Spenser had learned to doubt the stability of heterosexual intimacy and the possibility of pleasure free from pain.

'In the thickest couert of that shade'

It must be apparent, from my argument in this chapter and in earlier parts of the book, that I do not accept the idea, found in a number of important accounts of the Garden canto, that Spenser represents the femininity ascendant there as threatening, even fatal to proper masculine interests. There is certainly some basis for these readings. Everyone who has pondered the canto recognizes that its account of sexuality and gender roles is unconventional, enigmatic, even baffling. Critics do not agree on whether Spenser was pro- or anti-feminist, a proponent or a critic or a prisoner of patriarchal discourse. Perhaps our poet failed to heed the advice that Venus gave to Adonis, to be bold, but not too bold (*Metamorphoses* X 543–4).

I readily agree that the Garden, although it is a fine and private place, is also dangerous. The critics who have highlighted its dangers have shed light on its authentically *mysterious* character, and even when they seem to be more driven by the present-day concerns of feminism than by curiosity about the forces at work in Elizabethan culture, they have contributed generously to our understanding of Spenser's perennial appeal. Spenser did, like other Elizabethans, regard powerful femininity as dangerous, even 'an object of nausea' (Miller, *Poem's Two Bodies* 218); this is apparent as early as *The Shepheardes Calender* and his correspondence with Harvey. With regard to the dominance of feminine over masculine energies in the Garden, however, we need to ask what kind of masculinity Spenser regarded as appropriate in the circumstances. Should such a liminal space, devoted to celebrating and to some extent understanding the origins of life, have been imagined differently? Should other forces and forms have been put in control, or displayed in a more equal contest? And should the otherworldly union of a goddess and a mortal youth, which in some respects is as unnatural as Adonis's incestuous parentage, be examined as if it were either a paradigm or a cautionary example of heterosexual relations?

Harry Berger was the first to develop an account of the Garden that paid close attention to the dominance of feminine over masculine agency, and he returned to the Garden recently in a brilliant essay, responsive to several feminist readings. In 1961 he had described Adonis 'seen from the perspective of the female, imprisoned in the world of feminine experience of which the garden is mainly constituted' (*Revisionary Play* 152). In his recent essay, starting from 'the poem's discursive critique of androcentric vision,' Berger responds to Maureen Quilligan's account of the narrative's 'peculiarly female perspective' (*Milton's Spenser* 197) by arguing 'that we look at female power from the peculiarly male perspective of the narrative occasionally addressed to female readers to whose interests it is clearly sympathetic' ('Actaeon at the Hinder Gate' 93 and 109). Most of the canto 'is devoted to the project of domesticating male sexuality and placing it firmly under female control' (100), but Berger finds evidence in Spenser's language of a residual 'anxiety,' even 'hints of terror and symbolic castration,' darkening his representation of the supposedly benign figure of Venus (115 and 113).

While I suppose that anxiety was inescapable for a poet in Spenser's situation, as for a male critic today, I will argue that terror is an inappropriate response to everything the Garden contains. The broad basis for Berger's misreading is apparent, I believe, in his support for 'Quilligan's claim ... that Book III of *The Faerie Queene* privileges the female perspective and censures the male perspective on its narrative,' and his proviso that the text also contains 'a kind of backlash, a subversive countermovement of gynephobia' (107). Both Quilligan and Berger subscribe to the questionable assumption that any ceding of power to the female perspective will entail some loss of power by the male. Gender theory in its subtler and more persuasive forms invalidates that fear, and enables us to entertain the possibility that Spenser's authorial interests were not circumscribed by his gender. In my opinion, in the Garden canto Spenser writes as if The Feminine in its many manifestations – Chrysogone, Belphoebe and Amoret, Venus and Diana, 'euery substance ... conditioned / To change her hew' (38.3–4), and Psyche with her daughter Pleasure – is other than Other. Androgyny, understood in Renaissance terms as a way of being and a way of knowing human nature in its original form, provided Spenser with an alternative to the 'Endangered Male Viewpoint' that Berger so ingeniously analyses.

A basic principle is at stake in my difference with other critics here; it concerns what Spenser's poem has to show us about conflicts and their resolution. I take it that for Berger, no conflict can be resolved satisfactorily: it will only persist in different terms, attracting a more suspicious response as the terms for resolving tensions become more abstract. Having been for many years a reader for whom Spenser was a poet of concord, I am now persuaded that the important conflicts – with gender conflict arguably the most basic of all, supportive of endless elaboration – remain unresolved in Spenser's fiction, which is dedicated to unity but dependent upon difference. I submit, however, that readings intent upon the discovery of conflict, and especially upon subliminal conflict (e.g., 'a kind of backlash'), can inadvertently simplify the poem. I will suggest that for Spenser, the meaning of difference is to be found first in conflict, but more deeply in complementarity. As I argued in chapter 5, Spenser asks us to accept love and strife as sibling principles, each maintained in full strength by Concord. The proper response to Concord's firmness is reverent awe, but the 'envious have-nots' in *The Faerie Queene*, about whom Berger has written so brilliantly ('Actaeon at the Hinder Gate' 111 and passim), discover all their strength in vain attempts to nullify the knots of discipline. The power exercised by Concord is in some sense responsible for the intractability of Hate, but 'her blessed hands' confer a greater strength upon the younger brother, Love (IV x 35).

The difficulties on which Berger practises his hermeneutics of suspicion are all connected, I think, with the attention Spenser pays to death in his account of life, both within the Garden's walls and beyond them. Berger does not find Time's dark presence in the Garden anomalous, but I believe he exaggerates the threat posed by temporality and death in the total scheme of things. In what remains of this chapter, I will be interpreting the significance, within the affirmative emphasis of the Garden canto, of Spenser's unblinking acceptance of mutability and mortality.

In the Garden of Adonis, death is not avoided, but is treated as subject to recuperation, involved in a complementary relationship with love and its fruition, childbearing and other creative activity. In this connection, the pivotal position of the Garden canto becomes apparent, in relation not only to such later episodes as Scudamour's adventure in the Temple of Venus, but to Guyon's temptation in the Bower of Bliss and other distorted visions of the world's dangers and pleasures. What is crucial to an understanding of all these episodes is a grasp of the distinctions being made between the world of a reader's flesh-and-blood experience and another world in the book. What raises the Garden of Adonis above 'All other pleasant places' (29.7) is the distinction made within its own description between our 'mortall state' (32.8), 'the chaungefull world' (33.7), and another place, also full of change, where spring and harvest are 'there / Continuall, both meeting at one time' (42.1–2). This place, a world apart from the stasis and willed oblivion of the Bower of Bliss, also offers an alternative, admittedly idyllic and visionary, to the contestatory triumphs and frustrations that punctuate the rest of the poem's inescapable romance.

The ruin and rescue alternatives presented by Guyon and the Palmer in Book II, where good and evil are sorted out and lonely self-control is made the burden that defines a noble life, give way in the Garden to a chiaroscuro vision of the cycles animating all of life, with creation and destruction put in place of good and evil. Cyclical changes link together not only temporal phases of life, but distinctions between high and low, inner and outer, subjective and universal, spiritual and bodily phenomena. This view 'Of all things, that are borne to liue and die' (30.5) ought to discourage us from fixing the blame for death on any person or personification. (Berger enjoys catching Spenser in this erroneous fantasy, but the error could be in the reading, not the writing of death.)

The series of stanzas referring to Chaos and Time (36–41), the sources of mortality in the physical world and of decay even in the Garden, require that we recognize death as a fact of life, present at its creation and not, in Rilke's terms, 'that part of life that is turned away from us.' Berger nicely observed in his 1961 essay that 'wicked *Time*' in stanza 39 enters the Garden as the shadow cast by Apollo's 'sunny ray' (38.9), which brightens 'the lilly fresh' only to make it fade away (*Revisionary Play* 148). The message here is superficially like that of the 'goodly lay' that had accompanied Acrasia's languid sexuality, but Spenser's rationale for Time's 'malice hard' in the Garden, in the midst of its simultaneous spring and harvest, implies that Venus's 'losse of her deare brood' there (40.3–6) accompanies their springing into mortal life apart from their mother, out in the physical world: 'For all that liues, is subiect to that law: / All things decay in time, and to their end do draw' (40.8–9). Apart from Cupid and Adonis, preeminent among her creatures, the progeny of Venus are far removed from her divinity.

Fear is among the forces driving Spenser's imagination of the Garden, and the poem permits us to trace that fantasy-forming emotion back to its roots, not in Freudian castration anxiety but in a fear of death that is simpler and more profound. *Et in Arcadia ego*: in its most idyllic flights, his imagination is chastened by this reality principle.[28] I follow Quilligan (*Milton's Spenser* 196) and Berger ('Actaeon at the Hinder Gate' 109) in emphasizing that Spenser, like Ovid and Petrarch, long before Freud, always shows us Eros haunted by Thanatos. The consolation offered by Venus to both Adonis and Psyche is that generous love is stronger than death. This consolation must be 'by succession made perpetuall' (47.6), however; mourning and melancholia remain, at best, in abeyance. Time and death, with such life-denying impulses as lust and jealousy in their train, are included in Spenser's account of the Garden but denied dominion over it. Since we are in the account rather than in the Garden, everything included in order to be excluded tends to 'returne backe by the hinder gate' (32.9).

It is in this light that I interpret the return of 'that wilde Bore,' crashing into the middle of a stanza (48) that places Adonis securely 'in eternall blis,' hidden in the secret 'gloomy groue of mirtle trees' on top of Venus's 'stately Mount' (43.2–3). Although Spenser has rewritten the myth to make Venus rather than the boar victorious, with Adonis as proof of her power and essential to her perpetual fertility, he makes the boar no less permanent than Adonis, and similarly under the great mother's control:

> For that wilde Bore, the which him once annoyd,
> She firmely hath emprisoned for ay,
> That her sweet loue his malice mote auoyd,
> In a strong rocky Caue, which is they say,
> Hewen vnderneath that Mount, that none him losen may.   (48.5–9)

In the explications of mythographers and in critics' discussions of this passage, the boar is variously glossed as Lust, as Winter (conspicuously absent from the Garden's oscillating seasons), and as 'Spenser's metamorphosis ... of Time-Death' (*Revisionary Play* 149). Equally important, the imprisoned boar is roughly homologous with Chaos, the source of 'The substances of natures fruitfull progenyes' (36.9). The description of Chaos in stanzas 36–7 prompts some of Berger's most colourful commentary ('Actaeon at the Hinder Gate' 110–11), and he rightly observes that the boar, in all his emblematic significance and wild animality, is 'kept alive directly underneath the bower' where Adonis is hidden (*Revisionary Play* 149). He is another manifestation of the reality principle, Adonis's shadow, reminiscent of the beasts outside of Acrasia's bower.

Spenserian narrative accumulates meaning by echoing, analogy, and juxtaposition; it employs structures that provide for inclusion, exclusion, and hierarchical disposition. In the dense texture of the stanzas devoted to the Garden, especially in those that take us to 'the middest of that Paradise' (43.1), Venus's mount and Adonis's hideaway (stanzas 43–9), things lose their outlines in an unusually dark conceit. Intense impressions and emotions are evoked, and contradictions don't seem incongruous: the 'gloomy groue of mirtle trees' associated with Venus produces 'sweet gum ... precious deaw ... most dainty odours, and most sweet delight' (43); this 'pleasant arbour' is decorated by floral tributes to 'sad louers,' most of them 'transformd of yore' although 'Sad *Amaranthus*, made a flowre but late,' is conspicuously included (44–5).

Adonis's mortal foe has a place in this design, but he is included to be excluded, like '*Phebus* beams' and '*Aeolus* sharp blast' (44.8–9). In his solitary confinement, what threat does the boar pose to Adonis? Has

Venus defeated him by taking his wild appetite within herself? Back in 1961, Berger observed that with the Garden's grounding of life and love in a profusion of vegetative forms, 'Form has become passive; the force breaks loose and asserts itself, revealing its source in death and chaos' (*Revisionary Play* 144). Adonis is aligned with form, and for Berger, Venus is force. Readings of Venus as a fierce, voracious figure have become fashionable since Lauren Silberman suggested, first in a 1982 conference paper and in print in 1986, that the boar's imprisonment 'promises Adonis's safety while figuring forth the *vagina dentata*, ultimate expression of Venus's fearsome power' ('Singing Unsung Heroines' 271; cf. *Transforming Desire* 47–8, 58). Both Quilligan (*Milton's Spenser* 195n.) and Berger cite Silberman approvingly; Berger comments on stanzas 46–8, 'In such moments the narrative perspective seems trapped in ceaseless oscillation between the desire and the fear of Venus' ('Actaeon at the Hinder Gate' 114).

Representations of Venus and her avatars have always been influenced by fear of the appetite associated with a feminine Other, and of the threat it poses to a masculine will, the ideology of rational self-control, and maturity understood as separation from maternal care and feeding. It is also true that the culture in which Spenser sought a man's public role was replete with reasons for fearing women and seeking control over them, rather than enjoying a minion's place in the shade, such as Adonis is given in stanza 46:

> There wont faire *Venus* often to enioy
> Her dear *Adonis* ioyous company,
> And reape sweet pleasure of the wanton boy;
>
> ...
>
> But she her selfe, when euer that she will,
> Possesseth him, and of his sweetnesse takes her fill.

This is a radical alternative to the more common images of the masculine role in love; perhaps it is a cautionary example, and Spenser is lending support to those (his friend Harvey among them) who thought that domesticity and devotion to pleasure were emasculating. Discussing in chapter 1 the Latin verse letter in which Spenser imagined for himself a long European adventure, we found him complaining, right at the time of his first marriage, that lack of opportunity had confined him in *tenebris pudendis*, 'shameful shade.' Could he have thought that for Adonis to overcome mortality, to be 'Transformed oft, and chaunged diuerslie,' becoming 'the Father of all formes' (47.7–8), he had to yield to Venus? I believe so. If negative connotations adhere to her power over Adonis, it is hard to read the account of his apotheosis as anything but the poet's loss of control over his fiction.

It will be helpful to return to Venus, seeking a clearer understanding of her agency – her ascendancy – in the Garden. The question to be answered could be stated in these terms: did a fear of premature death, or of emasculation (both active thematically in the traditional account of Venus and Adonis) provide Spenser with an unmanageable occasion for gynephobia, such that his image of Venus is, at bottom, a caricature of maternal sexuality, with her darling Adonis eminent among the poem's pallid victims of a desire that he could not represent in wholesome terms? Or did the poet represent Venus as an embodiment of faithful love, self-seeking but not selfish, that outlasts death and other dangers by steadily confronting them, representing Adonis in turn as an idealized object of love, whose youthful beauty is worth treasuring in spite of its vulnerability? The latter reading of Venus in the Garden would be consistent with the moral of Psyche's story, with Britomart's education in love, and with the tough-mindedness about the human condition that we find throughout *The Faerie Queene*. The latter account of Adonis involves a view of Spenser's attitude toward masculinity and the male form that has received little attention; it deserves more. Having described Spenser's viewpoint throughout the canto as androgynous, I will claim now that his interests are evenly divided, in what Judith Butler would call 'identificatory mimetism,' between the complementary figures of Adonis, 'the Father of all formes' (47.8), and Venus who, 'when euer that she will, / Possesseth him, and of his sweetnesse takes her fill' (46.8–9).

Just as I argued earlier that the Garden's integrity as a source of forms, animated by love of beauty that flows outward into the world, depends on a supply of substances from a Chaos external to the Garden, I will argue here that we should keep Adonis's nemesis in the picture but separate from Venus's fertility, confined 'vnderneath that Mount.' Evocation of the *vagina dentata*, an archaic image that is phobic in origin but furnishes a comic turn for critics today, offers in its *frisson* of naughtiness a release of tensions accumulated in the poem's 'thickest couert,' but it is a clumsy response to the frankness with which Spenser displays his goddess's anatomy, and the anatomy of his imagination, in the Garden's maze. Seen in relation to both Adonis and Venus, the boar's prison must be cloacal, not vaginal.[29] Just as Genius presides over two gates, so Venus, gathering life and death together as she does, still invites us to distinguish fair from foul. To impose the boar's fierce animality upon the mysterious union of Venus and Adonis is to erase a distinction that is vital to Venus's fertility as the *magna mater* who brings life out of death and leads the way from losses to the possibility of joy.

What is wrong, then, with Adonis as an embodiment of the male partner in a tableau dramatizing fertility? He is subordinate to Venus, but what mortal man would not be? After his apotheosis he is not so much passive as impassive, at ease in his vulnerable and subject status. He is also mercurial: a 'wanton boy' in one moment (46.3), and in the next lying 'Lapped in flowres and pretious spycery' (46.5). If Spenser's picture of his 'eternall blis' (48.1) suggests effeminization, the sensational popularity of Shakespeare's *Venus and Adonis*, deeply indebted to the episode I have been discussing, is evidence that the smart young men buying erotica in the 1590s were taken with this sort of masculinity, objectified and set apart as beautiful, rather like the mistress in a sonnet sequence.[30]

I regard Venus's enthralling of Adonis as entirely beneficial. Venus in the Garden is more lovely than the 'Great *Venus*, Queene of beautie and of grace,' who is idolized in a statue and honoured with a hymn in the Temple devoted to her in Book IV (x 44–7). There her favour is desired from afar by a frustrated lover 'Tormented sore' (43.8), and she is represented as self-sufficient in creation: 'She syre and mother is her selfe alone, / Begets and eke conceiues, ne needeth other none' (41.8–9). In the Garden canto, which I take to be the more original and authoritative myth, Venus alone is incomplete, and she knows it. Indifference to the company of those beneath her is characteristic of Diana, as it is of Belphoebe in canto v of Book III; the coupling of Venus and Adonis is a thorough-going revision of the painful discrepancies between Belphoebe and Timias. Unlike other places in the poem where femininity is self-assertive and represented as threatening or dominant, the Garden shows us goodness and vitality in control despite the presence of other less lovely aspects of the natural order. It is a place where some men might become unhealthily enthralled (I think of my own long history of irresolute engagement with the Garden's mysteries), but the author says that he knows its excellent pleasures 'by tryall' (29.6) and he recommends them; the phrase contains only a hint that as a lover he has found himself uncomfortably on trial.

Berger has happily suggested that in the Garden canto our poet composed a 'discourse of Venus' in answer to the misogyny of Orpheus in Book X of Ovid's *Metamorphoses* ('Actaeon at the Hinder Gate' 91, 114–15). We still lack a secure understanding of the terms in which Spenser, without the benefit of modern feminism and gender theory, would be apt to construct such a discourse. At every turn in the Garden's labyrinth we encounter gendered dualities, reminders that the 'one-sex model' basic to Renaissance constructions of gender and sexuality supported androgyny as a description of human nature's full potentiality at the same time that it marked effeminacy as a danger, presented not only by involvement with strong women but by the inherent instability of gender and identity (cf. Enterline, *Tears of Narcissus* 8–10). Participating in the assumptions about sex and gender that were traditional in his time, but participating with noncommittal attention to the discrepancies between conventional thinking and emergent possibilities, Spenser was apt, I believe, to regard aspects of both genders as Other, and to find both genders essential to the complex ideal that takes shape, but never a finished shape, as the poem unfolds through many reiterations of its complementary patterns. I regard Venus and Adonis together as parts of a single originary figure, the equivalent in Spenser's terms of Blake's 'human form divine.' My grounds for this argument were laid out partially in chapter 1, and the picture will be completed in the next chapter.

The Work of Mourning

Although the Garden canto involves, on the poet's part, a strenuous quest for terms appropriate to representation of the origins of life, and this involves harking back to Eden and other versions of paradise, Spenser does not attempt what Milton does in *Paradise Lost*, evocation of the earliest experience of the human race, in a time and place prior to all suffering. Love in the Garden may be wholly natural and therefore innocent, but its premise, evident especially from the viewpoint of Venus, is a prior experience of loss. Adonis is Venus's 'lost louer' (29.8), and she earns her title as 'great mother' not only by creating but by lamenting 'The losse of her deare brood, her deare delight' (40.4). If for the poet the Garden is *'fraught /*
With pleasures manifold' (Argument 3–4; my emphasis), perhaps the sadness preceding and inevitably succeeding them is implied in the intensity of those pleasures. There is a dark side, then, to the marvellous coincidence of 'continuall spring, and haruest there / Continuall' (42.1–2).

A number of recent studies have demonstrated the centrality, within early modern culture and the earlier experience that it reinterpreted, of melancholia, mourning, and consolation.[31] In *Eros in Mourning*, Henry Staten locates 'the *origin of idealism*' in a desire 'to transcend all merely mortal loves, loves that can be lost.' He aptly describes this desire as fundamental to Platonism and to the Platonizing Christianity typified in the Latin tradition by St Augustine. Diotima had explained to Socrates that 'love is wanting to possess the good forever' (*Sympos.* 206A), and this motive links sublimated sexuality with ascent to the only place where a love object can yield lasting satisfaction, the unchanging realm of Ideas. What is desired in all such striving is 'the overcoming of mourning,' attempting to solve the problem of unhappiness as defined by St Augustine: 'I was unhappy, and so is every soul unhappy which is tied to its love for mortal things; when it loses them, it is torn in pieces, and it is then that it realizes the unhappiness which was there even before it lost them' (*Confessions* 4.6).[32]

Plato and St Augustine can be placed appropriately in a historical perspective with reference to George McClure's study of *tristitia* and consolation within the humanist tradition founded by Petrarch.[33] The distinction made by St Paul in 2 Corinthians 7:10 between 'godly grief' (*tristitia secundum Deum*) and 'worldly grief' (*tristitia saeculi*) had urged Christian thinkers and officers of the church to proscribe sorrow over the loss of loved ones as sinful and an occasion for repentance (*Sorrow and Consolation* 10), but humanists of the fourteenth and fifteenth centuries, rediscovering such authors as Cicero, Seneca, and Ovid, made legitimate once again their themes of worldly sorrow and the remedies of consolation in secular forms of the 'cure of souls' (*Sorrow and Consolation* 12–17). It is in this light that I would interpret the Garden as a prime instance of Spenserian allegory. Its appeal is twofold. It accounts causally, at their source and 'According to their kindes' (30.6), for the loveliness and vitality of mortal things, showing us the world not as it appears in real time, filled with fully substantial individual creatures, but in terms of a perennially valid typology of forms. The Garden also displays the obverse of this view of allegory, Walter Benjamin's idea that it is a discourse responsive to decay and to the crumbling of a transcendentally guaranteed old order (cf. William E. Engel, *Mapping Mortality* 47, 98, 178). Enclosed within the celebratory and idealizing rhetoric of the Garden passage is a throbbing melancholia, and one effect of the fiction is to rationalize the melancholic stance that Spenser and his personae often take toward the things of this world.

Like St Augustine, Spenser treats happiness as the goal of consciousness but traces subjectivity back to the sadness of a fallen state. Melancholia complicates the world's erotic appeal, marking it as distant and unmanageable. How is melancholia to be managed, short of a wholesale renunciation of the world? Spenser's response to this problem was a fiction interpreting the world's imperfections in the light of a different origin and destiny. Ultimately, he was committed to the transcendental orientation represented by Henry Staten as an antidote to loss, but the Garden passage describes a cycle to which transcendence would be tangential. Not only does Venus have to mourn Time's passing like a reckless mower through the Garden's thriving beds (stanzas 38–40), but I will argue that the impulse on which the Garden was founded was memorial, involving what Elizabeth Mazzola has nicely termed 'a mortuary poetics.'[34] Mortal life in 'sinful mire' (32.7) originates in and returns to bliss, we are assured, but an understanding of this life cycle will be blocked if, like Verdant and Grylle in the Bower of Bliss, we are too eager to forget the pain of being human; or, like Sir Guyon, too eager to inflict it on others.

Spenser's aim in the Garden of Adonis, and more generally in the poem containing that mysterious *omphalos*, resembles not the rigorous transcendental orientation of Plato's doctrine of Ideas, with its denial of the physical world's substantial significance, but the archaic project found in Plato's earlier dialogues and still present in *The Symposium* and *Phaedrus*: the making of a memorial to Socrates and his teachings, not 'the overcoming of mourning' but a transformation of loss by reflecting on the soul and the nature of love. Throughout the Garden passage, death is credited with a huge part in making the things of this world valuable. Adonis is not called 'the Father of all formes' (47.8) until he himself has been 'Transformed oft, and chaunged diuerslie' (47.7). After death Adonis retains his identity, thanks to Venus's love and his cult following. Spenser's account of mankind's desire for permanent possession of the Good and the Beautiful is quite different from the renunciations – first of one body, then of all bodies – preached by Diotima in *The Symposium* and subsequently, to a larger audience, by Pietro Bembo in *The Courtier*.

The 'secret' state in which Adonis lies protected by Venus, 'Lapped in flowres and pretious spycery' (46.5), strongly suggests the living death of mummification. Venus resembles Acrasia as Adonis resembles Verdant, but as I will show in the next chapter, several significant details in the Garden canto establish, in terms taken from the discourse of spiritual magic, a contrast to the witchcraft and adverse effects of Acrasia's beauty. The figure of Adonis offers a perfect nexus for Spenser's paradoxical pondering of mourning, sexuality, and a Platonic poetics within what Berger has termed Book III's 'discourse of Venus.' He seems to have known, from ancient literary texts or interpreters such as Natalis Comes, that Adonis had been venerated in a fertility cult patronized by women, and even that the Adonis festival was 'a living ritual celebrating the sacred drama of love, death, and anticipated resurrection enacted by Adonis and his consort Aphrodite.'[35] The beauty and pathos associated with Adonis belonged to the world that Socrates (according to Plato) had rejected, just as he rejected the little 'gardens of Adonis' mentioned in the *Phaedrus*, analogous in their short-term value to the memory-destroying technique of writing.[36] Spenser's own memorial project, firmly committed to writing, obliquely invokes this context along with the better-known Ovidian one in a myth-making process that connects Adonis with the floral tributes of pastoral elegy. He may also have been aware of memorial tributes by Ronsard and by the artist Rosso Fiorentino, in which Adonis was transfigured in honour of François, Dauphin of France, who had died suddenly in 1536 at the age of eighteen.[37]

In the stanzas leading to Adonis's hideaway, he is placed at the head of a class of loved ones lost and transformed, 'giuen endlesse date' by poets' verses (stanzas 43–6). By the sequence of his tributes in stanza 45, Spenser invites us to gather these lost loves under the aegis of Adonis: 'euery sort of flowre,' from 'Fresh *Hyacinthus*, *Phoebus* paramoure,' to 'Sad *Amaranthus*, made a flowre but late.' Seen in this light, the figure of Philip Sidney, artfully concealed in Amintas and his transformation as the amaranthus, biblically associated with a canonized saint's 'crown of glory,'[38] is a recent instance of the fertility god's vulnerability and recreative potency. No less than Adonis, in Spenser's verses Sidney is 'Lapped in flowres and pretious spycery.'

Adonis and, by implication, Sidney figure prominently in the apparatus of patrons and patterns that constitute *The Faerie Queene*'s fabric of memorial homage. Just as Gloriana is represented as Queen Elizabeth's 'true glorious type,' Adonis is the mythic archetype whose transformation promises that lovers and poets such as Sidney will not lose in death their connection with an immortal beauty. In Spenser's revision of Platonism, consistent with Plato's earliest responses to the death of Socrates, the transcendent value of a specific earthly avatar motivates apprehension of a 'type,' an ideal beyond the reach of representation. As part of the dialectic of love, idealization interacts with mourning to turn transient life into memorable language. Philip Sidney is both lost and found in the versions of '*Amintas* wretched fate' and his floral 'endlesse date': Spenser brings Sidney's death and blessed memory into his poem by alluding to other poets' efforts to immortalize him, thereby confirming his claim to fame.[39]

The elegiac tone of stanzas 43–9 can be understood as Spenser's earliest contribution to the mourning of Sidney's premature death, an undertaking that began in 1586 and engaged the interests of many writers and circles of readers until well beyond the end of the century. The belatedness of Spenser's tribute in *Astrophel*, published in 1595 with other elegies composed within the Sidney circle, attracted speculation about the sincerity of his grief, beginning in the poet's lifetime and a recurrent theme in modern criticism.[40] Sidney is explicitly, if not crudely, identified with Adonis in *Astrophel*, and I am suggesting that when he assimilated Amintas's fate to that of Adonis in his approach to the inner sanctum of the Garden, Spenser was engaged in his own imaginative mourning of the knightly poet who had praised *The Shepheardes Calender* and, early in its evolution, *The Faerie Queene*. If, as Raphael Falco has argued, 'The *Astrophel* collection contains the roots of Sidney's canonization as a poet' (*Conceived Presences* 94), the seed is to be found in Spenser's 'first seminarie.'

Abraham Fraunce honoured Sidney's memory not only with his English version of Thomas Watson's *Amyntas*, but in later books dedicated to the Countess of Pembroke after she had assumed leadership of a circle devoted to his memory and his literary interests. The most important and informative of these is *The Third part of the Countesse of Pembrokes Yuychurch: Entituled, Amintas Dale* (London: for Thomas Woodcocke, 1592), a cento of mythological narratives embellished with moralizing comments, natural history, and metaphysical lore, offered in dialogue fashion by 'nymphs and pastors' who have joined 'Pembrokiana' to observe the 'solempne feast of murdred *Amyntas*' (sig. A2). Fraunce also alludes at the book's conclusion (sig. P5) to what seems to have been an annual event for the Sidney circle, marking the death and transfiguration of their lost leader.[41]

Emulation of the annual festivals devoted, in antiquity, to divinized mortals such as Adonis may have been part of the rationale for an annual event mourning Sidney's death. In this connection, it is significant that Spenser describes the transfiguration of Adonis as a matter of faith rather than fact: 'There yet, some say, in secret he does ly' (46.4), 'And sooth it seemes they say' (47.1), 'For him the Father of all formes they call' (47.8). We rightly think of Spenser as a myth-maker, but in this instance the myth he has codified is represented as a collective and coterie enterprise. The evidence will not take us beyond conjecture, but I am willing to suppose that on some occasion – perhaps an Amintas Day at Wilton – between 1587, when Fraunce's version of Watson's *Amyntas* was published, and 1590 when *The Faerie Queene* appeared in print, Spenser presented to Sidney's sister his own tribute to Venus, Adonis, and the transformed 'Father of all [poetic] formes.'[42]

It is noteworthy that one of the stories of metamorphosis in Fraunce's *Amintas Dale* concerns Venus and Adonis (sigs. M1v–M3). Fraunce's commentary first draws a lesson from the birth of Venus after Saturn's castration of his father, who thereby becomes Venus's father. 'So *Saturne* destroyeth, *Venus* bringeth foorth; and both are necessary for the continuall propagation of these inferior bodies, sith the corruption of one, is the generation of another' (sig. M3). In keeping with a mythographic commonplace, Saturn (Kronos) stands for Time (Chronus); Saturn is also, of course, associated with melancholia and with the *vita speculativa*. One can discern a reiterated pattern in this and the other narratives of metamorphosis in *Amintas Dale*: a catastrophe or violation evokes the generous action of love. Such narratives do the work of mourning, with a bearing on the memorial occasion for the dialogue. (Elpinus comments on Cassiopaea's performance that she 'hath so passionately discoursed of *Venus* and *Adonis*, that I feare me, vnder these names, she mourneth her owne loue, and vttreth her owne affection' [sig. M3].)

Although the Countess of Pembroke and her circle earned a reputation for piety and the transcendental orientation that Henry Staten has interpreted as 'the overcoming of mourning,' the emotional and intellectual commitments made by sophisticated Elizabethans were more complicated than Staten's account of idealization would suggest. Their experience included a deep involvement in the current of *tristitia saeculi* that George McClure and others have interpreted. Another reference to *Amintas Dale* will substantiate this point. The book ends with a mock-serious account, comparable in some respects to Spenser's description of the Garden, of the order of things superintended by Time. The last person to contribute to the 'solempne feast of murdred *Amyntas*' is 'good old *Daphne* ... odd in conceit, and therefore very like, either to say nothing or nothing like to that which had been said before' (sig. O1v). She tells an amusing story, at such length that she must be interrupted so that the book, and the occasion it commemorates, may be brought to a light-hearted end.

Daphne's story begins with 'certayne schollers of *Cambridge*, who would needes finde out some way to mount vp to heauen, and vnderstand those mysteries which bee aboue the Moone,' and then it shifts to an inset traveller's tale about another group of academics 'in the Vniuersitie, called the *Garden*, whereof we all were named Gardiners.' This university ('seminarie' would be a better term) is both make-believe and down-to-earth, devoted as it is to singing 'of the vertue of hearbs, the pleasaunt liquor of the vine, the sweetnes of fruits, the profite of husbandry, and dressing of Gardens and Orchyards' (sig. P1). Having devised a ladder to heaven from 'the poles that bare vp their hoppes' (sig. P1v), three of the Gardiners set out to test the truth of astrologers' prognostications. They meet *Intellectus* and his sister *Fantasie* riding on a cloud, and with them they are carried to the top of Olympus. After two of them, *Hemlock* and *Pasnip*, have been thrown out of heaven by Jupiter, the more circumspect

Thistle is blessed by the gods, who predict a bright future for his 'nephews and succeeding posteritie,' the *Artichauks* (sig. P4v). He is then taken to visit *Time*, who presides over an 'auncient pallace,' full of servants responding busily to his mood changes.

Time appears to be answerable to no one; *Destiny, Fortune,* and *Chaunce* are his ministers, and the executors of his will include such personages as are summoned by Mutabilitie in Spenser's *Cantos* (sig. [P5]; *Cantos* vii 17–46). Daphne's story ends abruptly, not with a synthesizing judgment offered by Nature but with a double interruption: first the discoursing stranger in the inset narrative is silenced by 'an outragius tempest of snowe, hayle, raine, winde, thunder, and lightning all together,' and then Daphne's account of the shipwreck that the tempest causes is put off by 'the Lady Regent' Pembrokiana until another gathering to commemorate the death of Amintas.

Abraham Fraunce offers no perspective on the cosmos and human life superior to the inscrutable figure of Time. This is consistent with the limits usually set for the scope of classical mythology as codified by Ovid: it pertains to the domain of God's creatures, not to first and final causes. An abyss, honoured only by silence in the text, seems to separate this world from the true transcendental consolations of Christian faith. An escape from mourning might be found through appeals to faith, or through the mediating discourse of Platonism, and Spenser often makes such appeals, but Fraunce's aims are more modest and playful. They imply the presence of sceptical and fideist attitudes in the social world that during the 1580s sustained Sidney's death and the deaths of several more mature leaders. Such attitudes are evident in Sidney's own literary work and more extensively in Spenser's. In the world defined unpredictably by Time, a world that is none too clearly connected with anything unchanging, mourning is a source of meaning and melancholia is an occupational hazard.

Love is dialectically paired with mourning and melancholia throughout *The Faerie Queene*. Eros is at the heart of Redcrosse's quest to prove himself worthy of divine grace, and his quest is paradigmatic, in that eros finds its way under conditions imposed by the work of mourning. Redcrosse is 'Right faithfull true ... / But of his cheere did seeme too solemne sad' (I i 2.7–8), and a similar seriousness burdens many other characters in the poem, beginning with the mournful Una and writ large in Prince Arthur. Mourning can be distinguished from the pathology of melancholia: Duessa, in her phony devotion to the 'dearest Lord' whose 'blessed body spoild of liuely breath' has been hidden from her, presents a cautionary example of the melancholic's 'deepe wounded mind' (I ii 23–4). At the beginning and the end of Book I we find images of more authentic piety, and they form the basis for the veneration accorded to Adonis in the different context of Book III. The 'bloudie Crosse' by which the 'Patron of true Holinesse' is identified promises life after death through the Saviour's absent presence, and we are told that Redcrosse 'dead as liuing euer him ador'd' (i 2). After his successful *imitatio Christi* the 'betrouthed' couple enjoy their union in paradise for a time, but in the midst of a long swim 'in that sea of blisfull ioy,' duty calls the hero to return to Gloriana's service, 'The which he shortly did, and *Vna* left to mourne' (xii 41). So must Redcrosse be mourning on his lonesome highway back to Cleopolis and Gloriana.

Like Gloriana, and like other daemonic and angelic figures in *The Faerie Queene*, Adonis participates in the *aevum*, between time and eternity;[43] alternatively, in the terms favoured by Ficino and his followers, Adonis united with Venus participates in the generative activity of the world soul.[44] 'All be he subiect to mortalitie, / Yet is eterne in mutabilitie' (III vi 47.4–5): Adonis figures forth within the secular order a resolution of the work of mourning, which is possible when art imitates the cyclical yieldings of nature. The recreative love exemplified in Venus comes to terms with loss as fundamental to the human condition, dialectically entwined with any claim to immortality.

chapter seven

The Platonic Program of the Garden Canto

Having given cursory attention in the previous chapter to contexts and sources for the distinctive features of the Garden of Adonis canto, I will now shift my focus to include a few texts that will illuminate obscurities and clarify some basic elements in the poem's design. In such passages as the canto under discussion, Platonic motifs are so coherent as to constitute an intentional program. We cannot, with any confidence, trace all the elements of that complex design to specific sources, but I will argue that in its main outlines we can discern intertextual echoes of *The Symposium* and the responses to its myths that were initiated, for the Renaissance, by Ficino's commentary.

Basic features of the canto's program were mentioned in the previous chapter (196–200). First, there is its two-part structure, 54 stanzas in balanced 27–stanza segments, with the number 27 alluding to the Lambda Formula from the *Timaeus*. Like 6, 'the lambda's key' and for Pythagoreans 'the spousal number,' 27 bears a significance related to the *anima mundi* and the generation of life forms.[1] Whether this symbolism was meant to be discovered or to remain hidden, we cannot say: perhaps, for Spenser, numbers were sometimes the soul and sometimes the skeleton of his poem. Related to these numerically ordered patterns, there are others with a Platonic provenance in the canto's imagery and narrative elements, and in my opinion these are more significant. Scholars interested in the source-related significance of our 're-sourceful' poet's most elaborate display of his learning have tended toward superfluity in their appeals to many strands in the tangled skein of Plato's legacy.[2] If a program based upon specific source texts can be discovered, it will bring economy and perspective to the enterprise of interpreting a canto 'fraught,' if I may vary the phrasing in its Argument, with *problems* manifold.

To say that the canto's poetry involves echoes of specific intertexts is not to deny the relevance of broader and historically deeper contexts, but to bring them into sharper focus. Take, for instance, the canto's master trope, in which the natural cycle of germination, growth, decay, and regeneration provides images for virtues that, if carefully cultivated, keep the distinctively human yearning for self-transcendence and immortality in harmony with nature. This way of thinking draws upon the doctrine of *logoi spermatikoi* or *rationes seminales*, the causal principles by which reason and energy are infused both in consciousness and in all living things. That doctrine, developed by the Stoics, was taken up by Plotinus and elaborated by Augustine; it seems to have been as pervasive in Renaissance culture as the idea that the universe is threefold, and perhaps it was just as fundamental to allegory as a mode of perception and discourse. As Maryanne Cline Horowitz has shown in *Seeds of Virtue and Knowledge*, the Stoic, Neoplatonic, and patristic traditions provide a choric background for Renaissance representations of the virtues, and also for the ways in which obsessive interests in social distinction, lineage, and the perpetuation of individual and family names were articulated in courtly cultures. Ficino, whose commentary *On Love* incorporates *rationes* and *semina* in its hierarchical ontology and epistemology, would not have understood modern scholars' interest in separating the opinions of Augustine from those of Plotinus. When I focus attention on Ficino and single out *On Love* among his many influential writings, I do so for two reasons: first, to bring a measure of simplicity to a subject already thoroughly discussed in historically oriented scholarship; second, because I am convinced that a few intertexts provided the basis for Spenser's program in the Garden canto and parts of *The Faerie Queene* affiliated with it.

My first undertaking in this chapter will be to show that the two halves of the Garden canto work variations on the themes in two myths from *The Symposium*: (1) Aristophanes' account (189D–93D) of the original form of mankind and its splitting by Zeus and Apollo into two halves, with love understood as desire for a return to the lost state of unity; and (2) Diotima's account (201E–4C), within the climactic speech by Socrates, of Love as a 'great daimon,' intermediary between the gods and mankind, begotten in the Garden of Zeus on the birthday of Aphrodite. I will argue that Spenser took his understanding of Plato's myths and the terms for his own variations on their themes from an allegorizing interpretive tradition renewed in the Renaissance by Ficino, reinterpreted by Leone Ebreo, and disseminated further by Plato's French translator and scholiast, Louis Le Roy. As with the number-based patterns informing *The Faerie Queene*, we cannot be sure that the myth-related patterns I will be interpreting were meant to be seen, but I believe that just as Spenser's allusions to lines and whole episodes from canonical poets confirm his claim to laureate status, so textual motifs in the Garden canto set up elaborate echoes that place the poem within the traditions of esoteric humanism, confirming more than any other part of *The Faerie Queene* the author's maguslike stature.

Leone Ebreo's Exposition of Two Myths in *The Symposium*

The ideas most important to Spenser's poetry, even in this most esoterically oriented passage, can be found in texts that were widely known in the poet's time, not only by the learned but by amateurs in the audience for literature and philosophy. My argument will lead back to Ficino's commentary on *The Symposium*, but I will begin with Leone Ebreo's *Dialoghi d'amore*, a book containing distinctive contributions to the interpretive tradition, and one that had a decisive impact on Spenser's thinking about love. Comments on Aristophanes' and Diotima's myths, dispersed in Ficino's and other commentaries, are juxtaposed by Leone, and his dialogue also provides a solid basis, clearer than any other known to me, for an understanding of the 'discourse of Venus' that my differences with Berger and other critics called for in the previous chapter.

When the *Dialoghi d'amore* were first published in 1535, the author was identified as 'Leone Ebreo.' Yehuda or Judah (i.e., Leone) Abravanel was the son of Isaac Abravanel, who was renowned both as a physician and for his Talmudic scholarship. Despite the family's prominence and the interest of modern scholars in the lives of both father and son, plus extensive recent scholarship on the Jewish communities established in Italy after the expulsions from Spain and Portugal in 1492, Leone remains a mysterious figure.[3] The frame of reference for his account of love and beauty and a host of related topics is in some respects distinctively Jewish, but he achieved a synthesis of ideas from several traditions that many broad-minded and curious Christian readers found appealing. Leone combines an earnest otherworldliness with elaborate attention to the subjective and interpersonal dynamics of courtship and love leading to marriage; in his *Dialoghi* love and beauty are not contemplated, as in Ficino's writings, within a circle of men for whom the dominant model of an ideal love is homoerotic, where the legacy of Dante and Petrarch prescribes an asymmetrical code of behaviour for men and for the women who are occasionally the absent objects of their reveries.

The *Dialoghi d'amore* are authentically dialogical, a lopsided but not one-sided conversation between Filone, a young man over-stuffed with both love and learning, and his beloved Sofia, a patient, curious, resistant audience for Filone's sometimes far-fetched demonstrations that reciprocal love is both the way of the world and in accordance with God's will, since it provides the means for the soul's return to God. Leone's view of the cosmos, like Spenser's, is gendered from top to bottom, from God to Chaos and its *prima materia*; Naomi Yavneh aptly terms the world of the *Dialoghi* 'a dualistic cosmos governed by a system of universal hermaphrodism.'[4] As I noted in the preceding chapter, concurring with the arguments of David Lee Miller and Lauren Silberman, in the 'imaginary' of *The Faerie Queene* androgyny is both characteristic of the idealized human body and the basis for a moral viewpoint. The *Dialoghi* can contribute significantly to our understanding of androgyny and desire in *The Faerie Queene*.

Leone's book consists of three dialogues, with the third, which will concern us here, constituting more than half of the whole and containing a synthesis of themes introduced in the first two dialogues. I will cite Pontus de Tyard's translation, published in Lyon in 1551; Spenser probably knew this version, and it is also the most readily available modern text.[5] Leone's account of the origin of love between human beings and throughout the cosmos, consisting primarily of commentaries on Aristophanes' and Diotima's contributions to *The Symposium*, is preceded by an analysis of the roles of lover and beloved in the generation of Love. This analysis is crucial to our understanding of Adonis in relation to Venus, and of other exemplary male figures in *The Faerie Queene*, including Arthur, Redcrosse, Artegall, and Colin. Philo asks whether the lover or the beloved is the 'first cause,' and Sophia replies that the lover is active like a father while the beloved receives love, like a mother; 'the first cause of Love is the lover, and the beloved is the second.' This seems unexceptionable, but here the argument takes a remarkable turn. Philo maintains, on the contrary, that 'the true father of Love is the beloved, who engenders it in the lover, and the lover is the mother, pregnant with love ... So the beloved is the first efficient, formal, and final cause of Love, as its only father, and the lover is only its material cause, as its pregnant mother who gives birth' (*D* 198). Thus the lover, who is apt to be male, is rendered feminine by the subjection involved in love. This transformation is not regarded as a loss, nor does Leone see the active role of lover as inconsistent with a feminine subject position. (It should be remembered that one of the motives driving Philo's long discourse is a desire to convert Sophia from his beloved to his lover.) Even when the lover is superior to the beloved, in inclining toward the beloved 'he does not remain defective and of less dignity and perfection, but gains something through the union and perfection of the object beloved' (D 199).

When Sophia raises questions about the dynamics of love between two people, when 'one and the other are equally lover and beloved,' it becomes clear that Leone's gender-based terms are independent of the partners' sexual identities, but correlate with the basic principle that 'each, insofar as he loves, is inferior, and insofar as he is beloved, is superior to the other' (D 199). His alignment of the beloved with a superior position and a paternal role is not inconsistent with ideas derived from *The Symposium*, as we will see, but it follows more directly from the emphasis, in Jewish and Christian traditions, on the involvement of God with His creation. Sophia asks, 'How can it always be true that the beloved is God to the lover? For it would follow that the creature beloved by God would be the God of God: this is too indecent, not only concerning God toward His creatures, but even concerning the spiritual toward the corporeal, the superior toward the inferior, and the noble toward the common.' Philo concedes the point with reference to God, but observes that all creatures are imperfect, and love is a consequence of imperfection. 'Any creature, loving not only its superior but even its inferior, increases its perfection and approaches the sovereign perfection of God.' This perfection is also communicated to the inferior partner: 'by this increase in perfection, both in itself and in the universe, the inferior beloved becomes divine in the superior lover, for being beloved, it participates in the divinity of the sovereign Creator' (D 201).

Such an argument might have been wasted on Belphoebe, except in the first flush of her interest in the wounded Timias, but courtiers like Sidney, Ralegh, and Spenser must have found that it spoke to their conditions. The bearing of Leone's ideas upon some of Spenser's themes in the Garden canto may already be apparent to a reader who has reflected on the seemingly 'miraculous' yet natural conception and childbirth by which Belphoebe and Amoret come into the world, each to be fostered by a goddess and eventually presented to the world as a paragon. The apotheosis of Adonis is also intelligible in the light of Leone's ideas. Both Leone and Spenser emphasize clear distinctions between inferior and superior figures, whether lover or beloved, but describe a gender-bending movement toward the perfection of reciprocal love. We saw that Philo describes the lover as maternal and the beloved as the father of Love. This somewhat paradoxical notion, at odds with the conventional alignment of masculinity with rhetorical and sexual dominance while the feminine role is passive, explains the activity of Venus in both halves of the canto. She searches for her lost Cupid, is the clear winner in her debate with Diana, takes up Amoret, has revived Adonis and imprisoned his adversary, couples with her beloved through both spring and harvest, shows a mother's solicitude toward the creatures who must depart from the Garden to be born in the world, and finally sees Cupid and Psyche reconciled under her roof. Leone helps us to put the much-discussed 'dominance' of Venus in perspective, and to understand the centrality, in Spenser's 'discourse of Venus,' of her words to her sister Diana: 'We both are bound to follow heauens beheasts, / And tend our charges with obeisance meeke' (22.7–8).

Leone's commentaries on the myths of Aristophanes and Diotima are prefaced by a review of several opinions from classical antiquity on the parentage of Cupid, and of a different figure, the ancients' Eros or Amor. Chief among the figures named Cupid is 'that blind child, nude, winged, and armed with a bow and arrows, of whom some say he is the son of Mars and Venus, while according to others he was born to Venus alone, without a father.' Cupid represents love that is 'voluptuous, delightful, and given to wantonness [*l'uxure*]'; for this reason Pleasure (*Volupté*) is said to be his daughter (*D* 240). Several accounts of the parentage of Love (understood both as a force of nature and 'the first of all the passions of the soul') are mentioned. Love was the first child of the primal parents, Erebus and Night (*D* 241; cf. *D* 114); another Love was the son of Jupiter and '*la grande Venus*'; this Love is said to have been twins.

With Leone's exposition of the nature of Love and the meaning of its parentage, we enter a discussion that corresponds in many respects to Spenser's narrative in the first half of the Garden canto, containing themes that carry over to the second half as well. Leone's twin Loves and their two parents provide tropes by which several aspects of 'virtuous [*honneste*] and temperate love' can be presented schematically, as desire for profitable and pleasurable objects, both corporeal and intellectual. Love's father is Jupiter, 'the poets' sovereign God,' and he is objectified as the beloved; his lover, Venus, is not 'she who inspires lascivious and impudent desires, but that great Venus whose influence is the cause of honest, virtuous, and intellectual desires' (*D* 241). Jupiter and Venus are termed by astrologers 'the two Fortunes,' and together they make both corporeal and spiritual desires virtuous. These ideas, available to Spenser from several sources, form the basis for his account of the favourable influences blessing the conception of Belphoebe and Amoret.[6]

When Philo explains to Sophia why Love is depicted as twins, he helps us to understand the programmatic significance of Belphoebe and Amoret;

in both Leone's argument and Spenser's narrative, other distinctions follow easily from the splitting of one personification into two. The ultimate authority for Philo's mythography is the speech of Pausanias in *The Symposium*, with its distinction between two Loves because there are two Venuses (*Sympos.* 180D–E); as we will see, Leone's interpretation of Aristophanes' androgyne myth is also relevant. Leone's Philo deftly summarizes ideas that are dispersed in Ficino's *On Love*, then finds his own way to analyse the mythology of Love. A distinction between virtuous and base or passionate love is less important to Leone than recognition that virtuous love is itself twofold, directed toward 'corporeal and spiritual things: toward the corporeal by the moderation of a little [desire], and toward the spiritual by all the increase and abundant growth to which desire can be extended.' Leone's focus here is on the ideal possibility, two loves balanced in one person: 'Whoever is virtuous in one love is equally virtuous in the other' (*D* 242).

The *Fowre Hymnes* are dedicated to 'two honorable sisters, as to the most excellent and rare ornaments of all true love and beautie, both in the one and the other kinde.' In *The Faerie Queene*, Spenser develops his account of a twofold virtuous love differently. His stories of twin daughters separated at birth, whose kinship only the hapless Timias is (much later, in canto vii of Book IV) in a position to recognize, add more than one twist to ideas found in the *Dialoghi*. When he ends the story of Venus's search for her runaway Cupid with the discovery of Chrysogone's twin daughters, Spenser creates a correlative to Leone's distinctions between wayward Cupid and virtuous Love. Something similar to the twins' separation appears as the dialogue between Philo and Sophia continues.

After his passing mention of Pausanias's speech, Philo offers an extended interpretation of Aristophanes' myth (*D* 242–56), which he treats as an explanation of the birth of love between human beings. Paired with this is an exposition of Diotima's myth from Socrates' speech, which accounts for the parentage of 'universal love in all the corporeal world' (*D* 256–9), and Philo goes on to explain, with reference to the higher level of God and the angelic world, the parentage of all love, both intellectual and physical (*D* 259–62).

According to Aristophanes, human beings were originally spherical in form, with double our number of arms, legs, and other parts. In this form there were three genders: males, children of the sun; females, children of the earth; and androgynes composed of both sexes, children of the moon. To restrain their proud and rebellious natures Zeus had Apollo cut them in half, relocating their genitals so that each gender would derive some sexual satisfaction from the face-to-face reunion that they desired, and by the coupling of the male and female parts of the androgyne, the human race would be perpetuated. Aristophanes' myth accounts for both homosexual and heterosexual desire, and represents sexuality in all its forms as an instinctual response to a primal loss, a yearning to return to wholeness that develops with our attainment of bodily consciousness.

> Love is born into every human being; it calls back the halves of our original nature together; it tries to make one out of two and heal the wound of human nature.
>   Each one of us, then, is a 'matching half [*symbolon*]' of a human whole ... and each of us is always seeking the half that matches him. (*Sympos*. 191D)

Julia Kristeva, one of several psychoanalytically oriented contemporary writers on love, notes Plato's use of the term *symbolon* here in its root sense (referring to the half of a disk used in voting): 'One should understand that each sex is the "symbol" of the other, its complement and support, its bestower of meaning.'[7] Receptive readers of Leone's *Dialoghi* would have understood this.

Philo's interpretation of Aristophanes' myth simplifies its terms and complicates their significance. After describing the androgyne at first as 'a third kind [*gendre*] of men' (*D* 242), he focuses his interpretation exclusively on this prototype, and finds in its original and divided forms an analogue to the biblical myth of Adam and Eve. The idea that much of Plato's wisdom came originally from Moses had been developed by Philo of Alexandria and Origen, with the androgyne myth as a prime instance, and the idea enjoyed wide currency in the Renaissance.[8] Leone goes further than other *trattatisti* in his careful exposition of Genesis (*D* 244–54) in order to validate Plato's myth; only Louis Le Roy, following Leone's footsteps in the eclectic commentary that is a large part of *Le Sympose de Platon*, provides ampler coverage (see 241 below). In effect, Leone and those he influenced use Plato and Moses intertextually, to explicate one another. Plato explains the 'obvious contradiction' between Genesis 1:27, where man is created 'male and female' on the sixth day, and Genesis 2:18 and 21–3, where Adam is alone and Eve is made out of his rib: inconsistencies in the scripture's literal sense indicate a 'hidden sacred mystery,' that in the beginning Adam was androgynous (*D* 245–6). The reference in Genesis 2:24 to marriage as a restoration of 'one flesh' conveys the same understanding of love as is found in Aristophanes' myth: 'Love is in every human being [*chacun homme*], whether male or female, because each is half human and not whole, whence each half desires to be restored to wholeness with its other half' (*D* 244; cf. *D* 247). The differences between Moses and Plato are insignificant: 'since sin and division are virtually the same thing, or two things inseparable and convertible one into the other, it can be said according to the Bible that sin comes from division, and according to Plato that division is the consequence of sin' (*D* 247).[9]

According to Leone, each sex or gender is not an autonomous entity but an aspect of mankind ('*l'homme*' in Tyard's translation). 'The first man, and all others that you may see, were made in the likeness and image of God, male and female.' When Sophia wonders how men and women can be both male and female, Philo insists: 'Each of them has a masculine part, perfect and active, which is the intellect, and a feminine part, imperfect and passive, which is the body and matter: whence the image of God is imprinted in matter, for the form, which is male, is the intellect, and the thing formed, which is female, is the body' (*D* 249). This response is not entirely satisfactory; Philo's explanation of the mother and father roles in reciprocal love had been subtler, and the next turn in the dialogue involves a return to subtlety.

In Leone's exposition of Plato's and Moses' explanations for gender and sexuality in the fallen state, a real duality results from the original organism's splitting. The two sexes are each regarded as imperfect outside of a heterosexual union. The full implications of Leone's dualistic world view emerge when he interprets Diotima's account (*Sympos.* 202D–7A) of the parentage and birth of the *daimon* Love. Aristophanes' myth had explained the origin of love between human beings (man being a 'little world'); Diotima describes the origin of 'universal Love in the great world of corporeal creation' (*D* 256). As befits the analogy of microcosm to macrocosm, the two myths are thematically similar. In the cosmos there is no self-division to account for, but in the proliferation of forms, a metaphysical equivalent of the fall of man is readily apparent in departure from the source and descent into matter.

Diotima's myth tells of the gods' festival on the birthday of Venus, at which Poros (Plenty), drunk with nectar, fell asleep in the Garden of Jupiter, where Penia (Poverty) lay with him and conceived Love. Having been begotten on the birthday of Venus, Love is a follower of Venus, desirous of beautiful things because Venus is beautiful. He also resembles his parents, and is 'not entirely mortal nor (because of his mixed nature) entirely immortal, but in a short time, within a single day dies and lives, reviving one moment and failing in another, repeating this behavior over and over' (*D* 256–7; cf. *Sympos.* 203B–E). Philo's paraphrase also includes

Diotima's comparison of Love to a philosopher who is 'a mean between the sage and the ignorant man'; Love likewise is 'truly a mean between the beautiful and the ugly, between wisdom and ignorance' (*D* 257; cf. *Sympos.* 204A–B). The resemblance of Love to Socrates as Plato portrays him is unmistakable.

In his allegorical interpretation of Diotima's myth, Philo explicitly rejects the interpretation developed by Plotinus and followed by Ficino, in which the formation of first the angelic mind and then the world soul is implied: 'we don't delude ourselves with such an abstract allegory, remote from the text of Diotima's fable' (*D* 257). The birth of Venus signifies, in his view, the coming into being in 'the created corporeal world' of a beauty resembling that of God and the angelic world. Poverty's coupling with Plenty shows how 'prime matter, needy but capacious and potential ... is desirous of participating in the beautiful forms and perfections' of the divine and angelic levels in the hierarchy of being (*D* 257–8). The Venus whose birth provided the occasion for the generation of Love is not 'the great Venus, i.e. the beauty of the world of intelligences,' but 'the inferior Venus, i.e. beauty imparted to the generated body' (*D* 259).

Pressed now by Sophia for a statement about 'the father and mother of all love in general,' Philo says that 'the father of all love is beauty, and its mother is knowledge of beauty mingled with lack of it.' He reiterates the principle that the beloved is the father in love and the lover plays a maternal role. 'Beauty beloved is the father who engenders Love, and the mother is the soul of the lover made pregnant with the seed of this beauty' (*D* 260). In Pontus de Tyard's translation, the mother's engendering of Love involves both '*congnoissance*' and an '*acte de jouissance.*' 'Love is truly a child of both [parents], taking its material part from maternal consciousness and its form from the father's beauty' (*D* 261). Love is understood not as pursuit and possession of another, but in terms of its purpose, which is generation; it is traced to the instinct for self-preservation that human beings share with other animals (cf. *Sympos.* 206E–8B). 'For as Aristotle says, individual animals, unable to exist perpetually, desire and strive to perpetuate themselves in the generation of their likenesses ... for it seems to each of them that their life passes away, and that the other is that part of oneself that must survive, through which it must be immortal with the continual succession of its likeness.' Philo ends his explanation by describing how the human soul, unlike lesser animals, develops and perpetuates itself: the soul, 'pregnant with the beauty of virtue and intellectual wisdom, desires to engender similar beauties in virtuous works and wise habits, because through the generation of such actions it acquires true immortality' (*D* 261; cf. *Sympos.* 209A). Leone follows Plato in privileging intellectual creativity over the making of babies, but he does not draw the comparison made by Diotima within Socrates' speech, between copulation with women and the intellectual intercourse by which a man who is 'pregnant in soul' can beget children with the help of a beautiful young man (*Sympos.* 208E–9E).

Summing up what she has learned about the union of father, mother, and child in the begetting of love, Sophia notes that love is inseparable from beauty, 'for the father is beautiful, the pregnant mother is the exemplary form of knowledge of this beauty, and the son desired is to be transformed into beauty through delight in union with that which is beautiful' (*D* 262). This observation opens the door to a discussion of universal beauty, which begins and ends with accounts of the love uniting God with divine Beauty, through which the beautiful universe was created and is sustained (*D* 262–95). Through a series of analogies, the marriage of Adam and Eve is eventually linked with the union of sun and moon by which 'everything in the inferior world' is engendered, and also seen as an 'image [*simulacre*] of the sacred and divine marriage of the supremely [*souerainement*] Beautiful and the supreme Beauty' (*D* 293), God and his beloved '*Sapience*' (see *D* 285–92).[10]

While Leone's account of love is structured consistently in terms of gendered pairs with masculine and feminine partners aligned as superior and inferior, the emphasis falls on their blissful complementarity. In the absence of a will to power, there seems to be no basis for a fear that hierarchy might be upset by a reversal of gender roles, with the inferior partner taking the initiative in desire. A conventional alignment of the intellect with masculinity and the body with femininity figures intermittently in the argument, but we have seen that '*congnoissance*' and even '*Sapience*' are attributed to maternal figures, who turn toward the sources of their own form-giving capacity and distribute their beauty and desire in the world below them.

The dynamism of universal love is imitated in the dialogue that Leone stages between Philo and Sophia. Near the end, Sophia takes exception to the flattery she has been hearing, saying that since she obviously lacks wisdom, she is unworthy of being compared to such entities as '*la sapience divine*' and '*la souveraine beauté*.' Philo responds that the beauty and intelligence he admires in her are 'natural,' superior to qualities gained through artifice and effort. He goes on to explain how love transforms its object into something divine. Sophia protests that such love must be an error: 'How without error can such a great distinction and change be made between the thing beloved and its image in the lover's mind, that something human is made divine' (*D* 317)? The question is worth pondering here, since it goes to the heart of Spenser's imaginative strategies throughout his career as a poet, nowhere more subtly than in Book III of *The Faerie Queene*.

Philo's reply describes a natural appetite that he attributes to both men and women. While in a similar earlier passage (*D* 199–201) the lover is male, here both the soul and its beloved are consistently gendered female:

> Our soul, being only a picture [*vne image depeinte*] of the sovereign beauty, naturally desiring to return to its divine source, remains pregnant with a natural desire for this sovereign beauty; for this reason, in another person who is herself beautiful with a beauty corresponding to her own, she recognizes divine beauty, both in her and through her, because this person is recognized as equally an image of divine beauty. And the image of the beloved reveals and reflects vividly, through its beauty in the lover's intellect, the divine beauty, latent and hidden, which is the soul itself ... And the image of the person loved is more adored and reputed divine in the lover's intellect, to the extent that the beauty of its soul and body is excellent, similar to divine beauty, and reflects its sovereign wisdom. (*D* 317–18)

According to this teaching, idealization of the beloved, regarding her as 'divinely born' and more worthy than she knows herself to be, enables the soul to know its own ideal form. Such a spiritual intimacy, in which the self and its internalized Other are both objectified as mirror images, is expected to lead both lover and beloved back to their source in God. Leone is but one of the interpreters of this mode of abstraction and self-knowledge, which was originally and most elaborately articulated by Ficino (*On Love* II viii 57 and VI vi 113–15; see below, 260).

This way of representing the value of a contemplative interpersonal love enters *The Faerie Queene* at several points, but it is not so earnestly pursued there as in the *Amoretti* and *Fowre Hymnes*, where more than once the lover is shown admiring what he knows to be 'the mirror of his own thought.' In *The Faerie Queene*, love is most virtuous when the absent beloved serves as a spur to heroic action, but self-knowledge is basic to Spenser's conception of the moral virtues, and striving for that goal often involves a wish for contemplative relief from the world's snares. Arthur's pregnancy with the image of Gloriana conforms to Philo's rationale for devotion to a 'face divine' even though his princely quest takes him through a world that ironically denies him reciprocation, offering in

Florimell only a fleeting reminder of his dream. But the author himself, detached from his Arthur, seeks his title as a poet by making eikastic images that lead beyond themselves, pointing toward their divine source. The blazons of Belphoebe in II iii and III v are clear instances of such images, and there are many others, the last and most elaborate within Spenser's six-Book structure being the revelations on Mount Acidale.

Louis Le Roy's *Le Sympose de Platon*

The cumulative effect of the Garden of Adonis canto is to stimulate, but only partially to satisfy, what Leone Ebreo calls the soul's natural desire 'to return to its divine source.' This complex intention is at the heart, I believe, of Spenser's 'discourse of Venus,' which refers to several levels in the hierarchical order manifesting being and beauty answerable to the soul's nature. In the Garden canto and in most of *The Faerie Queene*, Spenser focuses upon the conditions of the soul's embodiment, but the horizons of its heavenly origin and destiny are in the background, and are often foregrounded in metaphors. The *Dialoghi d'amore* may have been the immediate source for the Garden canto's program, but for a deeper under-standing of it, and of many significant details in the canto, we should go back to the wellspring, for the Renaissance, of ideas about love, beauty, and the soul's nature, Ficino's commentary on Plato's *Symposium*. For per-spective on Ficino's dialogue, and to assess its own contribution to Spenser's understanding of *The Symposium* and his design in the Garden canto, I will describe first a text closer in time and cultural circumstances to Spenser, *Le Sympose de Platon* (Paris: Pour Vincent Sertenas, 1559).

Robert Ellrodt, who did all he could to minimize the relevance of Ficinian Platonism to Spenser's poetry apart from the *Fowre Hymnes* and a few of the *Amoretti* sonnets, conceded with reference to Louis Le Roy's translation and its encyclopedic commentary that 'Affinities are conspicu-ous. Influence is at least likely' (*Neoplatonism in the Poetry of Spenser* 105). Ellrodt's favourable but perfunctory notice has not prompted many Spenserians to look further into *Le Sympose*, a rare book which should be made more accessible. Le Roy's influence would be impossible to prove beyond a reasonable doubt, since by design his book is, on the one hand, a faithful French translation of Plato and, on the other, a compendium of commonplace ideas, references, extracts from ancient and modern authors in prose and verse, and many unacknowledged borrowings from such predecessors as Ficino, Pico della Mirandola, and Leone Ebreo. Le Roy exceeds his learned predecessors in his range of reference, and he adds accuracy and critical detachment to their scholarship; to a remarkable degree his aims and methods as a commentator on Plato anticipate those of Spenser's most resourceful historicist interpreters, John Hankins and James Nohrnberg. Le Roy's work carries further the trend evident in Leone's *Dialoghi* and the more elegant courtly discussion found in Castiglione's *The Courtier*: in keeping with the principles of Erasmian humanism, while addressing an audience interested in erudition but at ease only in the vernacular, he treats philosophical texts and doctrines as both basic and decorative elements in a culture that is pious and literary. On his title page, the description of his three books of Commentaries puts '*toute Philosophie*' on an equal footing with '*meilleurs autheurs tant Grecz que Latins, & autres.*' (The 'others' include neo-Latin poets such as Poliziano and Pontano, and contemporary French poets such as Marot and Héroet; an appendix contains translations by Jacques du Bellay of passages from the Greek and Latin poets.) Le Roy's book is indicative of the erudition, tastes, and interests to which the Pléiade poets and other French intellectuals were committed, which decisively influenced Spenser's intellectual development.[11] Le Roy's selective borrowings from Ficino, Pico, and Leone Ebreo can help us to understand how Spenser, later in the century, received ideas derived from quattrocento philosophical culture.

A short summary cannot do justice to the rich and varied contents of Le Roy's commentary; I will only provide a few details and account for the principal motifs that organize the book. Leone had transformed Ficino's idealization of homosocial love into a romantic heterosexual agenda; Le Roy carries further the reconciliation of Plato's teachings on love and beauty with the institution of marriage and the practice of courtship. His labours are dedicated to Mary Stuart and the dauphin of France, François de Valois, on the occasion of their marriage: Plato's dialogue 'recommends the honest love which consists principally in marriage, and celebrates perfect beauty, the first model [*patron*] and true exemplar of all beautiful things' (sig. a2r–v). Considering the reputations in England of this married couple and the short life of their union, we can only guess how Spenser and other Elizabethans responded to such pieties.

Le Roy's commentary gives by far the most elaborate attention to Socrates' dialogue with other speakers and his own speech. Book I (fols 1–67v) contains the text of *Sympos.* 172A–97E, to the end of Agathon's speech; the contributions of Phaedrus, Pausanias, Eryximachus, Aristophanes, and Agathon are each carefully elucidated. Books II and III are devoted to a more meticulous and digressive examination of smaller portions of Plato's text: *Sympos.* 197E–209E in Book II (fols 72v–133v) and

209E–12C in Book III (fols 142–80). The last part of Plato's text (212C–23D), beginning with the disruptive arrival of Alcibiades, is omitted entirely from Le Roy's translation; he explains that out of respect for the persons to whom his work is addressed, he has excluded 'what Plato included only for fun, suiting his times and the licentious life of his country' (fol. 180).

Le Roy interprets *The Symposium* as a dialectical progression through the evidence of Love's power in the physical phenomena of the cosmos and human desires, toward the soul's eventual fulfilment in transcendental knowledge of beauty and immortal life. In an 'Epilogue' to Book I, he summarizes the message of the speakers preceding Socrates: 'All the things of this world depend upon Love, and take from him their being and continuance. In the first place this machine – spherical, great, and beautiful – could not last and would not be able to hold together in its entirety without friendship within its inferior and superior parts, which holds the elements in discordant concord.' Love is responsible for the reproduction of all species, and for 'drawing humanity from the savage state into civilization, first by marriages, then by clans and alliances, and afterwards by the communion of writing and language' (fol. 66).

Considering Le Roy's interest in heterosexual love and marriage, it is not surprising that he provides an elaborate commentary on Aristophanes' myth (see fols 42–57v). Right from the start, he reduces the three kinds of humans to 'an androgyne, who was not only man, and not only woman, as we are today, but male and female together' (fol. 42). Following Eusebius's opinion (*Preparation for the Gospel* XII vii) that Plato derived this image of mankind's original form and its splitting into separate sexes from Genesis in the Pentateuch, Le Roy proves the point with several references to the Bible and rabbinical commentaries; Leone is not mentioned but his opinions are included (fols 42–5; see also fols 46v–7). He takes from Ficino's commentary the idea that the essence of a human being is in the soul, not the body, and he mentions briefly the most important themes in Ficino's interpretation (fol. 45v; cf. *On Love* IV ii–v 72–9, discussed below, 252–3).

In subsequent comments (fols 47v–9), the sun, moon, and earth are all assigned roles in the creation of the androgyne, which as a sphere resembles all of them. Here Le Roy's interpretation of the myth is distinctive, differing from Ficino's and Leone's, and it may have contributed to Spenser's variations on these themes in his account of Chrysogone's conception of her twins. The sun is their father ('Great father he of generation / Is rightly cald, th'author of life and light,' III vi 9.1–2), and the moon, 'his faire sister for creation / Ministreth matter fit' (9.3–4), making the earthy matter of Chrysogone's womb fit to conceive.[12] Le Roy's comments on the sun and moon pull together ideas from several sources that are pertinent to Spenser's myth-making lesson in the natural history of beauty. Mentioning Aristotle, Plotinus, Avicenna, and Averroes, and citing Book III of Pico's *Disputationum in Astrologiam*, Le Roy says that from the sun's movement and light in its heavenly sphere, heat is generated which is

> heavenly, of great efficacy and most salutary, penetrating, warming, moderating, enlivening all things; containing the elements' qualities by its simple eminence, as heaven's nature contains all bodies and circular movement contains all other movements. In all living things there is a subtle and invisible spirit, midway between the body and the soul; this is the fountain of life, residing principally in the heart, by which it distributes and expands its powers to visible and terrestrial bodies. This spirit is hidden in seeds, in which divine virtue is stored for bringing things to life and continuing the engendering species in suitable matter. Life, then, consists principally in heat, animating moisture ... Since the sun is the minister of this heat, for good reason we call him author of life, and father of living things. (fols 47v–8)

Le Roy observes that the moon, which receives light from the sun and gives it to the elementary world, can be said to have a 'double nature,' while 'The earth, which receives from all, resembles woman, and is called by some the bowels [*ventre*] of the universe, since in it, as in the woman's bowels, the excrements needed for generation are assembled, and after being warmed by the sun's heat, they conceive, and in time produce their fruits' (fol. 47v). Commenting further on the moon's double nature, he says that the sun and moon together 'do the work of father and mother. The sun furnishes heat, the moon moisture; one the form, and the other, matter. One provides the vital and animal spirits, the other the body and its nourishment' (fol. 48v).

Le Roy has used the occasion provided by a few words in Plato's text to account not only for the generation of human nature in its original form, but for the means by which life continues in all species. Similarly, Spenser uses Chrysogone's 'straunge ensample of conception' as the basis for saying that 'reason teacheth that the fruitfull seades / Of all things liuing' spring to life when 'matter fit, which tempred right / With heat and humour, breedes the liuing wight' (III vi 8–9). Le Roy's explanation of the role of 'vital and animal spirits' is crucial here, considering the importance of the 'spright' or 'spirit' in Spenser's analysis of human nature: its vitality if not its occult presence within seeds and in the blood of animals depends upon the sun's heat and the moon's moisture, which it tempers as a mediating third term.[13] With the soul and body, the spirit constitutes a triad analogous to that of the sun, moon, and earth. While I don't believe that the passage I have been examining supplies germs either sufficient or necessary to account for Spenser's development of his images and themes in the Garden canto, it does put together many significant and suggestive details, useful to an interpreter and possibly, if not probably, among the texts Spenser consulted for insight into *The Symposium* and its myths. The learning and ingenuity displayed throughout Book II of *Le Sympose*, the heart of Le Roy's three-part design, also point in this direction.

Dividing Socrates' contributions in two, Le Roy presents Book II as a reexamination of themes from the preceding speeches, with an emphasis on desire for immortality. His interests are secular, in the sense that he is concerned with experience in this world rather than anticipating the life to come, but Le Roy follows Plato in treating secular matters as spiritual. Introducing Diotima 'to give greater authority to [Socrates'] disputation' (fol. 72), Plato teaches two lessons in the text analysed in Book II. First, Love is not a god but 'a great demon,' and 'the nature of demons mediates [*est moyenne*] between God and mortal men' (*Sympos.* 202E; fol. 86). Le Roy expatiates on the nature of demons and their activity in communication between God(s) and men, in all the priestly arts, and in enchantment and magic (fols 86–92).[14] Many demons are distributed throughout the world below the level of the planetary divinities, and Love's intermediate character, which 'fills the universe,' typifies all of them.

Commenting on Diotima's rejection of conventional ideas about Love as a god (*Sympos.* 201E–2D), Le Roy explains that the ancient poets' portrayal of a god responsible for many miraculous transformations arose from the ignorance of men in those early times. He pays elaborate attention to the iconography of Cupid, adding admonitory moralizations to such attributes as nudity, infancy, blindness, and wings (fols 81–2). 'It would not only be heretical to believe he is God, but a detestable offense to think it, for he is nothing but that which pleases our fantasies. Without necessity, he is the child of our corporeal affections, without which he could not survive, any more than a plant without soil' (fol. 82). Such sentiments would be an appropriate comment on Spenser's description of Busirane's castle; Le Roy's comments precede a selection of poems illustrating Love's attributes, which signify a charming but dangerous irresponsibility. He includes a sonnet by Antoine Héroet (*I'ay veu Amour pourtrait en diuers lieux*, the opening lines of *La Parfaict Amye*, Book I), 12 lines from Propertius on the conventional image of Amor as a winged boy armed with arrows (*Elegies* II xii, *Quicunque ille fuit puerum qui pinxit amorem*), the Greek text of Moschus's *Eros drapetes* ('Runaway Love'), and Clement Marot's French translation of a Latin version, '*L'Amour fugitif*.'[15] All of this poetry is relevant to the occasion that, in Spenser's Garden canto, brings Venus to earth and leads her to the newborn Amoret; so is Le Roy's comment at the end of this segment, on Diotima's classification of knowledge of Love as 'opinion, midway between wisdom and ignorance' (*Sympos.* 202A; fols 85–6). Book III of *Le Sympose* carries the reader on an ascent to wisdom ('*Sapience*,' the transcendental idea of beauty), but Book II examines the realm of opinion, the epistemological equivalent of the ontological space occupied by the *daimon* Love.

Le Roy's commentary on Diotima's myth (fols 93v–100v) cites without attribution ideas found in Leone, among them the observation that Aristophanes' myth of the androgyne accounts for the origin of human love, while Diotima's explains 'the birth of universal Love throughout the world' (fol. 95). According to Le Roy, Plato 'teaches us by this fable that the father of universal Love in the inferior world is that which knows beauty; the mother is a lack of the same. It is necessary that what one loves and desires is first known to be beautiful; that it decays, or is apt to decay; and that one desires to preserve it forever' (fol. 95v). Diotima's statement that love is 'an engendering in beauty, both in the body and the soul' (*Sympos.* 206B; fol. 102), becomes the basis for a distinction between lower and higher forms of pregnancy and child-bearing (*Sympos.* 206C–9E); this striving to perpetuate oneself becomes the second theme of Book II. Le Roy breaks Diotima's lesson in Love's creative capacity into small segments, commenting at length (see fols 105v–35) on different kinds of 'conception and generation,' each of which is a 'divine and immortal work within the mortal animal' (*Sympos.* 206C; fol. 105). Book II ends with Diotima's reference to the many memorials honouring men for the virtues and intellectual achievements that live after them (*Sympos.* 209E; see fols 133v–5). This emphasis resembles the memorial intention enclosed within Spenser's garden of Adonis, and the tribute paid at the end of canto v to Belphoebe's 'ensample dead' (54.9).

It seems obvious to us that Plato invented the exotic figure of Diotima to lend authority to Socrates' argument that begetting metaphorical children in a young man's soul is superior to bodily begetting through marriage; the dialogue appropriates a wise woman's voice to promote a masculinist agenda (see Stephens, *Limits of Eroticism* 29–30). Such thoughts did not cross Le Roy's mind. The idea that men as well as women 'conceive,' both physically and metaphysically, is to him unremarkable. He responds in long-winded comments to Diotima's account of 'generation and conception in beauty' (*Sympos.* 206E, fol. 105) and the reproductive instinct that humans share with other animals, quoting from Aristotle's zoological treatises and Galen, among others (see 105v–24). 'All men [*Tovs hommes*; i.e., mankind] conceive both according to the body and the soul' (*Sympos.* 206C; fol. 105). Le Roy's gloss on this statement discloses his emphasis in this part of *Le Sympose*:

> We conceive and engender children by the body, and by the soul good manners, virtues, laws, disciplines, books. The body has seeds sown in it from the beginning, so that at certain times teeth come to it, hair emerges, the beard increases, and semen flows. If the body is fertile, so much more the soul, and when it is well cultivated, it produces in due time fruit that is nobler and more admirable than those of the body. (fol. 105v)

Le Roy explains the male and female roles in the begetting of children with reference to Aristotle's *De Generatione animalium* (I i–ii: 715a18–25, 716a5–18): 'Some animals are engendered by corruption, others by the conjunction of the male and the female. The male preserves the origin of movement and generation, the woman that of matter; the male engenders in another, the woman in herself' (fol. 105v). From Book II of the same treatise, Le Roy takes the idea of an instinct for self-preservation in a 'sempiternal' existence, which can be satisfied by perpetuation of the species or kind, although not in the substance of an individual (fol. 106).[16] He ends his comments devoted to the preservation of species with a passage from another zoological treatise, recommending the pleasure that comes from scientific knowledge of forms inferior to our own 'eternal part, which is more noble and divine' but not directly knowable.[17] We can understand in these terms Spenser's strategy in the Garden canto, which embeds the origins of exemplary moral natures and of his own poetic genius in a *locus amoenus* crowded with metamorphosing lower forms of life.

In Plato's and Le Roy's discussions of the higher form of love and its engendering of beauty in the soul, the soul's immortal nature is assumed but the stress falls on the creation of lasting monuments here on earth. Le Roy pays attention where it is due to the value of friendship and the bond between a master and his student, but Plato's reference to the 'children' left by 'Homer, Hesiod, and other excellent poets' (*Sympos.* 209D; fol. 127v) justifies more elaborate attention to the importance of writing. 'For if letters had not been found, if the deeds of many centuries had not been recorded in writing, and if these excellent persons had not left their beautiful and useful books to posterity: what would our life be today, in that great obscurity of nature, and human ignorance' (fol. 129v)?

Marsilio Ficino's *De Amore*

I turn now to Ficino's commentary on *The Symposium, On Love*, adding a discussion of the ideas structuring Ficino's way of thinking to the attention given in earlier chapters to a few indications of Spenser's affinities with Ficino. *On Love* should be set somewhat apart from other sources of the lore found in the Garden of Adonis canto. Le Roy's *Sympose* may have been a conduit for that lore, and it serves us as a guide to it, in addition to providing Plato's dialogue itself in a reliable translation; it bears comparison to Landino's commentary on Book VI of Virgil's *Aeneid*. Ficino's treatise was more than a conduit or guide, however; by Spenser's time it had been for several generations a seminal interpretation of motifs from Plato and the Neoplatonists, together with their putative sources in Orpheus and other creators of the *prisca theologia*; it also provided a digest of Ficino's distinctive reformulation of Plato's legacy. In the author's own Italian translation and other vernacular versions, by 1590 it had been published separately in numerous editions; it was known to many courtly and scholarly readers who may not have read *The Symposium* itself, and may not have had other direct access to Ficino's ideas. If Plato's *Symposium* offers an allegorical account of Love's imprint upon the cosmos and the microcosm of human nature, Ficino's commentary provides an authoritative reading of that allegory which defined the terms for later readings.

Ficino's *On Love* and other writings have been cited since 1960 by several interpreters of *The Faerie Queene*, beginning with William Nelson and Thomas P. Roche, Jr; the largest and best-supported claims for Ficino's importance are those of Hankins and Nohrnberg. Some difference with my predecessors will appear in my stress on the programmatic design of the Garden canto and my treatment of *On Love* as an intertext: I will apply the principle of parsimony to the extent of excluding from my account other writings by Ficino, such as his commentary on Plotinus, and other authors, such as Boethius and St Augustine, whose writings contributed to the contextual matrix available to Spenser and his readers. I will argue that where Spenser alludes to an idea available from several strands in the skein of literary and philosophical traditions – for example, the idea that the principles constituting separate species are contained in *rationes seminales*, 'seminal reasons' – the most significant connotations can be thoroughly understood with reference to Ficino.

While Spenserians and students of other Renaissance literature are apt to encounter many passing references to Ficino's treatise, and to individual ideas such as his distinction between two Venuses and two Loves, accounts of the whole text's organization and imaginative integrity are not numerous. Of the few studies of Ficino's thought that focus on the *Symposium* commentary, the best are Michael J.B. Allen's article on the first three Speeches and the role of Giovanni Cavalcanti representing Phaedrus ('Cosmogony and Love'), and Sears Jayne's precise analysis of the dialogue's argument and its fictive method (*On Love* 4–18).[18] They provide the basis for my interpretation, which I have shaped in accordance with assumptions about Spenser's interests in the dialogue during the years of his engagement with *The Faerie Queene*.

We have seen that for some interpreters of the Garden of Adonis, the presence of 'An huge eternall *Chaos*,' within the Garden itself or elsewhere 'in the wide wombe of the world' (36.6–8), presents an obstacle to any idealization of Venus. The commentary's first substantive doctrine concerns Love in relation to Chaos. Commenting on the beginning of Phaedrus's speech (*Sympos*. 178B), Ficino cites Orpheus, as a follower of the theology of Hermes Trismegistus, for the opinion that Chaos preceded the world's formation and Love, 'in the bosom [*sinu*] of that Chaos,' came into being before the world and before the other gods (I iii 37–8). The literal sense of Latin *sinus* refers to the hanging fold of a toga, used as a purse; figuratively, it can mean a hiding place, or a person's bosom, lap, or womb. Ficino's choice of words, then, makes Chaos analogous to the generative and nurturing Venus; Orpheus and Plato offer similar versions of the same truth. The point of this chapter, elaborated throughout *De Amore*, is that Love is *the* worldmaking principle, conferring form and intelligibility upon the primal chaos of existence external to God. 'The Platonists define *chaos* as an unformed world, and *world* as a formed chaos. According to them there are three worlds, and likewise there will be three chaoses' (38): the first world created is the Angelic Mind, then the World Soul, and finally the World Body. In each phase of the emanating order that creates a threefold cosmos, love is an appetite within chaos, beginning with a turning toward God. The process of creation is compared to an eye's turning, in darkness, toward the sun's light; after seeing the sun and being illuminated it can see colours and the shapes of other things (39). Chaos, like darkness and other types of privation, resides eternally within the world just as love resides within chaos.

In keeping with the formation of three worlds in the first Speech, in the opening chapters of the second we are told that all things are created, governed, and perfected 'by the ternary number': the Pythagoreans, Virgil, and Orpheus are called upon to underwrite a trinitarian theology. All is ordered by a threefold movement, flowing from and returning to God; the creation, attraction, and perfection of things is also aligned with the triad of goodness, beauty, and justice or truth (II i–ii 45–7). This ternary pattern is manifested in a fourfold schema, with 'goodness in a single center, but beauty in four circles. The single center of all is God. The four circles around God are the Mind, the Soul, Nature, and Matter' (II iii 47). Dividing the intermediate realm of the world's Soul into two terms here, Ficino distinguishes between *anima*, understood as 'the power placed in the Soul's reason and sensation,' which tends upward, and *natura*, understood as 'the power placed in the Soul's faculty of procreation' (II iii 48–9). In the microcosm, *anima* is 'properly Man' and *natura* is 'an idol or image of Man,' since the latter power is active not within itself but '*in* the mass of the body.' Later, Ficino will be concerned to show how, at the level of *natura*, soul and body are connected by the apparatus of organic spirits (see VI vi 113–15).

Subsequent chapters do not always maintain the distinction made here between *anima* and *natura* (see V iv 89–91), but it should be remembered in connection with Spenser's appropriation of Ficino's cosmology. When he locates in the Garden of Adonis 'the first seminarie / Of all things ... / According to their kindes' (30.4–6), Spenser shows a precise understanding of the sequence of formative principles that Ficino articulates at the end of chapter iii in Speech II: 'Those species we are accustomed to call in the Mind, Ideas; in the Soul, Reasons; in Nature, Seeds; and in Matter, Forms' (49). Ficino's reasons, seeds, and forms are all found in appropriate places in *The Faerie Queene*, in a hierarchically ordered system of representations. 'Idea,' a loan-word with a technical meaning that was still uncommon in Spenser's day, is not in the lexicon of *The Faerie Queene*; ideas per se lie beyond the poem's horizon even in such privileged moments as Redcrosse's experience on the Mount of Contemplation, when he sees 'The blessed Angels to and fro descend / From highest heauen' (I x 56.2–3).

What is present all at once in the Mind as ideas is known as 'reasons' in the course of time, at the level of the Soul. The named personifications in *The Faerie Queene*, with their allegorical 'intendments,' refer to concepts at this level. Reasons are ideas reduced to discursive language; such language connects rational consciousness with the norms by which the world is supposed to be governed. We are briefly shown such reasons in the room at the top of Alma's castle where an anonymous sage (presumably representing discursive rationality, Sidney's 'erected wit') sits in the presence of 'All artes, all science, all Philosophy, / And all that in the world was aye thought wittily' (II ix 53.8–9). The elaborate attention given in this passage to the less stable and trustworthy faculties of imagination and memory (see stanzas 49–52, 55–60) shows both how reason is compromised in practice, and how much Spenser's poetry has to do with an imaginary future, confused by fantastic wishes and fears, and records of past events that may not accord with reason's dictates. The imagination, personified by Phantastes, dwells in a chamber where 'Infinite shapes of things' are depicted, 'Some such as in the world were neuer yit' (II ix 50.3–4). These are the counterparts in a hyperactive consciousness of the 'Infinite shapes of creatures ... / And vncouth formes, which none yet euer knew,' bred in the Garden of Adonis (35.1–2). In both places, the shapes presented to the imagination are insubstantial *semina rerum*, seen in the light of their future-oriented potential as forms embodied in matter. The links between the contents of consciousness and the world's real substance are tenuous, apt to be disrupted. In his description of Phantastes' chamber, as in the scene of Archimago's conjuring (I i 38) which it echoes, Spenser emphasizes the imagination's involvement with 'all that fained is, as leasings, tales, and lies' (II ix 51.9). The Garden of Adonis, on the other hand, shows how a healthy imagination can be nurtured at the source 'Of all things, that are borne to liue and die' (30.5), and involved in the circular movement from creation through an upward-tending attraction to perfection in a return to the source of being.

   In several chapters at the end of the climactic sixth Speech, which analyses Socrates' contributions to the phenomenology of love and beauty, Ficino again describes the orders of being below God, tracing the path on which Diotima leads Socrates (*Sympos.* 210A–12B), from the beauty of bodies to that of the Soul, above that to the Angel or Mind, and finally to God (VI xv–xix 136–45). Once again the angelic Mind is located in eternity, where knowledge 'is motionless, complete, continuous, and absolutely certain.' In the domain of the Soul, by contrast, being and knowledge of being are characterized by 'temporal progression.' 'Plato was right to locate in the soul the first motion and the first interval of time; from the soul both motion and time pass into bodies' (VI xv 136–7; see *Timaeus* 37D–8C). This statement establishes conclusively where Venus and the Garden's progeny, with '*Time* their troubler' (41.1), stand in the total scheme of things. 'The Soul is equally in stability and in motion, and the Body is only in motion ... The Soul has multiplicity of parts and passions, and is subject to change, both in the process of thinking and in fluctuations of mood, but it is exempt from limits of place. The Body, however, is subject to all of these' (VI xvi 139). Spenser's fiction in the Garden evokes the universal and spiritual source of motion and form; it contains *rationes* and *semina* and their potential for mortal life in the natural world that we inhabit physically, while we also inhabit, more or less consciously, the order of things designated by Ficino as Soul.

The second Speech, ostensibly devoted to exegesis of Pausanias's speech in *The Symposium*, includes a substantial chapter on his most famous contribution, a distinction between two Venuses and two Cupids (*Sympos.* 180C–E). In keeping with his division of the created order into three worlds, he locates the heavenly Venus, born of Caelus ('Uranus' in Jayne's translation, following Plato) without a mother, in the Mind as its intelligence; the vulgar Venus, born of Jupiter and Dione, is placed in the world Soul as its 'power of procreation,' virtually identical with *natura* as defined in chapter iii of this Speech. The two Venuses, then, represent the highest aspect of the Mind, a contemplative intellect devoted to God, and the lowest aspect of the Soul, devoted to procreation of beautiful forms in the physical world. When he places Venus in both the Mind and the Soul, and also makes Saturn and Jupiter parts of both worlds, Ficino is devising what may seem a static and artificial structure, but in practice, this ingenious mythologizing suits his interest in mobility and rationality within a spectrum of choices.[19] Saturn personifies being (*essentia*) in the Mind, but in the Soul he signifies understanding of higher things; Jupiter personifies life in the Mind, and in the Soul he is that which moves the heavens. Ficino's analysis of the nature of things in the cosmos and in consciousness is relentlessly twofold, as is Spenser's, with an emphasis more on complementarity than on opposition. Saturn in the Mind and Soul together can be understood as being reflecting on itself; Jupiter, the middle term in the tripartite organization of both Mind and Soul, transmits vitality from its transcendental source to all that is visible: hence Spenser refers to Jove's 'soueraigne see' (III vi 2.7).

In its emphasis on both distinctions and continuities, unfolding and infolding, Ficino's way of thinking profoundly resembles Spenser's. This is nowhere more evident than in the significance he gives to sexual difference, anticipating the 'universal hermaphrodism' that has been identified as a hallmark of Leone Ebreo's thought. Bisexuality is a feature of both the Mind and the Soul, and with the two Venuses personifying first the Mind's highest faculty, contemplative intellect, and then the generative capacity that connects the Soul with matter, Ficino accentuates the presence of feminine entities within the family of gods. A similar structure, of course, organizes consciousness and bodily activity in the microcosm: men and women both contain, at least potentially, two Venuses and two Loves. In both macrocosm and microcosm, reflection on the relationship of Love to Venus discovers another instance of complementarity, if not androgyny: since Venus personifies desire as well as beauty, and according to Orpheus Love is the oldest of the gods, he is related to Venus as both father and son. Together and separately, Venus and Love or Cupid put feminine and masculine faces on the various forms of love and beauty.

The last two chapters of Speech II and the whole of Speech III are devoted to the ups and downs of reciprocal love. Ficino first puts in Giovanni Cavalcanti's mouth an account of the emotional and spiritual bonding of friends such as Damon and Pythias, Orestes and Pylades, not to mention himself and Cavalcanti; this love involves mutual death, regeneration, and growth in virtue (II viii–ix 54–8). Then, in a short exposition of the speech of Eryximachus, the focus shifts to the cosmos, where 'love attracts like to like'; it is 'the eternal knot and link of the world [*nodus perpetuus et copula mundi*]' (see III i–iv 63–8; for the quotations, 65 and 68). The emphasis in these chapters falls on an intellectual love that is homoerotic, not sexual. The same emphasis dominates Speech IV, Landino's interpretation of Aristophanes' myth: the facts of sexual difference and desire are inescapable in Plato's text, but the account of its meaning offered by Ficino does not dwell, as we have seen Leone and Le Roy do, upon the androgyne figure and its splitting as an explanation for heterosexual coupling and the institution of marriage.

Aristophanes' Myth and the Daughters of Chrysogone

I have argued that the impetus for Spenser's adaptation of themes from Aristophanes' myth came from Leone Ebreo's interpretation of it, and proposed also that he may have found some useful ideas and relevant literary lore in Le Roy's elaborate commentary. The allegorical interpretation of the myth that Landino offers in Ficino's dialogue is, by comparison, both simpler and more abstract or obtuse. I will show that in the first half of the Garden canto, Spenser's troping of motifs from Aristophanes' myth pays homage to Ficino's interpretation at the same time that it reconfigures ideas that later interpreters had assembled from patristic, rabbinical, kabbalistic, and hermetic sources around the Platonic androgyne, understood as an image of human nature's primal wholeness. The resonances that Spenser discovers in this mythological material are in part ironic: the innocence in which Chrysogone conceives her twins is preserved up to a point in their upbringing by Diana and Venus, but the splitting that was traditionally interpreted as a fall from grace is part of their story from the start, and although each twin is called 'perfect' at crucial junctures, they are never reunited. The nature of the difference between Belphoebe and Amoret is one of several important themes in *The Faerie Queene* that Ficino's commentary helps us to understand: *On Love* articulates an agenda for the soul's recovery from its fallen state that Spenser represents in his own fashion, while indicating in the conduct of his polyphonic narrative that any reintegration of human nature is bound to be fitful, incomplete, fraught with misunderstandings.

The interpretation of Aristophanes' myth, which Ficino calls 'obscure and involved,' is concise (see *On Love* IV i–vi 71–80) and can be summarized briefly. The first two chapters preserve the attention paid in the myth to the three genders of humanity (*tria genera* in i, *tres sexus* in ii) in its original state. The male creature was born of the sun, the female of the earth, and the 'mixed [*promiscue*]' of the moon. The originally spherical creatures, becoming proud, were punished by division, and the reciprocal love that resulted can lead to the restoration of wholeness and God's blessing of those who worship him piously (71–3). Ficino acknowledges the obvious purpose of the myth as an explanation of sexual desire for one's 'other half,' but he is more interested in a hidden meaning: sexuality is only a metaphor. With no basis in Plato's text, he develops in chapters ii–vi a Thomistic distinction between 'two lights, one innate and the other infused,' that were present together in the original form of humanity and must be reintegrated if the soul is ever to return to bliss. Falling into the divided body, souls retain the innate light by which they perceive 'inferior and equal things,' and in adolescence that light arouses them 'to recover, through the study of truth, that infused and divine light, once half of themselves, which they lost in falling' (73). This rosy scenario, quite different from the plain sense of Aristophanes' bawdy myth, is placed appropriately in the mouth of Cristoforo Landino, the renowned teacher of Florence's best and brightest adolescents.

Landino makes familiar distinctions between the immortal soul and the body, 'perpetually in flux.' 'Man is the soul alone; the body is merely a work and instrument of Man' (IV iii 75), and the innate light should not confine the soul to bodily appetites. Properly educated, 'the natural light shines forth and searches out the order of natural things'; this searching is consistent with development of the cardinal virtues, which involves recovery of the light infused by God (IV v 77). The virtues are all, by this account, derived from God, with Prudence being the basis for the other three (Courage, Justice, and Temperance). The triad of virtues that are reconciled to Love in Agathon's speech (*Sympos.* 196C–D) are linked in the commentary on Aristophanes' myth with the sources of the three original genders: the masculine virtue of Courage (*fortitudo*) is derived from the sun, feminine Temperance is from the earth, and the 'mixed' virtue of Justice is the androgynous child of the moon (IV v 77–8).

Some reference to Spenser's handling of various schematic descriptions of the moral virtues will not be digressive at this point. The importance of the four cardinal virtues within a larger enumeration in *The Faerie Queene* is well known; I believe that Ficino's account was among those to which Spenser paid attention. His thinking does not seem to have been governed by one tradition dominant over others, and several overlapping and different schemas, none of them accounting fully for the scope of the poem, can be seen to confer significance on its structural members and narrative moments. It makes some sense to understand the three-Book structure of the 1590 *Faerie Queene* in accordance with the sequence of Courage / Sun (I), Temperance / Earth (II), and Justice / Moon (III). Book III introduces the androgynous Britomart, and the story of her affiliation with the moon – and with England's once and future sovereign – is not complete until Book V, the Legend of Justice. It could be argued that from the beginning of her quest, to right a wrong as well as to fulfil her desire and her destiny, Britomart is engaged in seeking justice, a complex of private and public virtues that is only partially embodied in Artegall.

Episodes involving Belphoebe and Amoret begin with the epiphany of Belphoebe in Book II and stretch to Book IV; they are not consistently organized by any of the three virtues just mentioned, but other motifs from Aristophanes' myth pertain to the twins' allegorical identities. Spenser's account of Chrysogone's conception of her daughters provides the clearest textual clues to a connection with the terms of Aristophanes' myth and Ficino's interpretation of it. Belphoebe's natal horoscope (III vi 2), shared of course with Amoret, probably alludes to the significances that Ficino assigned to Jove, Venus, Apollo, and the Graces, but these are not spelled out in *On Love*. As noted above in discussion of Le Roy's *Sympose* (see 241–3), when Spenser tells how 'wondrously they were begot' (III vi 6.1) and how this seemingly 'Miraculous' and 'straunge ensample of conception' (8.1–2) agreed with reason and the course of nature, his explanation brings the sun, 'his faire sister' the moon, and earth as the source of 'matter fit' all into the process of generating 'the fruitfull seades / Of all things liuing.' Thanks to the moon's ministry, aided significantly by Jove and Venus, the elements of fire and water, often seen in barren conflicts in Book II, combine in matter that is 'tempred right / With heate and humour' (9.1–4, 8.3–4). The principle of androgyny, important in Plato's text in connection with the moon, and in Ficino's alignment of Justice with the moon, remains in the background of Spenser's narrative, hinted at in the 'double nature' of Chrysogone's single parent, Amphisa. Chrysogone is virtually androgynous, and her virginal singularity aligns her with Diana and the moon. She is prepared for motherhood by bathing 'In a fresh fountaine, farre from all mens vew' (6.6), in a scene resembling that in which Diana and her company are discovered by Venus a little later in the canto (16–19).

Androgyny is only one of the forms that twofold wholeness takes in Ficino and Spenser, and for both of them, duality contains a centrifugal tendency as well as potential for mediation and unification. The two Venuses and their different Loves, tending upward toward God and downward in physical reproduction of beautiful forms, are echoed not only in the androgyne figure but in the distinction between innate and infused virtues, the 'two lights' that figure prominently in Landino's account of the soul's creation, fall, and recovery. In their commentaries, Leone and Le Roy do not follow Ficino's lead in this respect, although the soul's *'double lumiere'* figures prominently in Héroet's 'L'Androgyne,' which Le Roy reproduces (*Sympose* fols 53–7v). Spenser's account of Chrysogone's impregnation emphasizes mediation and harmonious union, and in the balance of the first half of canto vi, the potentially fractious encounter between Venus and Diana ends in agreement at the 'louing side' of Chrysogone soon after her painless natural childbirth.

When he gives Chrysogone twins rather than a single daughter like Una, Florimell, or Britomart (single forms that each give rise to false copies), Spenser builds into his narrative many possibilities for analysis of the different forms that virtue takes. Belphoebe and Amoret are often glossed as adumbrating the divergent orientations represented by Ficino's heavenly and vulgar Venuses (see Roche, *Kindly Flame* 101–3). This is not inappropriate, since Belphoebe is obviously an avatar of nobility and an otherworldly way of life, while Amoret is motivated by the pleasures and anxieties of a more common nature. Belphoebe and Amoret are more completely understood in the light of Landino's distinction between infused and innate virtues. In his allegory of an original integrity, followed by division and the mere possibility of reintegrating the heavenly and natural forms of love, we have a close analogue for the common origin and divergent later lives of Belphoebe and Amoret. The moral that Landino adds to Aristophanes' myth introduces an emphasis on nurture and education that is entirely consistent with Spenser's allegory.

In the opening stanzas of canto vi we are told that Belphoebe, 'this noble Damozell' (1.2), was the firstborn of Chrysogone, who 'bore in like cace /

Faire *Amoretta* in the second place'; the twins 'twixt them two did share / The heritage of all celestiall grace' (4.4–7). These terms, with the attention given to the planetary and elemental influences on their conception, all go to show that the twins share in the harmony of divinely infused and innate virtues. In the climactic stanzas of the preceding canto, before mention of Belphoebe's status as a twin, her chastity had been praised to the skies in entwined images of light and flowering, celebrating the harmonious union of 'heauenly grace' and 'stocke of earthly flesh': this 'perfect complement' combines the two lights of innate and infused virtues, understood as present in the creation of Belphoebe and developed to full vigour 'in her Heroick mind' (51–5) under the tutelage of Diana.

The narrator's praise of the mature Belphoebe, capping his account of Timias's inner discord, sets the stage for the flashback in canto vi to the antique world in which Belphoebe and her twin were conceived and nurtured, one as the exemplar of 'Maidenhead' (v 54.6), the other 'in true feminitee' and 'goodly womanhead' (vi 51.5, 9). Both are said to 'ripen' to 'dew perfection' (vi 3.6–9, 51.3–52.3); each is presented as an 'ensample' to 'Ladies all' (v 54.7–9, vi 52.4–6). Though not equal, they are comparable in beauty and virtue, and Spenser's hyperbolic praises involve them in a kind of sibling rivalry, innocent only because they are ignorant of each other's existence. As noted in the previous chapter, the shift of focus from Belphoebe to Amoret in the course of canto vi works to Belphoebe's disadvantage. We are told that Amoret was presented at court while Belphoebe is sequestered 'farre from court and royall Citadell' (52 and 1.5), but this is disingenuous: we all know who Belphoebe stands for long before any topical allegory is attached to Amoret. Each 'ensample' of feminine virtue calls the other's perfection into question, and when the sisters encounter one another near the end of their stories, the dazed and confused mind of Timias only exaggerates the predicament in which Spenser has placed his readers.

The topical part of Spenser's allegory, prescient in 1590 and still poignant in 1596 when the story of Timias's involvement with both Belphoebe and Amoret was completed in cantos vii and viii of Book IV, could be read as a wish that Elizabeth Tudor and Elizabeth Throckmorton could be sisters under their skin, alike in more than the given names that decisively insert their natures in culture.[20] Such a reading would misconstrue, however, the grounding of Spenserian allegory in trans-historical and transpersonal norms ('reasons,' to use Ficino's term for the conceptual counterpart to the 'seeds' of individual forms). The different capacities that nature and nurture provide for the twins, and the divergent paths on which

they are placed, first have the effect of deconstructing the 'perfect complement' that was represented at the end of canto v in Belphoebe alone; then,
after bringing Amoret to 'perfect ripenesse' as 'th'ensample of true loue
alone, / And Lodestarre of all chaste affectione' (vi 52.1–5), Spenser hints at
the 'sore, / Sore trouble' she will endure (53.5–6) for loving Scudamour.

We see in the second half of Book III how vulnerable Amoret is, lacking
Belphoebe's self-sufficient nobility and finding herself in a world where
love, so easy and prolific in the Garden, is reduced to jealous rivalry. I take
it that Amoret's innate virtues had been fostered in the Garden, in harmony with 'the order of natural things' that supports development of the
cardinal virtues, but that lessons 'In all the lore of loue, and goodly
womanhead' (51.9), could not return her to the other half of her nature. In
the Garden's hothouse environment, Belphoebe's place beside Amoret is
taken by Pleasure, the daughter of Cupid and Psyche. How nice it would
be if this pleasure could be reconciled to virtue once and for all, but
Spenser indulges that recurrent fantasy only to expose it as regressive. His
moral seems to be that like Psyche her teacher, Amoret is obliged to gain
the virtues of Prudence and Temperance through pain and suffering, only
after she has left the Garden's 'seminarie' and placed her chastity at risk in
the marriage market.

Was Amoret mistaken to seek her own perfection in a husband? According to Ficino, who idealizes reciprocal love but not the institution of
marriage, this would be asking for trouble – even 'sore, sore trouble.' As
we have seen, later commentators domesticated the androgyne figure in
the interests of praising companionate marriage: Plato's myth became what
it had been for several patristic and rabbinical authorities, analogous to the
primal union and original sin of Adam and Eve. Using allegorical narrative
as a way of having things both ways, Spenser assimilates that development
while retaining, in the twin paragons of Belphoebe and Amoret, another
way of representing virtue in feminine forms.

The original ending of Book III, with its image of 'that faire *Hermaphrodite*' (xii 46.2), implies that Amoret was on the right path when 'she
linked fast / In faithfull loue, t'abide for euermore' with Scudamour (vi
53.1–4), but even in Book III it is clear that he does not complete her nature
in the way envisioned by interpreters of the Platonic androgyne. Seen in
the terms offered by Landino, Scudamour is mis-educated, limited even
more than Amoret by his body's promptings. When the story of Amoret
and Scudamour is extended and concluded, exquisitely unresolved, in
Book IV, Spenser uses the myth of Orpheus and Eurydice to account for
their dysfunctional marriage: as Eurydice is to some degree responsible for

her accidental death on the day of her wedding, Orpheus is responsible for failing to return her to life.

As many critics have noted, over the course of Book III and beyond Spenser develops Britomart's character as that of an androgyne who learns by trial and prudent avoidance of serious error how to temper the qualities that are seen separately in Belphoebe and Amoret, bringing to her heroic career qualities absent from both of them. But if she is capable of a larger life than Belphoebe, Amoret, and Florimell combined, at the end of Book III in 1590 she is reduced to an envious spectator's role as the young married couple enjoy the fruits of her triumph over Busirane's enchantments, and in the revised version she must soldier on into the next Book even more frustrated. Her androgynous condition declares not perfection, but instability and an ability to surprise us.

In the revised ending of Book III, Britomart is left with Amoret on her hands, 'whose gentle spright / ... was fild with new affright' (III xii 44.6–9), and at the beginning of Book IV, Britomart's behaviour toward her frail companion is called 'fine abusion': she maintains her disguise 'to hide her fained sex the better, / And maske her wounded mind' (IV i 7.2–4). She doesn't persist in her pretence. Coming to a castle that admits only couples, she fights first as a man in defence of Amoret, and then reveals herself as a woman to be paired with the knight she had defeated (9–15). The take-charge attitude that she shares with Belphoebe is essential to her heroic stature, but while Britomart enjoys androgyny, Spenser has fun with her. Revelation of her floor-length veil of 'golden lockes,' in combination with her armour, raises doubts in the castle's crowd: 'Some thought that some enchantment faygned it' (14.5). Amoret, however, can now see through her saviour's disguise and is 'freed from feare' (15.6); the two women can spend the night comparing their experience in love, united by the pain of separation from the men whom they hope will some day complete their lives.

This little episode illustrates Spenser's tendency to vacillate in his treatment of Britomart's gender: he plays for a while with an identity that is enigmatic to Britomart herself, but resolves it finally into terms that Amoret, the lowest common denominator of virtuous femininity, can enjoy in reciprocal friendship. Despite Britomart's embodiment of an androgyne's virtues, she never obtains anything like the rewards that the lovely end of Speech IV in *On Love* promises to the justified soul when it returns to God: 'by a certain love of his own he perpetually kindles pleasure as if new in the soul and renders it blessed with enticing and sweet fruition' (IV vi 80). Such joys may be reserved for Belphoebe; for characters less confirmed in a single life, they belong to a paradisal past or the future's receding horizon. In the conceptual distinctions and recesses that structure Spenser's allegory, the stress falls on complementarity, self-transcendence, and return to unity, but more often than not in the narrative, the centrifugal tendency inherent in dualities creates broken arcs, or circles so large that they cannot be completed.

Daemonic Love in the Gardens of Jupiter and Adonis

In Plato's text, and even more in Ficino's interpretation of the androgyne figure, its association with the moon identifies love with mediation between terms in a hierarchy. For this reason, for Ficino as for Leone, reciprocation in love is crucial: Ovidian and Petrarchan accounts of love as mastery and subjection are distortions, misunderstandings of a dynamic that is active in the cosmos and available to human nature in fulfilment of its innate desire for perfection. Within the domain of the Soul, all movement serves the purposes of mediation and eventual unification of the part with the whole. While Spenser's narrative shows us over and over how powerful Ovidian and Petrarchan preconceptions were for his culture and in his own imagination, Ficino's different way of thinking about love is also prominent in *The Faerie Queene*. An account of Speech VI of *On Love*, interpreting the ideas advanced by Socrates and his interlocutor Diotima, will shed some light on the second half of Spenser's Garden canto, which provides a metaphysical justification for reciprocal love.

As was noted earlier in discussion of Le Roy's *Sympose*, the first thing that Socrates does is to contradict conventional thinking about Love's divinity and idealized traits; Diotima, he says, explained to him that Love is not a god but a *daemon*.[21] Unlike Le Roy, Ficino is unwilling to give up the idea that Love is divine, and he follows Plato in treating the words of Diotima and Socrates as an initiation into 'divine mysteries' (VI i 108; cf. *Sympos*. 209E–10A); in effect, he redefines divinity to include the intermediate realm of daemons. The mysteries arise from Love's place in the scheme of things, 'midway between the beautiful and the ugly, the good and the bad, the blessed and the wretched, god and man.' Ficino explains that just as the soul of a lover 'is obviously partly beautiful and partly not beautiful,' so Love, as a daemon, 'occupies the middle ground between formlessness and form' (VI ii 109). These distinctions set the stage for an extended account of souls and subordinate daemons, on the cosmic scale and in individual human souls (VI iii–x 109–30), and these chapters contain Ficino's exegesis of the myth of Love's birth from the union of Poros and Penia.

In chapter iii, 'On the souls of the spheres and the daemons,' already discussed in part (96–7 above), Ficino presents his rationale for a single *anima mundi* enlivening the world's *prima materia*, and separate souls for each of the twelve spheres. In this chapter, daemons are said to inhabit the sublunary regions assigned to fire, pure air, and humidity, just as men inhabit the earth. Souls and daemons together function as intermediaries in a universe that is full of fine distinctions. 'The gods are immortal and impassible; men are both mortal and passible; daemons are of course immortal but are also passible.' Finding very little difference of opinion between Dionysius Areopagita and Plato, Ficino identifies 'good daemons, who are our guardians,' with Dionysius's 'angels, rulers of the lower world' (VI iii 109–11).

At the end of this chapter and in the next, Ficino conflates several authorities to create a rationale for the transmission of 'gifts,' derived from ideas in the divine Mind, through the planetary spheres and into the embodied souls of human beings. Ficino's doctrine is found in Landino's commentary on Book VI of Virgil's *Aeneid*; it is relevant in turn to the gifts bestowed on Belphoebe and Amoret in their conception, and to other passages (e.g., III v 52–3) in which Spenser gives the soul or some virtue an extraterrestrial source, prior to being 'enraced' in an earthly form. As souls descend from heaven, 'they are wrapped in a special transparent astral body,' and this 'mediating and pure covering' receives from the planetary gods and daemons an imprint of several gifts, varying in accordance with the alignment of planets at the time of the soul's descent. By Jupiter and Jovian daemons, 'power of governing and ruling' is strengthened; from the sun comes 'clarity of the senses and of opinion (whence comes prophecy)'; the moon 'encourages the function of procreation.' With reference to Venus and our 'instinct of love,' Ficino explains why Love is both a god and a daemon: it is a trait 'we have received from the supreme God, and from Venus, who is called a goddess, and from Venerean daemons' (VI iv 111–12).

With such a multitude of influences, susceptible to variation not only at the time of conception and birth but in later life, it is no wonder that love takes many forms in different individuals. Subsequent chapters of Speech VI interpret this variation, making it a matter of choice rather than an inexorable fate inscribed in the stars. The lore that Ficino gathers together would have been available to Spenser from many sources; what makes *On Love* especially significant in connection with the Garden canto is its conflation, in a complex pattern relevant to the distribution of love and beauty through the cosmos, of ideas constituting a *gynecology* as well as an ontology of spiritual love.

Chapter vi, explaining 'How we are caught by love,' describes not only the agency of the astral body in transmitting the soul's gifts from heaven to earth, but the activity of a corresponding organic 'spirit' (the *spiritus* discussed at several points in my earlier chapters) in the process of translating sense impressions into cognition and idealized images. As we have seen, the spirit plays a mediating role in the human body and consciousness, precisely analogous to that given to *demones* in the cosmos.[22] If the soul descending from heaven, carrying divine ideas within itself and reproduced in its astral body, 'finds on earth a seed which is similarly well disposed, the soul then imprints on that seed a third image' (113), which shapes the body's growth into a form ideally suited to the soul's beauty. Ficino describes two individuals, internally similar and destined for each other (Amoret and Scudamour or Britomart and Artegall would be good examples), of whom one, the lover, has a body not so suited to its soul. Admiration of his or her alter ego enables the lover to recover, through the spirit apparent in the beloved, a 'reformed image' that renders visible 'the likeness of its own innate idea' (114). The aim of this process is reconstitution of the wholeness lost when the original forms of humanity were split apart: the lover's innate desire leads, through an infusion from the beloved's gracious presence, to awakened consciousness of both souls' otherworldly origin and destiny. These themes inform the more idealistic references to love's value in *The Faerie Queene*, but Spenser reserves elaborate attention to the upward-tending imagination and intellection of lovers for his *Fowre Hymnes* and a few of the *Amoretti*, where his close reading of *On Love* VI vi can be traced.

Ficino takes up Diotima's account of Love's birth and the traits derived from his parentage in several chapters (vii–xii 115–34) that are relevant to Spenser's description of the Garden of Adonis and its place in the poem's imaginative economy. He begins by explaining that 'the birthday of Venus,' the occasion for a feast in the Garden of Jupiter, signifies the birth of the angelic Mind and the world's Soul 'from the supreme majesty of God'; it was then that the twin Venuses came into being. His interpretation pertains first to the Mind, so '*The garden of Jupiter* means the fertility of the Angelic life,' but the coupling of drunken Poros and devious Penia also transpires in the world's Soul, whose fertility Love transfers to the world's Body. Having first identified the twin Venuses as 'the intelligence in the Angel and the power of procreating in the World Soul' (VI vii 116; cf. II vii 53–4), he also finds two Venuses in the Soul: the 'power of the Soul to understand superior things' reproduces the activity of Venus in the Mind, while 'its power to create inferior things ... is peculiar to the nature of the

Soul.' Both Venuses, with their different procreative capacities (one work-ing internally, the other in matter), bear Loves that are daemons (117–18).

The 'mixed' nature of the androgyne had been derived from the ambigu-ous position of the moon, on the boundary defining soul and body, heavenly and elemental realms. As a daemon, Love possesses a similarly mixed nature, traced by Diotima to his father's plenty and his mother's poverty (*Sympos*. 203C–4B). Having devoted chapter ix to the passions that lovers derive from the mother's side, in the next Ficino discusses the qualities that come from Love's father. The bulk of this chapter (VI x 127–9) explains why Love is called a 'magician [*magus*],' and why '*He is neither entirely mortal nor also immortal*.' The achievements of 'true magic' are 'works of nature,' the magician's art being only a 'handmaiden [*ministra*]' or midwife. Ficino observes that 'the whole power of magic consists in love,' because it draws together things possessing 'a certain affinity of nature,' only perfecting by art what matter has rendered defective. The text identifies several nodes in a network of analogies: as art resembles nature, magicians such as Zoroaster and Socrates resemble the daemons whose friendship confers power upon them. Magic is like agriculture, on the one hand; physical beauty, eloquence, and songs also possess magical properties.

The account of Love's affinity with magic is followed by a discussion of its mixed nature, mortal and immortal, which is continued in subsequent chapters (xi–xiv 130–6). It is essential to Ficino's way of thinking that mortal creatures should contain an immortal potential for life and cogni-tion. As daemons, the two Loves are immortal within us, as in the world's Soul; as a passion, however, love is mortal, changing all the time. Love in its daemonic form, within the individual and communicating with what Virgil called the *Spiritus intus*, marks the boundary between mortal and immortal states, also enabling us to cross that boundary, even in this life. Elaborating upon Diotima's formula for the aim of love between human beings (*Sympos*. 206B), Ficino calls it 'desire for procreation with a beautiful object [*generationis in pulchro*] in order to make eternal life available to mortal things' (xi 130). We desire to preserve our own bodies, and acknowledging their mortality, we produce children; similarly, 'the cognitive part of the soul' seeks, stores, and renews knowledge, and in maturity it procreates by writing and teaching.

'*In all men*,' Plato says, '*the body is pregnant or fertile, and the soul is pregnant*' (xii 132; *Sympos*. 206C). In a passage borrowed by Le Roy in his comment on this line (see 245 above), Ficino comments, 'The seeds of all the body's own things are implanted in it from the beginning.' Similarly 'the soul, which is more excellent than the body, is much more fertile, and it possesses the seeds [*semina*] of all of its own things from the beginning. Therefore the soul long ago was allotted the Reasons [*rationes*] of the customs, arts, and disciplines, and from them, if the soul is properly attended to, it will bring its own progeny into the world at the proper time' (132). The distinction between *semina* and *rationes* resembles that made in the exegesis of Aristophanes' myth between innate and infused virtues. Ficino's *semina* are natural attributes of the body, and of the soul in connection with the body's nourishing and procreation, but the soul's *semina* mature into *rationes* with the benefit of an education that adds grace to the gifts of nature.

Spenser's Garden of Adonis reveals to us the occult source of all the world's mortal species; it locates emergent life forms in a hierarchy of intermediate causes that accounts for the vitality of seeds. Knowledge of such causes was valuable to farmers, gardeners, physicians and chemists, married couples desirous of healthy children, practitioners of natural magic – and fashioners of fictional worlds where culture is integrated with the order of nature. Metaphorically, and more important in Spenser's textual economy, the Garden's fiction accounts for the lives of human beings among the other species, and represents in its natural innocence the sexual appetite that we share with other creatures. To the extent that the Garden's cosmic womb is imagined as present, microcosmically, in the procreative activity of human beings, it represents the inchoate potential, intellectual as well as sexual, of individual men and women.

Spenser grounds human nature and mortality in bodies, but he also shows us something of the process by which the organic soul takes shape and is endowed with its *semina* and *rationes* prior to its being clothed 'with sinfull mire' (III vi 32.7). When he makes the Garden a home not only for Venus and a transfigured Adonis, but for Psyche, Cupid, and Pleasure, and when he makes it the site of Amoret's primary education, Spenser invokes the distinction made by Ficino between the body's and the soul's innate *semina*. All the claims made for the renewable vitality of the Garden's creatures and the life that Adonis enjoys there, 'eterne in mutabilitie' (47.5), remind us of Diotima's rationale for love – the achieving of immortality by bodily or spiritual means. The 'sweet Poets verse' by which Amintas is accorded his 'endlesse date' (45.9), along with the highly allusive character of Spenser's poetry throughout the canto, remind us of the right relationship of poetry to nature. The soul can be pregnant in imitation of the beauty it finds in bodies. To the extent that the entire Garden passage pertains to matters of the spirit and soul, the Garden's vitality is fundamental to an educative program far more complex than Amoret's 'lesson[ing] / In all the lore of loue, and goodly womanhead' (51.8–9); its developing *semina* are metaphors for *rationes* informing the poet's mind and the larger public world of thought and action, for which some of the 'thousand thousand naked babes' (32.3), remembering their antecedents in Virgil's cavalcade of future heroes, are destined.

Like Plato and Ficino, Spenser incorporated a feminine perspective on love, emphasizing reciprocity and procreation over the self-centred alternatives of conquest and failure, within a discourse that remains masculine. The whole interpretive tradition within which Spenser received *The Symposium* privileged soul over body, writing and other arts over childbearing and familial nurturing. In *The Symposium*, however, the difference between the soul and the body, and between the aims of knowledge and an interest in the bonds of love, is less acute than in many of Plato's dialogues; a transcendental orientation remains strong, but Love is represented as an immanent, ambiguous entity, capable of bridging distances and reconciling differences.[23]

Ficino helps us to understand what transpires at the 'double gates' of the Garden at the hands of 'Old *Genius*, the which a double nature has' (31.5, 9). Genius is a daemon: in the Latin Platonic tradition, following Apuleius, the Greek term *daimon* is translated as *genius* (Allen, *Platonism of Ficino* 20). For confirmation and elaboration of this point we can turn to Louis Le Roy's commentary on *Sympos.* 202E–3A. Glossing Greek *daimones*, Le Roy gives two Latin alternatives, *genios* and *Lares*, adding, 'We colloquially and commonly call them "*esprits.*"' Further, according to Philo Judaeus, the same order of creatures were called 'Angels' by Moses (*Sympose* fol. 86r–v). Hesiod's description of *daimones*, in their afterlife, as 'kindly, delivering from harm, and guardians of mortal men' (*Works and Days* 121–5) provides venerable testimony to the kind of spirit variously called daemon, genius, and angel. Le Roy's later reference (fol. 91v) to Hesiod's mention of the four kinds of creatures with souls – gods, daemons, heroes, and men – probably comes from the *Cratylus*, where good men who become daemons after death are termed *chryso genous*, 'of golden race,' and *hero* is derived from *eros* (398B–C). Translating *The Symposium* at 203A, Le Roy introduces a gloss apparently derived from the *Cratylus*: 'We call the man who is expert in such matters *daimonion*, i. e. blessed and wise [*heureux & sage*]' (*Sympose*, fol. 86; cf. *Crat.* 398C).

When we reflect, with ideas from Ficino and Le Roy in mind, on the cyclical processes over which Genius presides – conception and birth, life and death, return and regeneration – and on the heaven-sent conception of Chrysogone's twins, it becomes clear that in both places Spenser is invoking the activity of daemons within what Virgil had called the *Spiritus intus*. The in-between state ascribed to Love as a daemon, *'neither entirely mortal nor also immortal,'* aptly describes Adonis as well as Genius, and not him alone among the Garden's residents: Amintas's 'endlesse date' as a latter-day Adonis should be understood in these terms. And if 'the endlesse progenie / Of all the weedes, that bud and blossome there' (30.7–8), are best understood in Ficino's terms as *semina* becoming *rationes*, each of the 'thousand thousand naked babes' surrounding Genius must be, or must contain, an individual's twofold *daemon*, the seminal principle of love that is both mortal and immortal. The Garden's vegetative species are conspicuously mortal but enjoy a renewable life; the babes are destined 'to liue in mortall state' (32.8), but throughout their cycles of change they retain a soul-like vitality and identity.

According to Ficino and a host of authorities in the Platonic tradition, daemons resemble and communicate with both the organic *spiritus* and the rational soul. In the lore associated with them, they are more independent of bodies than the *spiritus*, yet not destined like the rational soul for immortality in either heaven or hell. They are fully at home, therefore, in myths, in poetry that represents a golden world of possibilities, and in philosophy such as Ficino's that imagines a cosmos suited to the soul's natural appetite for hierarchical order and its eventual transcendence. In *The Faerie Queene*, then, it is fitting that 'Faire *Venus* sonne' and Venus herself should be invoked in the first Proem (3); their aid of the poet can be rationalized by Ficino's teaching that the power represented by Venus and Cupid in the world's Soul extends to individuals in the form of daemons. The Cupid-like guardian angel who protects the exhausted Guyon after his encounter with the demonic figure of Mammon (II viii 1–3) is an even clearer instance of a good daemon.

The last theme in *On Love* that deserves attention is the involvement of daemons, and of Love in particular, in various forms of priestcraft, enchantment, and magic, including the use of eloquence and songs (VI x 127–8). Ficino's emphasis in this passage falls on the magician's mastery of forces inherent in the natural order of things, and this makes it particularly relevant to the Garden of Adonis. He is interpreting Diotima's account of the daemons' activity in all communication between the gods and men (*Sympos.* 202E–3A). Le Roy's comments on the same passage are also relevant. Explaining what is meant by 'magic' (*la Magie*), he says that in the ancient Persian tongue, the word means 'wisdom' (*Sapience*), and a magician is a 'wise man' (*sage*). He distinguishes between *natural* and *supersti-*

tious forms of magic, making a distinction that is more appropriate to the types of magic we encounter in Ficino and Spenser than D.P. Walker's terms, *spiritual* and *demonic*. Of natural magic, Le Roy says that 'contemplating the virtues of inferior and heavenly things, and considering their sympathies and antipathies, it discovers the powers hidden in nature, and putting these with those in due proportion and under a certain constellation, and connecting actives with passives, it produces great miracles naturally.' Superstitious magic, on the other hand, involves 'invocation of evil spirits, which is an obvious idolatry, and has always been prohibited in well-governed republics' (*Sympose* fol. 90). As Allen notes (*Platonism of Ficino* 15–19), Ficino often seems nervous about the difficulty of separating the good daemons or spirits (the 'sonnes of Day' in Spenser's terms) from infernal demons; Le Roy's distinction between mastering 'powers hidden in nature' and 'invocation of evil spirits' solves this problem, although it leaves both the magician's mastery and the agency of nature's occult powers rather mysterious. Not that Ficino is precise in *On Love*, with such statements as this: 'And all nature, because of mutual love, is called a magician' (127).

For a better understanding of the theory and practice of magic, which is beyond the scope of this study, one would have to go to Ficino's *Three Books on Life* and to other treatises, earlier and later, in the tradition to which Book III of *De Vita*, 'On Drawing Life from the Heavens,' contributed decisively. I will end this chapter with a suggestion that at various points in *The Faerie Queene*, most substantively in the Garden of Adonis canto, Spenser invokes the power of love, with the poet's imaginative art as its ally, to reform life by a kind of natural magic. This suggestion will be more cogent if we return to some of the ideas cited in chapter 4 from passages in *Batman vppon Bartholome*. Ficino, Agrippa, and Stephen Batman were interested in properties inherent in the four elements of the sublunary world, and showed a greater curiosity about the power to be derived by various arts from the *quinta essentia* of the 'spirite of the world,' the source of 'all vertue generatiue and of seede.' In line with Ficino's ideas, Agrippa makes the world's Soul and Spirit intermediary between God, in whom all Ideas reside 'by the manner of the cause,' and their mere 'shadowes' in the physical world. This intermediary place 'in the heuens' contains, as we read in *Batman vppon Bartholome*, 'so many seminall reasons of things in the world, as there bee *Idees* or conceites in the diuine mind,' and by the instrument of the world's *Spiritus intus* 'all hidden propertye is spread abroade, vpon hearbes, stones, and mettalls, and vppon liuing creatures: by the Sunne, by the Moone, by the Planets, and by the Starres, higher then the planets' (fols 170r, 173r; see 122–3 above).

The art or science of alchemy (to mention, as Agrippa does, just one form of natural magic) seeks to transform base materials into a purer form by using the 'spirite' that has been separated from matter in which it is most abundant and pure. The aim of this art, according to Agrippa, is to 'ingender and beget a thing lyke vnto' the more perfect, 'those things in the which that spirit is lesse plunged in the bodie' (fol. 173r). Similarly, a fiction that directs us back to the archaic and pure forms of virtuous life (temporally, with reference to paradise and a Golden Age; causally, with reference to ideas or reasons informing imperfect manifestations on earth) engages in a kind of alchemy when it presents idealized images for admiration and exemplary characters for imitation. Of course, most readers of Spenser who have reflected on parallels between his art and that of a magician or alchemist have taken the view that poetry is the noblest form of making; magic, by comparison, is base – the occupation of charlatans and dangerous men who have sold themselves to the devil. As Isabel MacCaffrey puts it, 'The perpetual temptation of the artist is to become a magician' (*Anatomy of Imagination* 254). Spenser supports this attitude to the extent that he stigmatizes practitioners of the magic that Le Roy called 'superstitious'; even Merlin, as MacCaffrey points out, is rendered shady by his 'dubious paternity' and 'ambiguous fate.' I am suggesting, however, that Spenser's persistent interest in parallels and dualities extended to include both parts of the twofold image of magicians and their arts, with the 'natural' aspect of the tradition and its philosophical rationale contributing powerfully to his conception of poetry's nobility and usefulness. If my argument in chapter 3 is plausible and my account of similarities between Ficino's ideas in *On Love* and Spenser's program in the Garden canto is convincing, the poet's worldmaking and the procedures of a magician whose power comes from the daemon Love may be much alike.

chapter eight

The Faerie Queene in 1596 and 1609

For Spenser 'All things,' as we noted at the end of chapter 5, 'decay in time, and to their end do draw.' This line from the Garden of Adonis comments specifically on the law governing 'all that liues' (40.8–9); it issues from a place in which spring and harvest happily coincide, where Time is 'wicked' but losses are made good. Art, typified by magic and by poetry, can be understood as an attempt to contradict, by nuturing sempiternal *semina* and *rationes*, the natural decay in which phenomena are swallowed. Spenser does not, however, set art over nature in *The Faerie Queene*; he makes no claim that either his genius or some quality inherent in his poem can transcend cyclical change. The greatest success he hopes for is participation in the generational 'succession' of species, and also in an office, such as 'poet' or 'sovereign,' that can claim to be sanctioned by heaven, to survive mortality though not to escape the *aevum*. Accordingly, he must accept the 'decay of might' noted in the Proem of Book VI as part of the truth on which his poem's survival depends. Things fall apart in *The Faerie Queene*, more in its continuation than in the first triad, so prodigiously organized, that was published in 1590. Already in 1590, the natural condition is shown to be limited by loss and division; as the poem succeeds itself the reintegration of divided parts, promised from time to time, is repeatedly deferred or denied.

Reflection upon several events and narrative strands in Books IV through VI, and upon motifs in the posthumous *Cantos of Mutabilitie*, will show that the poem repeatedly harks back to the terms for a stable synthesis that emerged in Books I through III, but the disjunctions present from its beginning gain more power as *The Faerie Queene* develops. A doubleness of indeterminate significance runs through that development: as the poem's scope is enlarged to address fundamental social and political concerns, returns to the leitmotifs of an all-embracing order help to hold the poem together and consolidate the poet's position at its centre, but those terms become anachronistic, and the poet's perspective on 'this state of life so tickle' (*Cantos* viii 1.6) risks irrelevance. Where chapter 5 of this study stressed structure and continuities in its account of Spenser's vision of the order of things, this last chapter will offer a few observations, themselves disjointed, on the disjunctions that develop as the poet struggles to remain true to his vision in a world that is less and less to his liking.

The Garden Remembered

Elaborating massively upon William Blissett's remark that 'Spenser is the poet of the second thought' ('Florimell and Marinell' 89), James Nohrnberg observes in *The Faerie Queene*'s second set of three Books 'a continual reversion of the poem to its own antecedents' (*Analogy* 647). Nornberg's account of the analogies linking large and small parts of the whole poem together provides the basis for my comments here.[1] The two triads are most obviously allied in Books III and IV, where Nohrnberg discovers 'a conjugation of the poem with itself.' Spenser's reversion is articulated first in the Proem to Book IV, modulated with an intensifying nostalgia in each of the subsequent Proems, and summed up finally in the *Cantos*. The poet's ability to carry on with his account of the poem's expanding universe of themes, all responsive to conditions in the 'state of present time' (V Proem 1.1), seems to depend on his returning to the source of vitality discovered in a former age, revealed most fully in the Garden of Adonis.

   In the second half of the Garden canto, Spenser had celebrated the inevitability of a return, after death, to the source from which everything must be separated if it is to exist with any semblance of autonomy. The integrity of any form is only temporary, flower-like. In the Proem to Book IV he harks back to the Garden's imagery of roots and flowers, recalling how the most basic form of life flows perennially from stock to scion. He has been provoked to defend his praises of 'naturall affection,' which 'of honor and all vertue is / The roote, and brings forth glorious flowres of fame' (2.3–7). His 'looser rimes,' though they circulate out of his control and may come into the hands of 'fraile youth,' are not to be mistaken for 'weeds' (1.3–9). The reference here to 'glorious flowres of fame, / That crowne true louers with immortal bliss' (2.7–8), seems to be a pointed reference to one of the flowers named in the Garden, the amaranthus, 'incorruptible crowne of glorie' (1 Peter 5:4), associated with martyrdom and with Sir Philip Sidney.

If in some respects his use of images plucked from the Garden is nostalgic, in this Proem Spenser is also revising the distinctions he had made between Venus and Diana, and complimenting Elizabeth in terms parallel to those used in the Proem to Book III: she is not only 'my soueraigne Queene, / In whose chast breast all bountie naturall, / And treasures of true loue enlocked beene,' but she takes the place of Venus as 'The Queene of loue, and Prince of peace from heauen blest' (4). Spenser does not, however, end his Proem on that exalted note: recognizing the Queen's 'high spirit,' he asks the 'dred infant' Cupid to chase from it 'imperious feare, / And vse of awful Maiestie remoue.' As Amoret and the ladies for whom she had been introduced as 'th'ensample of true loue alone' were 'lessoned' in the Garden, Book IV with its additions to the stories of Amoret, Belphoebe, Florimell, and Britomart, is presented to the Queen 'That she may hearke to loue, and reade this lesson often' (5). Considered as an anticipatory gloss on Belphoebe's failure to recognize her twin in canto vii, these lines are poignant and ironic.

In the Proem to Book V, the Garden and other lessons in love are regarded from a great distance. Spenser still treats 'faire vertue' as a 'blossome' (1.4), but the simple innocence of Hesiod's and Ovid's Golden Age, which in the Garden canto was accessible to an erected wit in a place just outside of history, is put back at the beginning of a series of degenerating ages, with 'a stonie one,' the present, added after the classical Age of Iron. The author's outraged sense of right and wrong is still derived from 'the antique vse, which was of yore, / When good was onely for it selfe desyred' (3.5–6), but the time when 'all things freely grew out of the ground' (9.7) seems beyond hope of recovery. The virtue of justice resembles God not in bounty but 'in his imperiall might' (10.2), far above the barren earth, and the poet's 'Dread Souerayne Goddesse' delivers her 'righteous doome' from on high like God (11.1–4). Outside of the Proem, as the opening stanzas of Book V describe the hero's education, the mythical Astraea resides on earth, but once Artegall has grown up and impressed his fellow men with 'his ouerruling might' (8.5), she equips him with a sword of heavenly origin and deserts him, leaving behind Talus, an iron robot whose unattractive character lacks even the ornamental gold that glitters 'In goodly wise' upon Artegall's 'steely brand' (9–12). The pageantry of the river marriage at the end of Book IV had hinted at prosperity in a future British empire, but nothing in these stanzas, or in events that follow in Book V, supports hope that Astraea's return in a new Golden Age is imminent.

Canto i of Book V begins by tracing back to the heroic age, 'In those old times, of which I doe intreat,' not only a love of virtue but 'the wicked seede of vice' (1.2–3); virtue is not, it now seems, a simple love of goodness for its own sake, but a 'heroicke heat' aroused by the dangers that vice presents. Astraea equips Artegall with civilizing skills by causing 'him to make experience / Vpon wyld beasts, which she in woods did find, / With wrongfull powre oppressing others of their kind' (7.7–9). This startling view of nature, brutal in disorder, takes us far from the Garden's menagerie of paramours and lemans, back to the wilderness surrounding Acrasia's bower, where men who have degenerated into animals threaten 'to deuoure those vnexpected guests' (II xii 39.9), the righteous Palmer and Sir Guyon.

The barren and conflictual world of Book V has much in common with the deserts and jungles of Book II, but it is also continuous with the scene near the beginning of Book IV, where we meet Ate, 'mother of debate, / And all dissention, which doth dayly grow / Amongst fraile men' (i 19.1–3). This survivor from Homer's heroic world adds her threats to those posed by Duessa. In addition to making the two hags visible and voluble, Spenser locates their evils in the order of things. To Duessa's witchcraft derived from the underworld of Book I, he adds the secular wickedness that Ate has sown around her house:

> ... all without,
> The barren ground was full of wicked weedes,
> Which she her selfe had sowen all about,
> Now growen great, at first of little seedes,
> The seedes of euill wordes, and factious deedes;
> Which when to ripenesse due they growen arre,
> Bring foorth an infinite increase, that breedes
> Tumultuous trouble and contentious iarre,
> The which most often end in bloudshed and in warre.   (25)

Ate's seeds and the toxins derived from them are antithetical to the vitality and virtuous potential flowing into the world from the Garden of Adonis. Coming late in the poem's parade of witches, Ate points up the difference between the good and evil forms of magic that are active throughout *The Faerie Queene*, also calling attention to the mischievous presence of magical thinking in Spenser's desire to attribute either creative or destructive power to language. Ate is an old crone, but more than that; her looks, her words, and everything about her, allegorically considered, can be held responsible for all sorts of discord. But while the seeds she plants enable her to cause trouble through her surrogates at least as effectively as Errour with her 'vomit full of bookes and papers' (I i 20.6), Spenser does not indulge in the fantasy of destroying her and all her works. He does, however, wishfully invoke the power of 'a God or godlike man' – the 'daimonic man' of *Symposium* 203A – to bring harmony out of discord, citing Orpheus, David, and Menenius Agrippa as opposites to Ate (ii 1–2).

Among the good characters in Book IV, the clearest antithesis to Ate is Agape,[2] whose 'skill / Of secret things, and all the powres of nature' (ii 44.1–2) recalls the recreative capacity of Venus in Book III and anticipates the concord to which the Temple in canto x will be dedicated. Agape's descent to the abyss of Demogorgon and the Fates on behalf of her three sons (ii 46–53) does not entirely prevent strife, but directs it to a good end. (Several episodes in Book IV involve strife within the bounds of civility, which Spenser treats as acceptable and none of Ate's business.) Agape's descent echoes and contradicts the nefarious purposes seen in Duessa's earlier descent to Night on behalf of Sansjoy (I v 19–44), and although the narrator comments, 'this Fay I hold but fond and vaine' (iii 2.1), the mother's interest in her three sons' lives also improves upon Cymoent's overprotective intervention in Marinell's fate. MacCaffrey was right to see in the arrangements Agape makes with the Fates 'a rationalized version of the same principle' expressed in the renewal of Adonis through his union with Venus, 'by succession made perpetuall' (*Spenser's Allegory* 338). In Book IV, the exchange of life for death that Ficino and Leone regarded as fundamental to reciprocal love is articulated with an expanded scope: from the pains and deferred gratifications of sexuality examined in Book III, we move in the Legend of Friendship to an examination of marriages achieved in the context of homosocial bonds.

Although it wraps up, under the aegis of Justice, several stories that began in Book III and provided much of the content of Book IV, Book V does not permanently unite Britomart and Artegall, and it ends with Artegall's labours on behalf of Irena interrupted. Journeying back to their beginning with little to show for their labours, Artegall and Talus seem to be 'captived to the truth of a foolish world,' outnumbered by figures reminiscent of Ate: Envie, Detraction, and 'A monster, which the *Blatant beast* men call' (xii 37.7). Artegall responds to their noisy and poisonous tongues only with silence, restraining Talus and refusing to 'swerue / From his right course,' not in pursuit of Justice but on his way back 'To Faery Court, where what him fell shall else be told' (43.7–9).

The Proem to Book VI begins the sequel to this most ambitious and least successful of the Legends with reference to the poet's own 'weary steps,' but his imagination finds a refuge that was not available to Artegall. Where the overburdened patron of Justice had confined himself to a single 'right course,' the poet contemplates several 'waies ... / In this delightfull land of Faery' (VI Proem 1.1–2). Spenser seems to have found a fresh perspective on the Wandering Wood in which his poem began so earnestly. The pleasures that led back then to 'diuerse doubt' (I i 10.9), even 'dreadfull doubts' (12.4), now provide an epiphany: 'I nigh rauisht with rare thoughts delight, / My tedious trauell doe forget thereby' (VI Proem 1.6–7). But the point of referring back to the poem's beginning is to note a difference in the frame of reference. The Virgilian *silva* haunted by Errour has been replaced, through the maker's 'tedious trauell' and his access to 'learnings threasures,' by a world of words; the material world that Artegall and many other characters experience as their souls' prison also encloses 'the sacred noursery / Of vertue' (3.1–2), open to those who enjoy the Muses' favour.

Echoes from the poem's 'first seminarie' in the Garden of Book III are apparent in everything that Spenser says in Book VI about the Muses' 'sacred noursery,' which was 'deriu'd at furst / From heauenly seedes of bounty soueraine' (3.6–7). Through the Muses' agency, and also in his Queen's 'pure mind, as in a mirrour sheene' (6.5), the poet enjoys access to a mediating daemonic virtue, 'Which though it on a lowly stalke doe bowre, / Yet brancheth forth in braue nobilitie, / And spreds it selfe through all ciuilitie' (4.3–5). As usual, however, in Book VI Spenser descends from his Proem's ideals to evidence in his opening canto of the fallen world's imperfections. In contrast to the 'ripenesse' of a bountiful virtue (Proem 3.9), reminiscent of Amoret's growth 'to perfect ripenesse' (III vi 52.1), we soon learn that Courtesie's *bête noire*, the Blatant Beast, 'was fostred long in Stygian fen, / Till he to perfect ripenesse grew' (i 8.4–5).

Here and there in Book VI Spenser drops hints leading us to suspect his sincerity along with Calidore's. Harking back to the climactic ending of Book IV, he pays tribute to his 'most dreaded Soueraine' as the oceanic source of all virtues, but when he returns on Mount Acidale with an ampler version of the Proem's message, his fourth Grace is no longer the Queen but only 'that iolly Shepheards lasse' (x 16.1), whose 'goodly presence' (12.9), witnessed briefly by Calidore, counters Arthur's dream vision of Gloriana in Book I. When Spenser observes in the Proem, 'But vertues seat is deepe within the mynd, / And not in outward shows, but inward thoughts defynd' (5.8–9), he is only emphasizing a truth borne out by the whole poem, but the dramatic difference between Calidore and Arthur, and the Prince's attenuated role in Book VI, can be correlated with the increasing prominence of the poet's personal voice. As *The Faerie Queene* ends, the enlightened consciousness of 'Poore *Colin Clout*' (x

16.4) is not so much a mirror of splendid complexities in the macrocosm as it is a refuge from its irremediable defects.

Scudamour, Florimell, and the Scope of Friendship

My study of Spenser's representation of the order and vitality of nature would be incomplete without a coherent account of the three cantos at the end of Book IV, which together constitute a set piece expanding upon themes from the Garden canto, and an alternative to the scenario developed in the *Two Cantos of Mutabilitie*. This discussion will include comments on Florimell, in whose character and narrative Spenser doubles and modifies the themes associated with Amoret and Belphoebe, alluding enigmatically to the Platonic doctrine of form and ideal beauty as he does so.

Florimell is introduced before Amoret in Book III, and she provides Spenser's prototypical instance of chaste (and chased) beauty. Although the double truth represented by Belphoebe and Amoret has more to do with Britomart's quest and the Garden at the Book's centre, Florimell and her false double, secular analogues to Una and Duessa, figure prominently in Spenser's anatomy of Book III's titular virtue, Chastitie. That subject inevitably entails its attribute, ideal beauty, and the not-so-ideal desire that responds to it. Over the course of Books III and IV, Amoret and Florimell are interchangeable in Spenser's variations on the theme of feminine vulnerability and yearning constancy in love. The narrator shifts his focus at the end of canto vi in Book III from the 'sore, / Sore trouble' to be endured by Amoret because of her 'faithfull loue' for Scudamour (53) to Florimell's similar predicament, anticipating in cantos vii and viii the captivity of Amoret in cantos xi and xii; the two victim heroines are linked again in a rhyme at the beginning of Book IV (i 1.4–5).

The 'idle feare' and 'vaine feare' (III vi 54.9, vii 1.6) attributed to Florimell while Arthur is chasing her becomes legitimate enough as others lust after her, and it is no longer played for laughs when Proteus becomes her rescuer and does his best to frighten her into 'losse of chastitie, or chaunge of loue' (viii 29–42). Florimell's fugitive virtue is a vehicle for development, outside the Garden of Adonis, of the conflict between a constant lover's ideal beauty and all the threats posed by mutability in the material world. Adonis's bestial adversary and his ill-advised pursuit are both suggested by Florimell's first pursuer, the grisly forester with his 'bore speare' (i 17), who is eventually replaced by the more versatile and persistent Proteus, not only lustful but associated with age and winter (viii

34–5). Thematic connections of Florimell with Adonis are complicated further by the development of her opposite number, Marinell, as an Adonis of the seaside. Over the course of Books III and IV Spenser seems to be unfolding, in the episodic stories of Florimell and Marinell, themes related to the enigmas at the centre of the Garden.

Many critics have interpreted the Platonic allegory suggested by Florimell's unhappy presence, first in the world above and then in a captivity suggestive of Proserpina's fate and her significance in the Eleusinian mysteries. She is compared to 'a blazing starre' (III i 16.5) and seen racing, terrified, through the 'forrest wyde' (i 14.5) to a rustic witch's house, to the seashore, into a fisherman's 'cock-bote' (viii 24.4), into Proteus's hands and finally to his cave 'in the bottome of the maine' (37.1). Florimell's transit from one encounter with crude matter and appetite to another suggests the fate of beauty, and of a pure soul, faced with mutability and eventual death.[3] Florimell's devotion to Marinell, who is virginal but also emasculated, a character associated with wealth redeemed from the mutable world, suggests wishful thinking about a lasting union in love that somehow transcends sexuality and change: is this a study in hysteria? MacCaffrey describes Florimell and Marinell together as 'characters in whom are crystallized certain of those forces we call "natural"' (*Spenser's Allegory* 293), but their behaviour puts fearful resistance to those forces in the foreground. The static beauty of a crystal, a form growing naturally out of inorganic matter, captures well their subject positions as self-absorbed sufferers, immersed in the natural world but separated from its fluctuations. Spenser also encloses the naive natural properties that he attributes to his odd couple in the conspicuous artifice of his poem, offering variations on the secret histories of Achilles and Helen, along with allusions to Ariosto's Angelica and his own Una. Florimell and Marinell are like jewels, unwrapped from time to time in the episodic narrative to catch the light and be admired, then hidden away for use on a different occasion. Their value (i.e., the basis and the scope of their allegorical significance) is only hinted at, as if to encourage speculation.

Seen in relation to her succession of admirers and along with the false *simulacrum* that is so generally mistaken for her, Florimell shows us how interpretation, responding to the demands of desire, confers value upon the forms supplied by nature. (Marinell's predestined suffering, misinterpreted by a mother who is ill-equipped to understand the natural course of love, offers a parallel lesson in hermeneutics.) Florimell's trials and her pursuers' frustrations do not oblige us to conclude that beauty is in the eye of the beholder, but they raise a troubling question: can beauty as elusive as Florimell's ever be known as it is in itself? Florimell may be a better instance than Elizabeth of the 'unreadability' that surrounds the extraordinary women of *The Faerie Queene*.[4] Such considerations as these arise, I think, from the poet's using Florimell and Marinell in a display of his ability to combine several dissimilar and discordant units of significance, some quite simple and others still obscure.

The last four cantos of Book IV make it obvious that, like the quartets whose stories fit neatly into that Book, the four young lovers whose stories began in Book III ought to be considered together. Cantos x through xii will provide, first, the last that we learn of Amoret and Scudamour, and then a contrasting account of the happy ending in store for the other long-suffering pair. Canto ix assembles the audience for Scudamour's story in the next canto, and in its opening stanzas we are given a plain statement of the principles, both illustrated and abrogated in Book IV, by which love leading to marriage is to be tested as Spenser completes the Legend of Friendship and carries its unfinished business forward to the Legend of Justice. 'Hard is the doubt, and difficult to deeme,' he says (ix 1.1), as if to explain his worrying at the inescapable problems of lovers. He cuts through the difficulty: allowing only 'three kinds of loue' to 'dispart the hart with powre extreme' (1.2–3) makes analysis possible, and at least provides useful terms and a developmental sequence, suited both to the exemplary episode of the -mond brothers with Cambell, Cambina, and Canacee, and now to the climactic episodes in the temple of Venus and the house of Proteus.

The first form of love, 'deare affection vnto kindred sweet' (1.5), is supposed to yield to the second, '*Cupids* greater flame' (2.2). The conduct of both virtuous and merely adventurous characters proves that this is the usual course of nature, making Marinell a case of arrested development. The third and highest form of love solves problems arising from the constraints of childish affection or stirred up by 'raging fire of loue to woman kind' (1.6):

> faithfull friendship doth them both suppresse,
> And them with maystring discipline doth tame,
> Through thoughts aspyring to eternall fame.
> For as the soule doth rule the earthly masse,
> And all the seruice of the bodie frame,
> So loue of soule doth loue of bodie passe,
> No lesse then perfect gold surmounts the meanest brasse.   (2.3–9)

This description of 'zeale of friends combynd with vertues meet' (1.7) is problematic as a prelude to the resolution of stories about marriage. Only if married love is understood as a type of 'faithfull friendship,' or if friendship's 'maystring discipline' leads an immature and passionate lover to dwindle into a husband, do the problems become manageable.[5] The ideals of friendship provide a foundation for Spenser's contribution to the emergent discourse of companionate marriage and the courtship appropriate to it, but many of the problems apparent in Book III remain unresolved at the end of Book IV. What is clarified in the concluding cantos, but has not been stressed in most of the attention given to the episodes I will be discussing, is that Spenser reads the ideals informing his vision of a sound social order into his representation of animate nature as a whole, so that 'the band of vertuous mind' (1.8) and 'loue of soule' (2.8), while contrasted to human nature's lower appetites, are grounded in the natural environment.

It is appropriate to ask why the end of the story of Amoret and Scudamour, an ending that is really a blighted beginning, is so hard to square with the orderly world in and around the Temple of Venus which is its setting. After examining the incongruities in Scudamour's story – a lover's boast that may cloak feelings of failure – we can go on to consider how the releasing of Florimell and Marinell from their separate prisons, and the prospect of a marriage in which '*Cupids* greater flame' has done no matchmaking, can be not only inevitable but satisfying. Perhaps the sequence from canto x to cantos xi–xii presents, on a large scale, a pattern that is common in Spenser's narrative: first we are given a false or flawed version of an idea, and then one that completes the idea by setting it in a larger context.

Spenser began Book IV by explaining how, and in part why, Amoret had been imprisoned by Busirane, and that explanation has a bearing on their meeting. First, 'from the time that *Scudamour* her bought / In perilous fight, she neuer ioyed day' (i 2.1–2): the narrator provides in one stanza a preview of canto x, Scudamour's own retrospective account of 'that atchieuement' (ix 41.6), the winning of his shield and purchase of his bride (see x 3). The next stanza in canto i explains how Busirane, using 'that mask of loue which late was showen,' spirited Amoret away. The enchanter succeeded because friendship, shown to both young lovers by Britomart after the event, had failed them on the wedding day. Busirane brought on his entertainment 'whilest euery man / Surcharg'd with wine, were heedlesse and ill hedded, / All bent to mirth before the bride was bedded,' and the bride herself was 'ill of friends bestedded' (3).

Throughout the central Books, one incident after another shows true friendship to be impossible for many characters, and even friends sometimes behave like gang members. Rivalry is the dark side of friendship between men, and women, objectified and unequal, provide occasions for both rivalry and friendship. In the chivalric environment of *The Faerie Queene*, single combat and jousts between teams are elementary forms of social intercourse, and this ritual violence, largely independent of Ate's malignant influence, keeps friendship and antisocial rivalry in an uneasy equilibrium (see Mallette 114–30). There are other signifying systems, of course. As Lauren Silberman points out, 'At the conclusion of Book IV, marriage figures as an alternative to the joust as a paradigm of institutional order and as a figure of textual functioning' (*Transforming Desire* 125). Scudamour's problem, and Amoret's too, is that he imagines marriage not as an alternative to jousting but as a reason for it. This puts his bride-to-be on a par with the elusive false Florimell, the cause of quarreling in canto ii's lesson in 'fayned friendship' (18.9) and again the focus of attention in cantos iv and v, which narrate Satyrane's almost disastrous tournament and the subsequent fiasco, a beauty contest that pits Amoret's 'vertuous gouernment' against the 'beauties wonderment' that many see in Florimell (see v 13–27). There is always some friction between the emotion-laden fabric of homosocial friendship and that of companionate marriage, and just as friendship is vexed by rivalry, marriage may include a struggle for freedom or dominance. These problems are not addressed as directly as we might wish, but they keep peeking out from the interstices of Spenser's fiction.

The Temple of Venus is obviously an addition, in the social world of Book IV, to the goddess's place in Book III, canto vi, but it is dedicated *to* Venus, not inhabited *by* her. Significant details in Scudamour's description and his actions also recall the Bower of Bliss[6] and Busirane's castle, but the principal connection, through the fragmentary story of Amoret's development 'to perfect ripenesse' (III vi 52.1), is with the Garden. 'It seem'd a second paradise to ghesse,' says Scudamour in some amazement: if the souls in Elysium that 'liue in lasting blesse' could see it, they would rather return to live there (23). Spenser must expect us to admire the place and learn from it, but the Temple's mysteries are more commonplace than those of the Garden, and our experience of them is mediated by the self-interested and defensive character of Scudamour, whose recovered memory of his 'hard aduenture' (x 5.1) contains hints that, like Chaucer, Spenser has contrived a tale suited to its teller and not to be taken at face value. The Temple, however, with its environs and inhabitants, is a speaking picture presented for our instruction and delight, over against the incongruous perceptions and actions that declare Scudamour's character.

Scudamour's experience in the outer precincts of the island containing the Temple of Venus deserves our close attention. The Temple will be a feminine space, but in the park-like pleasaunce that impresses him as 'a second paradise,' Scudamour finds exemplary men enjoying enviable intimacy and 'endlesse happinesse' (28.4). Some men are joined by women: first he sees 'Sweet springs, in which a thousand Nymphs did play' (24.3), then 'Delightfull bowres, to solace louers trew' (24.7), and then a periphery of 'walkes and alleyes dight / With diuers trees ... / And therein thousand payres of louers walkt' (25). Then, set apart from these nameless thousands, suggesting that Scudamour has shifted from wish-fulfilling reverie to a more substantial vision of the afterlife earned by heroes, he sees 'another sort / Of louers lincked in true harts consent' (26.4).

Of these exemplary friends, who 'on chast vertue grounded their desire' (26.6), six pairs are named; there are no married couples in 'endlesse happinesse ... / That being free from feare and gealosye, / Might frankely there their loues desire possesse' (28.4–6). From this lovely scene Scudamour must ruefully tear himself away. As he moves on, 'forst to seeke my lifes deare patronesse' (28.8) elsewhere, he shows himself to be one of the 'envious have-nots' that Harry Berger has discerned at many junctures in Spenser's poetry. As usual in *The Faerie Queene*, passage through an earthly paradise involves profound ambivalence: anyone is apt to envy 'endlesse happinesse,' but if it is unearned it must be unreal, and useful only as a reminder that 'Much dearer be the things, which come through hard distresse' (28.9). Stanza 27, filled with famous friends, locates them all in antiquity. Although their 'loues decayed neuer' (27.9), they were without issue: they are 'history.' While friendship between men retained great cultural significance in the Renaissance and Reformation, it was seldom celebrated as a heroic enterprise. Founding a family or continuing a noble lineage was far more significant and fraught with greater anxiety, as was the still uncharted territory of companionate marriage. It is appropriate, then, that Scudamour should devote much more precise attention to the famous 'louers lincked in true harts consent' than to the multitude of cozier domestic partners (not to mention the twenty rivals for his shield that he polishes off in stanza 10), but his future lies within the Temple of Venus.

The form and force associated with the Temple's two presiding maternal figures, Concord in the porch (31–5) and the statue of Venus 'Right in the midst' of 'the inmost Temple' (37–47), are 'antique' in the sense Harry Berger has given to that term (*Revisionary Play* 195–202). No single source or tradition explains them, but the speech of the physician Eryximachus in *The Symposium* (185E–8E) provides a *locus classicus*. In keeping with a medical tradition that guided practice from pre-Socratic times to well after Spenser's day, health and well-being are said by Eryximachus to come from the cultivation of concord and mutual love, which are found not only in the human soul, but by seeking harmony and avoiding discord between the opposite principles that define the cosmos. Love of the proper sort, noble and honourable, is basic to piety and good happiness. 'For what is the origin of all impiety? Our refusal to gratify the orderly kind of Love, and our deference to the other sort' (*Sympos.* 188C). Speech III of Ficino's *On Love*, devoted to Eryximachus's speech, caps the contributions of Giovanni Cavalcanti to the dialogue. It begins by summarizing themes that are important to the Temple of Venus, and to Book IV of *The Faerie Queene* as a whole: 'First, that love is present in all things and extends through all things. Second, that he is the creator and preserver of all works that are according to nature. Third, that he is the master and lord of all of the arts' (*On Love* III i 63). Rather than emphasizing the difference between orderly love and 'the other sort,' Ficino enumerates in this short Speech the many ways in which reciprocal love is prolific (see *On Love* III i–v 63–8, and cf. Le Roy, *Sympose* 27v–37v).

There is a harsh justice in Berger's observation that Scudamour's story 'is a fragmented and arbitrary collection of episodes'; I take this failure of Concord to be indicative of Scudamour's character, and also typical of the culture in which he was seeking his place. When Berger goes on to say, 'The mind which creates and then submits to the Temple of Venus closes down too quickly on experience' (*Revisionary Play* 201), he may himself be closing down too quickly. Compared to the Garden canto, as poetry and as an articulation of ideas about love the Temple canto is second-rate, but it is also, by design, secondary and supplementary. The virtues of the place are not vitiated by Scudamour's incongruity within it. As the acme of 'all that nature by her mother wit' and 'Art playing second natures part' can create (21.6–9), the Temple and its environs are more complete than the Garden, but also a cooler world, in which the lines dividing Self from Other are clearly drawn. Spenser is setting the scene for passage through adolescence into adulthood, and from the bosom of family life into society, which for Amoret is represented by 'Faery court' (III vi 52.7) and its resident matrons. Scudamour's world, the imaginary 'wide kingdome of loue' enjoyed by Cupid (42.7–9), is larger than Amoret's but his place in it is indistinct; he has no mentor, master, or mission beyond himself, and his interest in Cupid and Amoret can be understood in that light.

Concord's management of the sibling rivalry between Love and Hate (32–6) addresses in optimistic terms the instability of the self and the world that Scudamour must negotiate. He sees himself compelled like other creatures to obey Cupid but also seeks to exercise power in his own right. This is the reason, I take it, that he notes Cupid's absence from the 'flocke of litle loues' around the statue of Venus (42): he wants to take Cupid's place, in a move roughly symmetrical with the adoption of Amoret by Venus. Scudamour finds himself in the company of 'Great sorts of louers piteously complayning' (43.2), and the Lucretian hymn declaimed by one of them (44–7) directs his attention to the source of all that Cupid 'enioyes / ... with Lordly sway' (42.7–8). Here, more explicitly than in the Garden canto, the 'discourse of Venus' is presented in some tension with the imperatives of masculine will and wishful thinking. Anthony Esolen's analysis of Spenser's language in comparison to Lucretius's discovers internal tensions within the hymn: 'At virtually every opportunity Spenser overgoes Lucretius in celebrating the wildness of love's power ... Yet many of Spenser's alterations show his commitment to the un-Lucretian principle of divine control' ('Spenserian Chaos' 42–3). To modify Berger's point: Spenser's mind, and even more that of a scion like Scudamour, can often be seen 'closing down' on experience in some impatience, but with the author this can sometimes be understood as a capacious mind's response to the threat of sensory overload.

It should be borne in mind that the figure of Venus, introduced by Scudamour as 'the Goddesse selfe' (39.1), is not Venus but a statue that 'in shape and beautie did excell / All other Idoles, which the heathen adore' (40.1–2). Scudamour marvels at its workmanship as well as at the mystery of androgyny that is said to be 'The cause why she was couered with a vele' (41.1). His own attitude involves idolatry, most suspiciously when, having taken Amoret by the hand, he watches 'the Goddesse face / ... for feare of her offence' (56.1–2); throughout, he behaves as if he were in the presence of Venus herself, and there is some bad faith in his reverence. When he adds, 'Whom when I saw with amiable grace / To laugh at me, and fauour my pretence, / I was emboldned with more confidence' (56.3–5), I think his audience is supposed to be amused, but not to favour his pretence, which is either self-delusion or poetic licence. Spenser is reminding us here, as in his borrowing from Lucretius, that according to Plato and Ficino love 'is the master and lord of all of the arts' (*On Love* III i 63 and iii 66–8; *Sympos.* 187A–8D), and Venus has been honoured in art through the ages. The Venus who steps into Spenser's poem and meets Diana in the Garden canto also comes from culture, not nature uninterpreted, but the Venus in this Temple is much further removed from the *vis generandi*: her glassy statue and the costly altar on which it stands, both man-made, typify the 'discrete, self-centered parts' that Berger (*Revisionary Play* 201) rightly finds antithetical to the actual dynamics of love in the cosmos and society. This is a 'discourse of Venus' that betrays its source in masculinist rhetoric.

The knot of personified abstractions that contains Amoret and anatomizes the virtues in which she has been indoctrinated is significantly placed 'at the Idoles feet apart' (48.7). If Venus and her Temple are artificially 'antique,' Amoret and her several duennas are incongruously early modern, not yet free of medieval trappings. Amoret is described vividly enough, 'Shyning with beauties light, and heauenly vertues grace' (52.9), in clothing reminiscent of Una's garment when she is presented to Redcrosse by her father (cf. 52.4–7 and I xii 22.6–9), but as Elizabeth Fowler points out, 'personification allegory ... serves to dissipate rather than to collect Amoret's agency' ('Failure of Moral Philosophy' 58). A technique that worked well enough in the House of Holiness and the Castle of Alma, where character-building abstractions are seen from the point of view of the character being instructed, is tricky when the narrator's stance is unsympathetic. In his argument with Womanhood (54) Scudamour has all the good lines, and the coquette described in stanza 57 ('She often prayd, and often me besought, / Sometime with tender teares to let her goe, / Sometime with witching smyles') may not be all that unhappy to be separated from her caretakers, but she cannot have 'her wished freedom.' Scudamour's behaviour as a suitor belongs in a fabliau or the rustic subplot of a comedy. I wouldn't go so far as to call his impatience 'rape,' but his earlier admiration for 'louers lincked in true harts consent' (26.4) condemns in advance his desire, at the climax of his adventure, to possess 'so glorious spoyle' (55.9). Theresa Krier is right to argue that if Amoret is ever to grow up, the Temple's 'maternal *protectiveness*' must yield to 'a vigorous and healthy invasion' (*Gazing on Secret Sights* 146–7), but Scudamour uses his shield too aggressively, to frighten rather than to defend his chosen companion.

Either as a sign of Scudamour's limitations or because the poet himself was poorly equipped to record her subjectivity, Amoret is seldom more than a name and a sweet, hapless thing, a place-holder among the legendary good women of *The Faerie Queene*. Did Spenser, for whom the figure of Orpheus (Scudamour's self-image in x 58) is supremely important, think so little of his Eurydice? Amoret comes to life only in her friendship with Britomart. But if Amoret is colourless, denied agency and intelligible subjectivity most of the time, Florimell provides a vivid parallel to her character: strange and simple, but vivid. Some of her aura is derived from the narrator's melodramatic responses to her perils and pains, for which he assumes some responsibility. When Spenser shuts the door on Scudamour's Temple story and its audience, he shifts away from the mysterious disappearance of Amoret to show a guilty interest in Florimell, who like Amoret at a comparable point in Book III has been languishing 'In bands of loue, and in sad thraldomes chayne' (IV xi 1.5). The mutual love that eventually flowers and flows between Florimell and Marinell plays variations on the original ending of Book III, with Proteus in Busirane's place and Cymodoce a go-between less heroic than Britomart. Spenser's returns to earlier themes are never repetitive, however; Florimell and Marinell do not melt together as the other pair did in 1590; that is done for them, on a scale far grander than anything imagined by 'that rich *Romane*' for 'his costly Bath' (1590 III xii 46.3–4), by the rivers that join in the sea east of London, Penshurst, and the home base of England's naval power. (Gordon Braden, 'riverrun: An Epic Catalogue' 37–8, interprets the marriage site's geography.)

The plenitude that Spenser celebrates with lovely pageantry in the river marriage consolidates the claims made for Venus's sovereignty in canto x: summarizing the 'endlesse worke' of 'the flouds in generation' and his own attempt to 'recount' those present for the wedding feast, he says, 'Therefore the antique wisards well inuented, / That *Venus* of the fomy sea was bred; / For that the seas by her are most augmented' (xii 1–2). The alliance between Venus and Neptune that was important in Virgil's *Aeneid* – their love opposing Juno's hate – is crucial now to Spenser's sense of England's past and future. As already noted, in his first appearance Proteus has much in common with Adonis's boar, but at the end of Book IV his house becomes a marine extension of the Garden of Adonis, a place of renewal, reminiscent of the origins of both natural forms and cultures, ancient and modern.[7] As Florimell is the secular adumbration of Una, the pageantry of canto xi recalls the springtime festival atmosphere that greets the victorious Redcrosse and surrounds his unveiled bride-to-be (I xii 3–23).

Seen in relation to the pageant in canto xi, Spenser's handling of Florimell's reconciliation with Marinell is not without its incongruities. His emphasis on pity rather than desire as a basis for love and marriage seems stranger to us, no doubt, than it did to Elizabethan readers. 'But ah for pittie that I haue thus long / Left a fayre Ladie languishing in payne' (xi 1.1–2), the poet says when he takes up the narrative strand dropped in canto viii of Book III; of Florimell's need for a miracle he mourns, 'it inly pitties me' (1.9). This is awkward; the emotion seems inauthentic, and Silberman aptly observes that Florimell's 'fictional jailer' jangling his keys resembles Busirane when he 'pens' Amoret (*Transforming Desire* 126–7). Spenser betrays some ambivalence toward Florimell as an instance of the feminine Other. Like Gloriana, she is made mysterious by being omitted from representation, and the easy but empty availability of the false Florimell renders her absence more conspicuous.

Scudamour's story had been a Chaucerian experiment in ventriloquism in which the speaker remains wooden and all too predictable; with Marinell, who in Book III had been a character even more frail than Scudamour, Spenser attempts a surprising series of adjustments in which the male lover, while remaining comically weak, refracts the reader's and even the author's relationship to his text. We are told in Book IV that Marinell 'despysd' Florimell (xi 5.2); in Book III it had not been clear that he knew of her existence. He has been stuck in that stage of adolescence with which we see Guyon struggling, at which Arthur rides out to his dream encounter with Gloriana. Marinell is much less vital and vulnerable than Arthur, and the poet now reproves in him a 'pride' that he did not fault in his Prince (5.5). He was humbled, we are reminded, by Britomart's 'cruell stroke' (5.8), and Cymodoce, slow to find a surgeon for his wound, is quick to 'retain' her son when he returns to health. He is being prevented from becoming a man. Time passes as slowly for him as it does for Florimell, and the ageing boy who finds himself outside her prison in canto xii is happy to be away from home, having suffered 'long time ... / There with the Nymph his mother, like her thrall' (7.5–9). Marinell is excluded, however, from the feast that Cymodoce and the other sea-born immortals enjoy:

> But for he was halfe mortall, being bred
>   Of mortall sire, though of immortall wombe,
>   He might not with immortall food be fed,
>   Ne with th'eternall Gods to bancket come;
>   But walkt abrode, and round about did rome,
>   To view the building of that vncouth place,
>   That seem'd vnlike vnto his earthly home:
>   Where, as he to and fro by chaunce did trace,
> There vnto him betid a disauentrous case.   (xii 4)

Marinell's 'halfe mortall' nature resembles that of Achilles, and also of Aeneas; come to think of it, he is like any of the progeny of Venus and Adonis. His position as a solitary, somewhat alienated listener, overhearing a complaint that turns out to be intended just for him, resembles the reader's position as Spenser intends it in his nondirective, overdetermined text. That position is also, as the reader may have learned by this late stage in the narrative's unfolding, a relationship to the flow of natural events through time, both circular and progressing toward an end, capturing individual lives and resolving lesser things in greater.

What Marinell hears in Florimell's complaint is pathetic; it would be less instructive if it contained more truth. While not denying Florimell a virtuous victim's status, Spenser makes her monotonously self-absorbed, not 'the paradigmatic psychotic' that Marinell has been called (Bellamy, *Translations of Power* 198), but a match for him, with an indefinitely renewable commitment to 'her wretched case' (8.9). Hope that 'griefe may lessen being told' (6.3) carries Florimell forward. A conviction that 'greedy seas doe in the spoile of life delight' (6.9) is well founded in her individual experience, but it has been elaborately contradicted in the preceding canto, and by the narrator's comment on his effort 'to recount the Seas posterity: / So fertile be the flouds in generation' (xii 1.7–8). As a witness to 'The manner of the Gods when they at banquet be' (3.9), Marinell knows that Florimell is wrong about life but right about him. The narrator comments that, having been 'toucht with soft remorse and pitty rare' (12.5), he submits to Cupid's 'maystring bridle' (13.6); 'Then gan he make him tread his steps anew, / And learne to loue, by learning louers paines to rew' (13.8–9). Under Cupid's discipline, Marinell has learned to read, and he proceeds to discover in himself 'the author of her punishment' (16.3). Spenser quickly makes his delicate condition desperate again: he loses himself in melancholia (17–18), and

> Being returned to his mothers bowre,
>   In solitary silence far from wight,
>   He gan record the lamentable stowre,
>   In which his wretched loue lay day and night,
>   For his dear sake, that ill deseru'd that plight: (19.1–5)

I don't suppose that Marinell has literally become a poet, but the suggestion is present in 'He gan record,' along with a hint that his painful musings on Florimell's ill-deserved plight remain pitifully self-absorbed.

Mother's intervention is necessary before the lovers can be freed from their separate prisons and brought together, with Proteus's claim on Florimell set aside by Neptune. Cymodoce first asks '*Apollo* King of Leaches' (25.4) to bring the heavenly light of reason to bear on Marinell's illness, which is found to come from 'some inward thought': the dark and watery underworld that Cymodoce and her son share with Proteus, promoting regressive, willful, and secretive behaviour, opens to reveal 'loue ... that leads each liuing kind' (25.9), and Neptune equitably affirms that principle when he grants Cymodoce's suit. She shows that he can claim Florimell 'by high prerogatiue,' rejecting a selfish claim in order to benefit others: 'So shall you by one gift saue all vs three aliue' (31.9). With her fear of fate and love set aside, Cymodoce is not losing a son but gaining a daughter, and the triad of 'vs three aliue' faintly resembles the reconciliation of Venus with Psyche and Cupid. Neptune's judicial resolution to the problem posed by Proteus looks ahead to Book V, and not only to the marriage that will be performed there with little ceremony (see V iii 1–3), but to the internecine rivalries, troubling Book V even more than Book IV, that make true justice impossible to sustain for any length of time, as Theresa Krier has shown in her discussion of canto iii in Book V (*Gazing on Secret Sights* 191–6). The enlarged perspectives on self-centred lives that are achieved at the end of Book IV go beyond not only the possessive desires of Scudamour and his fellow men; they also transcend defects in the social order that the code of friendship can neither repair nor avoid, since its one-on-one bondings and emphasis on competitive testing tend to commodify women and break society down into rival factions.

The gathering at the house of Proteus projects a vision of capacious order that is based in mutable nature but includes history, stretching back to mythic origins and obscurely including the future. This vision is utopian, and 'primitive,' as it is termed by Berger (*Revisionary Play* 195, 202–14), in the way that most utopias are primitive. I will have little more to say about canto xi, which has already been brilliantly discussed by others, but a few points deserve emphasis in the context of this book's argument, in preparation for closing remarks on Spenser's final representation of the natural order in the *Cantos of Mutabilitie*.

The utopian tendency of the entire *Faerie Queene* is nowhere more apparent than in the last two cantos of Book IV, and this serves Spenser's dialectical purposes, since Book V will be the poem's most dystopian part. And it would be wrong to conclude, as I think Berger tends to do in his account of primitivism in *The Faerie Queene*, that the poem's darker truths correct the lighter ones. In Spenser's world, the mirror image of Yeats's, foul needs fair. Like other Elizabethans, and more thoughtfully than most, he was alive to images of the Golden Age and devoted to the possibility of its return, in perennially useful fictions if not in a thorough transformation of the brazen world. In this connection, a passage from E.M. Cioran's reflections on the myth and its history is apposite: 'Suppose we put an end to such speculations: total stagnation would ensue. For we *act* only under the fascination of the impossible: which is to say that a society incapable of generating – and of dedicating itself to – a utopia is threatened with sclerosis and collapse' (*History and Utopia* 81).

The cosmogonic myths and cosmological scenarios articulated in *The Faerie Queene* could be described as a continued allegory of hierarchy and its discontents. In the marriage canto this enterprise becomes, as Silberman puts it, 'a full-scale exploration of fluidity as an intellectual paradigm' (*Transforming Desire* 126). With no room for a full-scale exploration of this paradigm, alternative to the vertical axis on which most of the poem is organized, I will focus on the first part of the procession, since for Spenser first principles contain all that follows. 'First came great *Neptune* with his threeforkt mace, / That rules the Seas, and makes them rise or fall' (xi 11.1–2). Kathleen Williams was the first to note that in the 'poetic theology' developed by Pico della Mirandola, Neptune 'presides over Generation.'[8] The idea applies to large and small cycles in the natural world (the lives of Florimell and Marinell and all that they imply), and to world-historical events such as the course of empire. In Aeneas's account of the fall of Troy, the city is 'Neptunia Troia' (*Aeneid* II 625), and as Anchises' son moves toward the founding of Rome, Neptune and Venus are linked in opposition to Juno (see *Aeneid* V 779–826). In *The Faerie Queene*, similarly, Neptune adds strength to designs sponsored by Venus.

The procession led by Neptune and Amphitrite continues with 'the royall issue ... / ... sprung by lineall descent' (12.6–7). These sons, mighty and dreadful, include founders 'Of puissant Nations, which the world possest' (15.1–2), among whom Albion, 'father of the bold / And warlike people, which the *Britaine* Islands hold,' is singled out for extended comment (15.8–16.9). Albion's battle with Hercules in France exemplifies the rough justice and the long views of the good over which Neptune presides:

> there his mortall part by great mischance
> Was slaine: but that which is th'immortal spright
> Liues still: and to this feast with *Neptunes* seed was dight.   (16.7–9)

Next after Albion comes an important pair whose presence establishes the radical difference between Neptune's reign and Jove's, which is hierarchical and therefore open to the subversive challenge mounted by Mutabilitie.

> Next came the aged *Ocean*, and his Dame,
> Old *Tethys*, th'oldest two of all the rest,
> For all the rest of those two parents came,
> Which afterward both sea and land possest: (18.1–4)

On the august authority of Orpheus, Natalis Comes makes Ocean 'the father of rivers, of all things living, and of the gods' (Hankins, *Source and Meaning* 229–30). The genealogical myths associated with Ocean and Neptune, and their silence on the matter of succession (which becomes more significant and ugly when land is being claimed), allow Spenser to portray the titanic and the newer race of rulers as at peace with each other: power flows between them untroubled by repression and resentment.

Ocean and Tethys, revered and contemplative in their roles as *éminences grises*, don't so much rule as enjoy 'the pleasures of merely circulating.' Their positions as the primal sovereigns are consolidated by their off-spring, and those children can be seen through Spenser's ambiguous syntax as both possessing sea and land and being possessed by it – and by their immortal parents (cf. Berger, *Revisionary Play* 205–6). Ocean and Tethys are not, like Neptune, held responsible for bringing power-hungry heroes into the world; the one person named as their direct descendant is '*Nereus* th'eldest, and the best' (18.5). He is 'expert in prophecies' and foretells the fall of Troy (19.1–7). Spenser does not mention the shape-shifting ability that he shares with Proteus, describing him rather as a source of civility, 'Most voide of guile, most free from fowle despight, / Doing him selfe, and teaching others to doe right' (18.8–9). In Nereus, power takes the form of true and useful knowledge. He may be regarded as a mask or ego ideal for the poet who provides, in the ensuing stanzas, a catalogue of the rivers who accompany the Thames and Medway to their marriage (stanzas 20–47), and the old man's goodness is seen, transformed, in the perennially youth-ful beauties of his daughters 'the Sea Nymphs' (48.1), whose mellifluous names and attributes provide Spenser with an occasion for his most musi-cal poetry (stanzas 48–51). The whole pageant, a merging of ancient and modern cultures within nature, complements the marriage of the traits Spenser associates with his groom and bride, who are well glossed by Quint: the Thames represents the poet's 'historical moment' while the Medway brings to it 'the presence of consecrated nature' (*Origin and Originality* 159–61).

Mutabilitie and the End of Nature

The *Two Cantos of Mutabilitie*, Spenser's final display of his genius for visionary retrospection, involve the entertainment of creative energies that we would recognize more readily if they were not veiled in a figure opposed to virtue and subject to repression. The dialectical tension of prolific and devouring forces is evident throughout *The Faerie Queene*, and not only represented but theorized. In the *Cantos* it is articulated elaborately, synoptically, and too obviously for some tastes (Berger, *Revi-sionary Play* 267–8; Teskey, *Allegory and Violence* 176–7), but with a distinctively Spenserian vein of irony that complicates both the claims of Mutabilitie and the 'doome' of Nature, also revealing Jove's 'imperiall see' (vii 59.7) to be a narrow perch, little more than a vantage point. The *Cantos* meditate for one last time on the predicament of human life, both social and solitary, within time's covenant, in circumstances that impose mortality and obscurely anticipate an immortality beyond the limits of nature.

The thoroughness and brilliance of existing commentaries on the *Cantos* provide my essay with a foundation and enable me to make it short. Recent interpretations, especially that of Gordon Teskey, call for a response that integrates the best new insights with older ones that are in danger of being forgotten. I regard Nohrnberg's account of Mutabilitie and the *Cantos* in relation to *The Faerie Queene* in six Books (*Analogy* 735–91) as the best part of his immense tract; it forms the basis for much that I will have to say. Nohrnberg provides a lucid and suggestive account of Mutabilitie in relation to an array of traditional figures within Spenser's poem and its context: Demogorgon, Night, Nature, Fortune, Strife, Momus, and Folly (737–53). Stepping free of the conventional thinking that the poem's deceptive rhetoric occasionally supports, according to which Nature and Mutabilitie are opposed like good and evil, right and wrong, he identifies the two personifications as 'differentiations out of a single theogonic principle.' Although one points toward Chaos, the other toward Eternity, they are 'related to each other dialectically' and can be understood, in part, in terms of 'the ancient pattern of Demeter-Kore' (741–2).

Seen in this light, the scapegoating of Mutabilitie that Berger discerned in the opening gambit of the *Cantos* (*Revisionary Play* 248–51) is a self-correcting exercise, more subtle than the representations of Errour, Night, Duessa, and Ate (grotesque fantasy figures who are only superficially similar to Mutabilitie). If Nature and Mutabilitie are understood dialectically, we can do without absolutes, accepting the gathering on Arlo Hill as somewhat larger in scope but no less fluid than the pageant that moves through the house of Proteus. The precise relationship of Nature to the God of nature can remain enigmatic, and references to 'Him that is the God of Sabbaoth hight' in the poem's final lines will involve, more clearly, a leap of faith beyond the poem's horizon. Also, the post-heroic character of the human world over which Mutabilitie and Jove contend, in which Nature presides as nurturer and arbiter, becomes poignantly clear. The virtue of Constancie to which this 'parcell' of a Legend is ostensibly dedicated can be found in nature, but it is more fully articulated in the poet's voice, interpreting all things as they bear upon the lives of georgic labourers in a land no longer enchanted with chivalry. When Spenser laments that through Mutabilitie 'we all are subiect to that curse, / And death in stead of life haue sucked from our Nurse' (vi 6.8–9), he voices the superstitious fear of an English colonist that in a savage environment even the pure race will decay, but his text asserts, even in its 'vnperfite' state, that a fuller life survives his death.

The *Two Cantos of Mutabilitie* encompass and reflect not only upon several themes developed without closure in the six Books of *The Faerie Queene*; they also deal with leitmotifs in the history of Western natural philosophy and metaphysics. Gordon Teskey has said provocatively of Spenser 'that he was not primarily a narrative poet but a poet whose main concern was to think' (*Allegory and Violence* 174), and I tend to agree with him. Teskey observes that, like Nietzsche but as 'a quiet apostate,' Spenser was 'preoccupied with the metaphysical authority of visual forms' (175). For my own argument's sake I will suppose that in the *Cantos* he was thinking about this passage from Plato's *Timaeus*, about the value of the sense of sight:

The sight of day and night, of months and the revolving years, of equinox and solstice, has caused the invention of number and bestowed on us the notion of time and the study of the nature of the world; whence we have derived all philosophy, than which no greater boon has ever come or shall come to mortal man as a gift from heaven. (47A–B, trans. Cornford)

Further, in connection with Mutabilitie's assertion, 'But all that moueth, doth mutation loue' (vii 55.8), with its corollary in Nature's finding of fact, 'that all things stedfastnes doe hate / And changed be' (vii 58.2–3), he may have been thinking about Aristotle's distinction in the *Nicomachean Ethics*, at the end of his discussion of pleasure, between that enjoyed by 'a simple nature,' such as the divine Unmoved Mover, and human nature:

There is no single object that continues to be pleasant forever, because our nature is not simple but contains another natural element, which makes us subject to decay ... If there is a being with a simple nature, the same action will always be the most pleasant to him. That is why the divinity always enjoys one single and simple pleasure: for there is not only an activity of motion but also an activity of immobility, and pleasure consists in rest rather than in motion. But 'change in all things is pleasant,' as the poet [Euripides] has it, because of some evil in us. For just as a man who changes easily is bad, so also is a nature that needs to change. (1154b20–30, trans. Ostwald)

Beginning with the pre-Socratics, the phenomenology and the moral implications of motion and change were knotty topics for thought in philosophy and poetry. (In our culture, with its plethora of technological and discursive means for examining, manipulating, and abstracting motion and change, it may be impossible to recover the forms that such preoccupations took in earlier cultures, with little more than words at their disposal.) It is partly in this connection that Lucretius, Ovid, and Boethius have been cited in interpretations of the *Cantos*. Aristotle's opinions on these topics were clear-cut but not determinative, and we should not be surprised to find Spenser pondering them. Aristotle's preference for rest over motion and for simplicity over complexity fell under scrutiny in the sixteenth-century critique of received opinions. Although he may have been ambivalent about the issues and the unsettled outcome of that critique, Spenser participated in it, nowhere more clearly and extensively than in the *Cantos of Mutabilitie*. Hence the relevance of Giordano Bruno's dialogue, *Lo Spaccio della bestia trionfante* (1584), which has long been recognized as at least remotely analogous to the *Cantos*.[9]

Bruno's *Spaccio* does not repay study as a source for Spenser's ideas or their narrative vehicle in the *Cantos*, but it remains a relevant intertext with something to contribute to historicist interpretation. Spenser was almost certainly aware of Bruno's controversial opinions; I expect that he was familiar with some of his writings, and stimulated or provoked by them in ways we cannot hope to recover. Different as they were, temperamentally and as participants in diverse discourse communities, Bruno and Spenser sometimes invoke similar principles. A committed Spenserian cannot read Bruno without some queasiness, however: he seems devoted not to plenitude, as Spenser was, but to excess, and his rhetoric, sometimes breathtaking in its daring, is more often either bewildering or boring. Bruno's *Spaccio* belongs with Lucretius's *De rerum naturae*, Ovid's *Metamorphoses*, and Boethius's *De consolatione philosophiae* in the context for the *Cantos of Mutabilitie*, but its most telling intertextual relations with the *Cantos* differ significantly from those explored in my discussion of the Garden of Adonis canto and the tradition of commentary on Plato's *Symposium*. Bruno's dialogue adds resonance to our wonder at Spenser's achievement, but its relevance is mostly ironic – usefully, I believe, since Spenser's own ironies are easily missed or misunderstood.

In Bruno's physical and moral cosmos, the changeable conditions that

Spenser treats as potentially catastrophic are treated enthusiastically; they constitute the point of departure in a systematic exercise of satire, demythologizing, and reform. Describing his scenario in the 'Explanatory Epistle' that dedicates the book to Sir Philip Sidney, Bruno says, 'We here, then, have a Jove, not taken as too legitimate and good a vicar of the first principle and universal cause, but well taken as something variable, subject to the Fate of Mutation' (*Expulsion* 75). He attributes to this well-intentioned but comical figure some pieces of his own sublime knowledge: 'one infinite entity and substance' contains 'infinite and innumerable particular natures (of which he is one individual)'; although all individual composites undergo change and will cease to be, both 'the eternal corporeal substance' and 'the eternal incorporeal substance' remain independently; there is also, within each individual, 'an efficient and formative principle,' the cause of growth and the eventual ruin of the organism; 'this principle ... that substance which is truly man,' is rational, and is rewarded or punished by a just Fate in a succession of bodily lives, in accordance with its behaviour 'in the immediately preceding condition and lot' (*Expulsion* 75–8). Chastened by this knowledge, Jove undertakes to produce new heavens and a new earth, putting virtuous abstractions in the places occupied, on conventional maps of the heavens and in the minds of superstitious humans, by various beasts and other detritus of a decadent mythology. The rationale for this reform is given in the Epistle (79–88), and it is discussed at length in a series of dialogues conducted by Sophia with several interlocutors.

Bruno's starting point in the dialogues closely resembles the conclusion supported by Mutabilitie's evidence, 'But all that moueth, doth mutation loue' (vii 55.8). We enter a conversation already under way: Sophia says to her ephebe Saulino, 'So that if in bodies, matter, and entity [*ente*, better translated as 'being'] there were not mutation, variety, and vicissitude, there would be nothing agreeable, nothing good, nothing pleasurable' (89). She goes on, 'Labor does not please except in the beginning, after rest; and unless in the beginning, after labor, there is no pleasure in rest,' and Saulino adds, 'If it be so, there is no pleasure without an admixture of sadness, since in motion there is the participation of that which satisfies and of that which wearies'; this leads to some comments on the wisdom of Cusanus's idea, 'coincidence of contraries' (90). Such shrewd, Montaigne-like reflections on experience season the dialogues. Bruno's rejection of Aristotle's opinions on pleasure and on change is evident from the start, and as the figures of Jove and other planetary divinities are fleshed out, the conventional distinction between a mutable sublunary world and an immutable supralunary one, an article of faith elaborately supported by the Aristotelian tradition in philosophy, is utterly disregarded. Bruno goes far beyond Ovid in treating the classical pantheon as projections of an anthropomorphizing culture, out of touch with the truths that once animated its fables and captivated by the falsehoods on their surfaces. Also, to the extent that mutability is represented as motion in the continuum of time and space, his account of events in both heaven and earth tends to break down Aristotle's distinction between violent, unnatural motion and that required by teleological thinking, for which Bruno has no use.

Bruno's cosmos may be de-centered and de-mythologized, but it is not normless. The place of the Christian God is taken by Fate, enigmatic but rational; the ways of Fate and Fortune, together with the old pantheon, are subject to interpretation by Sophia in the name of ideal truth and virtue; Nature is an intrinsic norm unifying all existing phenomena. In the first part of the first dialogue, Venus is introduced (with a free translation of Lucretius's opening lines) as 'she who alone governs the nature of things, and by virtue of whom everything prospers under heaven' (98), but in Jove's response to her it soon becomes clear that Venus, along with Jove, is the ageing symbol of a more mysterious vitality. That mystery is fully described in the middle of the last dialogue: Jove explains to Momus why the Egyptians, whom Bruno regards as the founders of religion and mythology, made idols and adored their divinities in bestial forms. Having debunked myths and idols, Bruno now takes a more paradoxical and dangerous position; magical practices and heterodox views from the hermetic and kabbalistic traditions enter the argument, for the purpose of renewing faith and restoring an awareness of God's presence in the world. Jove tells Momus, 'You know that animals and plants are living effects of Nature; this Nature (as you must know) is none other than God in things.' Saulino adds emphasis to Sophia's narration of the heavenly colloquy: 'So, *natura est deus in rebus*' (235). After providing a rationale for the Egyptians' and the Greeks' polytheism, and for the confusion of Paul with Mercury and Barnabas with Jove (Acts 14: 11–18), Sophia tells Saulino, 'You see then that there is one simple Divinity found in all things, one fecund Nature, preserving mother of the universe insofar as she diversely communicates herself, casts her light into diverse subjects, and assumes various names' (238). The divinity discovered in nature is, of course, the *anima mundi*, Virgil's *Spiritus intus*, revered sometimes as Isis, celebrated in poetry and myth-minded philosophy as Venus and Jupiter.[10]

That Bruno's *Spaccio* is relevant to the *Cantos of Mutabilitie* should be apparent from this selective survey of the dialogue's contents. It presents, idiosyncratically and with a rashness that led, famously, to a trial and burning for heresy,[11] ideas that Spenser is apt to have encountered in various other contexts. Bruno's *Spaccio* and Spenser's *Cantos* may both owe something to Sperone Speroni's 'Dialogo della Discordia,' in which the personification of Discordia paradoxically maintains, in an argument with Jove that is refereed by Mercury, that Jove's *imperio*, originally hers, should be returned to her. Mercury declares near the dialogue's end that Discordia is 'Nature's first-born, mother of the heavens, genetrix and conservatrix of the universe.'[12] The popularity of Speroni's collection (Fournel cites seven editions between 1542 and 1558, and a French translation published in 1551) goes to show that the theme he shares with Bruno and Spenser was not inherently scandalous; everything depends on its treatment. The relationship of the *Cantos* to the *Spaccio* resembles that of Donne's 'Nocturnall uppon St. Lucies Day' to Spenser's *Epithalamion*: in each instance the later work presents not variations on the themes of its predecessor, but the poetic equivalent of a musical *canone inverso*, taking the given subject in a contrary direction. While Donne's purpose could be called deconstructive, Spenser's is, as usual, recuperative: as he says in his first stanza, after alluding to Mutabilitie's 'cruell sports' and 'many mens decay,' 'Which that to all may better yet appeare, / I will rehearse that whylome I heard say' (vi 1.5–7). In these lines, as often in Spenser's allegory, the aim of making deep truths more apparent exists in some tension with an attempt to put the best face on things.

It would be difficult to summarize, even in many more pages than remain at my disposal, everything that eventually becomes apparent in the *Cantos*. I will focus on the figure of Nature and her 'doome,' closing with some thoughts on the poet's less-than-total satisfaction with it. Spenser's Nature is more elaborately clothed in tradition than Bruno's, and the evidence presented before her preserves the orderliness of a memory theatre where Bruno's unfolds unpredictably, neither representing nor explaining the relationship of decadence to fecundity throughout the universe. While in his substance and style Spenser constructs a conservative response to Mutabilitie's challenge, we will see that he also accommodates much that Bruno and other sixteenth-century innovators had contributed to the renewal of natural philosophy and the emergence of a modern world view.

Although Nature presides over a cosmos that is hierarchically ordered, she herself (both masked and revealed, it would seem, by the feminine gender that Spenser applies to her androgynous figure) is characterized by the coincidence of opposites and by dialectical tensions rather than higher and lower parts. She never possesses the simplicity that Aristotle attributed to divinity. Each adjective applied to her requires another, and each pair, another pair; she is described twice (vii 5–7, 13.1–4). Her speech as well as her person is constructed out of contrasting, even contradictory terms, 'yet being rightly wayd' (vii 58.3) they complete the account of a complex whole. As soon as she has fully revealed the fate of her domain ('But time shall come that all shall changed bee, / And from thenceforth, none no more change shall see'), she vanishes, 'whither no man wist' (59.4–5, 9). Her disappearance beyond the reach of language comments upon the horizons of the vast poem that her 'doome' draws to a close.

To reiterate James Nohrnberg's point about the dialectic that links together Nature and Mutabilitie, yet requires that at the end of the day they must be distinguished: Nature points ultimately toward Eternity, while her 'daughter' (vii 59.1) harks back to her origin (Nature's origin, too) in Chaos. We have seen at several junctures in this study that Spenser regards Chaos and anything close to it in nature's signifying chain with fascination, usually with horror. As others have already explained, Mutabilitie makes an elaborate show of respect for Nature, but if her revolt were to prosper she would dethrone Nature as well as Cynthia and Jove. Mutabilitie's claim to be the legitimate heir to the Titans overthrown by Jove reduces his claim to a conqueror's rights, but in the last analysis, her winsome ways mask an appetite as horrid as Saturn's, with his reaching hand and devouring maw.[13] Nature recommends temperance and content-ment with a limited domain, consistent with the bureaucratic character of Jove's regime, 'For thy decay thou seekst by thy desire' (59.3). As we have seen, desire and decay, dialectically entwined, constitute a deep theme in Spenser's work – perhaps the deepest and the most pervasive. To say that he reflects upon it obsessively tells half the truth; we must also recognize how prolifically his imagination responded to the limits imposed upon human aspirations, from within this nexus as well as from the censoring voices of authority figures.

Nature's response to Mutabilitie's evidence of her power begins with a finding 'that all things stedfastnesse doe hate / And changed be' (58.2–3). The emphasis here on 'hate' is striking; Mutabilitie had said to Jove, just before turning back to Nature, 'But all that moueth, doth mutation loue: / Therefore both you and them to me I subiect proue' (55.8–9), and it is this language that the poet echoes in his last stanza: 'For, all that moueth, doth in *Change* delight' (viii 2.6). Nature is a jealous mother, unwilling to admit that her creatures might love another woman, and her opinion contradicts the poet's earlier portrayal of Love as stronger than his elder brother, Hate. I take it that the heavenly bodies are included here in 'all things' and 'all that moueth'; this is consistent with Mutabilitie's preamble to the evidence she presents to Nature: 'For, heauen and earth I both alike do deeme, / Sith heauen and earth are both alike to thee' (vii 15.6–7). In thus representing heaven and earth as alike, and all things caught up together in centrifugal desire for change, not for rest, Spenser goes a long way toward accepting Bruno's vision of a cosmos in flux, with everything in heaven and earth made of eternal substances, shaped from within by mutable formative principles.

Accepting Mutabilitie's evidence of instability and a pervasive hatred of 'stedfastnes' is only Nature's beginning, however. She argues for an understanding of change as both cyclical and progressive, moving toward perfection at the end of time:

> yet being rightly wayd
> They are not changed from their first estate;
> But by their change their being doe dilate:
> And turning to themselues at length againe,
> Doe worke their owne perfection so by fate:
> Then ouer them Change doth not rule and raigne;
> But they raigne ouer change, and doe their states maintaine.   (58.3–9)

Nature's judgment on behalf of 'all things' answers both Mutabilitie and Jove, who had defended his sovereignty with a claim that the planetary divinities 'poure that vertue from our heauenly cell, / That moues them all, and makes them changed be' (48.6–8). Jove promotes the idea that he and his regime reign over Time, not within it, but Spenser's poem and the traditions on which it draws do not support his vanity. Mutabilitie, also known as Change and Alteration, captures much of the emotional significance borne by Time throughout *The Faerie Queene*, and Nature now adds a final emphasis to a principle implied more than once in the gathering for the marriage in Proteus's house (see above, 286–7, and IV xi 15 and 18): in nature, if not in human society, the sovereign is an artificial person, representative of his or her subjects, ruling in rather than over them. Time, Mutabilitie, Jove, and Nature have no being external to the domain they claim to govern; they are no more real, by themselves, than the 'author-function.'

The scholarship of Hankins, Nohrnberg, and others has explained well enough Nature's claim that in the course of time the 'first estate' of things undergoes 'dilation'; moving through their natural cycles they 'worke their owne perfection' (Hankins, *Source and Meaning* 287–93; Nohrnberg,

Analogy 729–30, 748). Nohrnberg observes that what is said of the cosmos is proven true of the poem; 'Nature emerges at that point where the poem has become an objective order in its own right, and can speak for itself' (*Analogy* 760). One implication of Nature's speech calls for further discussion: even though she finds a disconcerting 'hate' within them, she confers a self-determining power upon the innumerable parts of the world system, mentioning only 'fate' as their superintendent until such time 'that all shall changed bee' (59.4). Just as quietly as she invokes the Platonic doctrine of a 'great year' concluding at the end of time, when all things return through their different cycles to the positions defining 'their first estate,' Nature describes a universe like Bruno's, where all things are unified and governed not from the top down but from the inside out. Nature does not ratify Jove's claim to a 'vertue' by which the heavens rule things on earth; Mutabilitie's response, that his 'secret powre' is no more than a pretence (49), remains to be taken seriously. Although the narrator comments, 'So was the *Titaness* put downe and whist, / And *Ioue* confirm'd in his imperiall see' (59.6–7), Jove's power has been reduced to oversight, with Mutabilitie granted dominion in the world below the moon.

The two valedictory stanzas – one astringent, one ecstatic – give equal time to Mutabilitie and to Nature's promise of 'stedfast rest of all things firmely stayd / Vpon the pillours of Eternity' (viii 2.3–4). The poet appears unimpressed with the orderliness of the pageant offered in evidence of Mutabilitie's power, and the last two lines of Nature's speech prompt him to dilate upon it in a proleptic vision transcending the scope of her judgment. By contrast, in the first stanza's thoughts on 'this state of life so tickle,' we seem to be once more – as when the poet imagined sailing for the continent, leaving Harvey with nothing but his name, or when he made his poem a ship and was eager to reach harbour – at sea in a none-too-stable vessel (a 'ticklish' boat is one easily upset). Hence the desire for 'stedfast rest,' turning at last to imagining the kind of pleasure Aristotle attributed to simple and divine natures.

That Nature's account of the orderliness of her kingdom receives scant attention at the poem's end should give us pause. Intelligent critics have seen in Mutabilitie's own evidence a refutation of her claims; a few have doubted Spenser's willingness to admit into the poem any real threats to Jove's or Nature's sovereignty. We must let Spenser be Spenser, and his need to assume control limits his representation of disorder. It was within his character, I believe, to find Mutabilitie 'vnworthy ... / Of the Heav'ns Rule' (viii 1.3–4), and yet to be unsatisfied by Nature's reading of 'all things else,' which delivers the quotidian world from Mutabilitie's 'sway' and Time's 'consuming sickle' (viii 1.5, 9) only in a future when 'none no more change shall see' (vii 59.5). Nature's double negative here, followed by her vanishing act, has the effect of a total eclipse at midday.

The cold comfort offered by Nature requires an adjustment in the poet's point of view. He has schooled us well, in all the parts of *The Faerie Queene* examined in this book, in the taking of long views, but we should remember that the ground beneath Spenser's feet in this posthumous publication differs from that occupied in 1590 and 1596. After Nature's vanishing, the poet voices impatience with the fictional mode and the mass of cultural lore that his imagination had sustained – that had sustained him in turn – for so long. In the splendid order surrounding Nature on Arlo Hill, in the diverting story accounting for Diana's desertion of the district, and most of all in Mutabilitie's dilatory pageant, we are given both antidotes to anxiety and occasions for ennui. The wheels of the gods grind slowly, and Nature's wheels, disposing of the gods as anything more than appealing metaphors, grind exceeding small. The tableaux vivants of miniature human lives included with Mutabilitie's sequence of seasons, months, and other units of time (vii 28–46) pay tribute to georgic labour and patience but not to any form of intense experience, either self-defining or self-transcending. Such a disenchanted world invites detachment, even disgust. In their appended two stanzas, the *Two Cantos* have much in common with Yeats's poem 'The Circus Animals' Desertion,' even more with 'Meru':

> Civilisation is hooped together, brought
> Under a rule, under the semblance of peace
> By manifold illusion; but man's life is thought,
> And he, despite his terror, cannot cease
> Ravening through century after century,
> Ravening, raging, and uprooting that he may come
> Into the desolation of reality:
> Egypt and Greece, good-bye, and good-bye, Rome!
> Hermits upon Mount Meru or Everest,
> Caverned in night under the drifted snow,
> Or where that snow and winter's dreadful blast
> Beat down upon their naked bodies, know
> That day brings round the night, that before dawn
> His glory and his monuments are gone.

The Faerie Queene shows us how character and destiny are defined by desire, and in the end, the poet's character is defined by his ambivalence. He does not give Mutabilitie a coherent character, so we cannot say just what she wants, but it bears some resemblance to a personal apocalypse.

Nature offers instead a far-off universal eschaton, when every blessed thing returns simultaneously to 'perfection' at its point of origin. In his prayer for 'that Sabaoths sight,' with 'all things firmely stayd / Vpon the pillours of Eternity,' the poet expresses his urgent desire for something in between: both the fulfilment of his deepest individual aspirations, and an enduring union with the panoply of 'all things.'

Especially in its temporal dimension, the universe of 'all things' is mentioned repeatedly in Spenser's poetry. The phrase constitutes a leitmotif in the *Ruines of Rome* (iii.8, ix.10, xviii.14, xxii.13), where Time's cycles are contemplated in terms that duplicate, on a small scale, the philosophical perspectives found in *The Faerie Queene*. In the Garden of Adonis, of course, 'all things, that are borne to liue and die' are seen at their source (III vi 30.5; cf. 8.4, 34.3, 37.1, 39.1–5, 47.3), and many other passages – some discussed at the beginning of this chapter as echoes from the Garden – reflect upon their fate. 'All things' are threatened by Ate with decay (IV i 29.4); 'All things not rooted well, will soon be rotten' (IV i 51.5), as Blandamour says to Scudamour; the poet himself complains that 'Right now is wrong, and wrong that was is right, / As all things else in time are chaunged quight,' far gone from the time when 'all things freely grew out of the ground' (V Proem 4.5, 9.7); the egalitarian giant threatens 'all things' (V ii 32.9, 34.2, 37.2). As we have noted before, anxiety verging upon paranoia lurks in some of these passages, but the forces of negation are always answered vigorously, and on their own ground, with few appeals to the absolutes of eternity.

Personal immortality transcending both nature and history is important in *The Faerie Queene*, but such a future is represented only in Book I, with reference to the destiny of St George. Throughout *The Faerie Queene* Spenser's personal expressions of concern with the life to come dwell upon his book's reputation, not his soul's fate. In the *Cantos*, as is fitting in a testament published ten years after his death, desire for an eternal life is an undercurrent, erupting as a devout wish in the last stanza. Nature cannot be expected to satisfy this desire, but by confronting her limits, the author learns that his soul belongs elsewhere. Spenser's prayer for 'that Sabaoths sight' rests, as securely as any hope for the soul's immortality can rest, on the evidence in canto vii, which is consistent with the limits placed on 'all things' elsewhere in the poem's encylopedic account of mortal life. In the end, then, nature's elaborate order shows us what our end is not. An educated recognition that the soul can find no lasting satisfaction on earth was for some in the Renaissance the best evidence that after the book of this life has been closed, there will be another.

Conclusion

The assumptions governing this book have been those of the main stream in contemporary historicist scholarship: first, that the value of recoverable experience, literature, and thought from past ages is best established with a detachment that separates what we think about any text and historically defined contexts for its interpretation from what we know about ourselves; second, that what we know about ourselves is partial and historically conditioned, subject to correction and amplification in the light of all that we can learn from the past. I take it to be self-evident to my readers that *The Faerie Queene* constitutes, in large and subtle ways, much that is worth knowing about the Elizabethan era, and also that it offers a great lens, or a number of smaller lenses, through which far-flung components of Renaissance culture may be brought into focus. Spenser's poem also adds resonance, by the intermittent reinforcement of its delightful teaching, to what we know or wish to know about ourselves as creatures of history.

These things having been said, I will confess to a doubt that historicist interpretation can map Spenser's meaning entirely, or even adequately. Spenser is still honoured as 'the poet's poet' (see Alpers's entry on this topic in *SE*), and I believe that now, after Modernism and no longer in the Romantics' terms, he is more worthy of that title than ever. There is, then, an 'untimely' aspect to his achievement that historical understanding can approach but not encompass. Our author aspired to participate, through his poetry, in the *aevum*: to be gathered up, with his Tityrus, Amintas, Gloriana and Adonis, among the perennially vital 'reasons' through which the world of words can be renewed for as long as poetry has value.

How can we best apprehend the perennial Spenser, summoning him out of his own mythopoeia to another life in another time? Poets participating in the 'line of vision' show us one way of recapturing his *'unzeitgemässe'* qualities – 'untimely' but also 'unmodern' and 'unfashionable,' in different translators' renderings of Nietzsche's term – when they revisit some part of Spenser's world (as Blake does in his *Book of Thel*) or play variations on his themes, as some modern poets do deliberately, others subliminally. My way, in the end as elsewhere in this study, will go through Platonism, which I take to be at the root and in all the branches of Spenser's laureate life. Hitherto, I have been concerned with Platonism historically considered, and with a small part of that history; now I would like to adopt a different point of view. I will conclude *Spenser's Supreme Fiction* with some glosses, as if from the poet's perspective, on Gilles Deleuze's essay, 'Plato and the Simulacrum.'[1] Deleuze's intervention in an unfinished project, the 'overthrow [*renversement*] of Platonism,' announced by Nietzsche and echoing the critiques of Kant and Hegel, may help us both to measure our distance from the historical Spenser and to situate the poetry that survives him within the discursive regimes of postmodernism.

The Nietzschean and Deleuzean 'overthrow' of Plato's legacy is also an *understanding* of it, not a negation. It brings to light, as out of a cave or a shady grove, many features of Platonism in its Spenserian version. Deleuze finds the 'motivation' behind Plato's account of the worlds of essences and appearances in a desire not only to distinguish 'between the "thing" itself and its images, the original and the copy, the model and the simulacrum' (45), but more fundamentally, to settle disputes between rivals. When he observes that 'Platonism is the *Odyssey* of philosophy,' the apothegm applies to a son's quest, a faithful wife's stratagems, a wily father's errors and eventual homecoming, and the epic plot's climax in a massacre of illegitimate suitors. In keeping with the fundamentals of patriarchal culture from a long time before Socrates and after Spenser's day, Plato's legacy exhibits a concern with regulation of lineal descent, 'the sorting out of claims, the distinguishing of true claimant [*prétendant*] from false' (46). How fitting it was, then, that Edmund Spenser, whose humanist education was his principal source of status, should have drawn upon Platonism for the tropes with which to claim his descent from 'all the antique Poets historicall,' and to distinguish between the true and false claims on Redcrosse's faith, Guyon's will, Amoret's love, Florimell's desire for safety, Britomart's *amour propre*, and the other forms of desire and discipline that impel characters along the forking paths of Books IV–VI.

Deleuze's examination of the difference between *copies* and *simulacra* is useful with reference to Spenser's fiction. It helps us to understand why we are never delivered from twofoldness and deferral into the presence of a simple truth. Deleuze's 'true claimant' is at best a 'secondhand possessor,' not the father's son but a suitor for his daughter's hand. The best man among rivals, the *iconic copy*, proves himself worthy of sharing in the father's largesse, while the *phantasmatic simulacra*, on the contrary, all fail to qualify (46–8). What is lacking in the simulacra? 'Their claim – to the object, the quality, and so forth – is made from below, by means of an aggression, an insinuation, a subversion, "against the father" and without passing through the Idea' (48). In *The Faerie Queene*, simulacra such as the false Una and false Florimell lack souls; they have been made, not born in a lineage traceable to Eden or the Garden of Adonis. Such makers of simulacra as Errour, Mammon, Acrasia, and Busirane lack lineages themselves; they are parasitic upon nature and a well-born culture. Simulacral characters like Braggadocchio and Paridell lack all acquaintance with virtue that can be traced back to ancient roots or was once 'enraced' from heaven, and they don't even know what they lack.

'There is always a productive operation in the good copy and, corresponding to this operation, a correct *judgment*, if not knowledge' (49). One might suppose that Deleuze once read Sidney's *Apology*, or somewhere came across the famous passage about evidence of the poet's familiarity with 'that *Idea*': 'so far substantially it worketh, not only to make a Cyrus ... but to bestow a Cyrus upon the world to make many Cyruses, if they will learn aright why and how that maker made him' (*AP* 101.5–13). The good copy leads back to the original that makes it good; 'that true glorious type,' Gloriana, herself only indirectly revealed in the poem, provides the occasion for Arthur's display of virtues, which are more obviously proposed for imitation. Britomart and Artegall show us that it is praiseworthy to resemble Arthur, and possible even without a direct acquaintance, by being outstanding participants in the Faerie world.

We might be happier if simulacral images were less prolific than true copies, but the lesson illustrated in Errour's cave, where Spenser's fiction comes face to face with an allegory of its mechanical reproduction, is confirmed repeatedly in *The Faerie Queene*. The terms in which Deleuze describes the appeal of simulacra are useful to a reader of Spenser: 'The simulacrum implies great dimensions, depths, and distances which the observer cannot dominate. It is because he cannot master them that he has an impression of resemblance. The simulacrum includes within itself the differential point of view, and the spectator is made part of the simulacrum, which is transformed and deformed according to his point of view. In short, folded within the simulacrum there is a process of going mad [*un devenir-fou*], a process of limitlessness' (49).[2] Not even Arthur, chasing

Florimell with the best of intentions, reminded of his more distant beloved, can entirely escape this danger. He is not chasing the flirtatious false copy of Florimell's beautiful form, which sows such confusion among lesser men in Book IV, but it seems that there is something about Florimell herself, derived as she is from Ariosto's Angelica and reminiscent of Una but divergent from her sacrosanct type, that lacks authenticity.

Perhaps, in seeking to 'overgo' Ariosto, Spenser was obliged to flirt with limitlessness and maddening complexity. It was not a mistake or a betrayal of his allegiance to Plato's teachings, but a way of becoming modern, with his times and ahead of them, beyond the limits of a specifically early modern sensibility. The relationship between simulacra and true copies is dialectical even in Plato, and Deleuze shows that the less the simulacra are repressed, the better for art and its representation of experience. In his account, 'the essential character of the modern work of art' is 'a matter of different and divergent narratives' (51). Deleuze offers, as 'two readings of the world,' similar statements: '"only that which is alike differs," and "only differences are alike" ... The first one is an exact definition of the world as icon. The second, against the first, defines the world of simulacra' (52). Deleuze's second formulation defines modernity, and is far more applicable to Spenser's mode of discourse in *The Faerie Queene* than the first (his investment in the first is evident, I think, in *Fowre Hymnes*).

There is an inner divergence in Spenser's attitude toward the world of simulacra; on some occasions the twofoldness of his world is split again, along gender lines. Consider how he handles the contest between the true and false Florimells and, in the same canto (V iii), the 'uncasing' of Braggadocchio, who had introduced his 'snowy *Florimele*' (17.1) as superior to Marinell's 'fayre Franion' (22.7). The narrator clearly favours the interests of Marinell's 'noble Ladie' (23.1) over Braggadocchio's rival claimant, but he makes much of Marinell's astonishment when he sees 'that snowy mayd; / Whom euer as he did the more auize, / The more to be true *Florimell* he did surmize' (18.7–9). As soon as Artegall brings the two together, 'Like the true saint beside the image set' (24.2), the contest is over: 'Th'enchaunted Damzell vanisht into nought,' and only the true Florimell's 'emptie girdle' is left behind (24.7–9). The narrator takes an equal interest in the false Florimell's vanishing and the recovery of '*Florimells* owne girdle, from her reft, / While she was flying, like a weary weft, / From that foule monster' (27.4–6); he devotes two stanzas to the 'great astonishment' caused by the disappearance (25–6), and two more (27–8) to the recovered belt's power to single out the 'continent and chast' among the many ladies who try to wear it. For Spenser, the end of the enchantment wrought by the witch's counterfeit is a loss somewhat like other abrupt disappearances: of Gloriana in Arthur's dream, of Guyon's guardian from his sleeping side, of the beauties in Acrasia's bower before the tempest of Guyon's wrath, of the Tudor line's end in Merlin's prophecy, of the furnishings in Busirane's 'goodly roomes' after his spells have been reversed, of Astraea when she returns to heaven, of the dancers dispersed by Calidore's curiosity, of Diana when she deserts Arlo Hill, and of Nature once she has given 'her doome in speeches few.' The false Florimell is less legitimate than these temporary manifestations of meaning, and of less moment, but Spenser poignantly compares her evanescent beauty to that of a rainbow's 'glorious picture' (25.6): she is good, being gone.

Braggadocchio's pretensions to knighthood are treated as far more offensive than the false Florimell's simulacral beauty. When he first appeared, three Books before (II iii 6–46), Spenser's false knight had been the butt of topical satire and Belphoebe's scorn; while at first he seems incapable of doing real harm, when he presents himself for one last time to be disposed of in the Legend of Justice, he is 'the boaster, that all knights did blot' (16.3), a threat to the aristocratic order's legitimacy. Artegall is inclined to kill Braggadocchio when he reviles the justice that has been imposed upon him; 'our iudge of equity' is only pacified when Guyon argues that he would dishonour himself by wreaking vengeance 'on such a carle as hee: / It's punishment enough, that all his shame doe see' (36). The alignment of 'true' and 'false' with different stations on the social ladder is obvious here. After Talus has soundly punished both Braggadocchio and Trompart, stripping them of all semblances of honour and good repute, the narrator pauses to moralize:

> So ought all faytours, that true knighthood shame,
> And armes dishonour with base villanie,
> From all braue knights be banisht with defame:
> For oft their lewdnes blotteth good deserts with blame.   (38.6–9)

He ends the canto with a description of the merriment that follows the purging of their company: all enjoy remembering the knavery practised among them, and laugh at one another for having been fooled for so long. Shame, it seems, is to be felt only by the likes of Braggadocchio and Trompart, although Spenser may imply, in his parting reference to the 'deare delices and rare delights, / Fit for such Ladies and such louely knights' (40.4–5), that the present company are not entirely worthy of their status. While eager to defend the aristocratic order, Spenser shows how vulnerable it is to counterfeit behaviour.

What is the basis for different responses to the rivalry between the two Florimells and then to the judgment that ensues when Braggadocchio challenges Marinell, Guyon, and Artegall? The first dispute, brought about by the superstitious type of magic, is resolved by the dissolving of that magic, without the self-righteous violence that is visited upon the two scoundrels, and with the aesthetic effect seen in trompe l'oeil painting. The false Florimell was never more than an object, a trophy; the true Florimell has been more than that, but only for Marinell at the end of her long line of suitors, and for the narrator, who follows her story with extravagant pity. The subversive power of Florimell's simulacrum is seen in this: that her beauty, independent of her behaviour, reveals the extent to which Florimell herself is simulacral, implicated in a decadent courtly culture as well as in primitive nature. She is only valued as an object, not a participant in life. When the true Florimell was thought dead, her girdle had been venerated in her place (see IV iv 15–16). Perhaps Spenser was too willing to tolerate this aspect of masculine culture, but a deeper truth may lie concealed in his attitude toward loss. Florimell's long imprisonment, associated with seasonal death and rebirth, and the false Florimell's vanishing, associated with a rainbow that faintly echoes the promise made to Noah, may teach the same lesson that Colin offered to Calidore: that 'the truth of all' in the scene that so troubled Calidore survives the sudden disappearance of 'Diuine resemblance, beauty soueraine rare, / Firme Chastity' (VI x 18.9, 27.4–5). The whole truth that Colin shares with Calidore in stanzas 20–8 is not ecstatic but compensatory, constituted as much by disjointed experience – a primal and indefinitely renewable sense of loss – as by the privileged access to the Graces that Colin had enjoyed in solitude.

Deleuze finds that the way of reading based upon the proposition that 'only differences are alike' not only favours simulacra but 'posits the world itself as phantasm,' freed from the controls of hierarchical distinctions. Following Nietzsche, he seeks 'to raise up simulacra, to assert their rights over icons or copies' (52–3). While Spenser was not indifferent to the appeal of simulacra in a world that was fluid as well as hierarchical, he could not have gone so far. Deleuze quotes from *Beyond Good and Evil*: 'Behind every cave ... there is, and must necessarily be, a still deeper cave: an ampler, stranger, richer world beyond the surface, an abyss behind every bottom, beneath every "foundation"' (53, quoting *BG&E* §289). Spenser admits this kind of speculation into his poem, but only, I believe, in the persons of Mammon, Malbecco, and (perhaps) Florimell in the depths of her despair. The challenge to order presented by Mutabilitie also evokes such a view of the world's lack of a foundation, but it is accommodated in a dispensation profoundly different from Nietzsche's 'Eternal Return.' Some readers may find an abyss intimated in Spenser's lines about the contents of 'the wide wombe of the world' (III vi 6–9), but I do not: the 'huge eternall *Chaos*' there is a source of 'substances,' not subversion.

At the end of his essay, Deleuze says that modernity, as we know it now, offers two ways of proceeding toward the art and thought of the future: 'It is at the core of modernity, at the point where modernism settles its accounts, that the factitious and the simulacrum stand in opposition as two modes of destruction may: the two nihilisms' (56). A 'factitious' art remains committed to conventions and models, content with the diminishing returns to be derived from copies of copies; it takes refuge in familiar ironies. The other nihilism, which embraces the simulacrum freed from its dependent relationship to a purely hypothetical Idea and its 'true copy,' may be only marginally more appealing, although it is more radical; it requires a commitment to the eternal return of normlessness. Spenser's poetry offers a third alternative to those who read it now, not in an antiquarian spirit but as part of the history of the present: 'overgoing' may be preferable to 'overthrowing.' What *The Faerie Queene* contains of the *philosophia perennis* might only point us backward in time, but its 'untimely' fictions have the power to demonstrate that the overthrow of Platonism can never be complete, and that his poem will survive what remains of the postmodern condition to be part of the script for whatever pageant comes next.

Notes

Introduction

1 The most recent book-length contribution to this scholarship is Richard A. McCabe's *Pillars of Eternity*. See also Alastair Fowler, 'Emanations of Glory'; John Erskine Hankins, *Source and Meaning in Spenser's Allegory* (hereafter, *Source and Meaning*); and James Nohrnberg, *The Analogy of The Faerie Queene* (hereafter, *Analogy*).

2 Synthesis is already evident in the wisdom literature of the Old Testament, the writings of Philo of Alexandria, and the fourth gospel. The body of scholarship with a bearing on the transmission and transformation of ideas about the created order between Plato's time and Spenser's is, of course, enormous. For a recent and magisterial contribution to the subject, see Louis Dupré, *Passage to Modernity*. Elizabeth Bieman, *Plato Baptized*, provides a nuanced account of several strands in the traditions that suited Platonism to Spenser's purposes.

3 See also my article, 'Platonism,' in *The Spenser Encyclopedia* (hereafter, *SE*).

4 Paul Oskar Kristeller describes the Platonic tradition and the Renaissance revival of Platonism in *Renaissance Thought* 48–65; *Renaissance Thought II* 89–101; and 'The European Significance of Florentine Platonism.' See also James Hankins, *Plato in the Italian Renaissance*, and the chapter on Platonism in Brian P. Copenhaver and Charles B. Schmitt, *Renaissance Philosophy* (127–95), with its references to other scholarship.

5 I have explored this development and its bearing upon Spenser's poetry in 'Spenser's *Amoretti VIII* and Platonic Commentaries on Petrarch.'

6 Cited in R.M. Cummings, ed., *Spenser: The Critical Heritage* 157.

7 As I show in the article already cited, in the sonnet that became *Amoretti* 8 Spenser composed a poem significantly more 'Platonic' than his Petrarchan model and the poems by Ronsard, Sidney, and Greville that echo that model.

8 See S.K. Heninger, Jr, *Sidney and Spenser: The Poet as Maker*, and cf. Joel B. Altman, *The Tudor Play of Mind*.

Chapter 1: The Author in 1580 and 1590

1 'What is an Author?' 124–36. Richard Helgerson, *Self-Crowned Laureates* 55–100, provides the basis for an author-centred reading of Spenser; see also Louis Adrian Montrose, 'The Elizabethan Subject and the Spenserian Text'; Patrick Cheney, *Spenser's Famous Flight*; Richard Rambuss, *Spenser's Secret Career*; and Kevin Pask, *The Emergence of the English Author* 83–112.
2 The entry on 'allegory' in *SE* theorizes Spenser's position in a long tradition. On *The Faerie Queene* within the history of the heroic poem, see Elizabeth J. Bellamy, *Translations of Power*; Susanne Lindgren Wofford, *The Choice of Achilles*; and Patrick J. Cook, *Milton, Spenser, and the Epic Tradition*.
3 Daniel Javitch, *Poetry and Courtliness in Renaissance England* 132–59.
4 See 'Venus' in *SE*; John Manning surveys the goddess's connotations in Spenser's poetry, accounting for many of the sources of his thought; he gives little attention to the anti-Venerean sentiment that was common in Tudor culture, by no means limited to Lord Burghley's 'rugged forhead.'
5 It seems appropriate to flag my use of the first person plural here, to illustrate an indeterminacy intrinsic to writing. I don't pretend to determine the scope of the consensus I am describing; the statement is heuristic rather than legislative. My perspective is gender-specific, but I don't speak for all men, or only for men.
6 While I am interested primarily in rehabilitating the idealization of feminine objects of desire that we find in Petrarch, Sidney, and Spenser, I don't deny the potential for violence in Petrarchan poetics. To the extent that it accommodates obsessive desire, Petrarchism is susceptible to perversions of the kind encountered in Busirane's castle, as well as to the simplifications found in the Bower of Bliss and Scudamour's conquest in the Temple of Venus. On the rhetorical violence inherent in any allegorical project, regarded as a 'poetics of capture,' see Gordon Teskey, *Allegory and Violence*, chapter 1.
7 Barbara L. Estrin, *Laura: Uncovering Gender and Genre in Wyatt, Donne, and Marvell*. See also Dorothy Stephens, *Limits of Eroticism*.
8 Kari Weil, *Androgyny and the Denial of Difference* 2.
9 See Stephen Orgel, *Impersonations* 25–9; also Laura Levine, *Men in Women's Clothing*, and Mark Breitenberg, *Anxious Masculinity in Early Modern England*.
10 Thomas Laqueur, *Making Sex: Body and Gender from the Greeks to Freud*. Laqueur's account of the 'one-sex model' has been criticized as a simplifica-

tion of early modern thinking about sex and gender: see Winfried Schleiner, 'Early Modern Controversies.'

11 'Women in the Beehive' 195; cf. 203. (Elisions in the quotation appear in the text.)

12 The term is Julia Kristeva's. Lynn Enterline employs this and other concepts from Kristeva in *The Tears of Narcissus*; see 12 and 33 in particular. See also John Fletcher and Andrew Benjamin, eds., *Abjection, Melancholia, and Love: The Work of Julia Kristeva*, especially the essay by Elizabeth Gross, 'The Body of Signification.'

13 On Spenser's masking, usefully compared to Chaucer's, see Judith H. Anderson, 'Narrative Reflections.'

14 See 'Imitation and Gender Insubordination' in addition to Butler's *Gender Trouble: Feminism and the Subversion of Identity*.

15 For further development of these ideas along lines pertinent to my argument, see Estrin, *Laura* 26–36.

16 Gordon Teskey has commented on the centrality of gender difference in allegorical signification (*Allegory and Violence* 15–16).

17 The topic of 'imitation' is covered well in *SE*, and see Thomas Greene, *The Light in Troy*; for Spenser and *The Faerie Queene* in particular, the crucial study is Elizabeth J. Bellamy, *Translations of Power*. On imitation and courtly ambition, see Frank Whigham, *Ambition and Privilege* 78–87.

18 With a frame of reference quite different from Butler's, drawing on the work of Erving Goffman, Lloyd Davis argues that disguise is fundamental to characterization in the Renaissance: *Guise and Disguise: Rhetoric and Characterization in the English Renaissance*.

19 See Patricia Parker's chapter on the Bower of Bliss episode, *Literary Fat Ladies* 54–66.

20 Samuel Taylor Coleridge, from 'A Course of Lectures' (1818), in *Edmund Spenser's Poetry*, ed. Hugh Maclean and Anne Lake Prescott, 3rd ed., 670.

21 See Maureen Quilligan, *Milton's Spenser* 80–4; Teskey, 'From Allegory to Dialectic'; Stephens, *Limits of Eroticism* 60–1.

22 *Renaissance Self-Fashioning* 86. The quotation refers to William Tyndale's book, *The Obedience of a Christian Man*, in the course of revisionist remarks (85–99) on Benjamin's argument that mechanical reproduction eliminates the aura inherent in ritual acts and unique works of art. In Greenblatt's view, the printed book shifts the locus of authority from venerable persons and objects, and the institutions responsible for them, to multiple sites of subjectivity.

23 On Ponsonby and the production of the 1590 *Faerie Queene*, see Joseph Loewenstein, 'Spenser's Retrography: Two Episodes in Post-Petrarchan

Bibliography'; Michael Brennan, 'William Ponsonby: Elizabethan Stationer'; Wayne Erickson, 'William Ponsonby.'

24 Here and in what follows within this section, the argument alludes to and goes beyond the ground covered in my 'Questionable Evidence in the *Letters* of 1580.'

25 See Eleanor Rosenberg, *Leicester, Patron of Letters* 324–7, and Virginia Stern, *Gabriel Harvey: His Life, Marginalia and Library* 39–47. Harvey's response makes clear that he does not take Spenser's travel plans literally: 'me thinks I dare stil wager al the Books and writings in my study ... that you shall not, I saye, bee gone ouer Sea, for al your saying, neither the next, nor the nexte weeke' (*Prose* 444).

26 See David Lee Miller, *The Poem's Two Bodies*, under 'specularity,' for the best treatment of this theme.

27 I will cite my own translation, with phrases from Spenser's Latin quoted from the *Prose Works*, having checked both against the text and translation in Richard A. McCabe's edition of *The Shorter Poems*.

28 See *Prose* 449–62. Harvey's letters are chronologically later but more prominently placed, taking up most of the collection's first part.

29 See Richard Helgerson, *Self-Crowned Laureates* 25–54; Bruce R. Smith, *Homosexual Desire in Shakespeare's England* 79–115.

30 Jonathan Crewe, *Hidden Designs* 91, entertains the thought that Spenser, as a still untried poet, is implicated in the story of Redcrosse, an 'almost unbridled fantasy of the clownish, lowborn "knight," received into the court of Gloriana and ultimately reconstructed as the patron saint of the kingdom.' As a backdrop for this suggestion, see Crewe's discussion of 'sympathy' (35–69), and cf. Donald Cheney's earlier comments on the 'parallelism of narrator and protagonist' (*Spenser's Image of Nature* 19–20). Along similar lines, Richard Neuse has noted that it is easy to hear 'Author' in 'Arthur.'

31 On this point, see my 'Spenser's *Amoretti VIII*.' The poem is intertextually related to Greville's *Caelica* 3 and Sidney's *Astrophil and Stella* 42, substantiating Spenser's claims, in the contemporaneous *Letters*, to being 'in some vse of familiarity' with Sidney and his closest friends.

32 See Frank Whigham, *Ambition and Privilege* 24–31, on the tensions between learning and politics, which can be translated into tensions between two institutions, each containing conservative and activist factions. Whigham notes (25) that in 1579 the authorities at Cambridge protested to Burghley that because of the crown's interference 'the rewards of merit and studiousness are withheld, scholars being induced to look for preferment to the favour of courtiers rather than to their true deserts at the hands of the university.' It was a bad time for a man of Harvey's ambition and temperament to

be at Cambridge, but he serves as a valuable witness to the system's contradictions. Anthony Grafton and Lisa Jardine regard Harvey as a case study in the aspirations and practices of a man self-taught in the 'pragmatic humanism' of Erasmus, Sturm, and Ramus, and they note also the 'class conservatism' of his adversaries (*From Humanism to the Humanities* 184–96).

33 *Prose* 444, with 'woomanish' introduced from a copy emended in Harvey's hand; see David McKitterick 353.

34 I will cite the translation by James Sanford, ed. Catherine M. Dunn. Sanford's translation was published in 1569, reprinted in 1575; in Latin, Agrippa's treatise had been a runaway success, first published in 1530, with seven more editions in the next two years, nine others before the end of the century, and translations into Italian and French (Dunn, xxiv). Sidney's debts to Agrippa were first discussed by A.C. Hamilton, 'Sidney and Agrippa'; cf. Margaret W. Ferguson, *Trials of Desire* 157–8; and Ronald Levao, *Renaissance Minds and Their Fictions* 149–50.

35 *Gabriel Harvey's Marginalia* 160–1. This note appears in *The Surueye of the World*, signed by Harvey and dated 1574, within the years of his intimacy with Spenser, whose name is mentioned in other notes, in the company of such learned men as John Blagrave, Thomas Digges, Thomas Harriot, and John Dee (*Marginalia* 161–3).

36 McKitterick 349–50 notes that Harvey inscribed his ownership, '1580. Mense Aprile,' in Nicolaus Vigelius's *Iuris Civilis Totius Absolutissima Methodus* (Basle, 1561).

37 See Caroline Ruutz-Rees, 'Some Notes of Gabriel Harvey's in Hoby's Translation of Castiglione's *Courtier* (1561).' A note on the title page indicates that he acquired his copy in 1572.

38 As with the other topics discussed in the first three letters, Spenser provides the set-up: 'I thinke the *Earthquake* was also there wyth you (which I would gladly learne) as it was here with vs: ... *Sed quid vobis videtur magnis Philosophis?* [But what do you think, great philosopher?]' (*Prose* 15–16).

39 See S.K. Heninger, Jr, 'The Orgoglio Episode in *The Faerie Queene*' 172–3.

40 As stated by R.A. Markus, 'This is essentially the problem of distinguishing in natural processes and events between the divine activity present in everything that happens and the natural activity of each creature' ('Augustine. God and Nature' 397–8).

41 Abraham Fleming, *A Bright Burning Beacon, forewarning all wise Virgins to trim their lampes against the comming of the Bridegroome* B4r–v.

42 See *Prose* 458–9; Harvey cites the treatise *De rerum Praenotione, pro veritate Religionis, contra Superstitiosas vanitates,* of which the title alone makes clear

that its reasoning is in the service of orthodox religion. Harvey applies to the younger Pico his uncle's fame as a *'Phoenix* ... the odde, and in effecte the onely singular learned man of Europe' (*Prose* 459), which suggests that he was using the second of the two volumes in which the *Opera omnia* of both Picos were published (Basle: Sebastian Henricpetrus, 1572).

43 Charles B. Schmitt, *Gianfrancesco Pico della Mirandola (1469–1533) and His Critique of Aristotle* 6.

44 For Harvey's Latin, which I have translated, see *Marginalia* 202; the comment appears in John Foorth's *Synopsis Politica* (London: Henry Bynneman, 1582).

45 *'Ineptus'* was the word Spenser had used of himself (see 37 above). Within *The Faerie Queene*, we can compare not only Redcrosse's earlier rest with Duessa in the shade of Fradubio (I ii 28–30), but Una's solitary rest 'In secret shadow' (iii 4), where grace renders her both vulnerable and sacrosanct, and eventually, Redcrosse's well-earned rest by the side of a river in the shade of two hills (II i 24), suggesting even more than the pleasant places in Book I the female anatomy that will excite Sir Guyon's temperance.

46 On St George's nature, name, and destiny, see I x 52.2 and 60–1, 64–7, with Hamilton's notes.

47 The fullest discussion of Orgoglio in this light is J.W. Schroeder, 'Spenser's Erotic Drama'; see also James Nohrnberg, *Analogy* 264–70.

48 Cf. Kenneth Gross, *Spenserian Poetics* 81–4, for comments based on the 'mythifying and demystifying' efforts of Irenius and Eudoxus to identify the causes of Ireland's crisis.

49 Wofford's reading of this passage (*Choice of Achilles* 274–8) is the best as well as the most recent known to me.

Chapter 2: The World and the Book

1 There are other love stories, true and false: Fradubio's cautionary tale (I ii 33–43) contrasts with Duessa's lies in the same canto (22–6), and for comparison, Book II relates Amavia's sad story (i 36–56); Britomart gives a defensive account of her reasons for seeking Artegall (III ii 5–8), and the narrator steps in to account in a long flashback for the marvellous origin and destiny of her love (ii 17–iii 62).

2 In her discussion of Faeryland as 'a created and essentially unauthorized realm,' Jacqueline T. Miller emphasizes the Promethean theft involved in Spenser's imaginative conquest. This assertion of individual liberty is one aspect of the impulse I have called 'ludic.' See *Poetic License* 87–101, and cf. John Guillory, *Poetic Authority* 21–67.

3 A. Leigh DeNeef, 'Rereading Sidney's *Apology*,' offers a persuasive account of the logical basis for Sidney's theory of imitation.

4 Susanne Lindgren Wofford explores the ways in which the several giants and gigantic forms in the poem represent both illegitimate threats to Elizabeth's sovereignty and the poet's own ambivalence toward it (*Choice of Achilles* 334–53).

5 A descriptive and analytical survey of such developments, oriented to illuminate Spenser and Shakespeare, will be found in Herbert Grabes, *The Mutable Glass*. See also Grabes's entry, 'mirrors,' in *SE*.

6 In her otherwise subtle account of Spenser's 'characteristic swerve away from political critique' while offering 'a more radical moral analysis,' when Wofford comes to Venus and the gigantic Venerean locus of the Garden of Adonis, she makes an unwarranted claim that Venus stands for the Queen, and her Garden for the 'body politic' of England: *Choice of Achilles* 334, 347–58. This equation blurs Spenser's distinctions between Diana and Venus, Belphoebe and Amoret.

7 Spenser's indebtedness to Chaucer in this regard is stressed by A. Kent Hieatt, *Chaucer, Spenser, Milton*.

8 Although he does not deal with Spenser, Thomas M. Greene provides, in *The Light in Troy*, an eloquent account of the distances separating Petrarch and later poets from the classical predecessors they were bound to imitate.

9 See G.S. Kirk, *Myth: Its Meaning and Functions in Ancient and Other Cultures*. Myths in Spenser's poetry are 'speculative and explanatory' in function (*Myth* 254, 257–60).

10 Brooks Otis, *Virgil* 5–40. Otis says of the time of Euripides, 'Myth had finally lost its capacity to activate great poetry: in becoming incredible, it had also become symbolically irrelevant' (8). See also James E.G. Zetzel, 'Recreating the Canon.' Myth did, however, activate philosophy, and philosophically motivated criticism: see James A. Coulter, *Literary Microcosm*, and Robert Lamberton, *Homer the Theologian*.

11 I have in mind the work of Seznec, Panofsky, Wind, and Gombrich. Two studies with a more direct bearing on English literature can be cited, in which references will be found to the scholars just mentioned: Thomas Hyde, *Poetic Theology of Love*, and Leonard Barkan, *Gods Made Flesh*.

12 Chapter 2 in Angus Fletcher's *Allegory*, 'The Cosmic Image,' contains few references to Spenser, but much of the argument pertains to his poem; see also Fletcher's *Prophetic Moment*.

13 Douglas Brooks-Davies has traced Spenser's transformation of motifs from the Eleusinian mysteries, following Frances Yates in connecting Queen Elizabeth with Ceres as the goddess responsible for good harvests: see 'mysteries' in *SE*.

14 See Quintilian, *Institutio oratoria* I x 1; on the development of educational programs and their impact on imaginative literature, see the several papers in Peter Sharratt, ed., *French Renaissance Studies*, and Terence Cave, *The Cornucopian Text*. Giuseppe Mazzotta, *Dante's Vision and the Circle of Knowledge*, provides valuable medieval background. One testimony to English interest in this ordering of the liberal arts is James Sanford's translation of Agrippa's *De Vanitate*: he presents the treatise as a critique but not a rejection of 'the whole circle or compasse of Learning (the Seuen Liberall Sciences I meane, called *Encyclopoedia*).'

15 To these comments on nature and culture, compare Lawrence Manley's discussion of nature and convention, *Convention, 1500–1700* 1–25.

16 On the development of this idea, see M.H. Abrams, *The Mirror and the Lamp* 272–85. My thinking is deeply indebted to the 'ecological' criticism of Harry Berger, Jr, especially 'The Renaissance Imagination: Second World and Green World' (*Second World and Green World* 3–40). Angus Fletcher takes up some of Berger's themes in *Prophetic Moment*, and Sean Kane has pursued an argument related to mine in *Spenser's Moral Allegory*.

17 *Poetry of* The Faerie Queene 21; see 19–35, 107–34.

18 Harry Berger's criticism is notable for its emphasis on proto-modern characteristics of Spenser's mind and of the 'Renaissance imagination' in general, while Isabel G. MacCaffrey, in *Spenser's Allegory*, emphasizes proto-Romantic traits which are 'modern' in a broader sense.

19 In the courtly cultures of the Renaissance, play and festivity were of course central to the processes by which individuals and status groups defined themselves, their social positions and values, even the structure of their world. In this connection, see Jacques Ehrmann, 'Homo Ludens Revisited.' The most basic of Ehrmannn's principles is this: 'Play is not played against a background of a fixed, stable reality which would serve as its standard. All reality is caught up in the play of the concepts which designate it' (56). In *Sense of an Ending*, Frank Kermode develops a theory of fiction, analogous to Ehrmann's theory of play, that illuminates Spenser's practice.

20 A large body of scholarship bears upon my argument at this point. The seminal account is 'The Book as Symbol,' chapter 16 in Ernst Robert Curtius, *European Literature and the Latin Middle Ages*. For the medieval period see also Jean Leclercq, *Love of Learning and the Desire for God*; and Jesse M. Gellrich, *Idea of the Book in the Middle Ages*. On discursive practices developed in the sixteenth century, Lawrence Manley, *Convention, 1500–1750*, should be mentioned. Michel Foucault, in *The Order of Things*, offers a method and a vocabulary for the interpretation of early modern

discourse that is useful out of all proportion to the evidence it explicitly examines. Timothy J. Reiss, *Discourse of Modernism*, uses the work of Foucault and other theorists to interpret the impact on discursive practices of epistemological shifts accompanying the emergence of scientific world views. Largely independent of French structuralism and post-structuralism, and not yet assimilated by English and American scholarship, Hans Blumenberg has explored themes related to Foucault's (but more in line with the work of Cassirer and other neo-Kantians) in a series of massive studies now translated by Robert M. Wallace as *Genesis of the Copernican World-View*, *Legitimacy of the Modern Age*, and *Work on Myth*.

21 See Nicholas H. Clulee, *John Dee's Natural Philosophy*.

22 In this connection, see Maureen Quilligan, *Language of Allegory* 224–38, 254–60.

23 Galileo is quoted in Curtius, *European Literature and the Latin Middle Ages* 324. Curtius comments, 'The book of nature no longer legible? – a revolutionary change had occurred, which penetrated the consciousness of the humblest.' James J. Bono places Galileo's development of a mathematical language in the context of a shift 'from symbolic exegesis to deinscriptive hermeneutics': *Word of God and the Languages of Man* 167–98. The shift from pre-modern to modern ways of knowing, in which the sixteenth century was a critical period for England, has also been described as a transformation in the 'art of reading': see David R. Olson, *World on Paper* 160–78.

24 S.K. Heninger, Jr, documents in *Cosmographical Glass* 'a welter of differing images – many strongly appealing, none convincingly authoritative' (xvi). Brian Vickers, 'On the Function of Analogy in the Occult,' stresses the power of the occult sciences to assimilate ideas from many sources within a 'preformed interpretative model, often magical or mystical, which was neither derived from reality nor testable by it' (266). Further, see Vickers, ed., *Occult and Scientific Mentalities in the Renaissance*. Bono, *Word of God and the Languages of Man* 49–84, offers a valuable critique of Vickers's opinions as they relate to language.

25 *Poetry of* The Faerie Queene 327; cf. 330–1. Alpers returns to this theme in 'Narration in *The Faerie Queene*' 27–8. Seen in these terms, Spenser is a participant (one of the last) in the 'integrated civilisations' described by Georg Lukács (*Theory of the Novel* 29–39, 53–60). Harry Berger's description of the culture constructed by 'naive consciousness' and its transformation by 'the hypothetical attitude' is also pertinent (*Second World and Green World* 77–107).

26 Thomas G. Pavel, *Fictional Worlds*, provides an excellent analysis of the

issues raised by recent work in several disciplines, with a comprehensive bibliography. See also Felix Martinez-Bonati, 'Towards a Formal Ontology of Fictional Worlds.'

27 One excursus in that account might be the connections Spenser encourages us to make, through imagery and circumstances combining similarity with differences, between Una, Acrasia, Amoret, and Medua: see *FQ* I xii 21–3, II xii 77–8, IV x 52, and IV xi 45–6. More than the absent presence of Gloriana, the figure of Una becomes a memorable 'type' in the poem's deep structure, with whom other figures (Florimell, Belphoebe, and Pastorella among them) can be compared.

28 Pavel, *Fictional Worlds* 75–85, interprets distinctions between fact and fiction as cultural, characteristic (like political borders determined by treaties, in place of the vague borders of linguistic communities and feudal or tribal domains) only of the developed world in the modern period. See also Lorna Hutson, 'Fortunate Travelers.'

29 *Mannerism* 141. Shearman's entire discussion of 'Variety and Monotony' (141–51) is relevant. Wölfflin's distinctions between the 'multiple unity' of sixteenth-century art and the 'unified unity' of the baroque are also useful: *Principles of Art History* 155–95.

30 *Mannerism* 125. I use this architectural analogy advisedly; in general I agree with Kathleen Williams's statement that 'the kind of unity which Spenser achieves, though cumulative, is not architectural; he works not by adding section to section so that the structure is meaningless until it is finished, but by revealing new levels of a structure which we thought complete at our first sight of it' ('"Eterne in Mutabilitie"' 115).

31 Torquato Tasso, *Discourses on the Heroic Poem* 77–8, with Tasso's Italian inserted from the text published in 1594; cf. Alpers's translation and discussion (*Poetry of* The Faerie Queene 19–20). Further, see Robert M. Durling, *Figure of the Poet in Renaissance Epic* 124–6, 251, where Macrobius and Poliziano are cited as Tasso's sources. E.N. Tigerstedt, 'Poet as Creator,' explores in depth the idea that the poet is a kind of God, showing that it was first fully developed by Landino but has roots in Ficino's praise of man as godlike. Michael J.B. Allen offers some corrections to details in Tigerstedt's discussion of Ficino and Plato in 'Marsilio Ficino's Interpretation of Plato's *Timaeus*' 417–20. See also Annabel M. Patterson, 'Tasso and Neoplatonism: The Growth of His Epic Theory.'

32 See Eugenio Donato, '"Per Selve e Boscherecci Labirinti."' In *SE*, see the entry 'labyrinths, mazes.'

33 See 'The Elizabethan Subject and the Spenserian Text' and 'Spenser's Domestic Domain: Poetry, Property, and the Early Modern Subject.'

34 A good example of this mixed effect is his 'Epilogue' to *The Shepheardes Calender*, which moves from pride (*'Loe I have made a Calender for every yeare'*) to humility (*'Goe but a lowly gate emongste the meaner sorte'*) in a 'square' form emblematic of Aristotle's 'constant minded man ... *hominem quadratum'* (*Shorter Poems* 213).

35 *Prose* 16. This passage and Harvey's response are discussed by Richard Helgerson, *Forms of Nationhood* 25–32.

36 See Paul Alpers, 'Narration in *The Faerie Queene'*; the *SE* entries on 'narrative' and the 'narrator'; and Harry Berger, '"Kidnapped Romance": Discourse in *The Faerie Queene.'*

37 See *Poetry of* The Faerie Queene 24–5, and *Orlando Furioso* 7.1–2, referring to Alcina's island, Ariosto's first departure from the map of Europe for a place that is conspicuously allegorical.

38 The similarities and differences between Ariosto and Spenser, with regard to the poet's relation to his fiction and the fiction's relation to historical reality, are discussed brilliantly by Durling in *Figure of the Poet*; see 123–32 (on Ariosto's narrative as 'an example of the analogy between the poem and the cosmos and between the artist and God') and 224–37.

39 Pavel, *Fictional Worlds* 144–7, discusses 'the referential purposes of fiction' in terms of two principles, *distance* and *relevance*, which he aligns with a 'fantasy project' and a 'truth project.' 'Creation of distance could well be assumed to be the most general aim of imaginary activity' (145).

40 A. Leigh DeNeef, in his chapter on the Proems in *Spenser and the Motives of Metaphor*, observes, 'As we progress through the proems, we see Spenser's growing awareness of how thoroughly he is himself implicated in and even dependent upon the misrepresentations of the fictional false poets, of how both his manner and his matter duplicate theirs' (91). Here he affects a detachment from the world and access to an otherworldly source of virtue, but it is debatable whether inwardness generated his clear vision of the forgeries around him, or his defensive reaction to the pressures of social reality generated his own forgery of a false distinction.

Chapter 3: The Poet as *Magus* and *Viator*

1 In this connection, see Harry Berger's essay, 'Naive Consciousness and Culture Change,' in *Second World and Green World* 95–101.

2 I use the terms 'analytical' and 'synthetic' in the sense given to them by Isabel G. MacCaffrey in *Spenser's Allegory* 33–80.

3 See the papers now collected in *Second World and Green World*, especially 'The Ecology of the Mind: The Concept of Period Imagination – An Outline

Sketch' and 'The Renaissance Imagination: Second World and Green World.'
See also Ernst Topitsch, 'World Interpretation and Self-Interpretation.'

4 See also Ficino's *Theologia Platonica* XIV 3, quoted and discussed by Charles
Trinkaus, *In Our Image and Likeness* II 489–90.

5 In the last chapter of *The Individual and the Cosmos in Renaissance Philosophy*, 'The Subject-Object Problem in the Philosophy of the Renaissance,'
Ernst Cassirer discovers in a new attitude toward nature, and the beginnings
of 'the newer, deeper concept of "subjectivity,"' a 'complete parallel between
the *theory of art* and the *theory of science*'; the microcosm/macrocosm
analogy had a similar value for both kinds of theory (quotations from 141,
159; see also 84–111). Cassirer's book and a number of more recent studies
(including, crucially, Foucault's *The Order of Things*) form the foundation
for Arnaud Tripet's 'Aspects de l'analogie à la renaissance,' a useful synthesis
which offers support for some of the ideas presented here, as does Joan
Gadol in 'The Unity of the Renaissance: Humanism, Natural Science, and
Art.' For an essay that brings some of these themes to bear upon English
poetry of the Renaissance, see Robert B. Hinman, 'The Apotheosis of Faust.'
More recently, Ioan P. Couliano (*Eros and Magic in the Renaissance*) and
Gary Tomlinson (*Music in Renaissance Magic*) have interpreted the interplay
of the soul and cosmic forces as a central concern of erudite and esoteric
culture in the Renaissance.

6 *Selections from the Notebooks of Leonardo da Vinci* 111; cf. André Chastel,
Marsile Ficin et l'art 83.

7 'The Canonization,' ll. 42–3. Several other poems by Donne are based on the
idea that the world can be reduced to the lovers' minds, or brought into one
lover's presence in the form of the other; he also uses the corollary idea that
love makes it possible to rise above the sublunary world. 'A Nocturnall upon
St. Lucies Day' and 'An Anatomy of the World' make negative use of the
same analogy; having felt what it is to become all, the individual unsupported
by love can sink to nothing and the world also will collapse.

8 *Second World and Green World* 49. In Berger's model of the Renaissance
imagination, 'there is a world around man hemming him in and a world
within pressing out from the center of self, and these two worlds are discon-
tinuous, for the first is actual, the second imaginary or hypothetical' (ibid.).

9 Florentine Platonism is criticized on these grounds in Berger's 'Pico and
Neoplatonist Idealism: Philosophy as Escape' (*Second World and Green
World* 189–228). In *Music in Renaissance Magic* 247–52, Gary Tomlinson
responds to this view, imagining 'an enunciative space somewhere between
Ficino and us' (248) in which it is possible to recover the principles informing
spiritual magic, while admitting that much of Ficino's world remains irrecov-
erably other, beyond the reach of appropriation or rejection.

10 Petrarch's letter is discussed in the context of his life and his career as a writer by Hans Baron, 'Petrarch: His Inner Struggles and the Humanistic Discovery of Man's Nature,' and by Robert Durling, 'The Ascent of Mt. Ventoux and the Crisis of Allegory.' See also Miller, *The Poem's Two Bodies* 77–9.

11 Pico's ambition to embrace and unify all the branches of knowledge creates a problem for terminologists. Paul Oskar Kristeller, who would reserve the term 'humanist' for those who professed the *studia humanitatis*, emphasizes that 'humanism was merely one component of [Pico's] thought and work.' See 'Giovanni Pico della Mirandola and His Sources' 56–7. In applying the term 'humanism' to the totality of Pico's thought, as do Garin and others, I wish to stress its systematic character, but not to imply the existence of a systematic 'philosophy of humanism.'

12 The dichotomy I will describe need not be at odds with others. For example, Clark Hulse, in 'Spenser, Bacon, and the Myth of Power,' describes 'two quite distinct languages about power,' employed by 'poetic humanists' and 'politiques.' As Hulse's emphasis is on power and the state while mine is on knowledge and the individual, the domains we are mapping are dissimilar, but some agreement is to be expected between esoteric and 'poetic' humanists, and between the Socratic orientation and 'politique' or Machiavellian analysis of power.

13 In *The Poet as Philosopher*, Charles Trinkaus interprets the philosophical dimension of Petrarch's writings and their influence. Paul Oskar Kristeller's essay, 'Humanism' (*CHRP* 113–37), is the latest of that author's magisterial considerations of humanism in relation to philosophy. In the same collection, see also Lisa Jardine on 'Humanistic Logic' (173–98).

14 I will cite the translation of Elizabeth L. Forbes in *RPM*. In the second part of the 'Oration' (paragraphs 9–20), the progression from moral philosophy through dialectic to natural philosophy and then to theology is reiterated many times.

15 The implications and influence of these ideas are considered by Edgar Wind, *Pagan Mysteries in the Renaissance* 110–12, and at greater length by Frances A. Yates, 'Giovanni Pico della Mirandola and Magic.'

16 See Raymond Klibansky, Erwin Panofsky, and Fritz Saxl, *Saturn and Melancholy* 241–7.

17 See A.H.T. Levi, 'The Neoplatonist Calculus' 242–6; Hans Staub, *Le Curieux désir*; Peter Sharratt, ed., *French Renaissance Studies, 1540–70*; and Neil Kenny, *The Palace of Secrets*.

18 This phase of the 'ancient quarrel' is interpreted in Carl Rapp's essay, 'Philosophy and Poetry: The New Rapprochement' 124–9.

19 Roger Hinks, *Myth and Allegory in Ancient Art* 4. There is an instructive parallel in the history of the term 'ideology,' which means both the exposi-

tion and the critique of normative principles. See Terry Eagleton, *Ideology: An Introduction* 43–5.

20 Cf. the suggestions of Paul A. Olson in his review of Robert Lamberton, *Homer the Theologian.*

21 Gordon Teskey, 'From Allegory to Dialectic,' argues that 'moral deviation in *The Faerie Queene* is the condition of the narrative as a whole, and the turns and counterturns of romance are easily identified with error' (9).

22 *The Poetry of* The Faerie Queene 361. Alpers discusses (361–9) the way Spenser handles in Book I two different traditions of thought about the relation of human nature to divine grace.

23 I don't think the presence of contradictions in a text is always, or even typically, a weakness; it may be an indicator of the author's robust health and a register of contradictions within the culture, or in human nature. See Norman Rabkin, *Shakespeare and the Problem of Meaning*, for a suggestive discussion of contradictory interpretations and of what Rabkin calls 'complementarity' in literary texts. Carol V. Kaske, 'Spenser's Pluralistic Universe,' argues that '*The Faerie Queene* is somehow about contradictions' (123), but finds the contradictions between Christian and 'sub-Christian' or classical world views accommodated in a clear-cut 'intellectual structure' of three worlds (149).

24 See, however, Charles B. Schmitt, *John Case and Aristotelianism in Renaissance England*, a thorough account of academic philosophy which gives some attention to books addressed to lay audiences.

25 For an explanation of the texts and conventions used in citations from Ficino's *Commentary* (usually mentioned by its alternative title, *On Love*), see the headnote explaining abbreviations for frequently cited texts.

26 Jayne cites Chalcidius, Jamblichus, Proclus, and Apuleius (146, n. 9). See also Michael J.B. Allen, *Platonism of Marsilio Ficino*, chapter 1 ('Socrates' Inspiration').

27 A.C. Hamilton's analysis of the episode in the Wandering Wood, which 'inaugurates' the action of the poem, remains pertinent: *Structure of Allegory in* The Faerie Queene 34–43. Cf. Berger, *Revisionary Play* 23.

28 See 'The Scholastic Background of Marsilio Ficino,' Paul Oskar Kristeller's fundamental study, and Ardis B. Collins, *The Secular is Sacred.*

29 See Hamilton's note at III vi 30. The fame of Adonis's gardens in Spenser's time may have rested primarily on an item in Erasmus's *Adagia*, where they are glossed as 'trivial things ... suitable only for giving a brief passing pleasure.' Plato's *Phaedrus* is quoted, as are Plutarch (*Moralia* 560b–c) and Theocritus (*Idyll* 15). See *Adages* I i 4 in *Collected Works of Erasmus* 31: 51–3.

30 See Hamilton's note on Adonis at III vi 46–9, to which other discussions of

Adonis and the sun's role in generation should be added: Hankins, *Source and Meaning* 246–55, adduces a number of passages from Ficino in support of an identification of both Adonis and the sun with the power by which the world soul generates species; see also Nohrnberg, *Analogy* 552–4.

31 For another example of Spenser's reason and faith at work, see the stanzas that prepare for the appearance (straight out of Ficino, I believe) of Guyon's guardian angel, 'Like as *Cupido* on *Idaean* hill' (II viii 6.1), discussed below, [196–8].

32 Arthur O. Lovejoy, *Great Chain of Being* 50–5, 111–21; cf. S.K. Heninger, Jr, *Cosmographical Glass* 25–7.

33 Ficino's '*Unam esse oportet totius animam, sicut et una est materia, una constructio,*' could be translated, 'It is proper that there be one soul for the whole, just as there is one matter and one structure'; Jayne's translation, incorporating a phrase from Ficino's Italian version, reads, 'The soul of the Universe must be single, just as its matter is single and its structure is single' (VI iii 110). Paul Oskar Kristeller, *Philosophy of Marsilio Ficino* 68–73, discusses 'the argument in which some fact is called "meet" and is therefore admitted to be real.'

34 'Certainly it would be an absurdity if an imperfect body could possess a soul but a perfect body could neither possess a soul nor be alive. For who is so distracted [*mente captus*] as to say that a part is alive but the whole is not?' (VI iii 110).

Chapter 4: Platonic Natural Philosophy in the *Aeneid*

1 *Passage to Modernity* 15. In a similar spirit, C.S. Lewis wrote of 'Nature with a capital' as '*nature* in the dangerous sense' (*Studies in Words* 37; see 24–74 passim).

2 Levinus Lemnius, *Les Occvltes Merveilles et Secretz de Natvre* fol. 12r.

3 Dupré, *Passage to Modernity* 178–89, discusses several developments in the sixteenth century; see also *CHRP* 236–63, and Brian P. Copenhaver and Charles B. Schmitt, *Renaissance Philosophy* 285–328.

4 *CHRP* 469; cf. D.P. Walker, *Spiritual and Demonic Magic* 4.

5 *CHRP* 483–4, and D.P. Walker, 'Francis Bacon and *Spiritus*.'

6 *Origins of the Platonic Academy* 231. Landino is a central figure in Field's account of the 'Platonic revival' in Florence and its place within Florentine civic culture. On the early years of his career at the Studio, see 77–106, and for an account of his teaching and writings, 231–74.

7 I have used the British Library copy of the first edition (Florence: B. Nerli, 1487); for a description, see Giuliano Mambelli, *Gli Annali delle edizioni*

virgiliane, no. 55. It appears from Mambelli's bibliography (which is not without errors, and incomplete for the sixteenth century) that Landino's commentary was reprinted at least twice within the first year, and at least two dozen times in the next 35 years.

8 In what follows I will cite *Virgilius cum commentariis quinque* as published by Jacques Sachon (or Zachon) in Lyon, 1499 (Mambelli, no. 87; cf. Copinger 6078). Where the 1499 text is obscure or corrupt, I have taken readings from the first edition.

9 *Origins of the Platonic Academy* 231; cf. Don Cameron Allen, *Mysteriously Meant* 142–3. Craig Kallendorf, 'Cristoforo Landino's *Aeneid* and the Humanist Critical Tradition,' observes of the commentary in Landino's edition that he 'gave in here with some regularity to his love of allegorizing' (524), but his article concentrates on the *Disputationes*.

10 Eberhard Müller-Bochat, *Leon Battista Alberti und die Vergil-Deutung der Disputationes Camaldulenses* 13–16, argues that Landino's originality lay in his view of Aeneas in the first six Books as, like Odysseus, engaged in a process of purification and contemplation. On the Neoplatonic readings of the *Odyssey* and their influence, see Don Cameron Allen, *Mysteriously Meant* 83–94.

11 *Svpplementvm Ficinianvm* II, 184; cf. André Chastel, *Marsile Ficin et l'art* 143 and 152 n. 17.

12 *Virgilius* fol. 215v. This passage summarizes much of the exposition in the *Disputationes*.

13 *Virgilius* fol. 221r–v; cf. Ficino in *Svpplementvm Ficinianvm* I, 81.

14 *Virgilius* fols 111v–12r. Roberto Cardini's edition of Landino's *Scritti critici e teorici* includes this Preface to the *Aeneid* (I 226–33) with a valuable commentary (II 298–314). Cf. Charles Trinkaus, *In Our Image and Likeness* 713–14. Similar ideas are found at the beginning of Book III in the *Disputationes*, but Mercurius Trismegistus and the idea of a *duplex theologia* are not mentioned.

15 The appearance of Mercury as Jove's messenger to Aeneas at the end of Book IV provides an occasion in Landino's commentary for a long excursus on the various Mercurys of tradition, including the 'thrice-great' Egyptian, a philosopher, priest, and king in one person (*Virgilius* fol. 190r–v). Most of what Landino says about Hermes' antiquity ('*tempore Moyses*,' on the authority of Augustine), the arts he founded, his teachings, and their transmission by Plato, comes from the *Argumentum* with which Ficino prefaced his translation of the *Pimander* (first printed in 1471).

16 The *Hermetica: The Greek Corpus Hermeticum and the Latin Asclepius*, are now available in a scholarly translation by Brian P. Copenhaver, who pro-

vides an instructive Introduction, a copious commentary, and a *vade mecum* to the vast scholarly literature. See xxiii–xxxii for an account that places the *Hermetica* in their historical milieu, and xlvii–l for the rise and fall of Hermes within the myth of a *prisca theologia*.

17 *Virgilius* fol. 239r. Commenting (fol. 238v) on '*Principio*' in Anchises' discourse (*Aeneid* VI 724), after explaining that the word can mean several things in scriptural usage (God in John 1:1; the beginning of time and process in Genesis 1:1), he concludes, 'But I think that the meaning of a Platonic poet ought to be referred to the teachings of Plato.'

18 *Vergil-Deutung* 19. See the translation by Sears Jayne, *Commentary on a Canzone of Benivieni*.

19 'These three, Fate, Necessity, and Order, were effected by God's command.' Hermes' doctrine is found in *Asclepius*, 39–40: see *Hermetica* 91 and 257–8.

20 *Disputationes* 223; cf. *Virgilius* fol. 219r–v, a long note on *Aeneid* VI 98–101, explaining that by the four species of divine *furor* we may recover the wisdom enjoyed before the soul's descent to earth.

21 *Commentary on the Dream of Scipio* 157–8 (*In somnium Scipionis* I xvii 14).

22 Landino's distinction between two minds, '*separatus*' and '*coniunctus*,' follows Ficino's interpretation of the *Timaeus*: see *Compendium in Timaeum*, chapter 26, in Plato, *Omnia Divini Platonis Opera tralatione Marsilii Ficini* 684.

23 *Virgilius* fol. 220v; cf. Macrobius, *In somn. Scip.* I x 7 and xi 1. Much of what Landino says of the soul and the Underworld is drawn from *In somn. Scip.* I x–xiv, where ideas from the *Timaeus* are used to interpret *Aeneid* VI as well as Cicero's dream vision.

24 See Archimago's evocation of evil spirits in I i 37–44 and Duessa's descent in I v 31–44: both passages contain clear allusions to *Aeneid* VI, as does Mammon's Tartarean underworld in II vii.

25 *Compendium*, chapter 38; *Platonis Opera* 696: '*Adhibet & uehicula, id est aetherea corpora.*' The seminal study is D.P. Walker's, 'The Astral Body in Renaissance Medicine.' See also Michael J.B. Allen, *Platonism of Marsilio Ficino* 96–103, and *Marsilio Ficino and the Phaedran Charioteer* 100–6.

26 *Virgilius* fol. 239r. Explaining why Anchises calls the limbs of the body '*moribunda*' (l. 732), he says that 'only these bodies impede the mind, and not the etherial bodies with which they are clothed from the beginning' (fol. 238v).

27 *Disputationes* 125–6; cf. Ficino's *On Love* II vii 53–4 and VI vii–viii 115–20.

28 *Virgilius* fols. 183v–4r. Landino identifies the lovers' meeting in a cave after hunting (IV 165–72) as the point at which incontinence becomes intemperance. On Dido and her decline into intemperance, cf. *Disputationes* 182–4,

and Don Cameron Allen, *Mysteriously Meant* 151. Müller-Bochat, *Vergil-Deutung* 31, points out that in his edition of Virgil, Landino interprets the war for Latium as an embodiment of the purgatorial rather than the civic virtues.

29 Robert Ellrodt, *Neoplatonism in the Poetry of Spenser* 9; Erwin Panofsky, *Renaissance and Renascences in Western Art* 183.

30 E.H. Gombrich, *Symbolic Images* 64; cf. Panofsky, *Renaissance and Renascences in Western Art* 188.

31 On 'refeudalization' and 'uneven development,' see Agnes Heller, *Renaissance Man* 29–56.

32 *Batman vppon Bartholome, His Booke De Proprietatibus Rerum* ... (London: Thomas East, 1582). Having been Archbishop Matthew Parker's librarian, Batman became chaplain to Henry Carey, Baron Hunsdon; the book is dedicated to this patron. It is worth noting that Henry Carey was at least peripherally involved in the circle of learned and free-thinking men that included Ralegh and the Earl of Northumberland, and that Spenser was on some terms of intimacy with Lady Carey (née Elizabeth Spencer). For a further connection between Spenser and Bat(e)man, see Anne Lake Prescott, 'Spenser's Chivalric Restoration.'

33 *Batman vppon Bartholome* fols 165r–74v. The chapters included are as follows: I iii–xi, III xxi–xxii, I xii–xvii. Agrippa's account of the properties of One is found at the end of Bartholomaeus's Book I (on the triune God): see fol. 2r–v. Passages from Bartholomaeus and Agrippa are discussed with reference to Spenser in Rosemond Tuve, *Essays* 50–4. D.P. Walker, *Spiritual and Demonic Magic* 90–6, and Frances A. Yates, *Giordano Bruno and the Hermetic Tradition* 130–43, discuss Agrippa's exposition of different forms of magic.

34 See Walker, *Spiritual and Demonic Magic* 3–24, 91–3, for discussion of Ficino's treatise (Book III of *De Vita*) and Agrippa's use of it. Astrological medicine and magic in *De Vita* III are discussed by Raymond Klibansky et al., *Saturn and Melancholy* 258–74, and there is a modern edition and translation of Ficino's *Three Books on Life* by Carol V. Kaske and John R. Clarke.

35 On the genealogy of Genius, see the *SE* entry by John C. Ulreich, Jr, and Nohrnberg, *Analogy* 552–4 (citing *Batman vppon Bartholome* and noting the references to *rationes seminales*). For various accounts of the provenance of 'seminal reasons' as they appear in the Garden of Adonis, see Ellrodt, *Neoplatonism in the Poetry of Spenser* 76–82; William Nelson, *Poetry of Edmund Spenser* 210–22; Hankins, *Source and Meaning* 264–8; Nohrnberg, *Analogy* 533–62.

36 *The Institution of Christian Religion* I i–ii.

37 *Institution* I v, fol. 10r. See Edward A. Dowey, Jr, *Knowledge of God in Calvin's Theology* 50–147. Part of a study by Charles Trinkaus, 'Renaissance Problems in Calvin's Theology,' is also relevant (61–8).

38 Aristotelians and Stoics compete, according to Daneau, for 'the vpper hande in the Schooles,' and both are said to ascribe 'the chief and principall causes of engendryng of all thinges, vnto Nature, which is to bee founde in euery thing, and too thinges created, as vnto Heauen, the Sunne, and the Elements' (fol. 11v).

39 See Copenhaver and Schmitt, *Renaissance Philosophy* 240–3.

40 The scholarship on Bruno is extensive; for an excellent summary of his career and his thought on the subject of nature, with references to other studies, see Copenhaver and Schmitt, *Renaissance Philosophy* 290–303 and 314–17.

41 Bruno also alludes to Anchises' discourse in *Lampas triginta statuarum* and *De Magia*: see *Opera latine conscripta* III 60, 434. Cf. Frances A. Yates, *Giordano Bruno and the Hermetic Tradition* 265, 310.

42 *Dialoghi italiani* 232. My translation draws upon that of Sidney Greenberg in *The Infinite in Giordano Bruno*.

43 *Dialoghi* 244; cf. 246–7, where Dicson finds Ovid (*Metamorphoses* XV 153–9 and 165) and Solomon (Eccl. 1. 9–10) in agreement with Teofilo on the principle that all things change but nothing perishes.

44 *Studies in Medieval and Renaissance Literature* 160; cf. 140, and *Spenser's Images of Life* 8–17.

Chapter 5: Nature in *The Faerie Queene*

1 Richard A. McCabe, *The Pillars of Eternity*, grounds a reading of much that concerns me here in an excellent account of intellectual traditions.

2 *Kindly Flame* 8. Roche's rationale for 'The Elizabethan Idea of Allegory' is conveniently found in the Norton Critical Edition of *Edmund Spenser's Poetry*, 3rd ed., 705–7.

3 See David W. Burchmore, 'Triamond, Agape, and the Fates.'

4 *Spenser's Moral Allegory* 212. Cf. Gordon Teskey, *Allegory and Violence* 175–88: for Teskey the *Cantos* are 'too obvious in [their] metaphysical program, too affirmatively Neoplatonic' (177).

5 See the *SE* entry for 'Proteus.' Only his capacity for prophecy connects him closely with God's will; he is also conventionally associated with flattery. In mythography and in Spenser's 'physical' allegory, Proteus is associated with matter, the four elements, and the wintry death of transient life-forms; regarded positively, he is a giver of forms to matter, and his imprisonment of Florimell preserves her for eventual union with Marinell.

6 Edgar Wind discusses Renaissance responses to the Virgilian image of Venus as *virgo* in *Pagan Mysteries in the Renaissance* 75–80. See also Anthony di Matteo, 'Spenser's Venus-Virgo.' On Belphoebe, see Camille A. Paglia, 'The Apollonian Androgyne and the *Faerie Queene*.'

7 See *Muiopotmos* 45 and, in *Fowre Hymnes*, HB 29. In *FQ* see I x 42.6; II ix 21.8, 23.3, 47.2; II xii 83.3; III Pr. 2.8; III vi 12.5; IV vi 17.4, x 29.8.

8 To my account of some facets of this episode, compare Isabel MacCaffrey's discussion, *Spenser's Allegory* 143–50.

9 See 'Night' in *SE* for an account of the tradition and the full range of references in Spenser's poetry.

10 In Book V of the *Consolation*, Prose 3 and Prose 6, Boethius considers and resolves the apparent conflict between necessity and freedom of the will, responding to the counsel of despair. Cf. McCabe, *Pillars of Eternity* 158–62.

11 Twice, 'foresight' is used to mean divine providence: see I ix 7.1 and III iii 2.5.

12 On this point, see McCabe, *Pillars of Eternity* 124, and cf. 41–2: in his *View of the Present State of Ireland*, Spenser justifies a remorseless 'Course of reformacion' with an appeal to 'verye vrgente necessitye.'

13 Arthur and his shield are brilliantly interpreted by Kenneth Gross, *Spenserian Poetics* 128–44.

14 See 'Calvin, Calvinism' in *SE*, and McCabe, *Pillars of Eternity* 170–9.

15 See II x 9.8, 13.9, 45.5; III iv 27–8, ix 41–2 and 49, xii 46.9 [1590].

16 Cf. III iv 36–9, V iv 27, VI iv 30–1.

17 MacCaffrey (*Spenser's Allegory* 338) observes acutely that the 'lifes succession' allowed to the three brothers is a limited version of Adonis's state, 'by succession made perpetuall' (III vi 47.6). The word 'succession' appears in Spenser's poetry only in these two places.

18 See McCabe, *Pillars of Eternity* 159–63: Calvin rejected the Stoic and Boethian conception of fate as 'the perpetual connection and intimately related series of causes, which is contained in nature,' and thought that references to fortune ought to be avoided as foolish.

19 Hamilton's comment on the description of Concord in IV x 31 supports Osgood's suggestion that her costume alludes to the Queen's in several state portraits.

20 See 'alchemy' in *SE*: alchemical terms, images, and ideas pervade *The Faerie Queene*, but at least on the exoteric level, Spenser's attitude is 'negative in tone.'

21 See I vi 23.7, II v 5.6 and 39.9, III v 1.9, IV vi 43.6, IV ix 2.5, IV x 26.9, VI ii 34.5.

22 See I iv 11.8, II vii 48.3; VII vi 4.1, 21.2, 29.2; VII vii 59.1.

23 In Book III, see i 46 and 49–50, iii 1–2, v 1–2; in Book IV, Proem 1–4 and vi 31–3.

24 *Amoretti 72* is one of several places where Spenser suggests this; cf. Scudamour at IV x 28.3. The false Florimell made her lover 'thinke him selfe in heauen, that was in hell' (III viii 19.9).

25 See III xi 15.5, 22.4, 26.5, 29.6, 38.7, 45.1, 48.1, 52.5; xii 20.8, 22.9, 31.5, 38.1; IV i 4.5.

26 This topic is discussed sensibly by William V. Nestrick, 'Spenser and the Renaissance Mythology of Love' 60–7. Alastair Fowler, *Triumphal Forms* 47–58, places the episode in the context of pageantry and fictive triumphs. See also Kenneth Gross, *Spenserian Poetics* 162–8, and Lauren Silberman, *Transforming Desire* 58–67.

27 The Elizabethan fascination with jealousy shows in many episodes preceding this one, from Redcrosse's 'gealous fire' and 'furious ire' when he is finally aroused by Archimago's display of 'Una' in another man's arms (I ii 5) to the plight of Malbecco, reduced to a personification by his 'long anguish, and selfe-murdring thought' (III x 57.1).

28 S.K. Heninger, Jr, *Touches of Sweet Harmony*. For a broader perspective on cosmological and psychological schemata, see Yi-Fu Tuan, *Topophilia* 13–24. In *SE*, the entry on 'elements' is relevant here.

29 *Timaeus* 31B–32C; *Touches of Sweet Harmony* 160–3; in *SE*, 'tetrads.'

30 See I iv 10.2, ix 42.2, xi 7.5; *Cantos* vi 3.9, vii 15.6–7.

31 See Hamilton's note at I x 66 and William Nelson, *Poetry of Edmund Spenser* 151.

32 'Nothing is sure, that growes on earthly ground' (I ix 11.5); 'Nothing on earth mote alwaies happie beene' (III i 10.7; cf. VI xi 1.7); 'But what on earth can alwayes happie stand?' (V iii 9.1); 'So tickle is the state of earthly things' (VI iii 5.2; cf. VII viii 1.6).

33 *Batman vppon Bartholome* fol. 166r, from a chapter 'Of the meruailous or wonderfull natures of Fire and Earth,' a translation of Agrippa's Book I, chapter 5.

34 Hamilton's note cites Virgil's *Georgics*, II 323–8. To this vernal occasion, compare the autumnal storm that drives Aeneas and Dido together to their union in the cave, an event that Virgil glosses as 'that first day of death, and that the cause of evils' (*Aeneid* IV 169–70). It seems likely that the two passages were linked in Spenser's mind and both ironically present as intertexts for the devious detour that begins the poem's engagement with Errour.

35 MacCaffrey, *Spenser's Allegory* 148–50, takes 'protean' fire to be typical of 'the duplicity of the phenomenal world'; she cites Gaston Bachelard, *The Psychoanalysis of Fire*, for whom fire is 'a tutelary and a terrible divinity, both good and bad.' Cf. Yi-Fu Tuan, *Topophilia* 23–4.

36 Redcrosse's 'natiue virtue' or 'noble courage,' the basis for his Fortitude (first

among the cardinal virtues), is a 'spark' (I ii 19.1–2, xi 2.6). Virtuous love is a fire or flame: for a few examples, see I Proem 3.4, I vii 27.5 and ix 16.4; III iii 1.1 and v 1.8. Friendship is a 'zealous fire' (IV x 26; cf. ix 1–2); the same fire 'brings forth glorious flowres of fame' (IV Proem 1–2; cf. VI ii 37.3–4). Crowning his work in the *Cantos of Mutabilitie*, Spenser asks the 'greater Muse' to 'Kindle fresh sparks of that immortal fire, / Which learned minds inflameth with desire / Of heauenly things' (vii 2.4–6).

37 Circe, the classical prototype of Acrasia and her kind in Renaissance poetry, was begotten by the sun on the sea nymph Perse; accordingly, Natalis Comes glosses her as *commistio*, a harmony of the elements in the physical world and the human body. (In *SE*, see 'Circe.')

38 The quotations are from *SE*: W.H. Herendeen on 'rivers' (606c) and Terry Comito on 'fountains' (314b); see also Herendeen on 'sea.'

39 The creation story in *Colin Clout* (see 855–8) adds Empedoclean/Pythagorean principles to Genesis; cf. *F.Q.* IV x 44.8, based on Lucretius.

40 See I vi 1, xii 1 and 42; VI xii 1–2; and in *SE*, the articles on 'ship imagery' and the 'narrator.'

41 Cf. I i 53.4, ii 42.2, iii 16.3, iv 19.4; II viii 24.9; III i 59.3; V vii 12.6; VI viii 36.9. A person may also 'drown in dissolute delights,' as Phaedria tempts Guyon to do (II vi 25.7); cf. II v 36.9, III xii 6.5. Outside Mammon's cave Guyon is confronted with a choice between 'selfe-consuming Care' and Sleep; the choice seems easy, 'For next to death is Sleepe to be compard' (II vii 25.1, 7).

42 In *SE*, 'dreams' interprets both illusory and prophetic dreams, describing the similarity of Spenserian narrative to 'processes known usually to us only as mentation during sleep.'

43 On this subject, see 'fountains' in *SE* and Hankins, *Source and Meaning* 84–7.

44 Useful information on the physiological and psychological spirit or spirits, with specific reference to Spenser's poetry, will be found in *SE* under 'medicine' and 'psychology.'

45 A fascinating body of modern scholarship has interpreted the interplay between the cosmic and microcosmic *spiritus* as theorized by Ficino, Agrippa, and many others. Chapter 4 explored this subject: see 105–7, 122–4, 128–9. For Ficino, see also Michael J.B. Allen, *Platonism of Marsilio Ficino* 96–106; *Icastes* 184–5 and 194–204; and *Nuptial Arithmetic* 88–105. On the *spiritus* and the magical efficacy of verbal and non-verbal music, see Gary Tomlinson, *Music in Renaissance Magic* 101–44.

46 See VI i 2.2–3: we are told that Calidore was 'beloued ouer all, / In whom it seemes, that gentlenesse of spright / And manners mylde were planted

naturall.' That Belphoebe, Amoret, and Britomart each possess a 'gentle spright' is shown by their susceptibility to love (III vi 1.9; xii 44.6 and 46.7). Queen Elizabeth, on the other hand, is praised for her 'high spirit,' and the compliment comes with hope that she will, under the influence of Cupid and Venus, moderate her 'haughtie courage' and 'hearke to loue' (IV Proem 5).

Chapter 6: Reading the Garden of Adonis Canto

1 Jean-Pierre Vernant, in the Introduction to Marcel Detienne, *Gardens of Adonis* iii.

2 The most important contributions to the interpretation of doctrines and their sources are Nelson, *Poetry of Edmund Spenser* 206–25; Fowler, *Spenser and the Numbers of Time* 132–44; Cheney, *Spenser's Image of Nature* 117–42; Hankins, *Source and Meaning* 234–86; Nohrnberg, *Analogy* 490–567; McCabe, *Pillars of Eternity* 138–49. Richard Neuse, in 'Planting Words in the Soul' and in his *SE* article ('Adonis, gardens of'), offers both fresh insights into intellectual contexts and subtle responses to the Garden canto as poetry.

3 Berger, in an essay first published in 1961 (printed in *Revisionary Play* 131–53) and recently in 'Actaeon at the Hinder Gate,' has been the leader among Spenserians well-grounded in intellectual history but primarily interested in celebrating the Garden canto's difference, as poetry, from all the learning Spenser brought to his writing table. Other fine critics responsive to the canto in these terms include Kathleen Williams, *Spenser's World of Glass* 145–50; Alpers, *Poetry of* The Faerie Queene 5–8, 326–8, 391–2; MacCaffrey, *Spenser's Allegory* 254–90; Maureen Quilligan, *Milton's Spenser* 190–7; Gross, *Spenserian Poetics* 181–209; Miller, *The Poem's Two Bodies* 235–81; Lauren Silberman, *Transforming Desire* 35–48.

4 See Cheney, *Spenser's Image of Nature* 124–6; Nestrick, 'Spenser and the Renaissance Mythology of Love' 37–44; Hyde, *Poetic Theology of Love* 83–5, 166–8.

5 There is a modern facsimile edition of the Greek *editio princeps* and numerous translations: *Cebes' Tablet*, ed. Sandra Sider.

6 Elizabeth Bieman's discussion of *On the Cave of the Nymphs* (*Plato Baptized* 106–8) links its themes with those of the Garden canto and the story of Florimell and Marinell.

7 *Plato Baptized* accounts for several strands of patristic tradition and their bearing upon Spenser's poetry; see also Harold Weatherby's *Mirrors of Celestial Grace*.

8 In *SE*, the 'du Bartas' entry discusses the English reception of his poetry and considers the scope of Spenser's interest in it.

9 In *SE*, the article on 'Hermeticism' usefully supplements the viewpoint found in that on 'occult sciences.' See also 264–6 below.

10 In *SE*, see 'Orpheus.' Seminal articles by D.P. Walker on Orpheus and related topics are collected in his *The Ancient Theology*.

11 See Gross, *Spenserian Poetics* 200–9; Neuse, 'Planting Words in the Soul'; Miller, *The Poem's Two Bodies* 235–41.

12 In 'Spenser and the Patronesses of the *Fowre Hymnes*,' I have touched upon the challenges Spenser faced as he addressed his two audiences, men and women. There are many parallels to the story of Amoret in the experience of Margaret Russell Clifford, Countess of Cumberland (one of the two sisters to whom the *Hymnes* were dedicated), and the memoir and diary records that she and her daughter kept enable us to imagine some of her responses to *The Faerie Queene*.

13 For its multitude of unnamed inhabitants the Garden represents life before birth and after death; the awkwardness of imagining Amoret living there from the neonatal state in which she is discovered until her adolescence should not be finessed but is closed to interpretation.

14 My comments invite comparison with Miller's use of de Beauvoir: *The Poem's Two Bodies* 215–7. Jessica Benjamin, *The Bonds of Love*, also sheds light on Amoret's predicament and the characters of Britomart and Florimell; see chapter 3 in particular.

15 In *SE*, see 'courtesy,' 'courtesy as a social code,' and 'courtesy books.'

16 Sears Jayne's translation of the *Commentary* contains an introduction documenting its assimilation, with a list of later Italian treatises and mention of Ficino's translators and adapters in France, Spain, and Italy (19–23 and notes); Jayne's bibliography ranges far beyond studies devoted specifically to the treatise and its influence (183–213). For a more detailed account of translations and adaptations in Italy and France, see Raymond Marcel's edition, *Commentaire sur le Banquet de Platon* 114–29. Sem Dresden, 'Profile of the Italian Renaissance in France,' places Florentine Platonism and its assimilation in a context appropriate for Spenser. In *SE*, see 'Ficino.'

17 Cantos with an odd number of stanzas will have a central stanza, even a central line that may be significant; cantos with an even number will have a pair of stanzas forming a hinge. It so happens that the central line of canto i in Book III describes 'The faire *Adonis*, turned to a flowre' (34.5) in Malecasta's tapestry; in the two stanzas at the centre of canto ii (26–7), Britomart, having seen Artegall in her father's looking glass, is struck by Cupid's arrow and falls sick with love. The central line of canto vii, 'To that faire Mayd, the flowre of womens pride' (31.5), refers to Florimell, 'dearely loued' by Satyrane, who discovers her golden girdle with the remains of her

palfrey; at the center of canto viii, stanzas 26–7, the old fisherman attacks Florimell and she cries to heaven for help, which will come in the form of Proteus.

18 Quoting Hamilton at I i 28; see Mark Rose, *Spenser's Art* 14.

19 For further discussion of significant numbers in the Garden canto, see chapter 7, 227–9.

20 Though it is external to *The Faerie Queene*, the passage in *Colin Clouts Come Home Againe* describing the shepherds' religion of love is closely connected with this canto: Colin describes how Cupid was 'Borne without Syre or couples of one kynd, / For *Venus* selfe doth soly couples seeme, / … So pure and spotlesse *Cupid* forth she brought, / And in the gardens of *Adonis* nurst' (ll. 800–4). The twin girls' conception and birth is modelled, then, on Cupid's origin, and we should see both of them as alternatives to Cupid in Spenser's reformed religion of love.

21 Hamilton glosses 'indew' in 35.5 as 'assume, put on (as a garment)'; Latin *induere* can also mean 'to be entangled in.' Cheney observes sensibly that in the Garden Spenser remains within the limits of nature, and the rational soul has a higher origin and destiny (*Spenser's Image of Nature* 126–7).

22 Nohrnberg's discussion of Chaos in relation to the Garden (*Analogy* 554–7) is apt. 'Each functions as the other's allegorical "other," for in the actualizing of the potential of each, each must recruit, or "reap," the other' (555).

23 Comparing the Garden point-by-point to the Bower of Bliss, Nohrnberg notes that 'a similar trail of victims leads to the Garden of Adonis'; he refers specifically to Mordant and Verdant, Marinell and Timias (*Analogy* 491–4, 502). Cf. Berger, *Revisionary Play* 97–8, 139. For Redcrosse, see MacCaffrey, *Spenser's Allegory* 166.

24 Berger, *Revisionary Play* 147–8, 152, argues that 'Adonis stands for that which does not endure, that moment whose very act is an instantaneous spending of itself.'

25 See Berger, *Revisionary Play* 92–3, 109–17; MacCaffrey, *Spenser's Allegory* 254–7; Gross, *Spenserian Poetics* 199.

26 Cf. Miller, *Poem's Two Bodies* 240–1, 254–61.

27 *Inwardness and Theater in the English Renaissance* 182–209; for the quotation, 191.

28 Berger ('Actaeon at the Hinder Gate' 106–7) describes 'the logic of idyllic desire, which is autonomous desire, desire of escape from the power of the other,' but if this logic is at work in 'the conclusion of the *hortus conclusus*' and the womblike seclusion that Adonis is supposed to enjoy, it is crossed by abundant evidence that neither the life-affirming nor the death-dealing forces at work in the Garden permit autonomy as anything but a fantasy.

29 Jeffrey Masten's essay 'Is the Fundament a Grave?' supports my reasoning here, and Spenser's anatomy of Venus supplies an instance in response to the 'lack of examples of the fundament gendered female' that he notes, also answering his rhetorical question, 'to what extent did medical or religious discourses, for example, conceive of women as having "foundational" body parts?' (144 n. 43).

30 The best discussion of Shakespeare's debts to Spenser is A.C. Hamilton's in 'Venus and Adonis': he finds in Shakespeare's poem, as in Spenser, both prurient appeal and interest in what Abraham Fraunce termed 'hidden mysteries of naturall ... philosophie.'

31 In addition to the titles cited subsequently in the text, I have in mind Juliana Schiesari, Gendering of Melancholia; Bettie Anne Doebler, 'Rooted Sorrow'; William E. Engel, Mapping Mortality; and two essays by Jonathan Dollimore, 'Desire Is Death' and 'Death and the Self.'

32 Henry Staten, Eros in Mourning 1–8.

33 George W. McClure, Sorrow and Consolation in Italian Humanism.

34 'Spenserian Remains: A Mortuary Poetics'; cf. Pathology of the English Renaissance 13.

35 Richard T. Neuse in SE, 8b, interpreting Theocritus's Idyll 15, cited in Comes's Mythologiae, 5.16.

36 See Phaedrus 276A–E. Neuse, 'Planting Words in the Soul,' includes a sustained discussion of this dialogue in its complicated connections with the themes of the Garden canto.

37 Rosso's painting, The Death of Adonis, forms part of his elaborate decorative program in the gallery of François I at Fontainebleau; it was reproduced in an etching and in a splendid tapestry now in Vienna (see Eugene A. Carroll, Rosso Fiorentino 238–49). Ronsard's responses to Rosso's work and his handling of Adonis in poems concerned with human mortality and seasonal renewal are discussed by Philip Ford, Ronsard's Hymnes 10–18, 248–85.

38 See 1 Peter 5:4, cited in Hamilton's gloss.

39 On stanza 45 and its allusion to poetic tributes to Amintas, see Donald Cheney, Spenser's Image of Nature 132–7.

40 A recent discussion is Raphael Falco's, Conceived Presences 87–123.

41 Cheney, Spenser's Image of Nature 135, notes the reference in Fraunce's first Yuychurch volume (1591) to an annual 'Amyntas Day'; see also Margaret P. Hannay, Philip's Phoenix 110–12, and Mary Ellen Lamb, Gender and Authorship in the Sidney Circle 32–44.

42 The quotation of a stanza from FQ II iv in Fraunce's Arcadian Rhetorike, published in 1588 (ed. Ethel Seaton, 60), shows that some of Spenser's poem circulated within the Sidney circle well before its publication.

43 This term's applicability to Spenser's fiction is developed well by McCabe, *Pillars of Eternity* 36–7, 133–49; see also Frank Kermode, *Sense of an Ending* 75–81.

44 Adonis and Venus are interpreted in these terms by Hankins, *Source and Meaning* 237–9, 272–7; and Nohrnberg, *Analogy* 533–7.

Chapter 7: The Platonic Program of the Garden Canto

1 On the number 6 and its association with marriage and generation, see Fowler, *Spenser and the Numbers of Time* 37, 48–50, 56–7; Allen, *Nuptial Arithmetic* 67–8, 74, 130–5, 226–33. John MacQueen, *Numerology* 31–6, explains the Lambda Formula, which schematically presents the numbers that proceed from the monad (1), according to *Timaeus* 35B–C: 2, 4, 8, and 3, 9, 27. MacQueen observes that '27 is in fact the sum of all the other numbers in the Lambda Formula (1+2+3+4+9+8=27), and so in a sense contains them all' (*Numerology* 36); in a simpler sense, 54 contains them all. MacQueen discusses Robert Henryson's use of 27 as an organizing principle in his *New Orpheus*, which concerns the harmony conferred upon the cosmos by the world soul (*Numerology* 103–6). It should also be noted here that 28, the pivotal number in cantos of 54 and 55 stanzas, follows 6 as the second 'perfect' number, consisting of the sum of its factors (1, 2, 4, 7, 14).

2 James Nohrnberg's description of *The Faerie Queene* as 'our most resourceful poem' is excruciating but apt; I share wholeheartedly his interest in the poem's 're-creation of a source in a way that seems to illustrate those nuances or details that belong to the allegorical or interpretive future of that source' (*Analogy* ix–x).

3 On Leone's life and the cultural context for his *Dialoghi*, the best account is Riccardo Scrivano, 'Platonic and Cabalistic Elements in the Hebrew Culture of Renaissance Italy'; see also Arthur M. Lesley, 'The Place of the *Dialoghi d'amore* in Contemporaneous Jewish Thought.' The *Dialoghi* figure in many accounts of the *trattati d'amore* and their impact on courtly life and the literatures of Europe during the Renaissance. Two book-length studies should be mentioned: Marco Ariani, *Imago Fabulosa*, and T. Anthony Perry, *Erotic Spirituality.*

4 'The Spiritual Eroticism of Leone's Hermaphrodite' 86–7.

5 My quotations are based on Tyard's *Dialogues d'Amour*, ed. T. Anthony Perry, designated as '*D.*' (I follow Tyard in calling the participants in the dialogues 'Philo' and 'Sophia.') I have also used the Italian text, ed. Santino Caramella, and the English version by F. Friedeberg-Seeley and Jean H. Barnes, *The Philosophy of Love.*

6 See Richard J. Berleth, 'Heavens Favorable and Free: Belphoebe's Nativity in *The Faerie Queene*,' and Hugh De Lacy, 'Astrology in the Poetry of Edmund Spenser' 535–40. Ficino interpreted Jupiter, Venus, and Sol as astrological symbols of the Graces: see *Three Books on Life*, III v, discussed by Yates, *Giordano Bruno and the Hermetic Tradition* 74–9; Fowler, *Spenser and the Numbers of Time* 83, 96; and Nohrnberg, *Analogy* 466–7.

7 *Tales of Love* 70. See also John Brenkman, 'The Other and the One,' an analysis of *The Symposium* that incorporates Lacan's references to Aristophanes' myth.

8 See Nohrnberg, *Analogy* 600–8, for an account of several sources for images of the androgyne or hermaphrodite and their bearing on Spenser's fiction.

9 For a semiotic analysis of the myth in Genesis, similarly linking sin with division into two sexes, see Mieke Bal, 'Sexuality, Sin, and Sorrow.'

10 In 'Spenser's Image of Sapience' 200–11, I make a case for the decisive bearing of this passage on the account in *Fowre Hymnes* of 'The soueraine dearling of the *Deity*' (*HHB* 184) and her procreative role in the universe.

11 See 'French Renaissance literature' in *SE*.

12 Hankins, *Source and Meaning* 243–4, provides the best gloss on the sun and moon in this passage.

13 The physician Levinus Lemnius observes, 'there bee three especiall thinges, in whose temperature and moderation the health of mans body doth principally consist, *viz.* vitall moysture, naturall heate, and Spirite, which combineth all thinges, and imparteth his force, vertue & nature, vnto them': *The Touchstone of Complexions*, trans. Thomas Newton, 3rd ed. (London: Thomas Marsh, 1581), fol. 7v.

14 A list of the authors cited in fols 86–92 of the commentary (some mentioned several times) will give some idea of Le Roy's learning: Cicero, Pontano, Philo Judaeus, Plato, Eusebius, Plutarch, Xenophon, Caelius Rhodiginus, Aristotle, Pietro Pomponazzi, St Augustine, Pico della Mirandola, Lucian, Agostino Steucho, Agrippa von Nettesheim, Jean Fernel, Marsilio Ficino, Caspar Pencer, several books of the Old Testament, Iamblichus, Julius Caesar, Musaeus and Orpheus as cited by Plato, Isocrates, Acts in the New Testament, Clement of Alexandria, Pliny, Apuleius, Philostratus, Virgil, St Jerome, Proclus, Plotinus, Michael Psellus, Hesiod, Jerome Cardanus, Georgius Agricola, Porphyry.

15 See *Sympose* fols 82–5. A marginal note, fol. 82v, refers to Angelo Poliziano's Latin translation of Moschus's poem, which is not the version used by Marot. The conjunction of Propertius, Moschus, and Poliziano here is suggestive: E.K., in his gloss on 'March,' had referred the reader interested in 'Cupids colours and furniture' to 'ether Propertius, or Moschus his Idyllion of

wandring loue, being now most excellently translated into Latine by the singuler learned man Angelus Politianus: whych worke I haue seene amongst other of thys Poets doings, very wel translated also into Englishe Rymes' (*Shorter Poems* 64).

16 Le Roy cites *De Generatione animalium* II i: 731b25–732a12. Cf. *Sympose* fol. 107r–v, citing several places in Aristotle and the account in Plato's *Timaeus* of generation from the Same and Different; and fols. 119v–20, citing Galen.

17 *Le Sympose*, fol. 124, citing *De Partibus animalium* I v: 644b23–645a10.

18 In addition, Maryanne Cline Horowitz's *Seeds of Virtue and Knowledge* devotes a chapter to Ficino and focuses on the *Symposium* commentary.

19 The several roles Ficino devises in *On Love* for Saturn, Jupiter, and Venus are apt to confuse a modern reader, but the schematic arrangements found there are simple by comparison to his interpretation of Neoplatonic categories and the ancient pantheon in later works such as his *Phaedrus* commentary: see Allen's interpretation in *Platonism of Ficino* 113–64, which is relevant at several points to the ideas in *On Love*.

20 Spenser celebrates a happy parallel to Timias's predicament when, in *Amoretti* 74, he pays tribute to the three Elizabeths who, like three Graces, have blessed him 'With guifts of body, fortune and of mind.'

21 Here and elsewhere, I follow Jayne's spelling of this term, to distinguish the good daemons of the upper world from infernal demons. In Ficino's Latin text, *demon* is his equivalent to Plato's *daimon*. Le Roy, as we have seen, translates *daimon* as *Demon*.

22 Several chapters in Speech VII (iv–xii 159–68) describe the agency of spirits in vulgar love understood as 'enchantment [*fascinatio*]'; such spirits could be allied with infernal *demones* of the kind employed by Archimago and the witch who contrives the false Florimell.

23 On the bearing of Diotima's teachings on the development of demonology within Neoplatonism, see Philip Merlan in *The Cambridge History of Later Greek and Early Medieval Philosophy* (ed. A.H. Armstrong) 32–7, and E.R. Dodds, *Pagan and Christian in an Age of Anxiety* 37–68; on the daemons in Ficino's version of Platonism, see Allen, *Platonism of Ficino* 3–40, and Tomlinson, *Music in Renaissance Magic* 121–34.

Chapter 8: *The Faerie Queene* in 1596 and 1609

1 See also John Guillory, *Poetic Authority* 23–45. Guillory's account of 'Spenser's habitual recourse to origins' (27) also credits Nohrnberg's *Analogy* as its antecedent.

2 The four-square schematic design that Spenser pursues throughout Book IV supplies Agape with a counterpart in Canacee, 'Well seene in euerie science that mote bee, / And euery secret worke of natures wayes' (ii 35.3–4); see also iii 37–52, where Canacee completes the unions that Agape had made possible.

3 On the forest setting considered as *hyle* or *sylva*, see Hankins, *Source and Meaning* 65–73; for the other aspect of Florimell's predicament, see Hamilton's note on Proteus (at III viii 30) and Hankins, *Source and Meaning* 228–34. Nohrnberg, *Analogy* 568–98, provides the most ample commentary on Florimell and the myths and mysteries of form and matter; see also 'mysteries' in *SE*, and Blissett, 'Florimell and Marinell.' Sean Kane's comments on Florimell are many-sided: *Spenser's Moral Allegory* 94–103.

4 See Elizabeth Jane Bellamy, 'The Vocative and the Vocational: The Unreadability of Elizabeth.'

5 Richard Mallette, in *Spenser and the Discourses of Reformation England* 113–42, provides an excellent account of companionate marriage understood as a form of friendship, and shows how that set of ideals competes in Book IV, as in Elizabethan culture, with the codes of revenge and rivalry between men.

6 When he claims for himself the shield of Love and seeks a bride rather than falling in with a temptress, Scudamour is avoiding the fate of Verdant, whose 'braue shield, full of old moniments, / Was fowly ra'st' and 'hong vpon a tree' (II xii 80), but whether he can ever live up to the motto associated with his identity-defining shield – '*Blessed the man that well can vse his blis*' – remains in question.

7 David Quint, *Origin and Originality in Renaissance Literature* 133–66, interprets the river marriage and related passages in *The Faerie Queene*, referring to religious and philosophical accounts of sources and cycles. For Silberman, the marriage canto 'draws on Neoplatonic notions of reality as a series of unfoldings of an infolded wholeness' (*Transforming Desire* 125–42).

8 *Spenser's World of Glass* 144. The idea appears in Pico's *Commento* and is more fully developed in his *Heptaplus* (I iii), in comments on Genesis 1:2–9. Landino had also interpreted Neptune in these terms: see 118 above.

9 Bruno's dialogue, one of several published in England during his stay there from 1583 to 1585, was like *De gli eroici furori* dedicated to Sir Philip Sidney; it has been translated by Arthur D. Imerti as *The Expulsion of the Triumphant Beast*. For opinions on some points of comparison between *Lo Spaccio* and the *Cantos*, see the Variorum *Books VI–VII* (389–91, 400–1) and 'Bruno' in *SE*; see also McCabe's appendix, 'Spenser and Bruno,' *Pillars of Eternity* 232–6. The most substantial discussion of Bruno's thought in relation to Spenser's (in the river marriage episode and the *Cantos*) focuses on *De gli eroici furori*: see Quint, *Origin and Originality* 137–49, 163–6.

10 The main themes of Bruno's philosophy of nature are summarized well by Copenhaver and Schmitt, with references to other scholarship (*Renaissance Philosophy* 288–9, 296–305, 314–17). The excursus on 'polydaemonism' at the end of Nohrnberg's *Analogy* (763–86) pertains to Bruno's thought as well as Spenser's.

11 Bruno's trial took place in Venice between 26 May and 30 July, 1592; in February of 1593 he was extradited to Rome, where he was incarcerated and occasionally examined; his public burning took place on 16 February, 1600. Imerti's introduction includes a detailed account of the proceedings against him and the heresies found in *Lo Spaccio* (*Expulsion* 29–65). Of course, these contributions to Bruno's subsequent fame have little bearing on his reputation in England and Ireland during Spenser's lifetime.

12 See Sperone Speroni, *Dialoghi* fols 80v–103v; for the quotation, 99v–100r. Some discussion of the dialogue is found in Jean-Louis Fournel, *Les dialogues de Sperone Speroni* 82–6.

13 Teskey has written brilliantly (*Allegory and Violence* 171–84) on the violence played out in the Olympian and Tudor genealogies, conveniently suppressed but still traceable in Spenser's account of the status quo; I differ with him primarily in my reading of Nature's judgment, which effectively dethrones Jove at the same time that it partially suppresses Mutabilitie.

Conclusion

1 'Plato and the Simulacrum' is the first half of an appendix, 'The Simulacrum and Ancient Philosophy,' in *The Logic of Sense*, 253–66. I have consulted this, the standard English version of Deleuze's *Logique du sens* (1969), but I will quote from the translation of 'Plato and the Simulacrum' by Rosalind Krauss, which I find more accurate. At a few points I have added, in brackets, phrases from Deleuze's text.

2 On the return of the unlimited to the surface, which Deleuze traces back to the Stoics, see *The Logic of Sense* 6–9.

Works Cited

See also p. xiii, Texts and Abbreviations; frequently cited titles listed there are not repeated here.

Additional abbreviations used in the works cited are as follows:

BHR	*Bibliothèque d'Humanisme et Renaissance*
CI	*Critical Inquiry*
ELR	*English Literary Renaissance*
JEGP	*Journal of English and Germanic Philology*
JHI	*Journal of the History of Ideas*
JMRS	*Journal of Medieval and Renaissance Studies*
JWCI	*Journal of the Warburg and Cortauld Institutes*
RES	*Review of English Studies*
SEL	*Studies in English Literature*

Abrams, M.H. *The Mirror and the Lamp: Romantic Theory and the Critical Tradition*. New York: Norton, 1958.

Adorno, Theodor. *Minima Moralia: Reflections from Damaged Life*. Trans. E.F.N. Jephcott. London: New Left Books, 1974.

Agrippa von Nettesheim, Heinrich Cornelius. *Of the Vanitie and Vncertaintie of the Artes and Sciences*. Trans. James Sanford. Ed. Catherine M. Dunn. Northridge: California State University, 1974.

Allen, Don Cameron. *Mysteriously Meant: The Rediscovery of Pagan Symbolism and Allegorical Interpretation in the Renaissance*. Baltimore: Johns Hopkins University Press, 1970.

Allen, Michael J.B. 'Cosmogony and Love: the Role of Phaedrus in Ficino's *Symposium* Commentary.' *JMRS* 10 (1980): 131–51.

- *Icastes: Marsilio Ficino's Interpretation of Plato's* Sophist. Berkeley and Los Angeles: University of California Press, 1989.
- *Marsilio Ficino and the Phaedran Charioteer*. Berkeley and Los Angeles: University of California Press, 1981.
- 'Marsilio Ficino's Interpretation of Plato's *Timaeus* and Its Myth of the Demiurge.' In *Svpplementvm Festivvm: Studies in Honor of Paul Oskar Kristeller*, ed. James Hankins *et al.*, 399–439. Binghamton: Medieval and Renaissance Text Society, 1987.
- *Nuptial Arithmetic: Marsilio Ficino's Commentary on the Fatal Number in Book VIII of Plato's* Republic. Berkeley and Los Angeles: University of California Press, 1994.
- *The Platonism of Marsilio Ficino: A Study of His* Phaedrus *Commentary, Its Sources and Genesis*. Berkeley and Los Angeles: University of California Press, 1984.
Alpers, Paul J. 'Narration in *The Faerie Queene.*' *ELH* 44 (1977): 19–39.
- *The Poetry of* The Faerie Queene. Princeton: Princeton University Press, 1967.
Altman, Joel B. *The Tudor Play of Mind: Rhetorical Inquiry and the Development of Elizabethan Drama*. Berkeley and Los Angeles: University of California Press, 1978.
Anderson, Judith H. '"In liuing colours and right hew": The Queen of Spenser's Central Books.' In *Poetic Traditions of the English Renaissance*, ed. Maynard Mack and George de Forest Lord, 47–66. New Haven: Yale University Press, 1982.
- 'Narrative Reflections: Re-envisaging the Poet in *The Canterbury Tales* and *The Faerie Queene.*' In *Refiguring Chaucer in the Renaissance*, ed. Theresa M. Krier, 87–105. Gainesville: University of Florida Press, 1988.
Anderson, Judith H., Donald Cheney, and David A. Richardson, eds. *Spenser's Life and the Subject of Biography*. Amherst: University of Massachusetts Press, 1996.
Ariani, Marco. *Imago Fabulosa: mito e allegoria nei 'Dialoghi d'amore' di Leone Ebreo*. Rome: Bulzoni editore, 1984.
Ariosto, Ludovico. *Orlando Furioso*. Trans. Barbara Reynolds. Harmondsworth: Penguin, 1975.
Aristotle. *Nicomachean Ethics*. Trans. Martin Oswald. Indianapolis: Bobbs-Merrill, 1962.
Bal, Mieke. 'Sexuality, Sin, and Sorrow: The Emergence of Female Character (A Reading of Genesis 1–3).' In *The Female Body in Western Culture*, ed. Susan Rubin Suleiman, 317–38. Cambridge: Harvard University Press, 1986.
Barkan, Leonard. *The Gods Made Flesh: Metamorphoses and the Pursuit of Paganism*. New Haven: Yale University Press, 1986.
Baron, Hans. 'Petrarch: His Inner Struggles and the Humanistic Discovery of

Man's Nature.' In *Florilegium Historiale: Essays Presented to Wallace K. Ferguson*, ed. J.G. Rowe and W.H. Stockdale, 19–51. Toronto: University of Toronto Press, 1971.

Bartholomaeus Anglicus. *Batman vppon Bartholome: His Booke De Proprietatibus Rerum* ... Trans. John Trevisa. Ed. Stephen Batman. London: Thomas East, 1582.

Bellamy, Elizabeth Jane. *Translations of Power: Narcissism and the Unconscious in Epic History.* Ithaca: Cornell University Press, 1992.

– 'The Vocative and the Vocational: The Unreadability of Elizabeth in *The Faerie Queene.' ELH* 54 (1987): 1–30.

Benjamin, Jessica. *The Bonds of Love: Psychoanalysis, Feminism, and the Problem of Domination.* New York: Pantheon, 1988.

Benjamin, Walter. 'The Work of Art in the Age of Mechanical Reproduction.' Trans. Harry Zohn. In *Illuminations*, 9–23. New York: Schocken, 1969.

Bennett, Josephine Waters. 'Reply: On Methods of Literary Interpretation.' *JEGP* 41 (1942): 486–9.

– 'Spenser's Garden of Adonis.' *PMLA* 42 (1932): 46–80.

– 'Spenser's Garden of Adonis Revisited.' *JEGP* 41 (1942): 53–78.

Berger, Harry, Jr. 'Actaeon at the Hinder Gate: The Stag Party in Spenser's Gardens of Adonis.' In *Desire in the Renaissance: Psychoanalysis and Literature*, ed. Valeria Finucci and Regina Schwartz, 91–119. Princeton: Princeton University Press, 1994.

– '"Kidnapped Romance": Discourse in *The Faerie Queene.'* In *Unfolded Tales: Essays on Renaissance Romance*, ed. George M. Logan and Gordon Teskey, 208–56. Ithaca: Cornell University Press, 1989.

– *Revisionary Play: Studies in the Spenserian Dynamics.* Berkeley and Los Angeles: University of California Press, 1988.

– *Second World and Green World: Studies in Renaissance Fiction-Making.* Berkeley and Los Angeles: University of California Press, 1988.

Berleth, Richard J. 'Heavens Favorable and Free: Belphoebe's Nativity in *The Faerie Queene.' ELH* 40 (1973): 479–500.

Bieman, Elizabeth. *Plato Baptized: Towards the Interpretation of Spenser's Mimetic Fictions.* Toronto: University of Toronto Press, 1988.

Blissett, William. 'Florimell and Marinell.' *SEL* 5 (1965): 87–104.

Bloch, R. Howard. *Medieval Misogyny and the Invention of Western Romantic Love.* Chicago: University of Chicago Press, 1991.

Blumenberg, Hans. *The Genesis of the Copernican World-View.* Trans. Robert W. Wallace. Cambridge: MIT Press, 1984.

– *The Legitimacy of the Modern Age.* Trans. Robert W. Wallace. Cambridge: MIT Press, 1983.

– *Work on Myth.* Trans. Robert W. Wallace. Cambridge: MIT Press, 1985.

Boas, George. 'Philosophies of Science in Florentine Platonism.' In *Art, Science, and History in the Renaissance*, ed. Charles S. Singleton, 239–54. Baltimore: Johns Hopkins University Press, 1967.

Boethius, Anicius Manlius Severinus. *The Consolation of Philosophy*. Trans. Richard Green. Indianapolis: Bobbs-Merrill, 1962.

Bono, James J. *The Word of God and the Languages of Man: Interpreting Nature in Early Modern Science and Medicine*. Madison: University of Wisconsin Press, 1995.

Braden, Gordon. 'riverrun: An Epic Catalogue in *The Faerie Queene*.' *ELR* 5 (1975): 25–48.

Bréhier, Emile. *The Philosophy of Plotinus*. Trans. Joseph Thomas. Chicago: University of Chicago Press, 1958.

Breitenberg, Mark. *Anxious Masculinity in Early Modern England*. Cambridge: Cambridge University Press, 1996.

Brenkman, John. 'The Other and the One: Psychoanalysis, Reading, the *Symposium*.' In *Literature and Psychoanalysis: The Question of Reading: Otherwise*, ed. Shoshana Felman, 396–456. Baltimore: Johns Hopkins University Press, 1982.

Brennan, Michael. 'William Ponsonby: Elizabethan Stationer.' *Analytical and Enumerative Bibliography* 7 (1983): 91–110.

Bruno, Giordano. *Dialoghi italiani*. Ed. Giovanni Gentile and Giovanni Aquilecchia. 3rd ed. Florence: Sansoni, 1958.

– *The Expulsion of the Triumphant Beast*. Trans. Arthur D. Imerti. New Brunswick: Rutgers University Press, 1964.

– *Opera latine conscripta*. Ed. Fiorentino Tocco. 3 vols. Naples and Florence, 1879–91; reprint Stuttgart / Bad Cannstatt: F. Frommann, 1962.

Burchmore, David W. 'Triamond, Agape, and the Fates: Neoplatonic Cosmology in Spenser's Legend of Friendship.' *Spenser Studies* 5 (1984): 45–64 and 273–87.

Butler, Judith. *Gender Trouble: Feminism and the Subversion of Identity*. New York and London: Routledge, 1990.

– 'Imitation and Gender Insubordination.' In *Inside/Out: Lesbian Theories, Gay Theories*, ed. Diana Fuss, 13–31. New York and London: Routledge, 1991.

Calvin, Jean. *The Institution of Christian Religion*. Trans. Thomas Norton. London: widow of Reginald Wolffe, 1574.

Carroll, Eugene A. *Rosso Fiorentino: Drawings, Prints, and Decorative Arts*. Washington, D.C.: National Gallery of Art, 1987.

Cassirer, Ernst. *The Individual and the Cosmos in Renaissance Philosophy*. Trans. Mario Domandi. New York: Harper and Row, 1964.

Cave, Terence. *The Cornucopian Text: Problems of Writing in the French Renaissance*. Oxford: Clarendon Press, 1979.

Cebes' Tablet. Ed. Sandra Sider. New York: Renaissance Society of America, 1979.

Chanter, Tina. *Ethics of Eros: Irigaray's Rewriting of the Philosophers*. New York and London: Routledge, 1990.

Chastel, André. *Marsile Ficin et l'art*. Geneva: Droz, 1954.

Cheney, Donald. *Spenser's Image of Nature: Wild Man and Shepherd in 'The Faerie Queene.'* New Haven: Yale University Press, 1966.

Cheney, Patrick. *Spenser's Famous Flight: A Renaissance Idea of a Literary Career*. Toronto: University of Toronto Press, 1993.

Cioran, E.M. *History and Utopia*. Trans. Richard Howard. Chicago: University of Chicago Press, 1998.

Cirillo, A.R. 'The Fair Hermaphrodite: Love-Union in the Poetry of Donne and Spenser.' *SEL* 9 (1969): 81–95.

Clulee, Nicholas H. *John Dee's Natural Philosophy: Between Science and Religion*. London: Routledge, 1988.

Coleridge, Samuel Taylor. From 'A Course of Lectures' (1818). In *Edmund Spenser's Poetry*, ed. Maclean and Prescott, 668–71.

Collins, Ardis B. *The Secular is Sacred: Platonism and Thomism in Marsilio Ficino's Platonic Theology*. The Hague: Nijhoff, 1974.

Cook, Patrick. *Milton, Spenser, and the Epic Tradition*. Aldershot: Scolar Press, 1996.

Copenhaver, Brian P., and Charles B. Schmitt. *Renaissance Philosophy*. Vol. 3 of *A History of Western Philosophy*. Oxford: Oxford University Press, 1992.

Couliano, Ioan P. *Eros and Magic in the Renaissance*. Trans. Margaret Cook. Chicago: University of Chicago Press, 1987.

Coulter, James A. *The Literary Microcosm: Theories of Interpretation of the Later Neoplatonists*. Leiden: Brill, 1976.

Crewe, Jonathan. *Hidden Designs: The Critical Profession and Renaissance Literature*. New York and London: Methuen, 1986.

Cummings, R.M., ed. *Spenser: The Critical Heritage*. New York: Barnes and Noble, 1971.

Curtius, Ernst Robert. *European Literature and the Latin Middle Ages*. Trans. Willard R. Trask. New York: Harper and Row, 1953.

Daneau, Lambert. *The Wonderfvll Woorkmanship of the World: wherin is conteined an excellent discourse of Christian naturall philosophie, concerning the fourme, knowledge, and vse of all thinges created: specially gathered out of the fountaines of holy scripture*. Trans. Thomas Twyne. London: for Andrew Maunsell, 1578.

Davis, Lloyd. *Guise and Disguise: Rhetoric and Characterization in the English Renaissance.* Toronto: University of Toronto Press, 1993.

de Grazia, Margreta. 'The Scandal of Shakespeare's Sonnets.' *Shakespeare Survey* 46 (1994): 35–49.

– 'The Secularization of Language in the Seventeenth Century.' *Journal of the History of Ideas* 41 (1980): 319–29.

de Grazia, Margreta, Maureen Quilligan, and Peter Stallybrass, eds. *Subject and Object in Renaissance Culture.* Cambridge: Cambridge University Press, 1996.

De Lacy, Hugh. 'Astrology in the Poetry of Edmund Spenser.' *JEGP* 33 (1934): 520–43.

Deleuze, Gilles. *The Logic of Sense.* Trans. Mark Lester, with Charles Stivale. Ed. Constantin V. Boundas. New York: Columbia University Press, 1990.

– 'Plato and the Simulacrum.' Trans. Rosalind Krauss. *October* 27 (1983): 45–56.

DeNeef, A. Leigh. 'Rereading Sidney's *Apology*.' *JMRS* 10 (1980): 155–91.

– *Spenser and the Motives of Metaphor.* Durham: Duke University Press, 1982.

Derrida, Jacques. 'Women in the Beehive: A Seminar with Jacques Derrida.' In *Men in Feminism*, ed. Alice Jardine and Paul Smith, 189–203. Methuen: New York and London, 1987.

Detienne, Marcel. *The Gardens of Adonis: Spices in Greek Mythology.* Introduction by Jean-Pierrre Vernant. Trans. Janet Lloyd. London: Harvester Press, 1977.

Di Matteo, Anthony. 'Spenser's Venus-Virgo: The Poetics and Interpretive History of a Dissembling Figure.' *Spenser Studies* 10 (1989): 37–70.

Dodds, E.R. *Pagan and Christian in an Age of Anxiety: Some Aspects of Religious Experience from Marcus Aurelius to Constantine.* New York: W.W. Norton, 1965.

Doebler, Bettie Anne. '*Rooted Sorrow*': Dying in Early Modern England.* Cranbury, NJ: Associated University Presses, 1994.

Dollimore, Jonathan. 'Death and the Self.' In *Rewriting the Self: Histories from the Renaissance to the Present*, ed. Roy Porter, 249–61. London: Routledge, 1997.

– 'Desire is Death.' In *Subject and Object in Renaissance Culture*, ed. de Grazia et al., 369–86.

Donato, Eugenio. '"Per Selve e Boscherecci Labirinti": Desire and Narrative Structure in Ariosto's *Orlando Furioso*.' In *Literary Theory/Renaissance Texts*, ed. Parker and Quint, 33–62.

Dowey, Edward A., Jr. *The Knowledge of God in Calvin's Theology.* New York: Columbia University Press, 1952.

Dresden, Sem. 'The Profile of the Italian Renaissance in France.' In *Itinerarium Italicum*, ed. Heiko Obermann, 119–89. Leiden: Brill, 1975.

Dronke, Peter. *Fabula: Explorations into the Uses of Myth in Medieval Platonism.* Mittellateinishe Studien und Texte, 9. Leiden: Brill, 1974.

Dupré, Louis. *Passage to Modernity: An Essay in the Hermeneutics of Nature and Culture.* New Haven: Yale University Press, 1993.

Durling, Robert M. 'The Ascent of Mt. Ventoux and the Crisis of Allegory.' *Italian Quarterly* 18 (1974): 7–29.

– *The Figure of the Poet in Renaissance Epic.* Cambridge: Harvard University Press, 1965.

Eagleton, Terry. *Ideology: An Introduction.* London: Verso, 1991.

Edelstein, Ludwig. 'The Golden Chain of Homer.' In *Studies in Intellectual History*, ed. G.G. Boas et al., 48–66. Baltimore: Johns Hopkins University Press, 1953.

Ehrmann, Jacques. 'Homo Ludens Revisited.' In *Game, Play, Literature*, ed. Ehrmann, 31–57. Boston: Beacon Press, 1971.

Eisenbichler, Konrad, and Olga Zorzi Pugliese, eds. *Ficino and Renaissance Neoplatonism.* Ottawa: Dovehouse Editions, 1986.

Ellrodt, Robert. *Neoplatonism in the Poetry of Spenser.* Travaux d'Humanisme et Renaissance, 35. Geneva: Droz, 1960.

Engel, William E. *Mapping Mortality: The Persistence of Memory and Melancholy in Early Modern Writing.* Amherst: University of Massachusetts Press, 1995.

Enterline, Lynn. *The Tears of Narcissus: Melancholia and Masculinity in Early Modern Writing.* Stanford: Stanford University Press, 1995.

Erasmus, Desiderius. *Adages.* Trans. Margaret Mann Phillips. Annotated by R.A.B. Mynors. *Collected Works of Erasmus.* Vols. 31–4. Toronto: University of Toronto Press, 1982–92.

Erickson, Wayne. 'William Ponsonby.' In *Dictionary of Literary Biography*, vol. 170, ed. James K. Bracken and Joel Silver, 204–12. Detroit: Gale Research, 1996.

Esolen, Anthony. 'Spenserian Chaos: Lucretius in *The Faerie Queene*.' *Spenser Studies* 11 (1990): 31–51.

Estrin, Barbara. *Laura: Uncovering Gender and Genre in Wyatt, Donne, and Marvell.* Durham: Duke University Press, 1994.

Falco, Raphael. *Conceived Presences: Literary Genealogy in Renaissance England.* Amherst: University of Massachusetts Press, 1994.

Ferguson, Margaret W. *Trials of Desire: Renaissance Defenses of Poetry.* New Haven: Yale University Press, 1983.

Ficino, Marsilio. *Commentaire sur le Banquet de Platon.* Ed. and trans. Raymond Marcel. Paris: Belles Lettres, 1956.

– *Svpplementvm Ficinianvm.* Ed. P.O. Kristeller. 2 vols. Florence: Olschki, 1937.

– *Three Books on Life*. Ed. and trans. Carol V. Kaske and John R. Clark. Binghamton: Medieval and Renaissance Text Society, 1989.

Field, Arthur. *The Origins of the Platonic Academy of Florence*. Princeton: Princeton University Press, 1988.

Fleming, Abraham. *A Bright Burning Beacon, forewarning all wise Virgins to trim their lampes against the comming of the Bridegroome* ... London: Henrie Denham, 1580.

Fletcher, Angus. *Allegory: The Theory of a Symbolic Mode*. Ithaca: Cornell University Press, 1964.

– *The Prophetic Moment: An Essay on Spenser*. Chicago: University of Chicago Press, 1971.

Fletcher, John, and Andrew Benjamin, eds. *Abjection, Melancholia, and Love: The Work of Julia Kristeva*. London: Routledge, 1990.

Ford, Philip. *Ronsard's Hymnes: A Literary and Iconographical Study*. Tempe: Medieval and Renaissance Text Society, 1997.

Foucault, Michel. *The Order of Things: An Archaeology of the Human Sciences*. Trans. Alan Sheridan-Smith. New York: Random House, 1971.

– 'What is an Author?' In *Language, Counter-Memory, Practice: Selected Essays and Interviews*, ed. Donald F. Bouchard, trans. Donald F. Bouchard and Sherry Simon, 113–38. Ithaca: Cornell University Press, 1977.

Fournel, Jean-Louis. *Les dialogues de Sperone Speroni: libertés de la parole et règles de l'écriture*. Marburg: Hitzeroth, 1990.

Fowler, Alastair. 'Emanations of Glory: Neoplatonic Order in Spenser's *Faerie Queen*.' In *A Theatre for Spenserians*, ed. Judith M. Kennedy and James M. Reither, 53–82. Toronto: University of Toronto Press, 1973.

– *Spenser and the Numbers of Time*. London: Routledge and Kegan Paul, 1964.

– *Triumphal Forms: Structural Patterns in Elizabethan Poetry*. Cambridge: Cambridge University Press, 1970.

Fowler, Elizabeth. 'The Failure of Moral Philosophy in the Work of Edmund Spenser.' *Representations* 51 (1995): 47–76.

Fraunce, Abraham. *The Arcadian Rhetorike*. Ed. Ethel Seaton. Luttrell Society Reprints, 9. Oxford: Blackwell, 1950.

– *The Third part of the Countesse of Pembrokes Yuychurch: Entituled, Amintas Dale*. London: for Thomas Woodcocke, 1592.

Gadol, Joan. 'The Unity of the Renaissance: Humanism, Natural Science, and Art.' In *From the Renaissance to the Counter-Reformation: Essays in Honor of Garrett Mattingly*, ed. Charles H. Carter, 29–55. New York: Random House, 1965.

Gellrich, Jesse B. *The Idea of the Book in the Middle Ages: Language Theory, Mythology, and Fiction*. Ithaca: Cornell University Press, 1985.

Girard, René. *Deceit, Desire, and the Novel: Self and Other in Literary Structure*. Trans. Yvonne Freccero. Baltimore: Johns Hopkins University Press, 1965.

Gombrich, E.H. *Symbolic Images: Studies in the Art of the Renaissance*. London: Phaidon, 1972.

Goodman, Nelson. *Ways of Worldmaking*. Indiana: Hackett Publishing, 1978.

Grabes, Herbert. *The Mutable Glass: Mirror-Imagery in Titles and Texts of the Middle Ages and English Renaissance*. Trans. Gordon Collier. Cambridge: Cambridge University Press, 1982.

Grafton, Anthony, and Lisa Jardine. *From Humanism to the Humanities: Education and the Liberal Arts in Fifteenth- and Sixteenth-Century Europe*. Cambridge: Harvard University Press, 1986.

Greenberg, Sidney. *The Infinite in Giordano Bruno, with a Translation of His Dialogue*, Concerning the Cause, Principle, and One. New York: King's Crown, 1950.

Greenblatt, Stephen. *Renaissance Self-Fashioning: From More to Shakespeare*. Chicago: University of Chicago Press, 1980.

Greene, Thomas M. *The Light in Troy: Imitation and Discovery in Renaissance Poetry*. New Haven: Yale University Press, 1982.

Gross, Elizabeth. 'The Body of Signification.' In *Abjection, Melancholia, and Love*, ed. Fletcher and Benjamin, 80–103.

Gross, Kenneth. *Spenserian Poetics: Idolatry, Iconoclasm, and Magic*. Ithaca: Cornell University Press, 1985.

Guillory, John. *Poetic Authority: Spenser, Milton, and Literary History*. New York: Columbia University Press, 1983.

Gundersheimer, Werner L. *The Life and Works of Louis Le Roy*. Geneva: Droz, 1966.

Hamilton, A.C. 'Sidney and Agrippa.' *RES*, n.s. 7 (1956): 151–7.

– *The Structure of Allegory in* The Faerie Queene. Oxford: Clarendon Press, 1961.

– 'Venus and Adonis.' *SEL* 1 (1961): 1–15.

Hankins, James. *Plato in the Italian Renaissance*. 2nd impression with addenda and corrigenda. Leiden: E.J. Brill, 1991.

Hankins, John Erskine. *Source and Meaning in Spenser's Allegory: A Study of* The Faerie Queene. Oxford: Oxford University Press, 1971.

Hannay, Margaret P. *Philip's Phoenix: Mary Sidney, Countess of Pembroke*. New York: Oxford University Press, 1990.

Harvey, Gabriel. *Gabriel Harvey's Marginalia*. Ed. G.C. Moore Smith. Stratford-upon-Avon: Shakespeare Head Press, 1913.

– *The Letter-Book of Gabriel Harvey, A. D. 1573–1580*. Ed. Edward John Long Scott. Camden Society, n.s. 30. London: for the Camden Society, 1884.

Helgerson, Richard. *Forms of Nationhood: The Elizabethan Writing of England.* Chicago: University of Chicago Press, 1992.

- *Self-Crowned Laureates: Spenser, Jonson, Milton, and the Literary System.* Berkeley and Los Angeles: University of California Press, 1983.

Heller, Agnes. *Renaissance Man.* Trans. Richard E. Allen. London: Routledge and Kegan Paul, 1978.

Heninger, S.K., Jr. *The Cosmographical Glasse: Renaissance Diagrams of the Universe.* San Marino, CA: Huntington Library, 1977.

- 'The Orgoglio Episode in *The Faerie Queene*.' *ELH* 26 (1959): 171–87.

- *Sidney and Spenser: The Poet as Maker.* University Park: Pennsylvania State University Press, 1989.

- *Touches of Sweet Harmony: Pythagorean Cosmology and Renaissance Poetics.* San Marino, CA: Huntington Library, 1974.

Hermetica: The Greek Corpus Hermeticum *and the Latin* Asclepius. Ed. and trans. Brian P. Copenhaver. Cambridge: Cambridge University Press, 1992.

Hieatt, A. Kent. *Chaucer, Spenser, Milton: Mythopoeic Continuities and Transformations.* Montreal: McGill-Queen's University Press, 1975.

Hinks, Roger. *Myth and Allegory in Ancient Art.* Studies of the Warburg Institute, 6. London: for the Warburg Institute, 1939.

Hinman, Robert. 'The Apotheosis of Faust: Poetry and New Philosophy in the Seventeenth Century.' In *Metaphysical Poetry. Stratford-upon-Avon Studies,* 11, ed. Malcolm Bradbury and David Palmer, 149–79. London: Edward Arnold, 1970.

Horowitz, Maryanne Cline. *Seeds of Knowledge and Virtue.* Princeton: Princeton University Press, 1998.

Hulse, Clark. *Metamorphic Verse: The Elizabethan Minor Epic.* Princeton: Princeton University Press, 1981.

- 'Spenser, Bacon, and the Myth of Power.' In *The Historical Renaissance: New Essays on Tudor and Stuart Literature and Culture,* ed. Heather Dubrow and Richard Strier, 315–46. Chicago: University of Chicago Press, 1988.

Hutson, Lorna. 'Fortunate Travelers: Reading for the Plot in Sixteenth-Century England.' *Representations* 41 (1993): 83–101.

Hyde, Thomas. *The Poetic Theology of Love: Cupid in Renaissance Literature.* Newark: University of Delaware Press, 1986.

Jardine, Lisa, and Anthony Grafton. '"Studied for Action": How Gabriel Harvey Read His Livy.' *Past and Present* 129 (1990): 30–78.

Javitch, Daniel. *Poetry and Courtliness in Renaissance England.* Princeton: Princeton University Press, 1978.

Johnson, W.R. *Darkness Visible: A Study of Vergil's Aeneid.* Berkeley and Los Angeles: University of California Press, 1976.

Kallendorf, Craig. 'Cristoforo Landino's *Aeneid* and the Humanist Critical Tradition.' *Renaissance Quarterly* 36 (1983): 519–46.

Kane, Sean. *Spenser's Moral Allegory*. Toronto: University of Toronto Press, 1989.

Kaske, Carol V. 'Spenser's Pluralistic Universe: The View from the Mount of Contemplation.' In *Contemporary Thought on Edmund Spenser*, ed. Richard C. Frushell and Bernard J. Vondersmith, 121–49. Carbondale: Southern Illinois University Press, 1975.

Kenny, Neil. *The Palace of Secrets: Béroalde de Verville and Renaissance Conceptions of Knowledge*. Oxford: Clarendon Press, 1991.

Kermode, Frank. *The Classic: Literary Images of Permanence and Change*. New York: Viking, 1975.

– *The Sense of an Ending: Studies in the Theory of Fiction*. New York: Oxford University Press, 1967.

Kirk, G.S. *Myth: Its Meaning and Functions in Ancient and Other Cultures*. Berkeley and Los Angeles: University of California Press, 1970.

Klibansky, Raymond, Erwin Panofsky, and Fritz Saxl. *Saturn and Melancholy: Studies in the History of Natural Philosophy, Religion, and Art*. New York: Basic Books, 1964.

Knight, G. Wilson. 'The Spenserian Fluidity.' In *Elizabethan Poetry: Modern Essays in Criticism*, ed. Paul J. Alpers, 329–44. New York: Oxford University Press, 1967.

Krier, Theresa M. *Gazing on Secret Sights: Spenser, Classical Imitation, and the Decorums of Vision*. Ithaca: Cornell University Press, 1990.

Kristeller, Paul Oskar. 'The European Significance of Florentine Platonism.' In *Medieval and Renaissance Studies* 3, ed. John M. Headley, 206–29. Chapel Hill: University of North Carolina Press, 1968.

– 'Giovanni Pico della Mirandola and His Sources.' In *L'Opera e il pensiero di Giovanni Pico della Mirandola nella storia dell'umanesimo: Convegno Internazionale (Mirandola: 15–18 Settembre 1963)*. Vol. I: *Relazioni*, 35–133. Florence: Instituto Nazionale di Studi sul Rinascimento, 1965.

– *The Philosophy of Marsilio Ficino*. Trans. Virginia Conant. New York: Columbia University Press, 1943.

– *Renaissance Thought: The Classic, Scholastic, and Humanistic Strains*. New York: Harper, 1955.

– *Renaissance Thought II: Papers on Humanism and the Arts*. New York: Harper, 1965.

– 'The Scholastic Background of Marsilio Ficino.' In his *Studies in Renaissance Thought and Letters*, 35–97. Rome: Editioni di Storia e Letteratura, 1956.

Kristeva, Julia. *Tales of Love*. Trans. Leon S. Roudiez. New York: Columbia University Press, 1987.

Lamb, Mary Ellen. *Gender and Authorship in the Sidney Circle*. Madison: University of Wisconsin Press, 1990.

Lamberton, Robert. *Homer the Theologian: Neoplatonist Allegorical Reading and the Growth of the Epic Tradition*. Berkeley and Los Angeles: University of California Press, 1986.

Landino, Cristoforo. *Disputationes Camaldulenses*. Ed. Peter Lohe. Florence: Sansoni, 1980.

– *Scritti critici e teorici*. Ed. Roberto Cardini. 2 vols. Rome: Bulzoni, 1974.

Laqueur, Thomas. *Making Sex: Body and Gender from the Greeks to Freud*. Cambridge: Harvard University Press, 1990.

Leclercq, Jean. *The Love of Learning and the Desire for God; A Study of Monastic Culture*. Trans. Catharine Misrahi. 3rd ed. New York: Fordham University Press, 1982.

Lemnius, Levinus. *Les Occvltes Merveilles et Secretz de Natvre ...* Trans. I[acques]. G[ohory]. P[arisien]. Paris: for Galiot du Pré, 1574.

– *The Touchstone of Complexions*. Trans. Thomas Newton. 3rd ed. London: Thomas Marsh, 1581.

Leo Hebraeus [Leone Ebreo]. *Dialoghi d'amore*. Ed. Santino Caramella. Bari: Laterza, 1929.

– *The Philosophy of Love (Dialoghi d'Amore)*. Trans. F. Friedeberg-Seeley and Jean H. Barnes. London: Soncino Press, 1937.

Leonardo da Vinci. *Selections from the Notebooks of Leonardo da Vinci*. Ed. Irma A. Richter. London: Oxford University Press, 1952.

Lesley, Arthur M. 'The Place of the *Dialoghi d'amore* in Contemporaneous Jewish Thought.' In *Ficino and Renaissance Neoplatonism*, ed. Eisenbichler and Pugliese, 69–86.

Levao, Ronald. *Renaissance Minds and Their Fictions: Cusanus, Sidney, Shakespeare*. Berkeley and Los Angeles: University of California Press, 1985.

Levi, A.H.T. 'The Neoplatonist Calculus: The Exploitation of Neoplatonist Themes in French Renaissance Literature.' In *Humanism in France at the End of the Middle Ages and in the Early Renaissance*, ed. Levi, 229–48. Manchester and New York: University of Manchester Press/Barnes and Noble, 1970.

Levine, Laura. *Men in Women's Clothing: Anti-theatricality and Effeminization, 1579–1642*. Cambridge Studies in Renaissance Literature and Culture, 5. Cambridge: Cambridge University Press, 1994.

Lewis, C.S. *The Allegory of Love: A Study in Medieval Tradition*. Oxford: Clarendon Press, 1936.

– *Spenser's Images of Life*. Ed. Alastair Fowler. Cambridge: Cambridge University Press, 1967.

– *Studies in Medieval and Renaissance Literature*. Cambridge: Cambridge University Press, 1966.

– *Studies in Words*. Cambridge: Cambridge University Press, 1960.

Loewenstein, Joseph. 'Spenser's Retrography: Two Episodes in Post-Petrarchan Bibliography.' In *Spenser's Life and the Subject of Biography*, ed. Anderson et al., 99–130.

Lotspeich, Henry Gibbons. *Classical Mythology in the Poetry of Edmund Spenser*. Princeton: Princeton University Press, 1932.

Lovejoy, Arthur O. *The Great Chain of Being: A Study of the History of an Idea*. Cambridge: Harvard University Press, 1936.

Lukács, Georg. *The Theory of the Novel*. Trans. Anna Bostock. Cambridge: MIT Press, 1971.

Macrobius. *Commentary on the Dream of Scipio*. Trans. William Harris Stahl. New York: Columbia University Press, 1952.

McCabe, Richard A. *The Pillars of Eternity: Time and Providence in* The Faerie Queene. Dublin: Irish Academic Press, 1989.

MacCaffrey, Isabel G. *Spenser's Allegory: The Anatomy of Imagination*. Princeton: Princeton University Press, 1976.

McClure, George W. *Sorrow and Consolation in Italian Humanism*. Princeton: Princeton University Press, 1991.

McKitterick, David. Review of Virginia Stern, *Gabriel Harvey*. *Library* 3 (1981): 348–53.

MacQueen, John. *Numerology*. Edinburgh: Edinburgh University Press, 1985.

Mallette, Richard. *Spenser and the Discourses of Reformation England*. Lincoln: University of Nebraska Press, 1997.

Mambelli, Giuliano. *Gli Annali delle edizioni virgiliane*. Biblioteca di bibliografia italiana, 27. Florence: Olschki, 1954.

Manley, Lawrence. *Convention, 1500–1700*. Cambridge: Harvard University Press, 1980.

Markus, R.A. 'Augustine: God and Nature.' In *The Cambridge History of Later Greek and Early Medieval Philosophy*, ed. A.H. Armstrong, 395–405. Cambridge: Cambridge University Press, 1967.

Martinez-Bonati, Felix. 'Towards a Formal Ontology of Fictional Worlds.' *Philosophy and Literature* 7 (1983): 182–95.

Masten, Jeffrey. 'Is the Fundament a Grave?' In *The Body in Parts: Fantasies of Corporeality in Early Modern Europe*, ed. David Hillman and Carla Mazzio, 129–45. New York and London: Routledge, 1997.

Maus, Katharine Eisaman. *Inwardness and Theater in the English Renaissance*. Chicago: University of Chicago Press, 1995.

Mazzola, Elizabeth. *The Pathology of the English Renaissance: Sacred Remains and Holy Ghosts*. Studies in the History of Christian Thought, 86. Leiden: Brill, 1998.

– 'Spenserian Remains: A Mortuary Poetics.' Unpublished paper, delivered at the MLA Convention, 27 December 1996.

Mazzotta, Giuseppe. *Dante's Vision and the Circle of Knowledge*. Princeton: Princeton University Press, 1993.

Miller, David Lee. *The Poem's Two Bodies: The Poetics of the 1590 Faerie Queene*. Princeton: Princeton University Press, 1988.

Miller, Jacqueline T. *Poetic License: Authority and Authorship in Medieval and Renaissance Contexts*. New York and Oxford: Oxford University Press, 1986.

Montrose, Louis Adrian. 'The Elizabethan Subject and the Spenserian Text.' In *Literary Theory/Renaissance Texts*, ed. Parker and Quint, 303–40.

– 'Spenser's Domestic Domain: Poetry, Property, and the Early Modern Subject.' In *Subject and Object in Renaissance Culture*, ed. de Grazia et al., 83–130.

Müller-Bochat, Eberhard. *Leon Battista Alberti und die Vergil-Deutung der Disputationes Camaldulenses. Zur allegorischen Dichter-Erklärung bei Cristoforo Landino*. Schriften und Vorträge der Petrarca-Instituts Köln, 21. Krefeld, 1968.

Nelson, William. *The Poetry of Edmund Spenser: A Study*. New York: Columbia University Press, 1963.

Nestrick, William V. 'Spenser and the Renaissance Mythology of Love.' *Literary Monographs* 6 (1975): 35–70.

Neuse, Richard T. 'Planting Words in the Soul: Spenser's Socratic Garden of Adonis.' *Spenser Studies* 8 (1987): 79–100.

Nohrnberg, James. *The Analogy of* The Faerie Queene. Princeton: Princeton University Press, 1976.

Olson, David R. *The World on Paper: The Conceptual and Cognitive Implications of Writing and Reading*. Cambridge: Cambridge University Press, 1994.

Olson, Paul A. Review of Robert Lamberton, *Homer the Theologian*. *Spenser Newsletter* 18 (1987): 40–3.

Orgel, Stephen. *Impersonations: The Performance of Gender in Shakespeare's England*. Cambridge: Cambridge University Press, 1996.

Osgood, Charles Grosvenor. *A Concordance to the Poems of Edmund Spenser*. Washington, DC: Carnegie Institution of Washington, 1915.

Otis, Brooks. *Virgil: A Study in Civilized Poetry*. Oxford: Clarendon Press, 1964.

Paglia, Camille. 'The Apollonian Androgyne and the *Faerie Queene*.' *ELR* 9 (1979): 42–63.

Panofsky, Erwin. *Renaissance and Renascences in Western Art.* London: Granada, 1970.

Parker, Patricia. *Literary Fat Ladies: Rhetoric, Gender, Property.* London: Methuen, 1987.

Parker, Patricia, and David Quint, eds. *Literary Theory/Renaissance Texts.* Baltimore: Johns Hopkins University Press, 1986.

Pask, Kevin. *The Emergence of the English Author: Scripting the Life of the Poet in Early Modern England.* Cambridge: Cambridge University Press, 1996.

Patterson, Annabel M. 'Tasso and Neoplatonism: The Growth of His Epic Theory.' *Studies in the Renaissance* 18 (1971): 105–33.

Pavel, Thomas G. *Fictional Worlds.* Cambridge: Harvard University Press, 1986.

Perry, T. Anthony. *Erotic Spirituality: The Integrative Tradition from Leone Ebreo to John Donne.* University: University of Alabama Press, 1980.

Pico della Mirandola, Giovanni. *Commentary on a Canzone of Benivieni.* Ed. and trans. Sears Jayne. New York: Peter Lang, 1984.

– *Heptaplus,* trans. Douglas Carmichael. In *On the Dignity of Man, On Being and the One, Heptaplus.* Ed. Paul J.W. Miller. Indianapolis: Bobbs-Merrill, 1965.

Plato. *The Collected Dialogues.* Ed. Edith Hamilton and Huntington Cairns. Princeton: Princeton University Press, 1961.

– *Omnia Divini Platonis Opera tralatione Marsilii Ficini.* Basel: in Officina Frobeniana, 1546.

– *Plato's Cosmology: The* Timaeus *of Plato.* Ed. and trans. Francis MacDonald Cornford. Indianapolis: Bobbs-Merrill, n.d.

– *The* Republic *of Plato.* Ed. and trans. Frances MacDonald Cornford. New York and London, 1945.

Prescott, Anne Lake. 'Spenser's Chivalric Restoration: From Bateman's *Travayled Pylgrime* to the Redcrosse Knight.' *Studies in Philology* 86 (1989): 166–97.

Quilligan, Maureen. 'The Comedy of Female Authority in *The Faerie Queene.*' *ELR* 17 (1987): 156–71.

– *The Language of Allegory.* Ithaca: Cornell University Press, 1979.

– *Milton's Spenser: The Politics of Reading.* Ithaca: Cornell University Press, 1983.

Quint, David. *Origin and Originality in Renaissance Literature.* New Haven: Yale University Press, 1983.

Quitslund, Jon A. 'Questionable Evidence in the *Letters* of 1580 between Gabriel Harvey and Edmund Spenser.' In *Spenser's Life and the Subject of Biography,* ed. Anderson et al., 81–98.

– 'Spenser and the Patronesses of the *Fowre Hymnes*: "Ornaments of All True

Love and Beautie.'" In *Silent But for the Word: Tudor Women as Patrons, Translators, and Writers of Religious Works*, ed. Margaret P. Hannay, 184–202. Kent, OH: Kent State University Press, 1985.

– 'Spenser's *Amoretti VIII* and Platonic Commentaries on Petrarch.' *JWCI* 36 (1973): 256–76.

– 'Spenser's Image of Sapience.' *Studies in the Renaissance* 16 (1969): 181–213.

Rabkin, Norman. *Shakespeare and the Problem of Meaning*. Chicago: University of Chicago Press, 1981.

Rambuss, Richard. *Spenser's Secret Career*. Cambridge: Cambridge University Press, 1993.

Rapp, Carl. 'Philosophy and Poetry: The New Rapprochement.' In *Literature as Philosophy/Philosophy as Literature*, ed. Donald G. Marshall, 120–34. Iowa City: University of Iowa Press, 1987.

Reiss, Timothy. *The Discourse of Modernism*. Ithaca: Cornell University Press, 1982.

Roche, Thomas P., Jr. *The Kindly Flame: A Study of the Third and Fourth Books of Spenser's 'Faerie Queene.'* Princeton: Princeton University Press, 1964.

Rose, Mark. *Spenser's Art: A Companion to the 'Faerie Queene' I*. Cambridge: Harvard University Press, 1975.

Rosenberg, Eleanor. *Leicester, Patron of Letters*. New York: Columbia University Press, 1955.

Ruutz-Rees, Caroline. 'Some Notes of Gabriel Harvey's in Hoby's Translation of Castiglione's *Courtier* (1561).' *PMLA* 25 (1910): 608–39.

Schiesari, Juliana. *The Gendering of Melancholia: Feminism, Psychoanalysis, and the Symbolics of Loss in Renaissance Literature*. Ithaca: Cornell University Press, 1992.

Schleiner, Winfried. 'Early Modern Controversies about the One-Sex Model.' *Renaissance Quarterly* 53 (2000): 180–91.

Schmitt, Charles B. *Gianfrancesco Pico della Mirandola (1469–1533) and His Critique of Aristotle*. The Hague: Nijhoff, 1967.

– *John Case and Aristotelianism in Renaissance England*. Kingston and Montreal: McGill-Queen's University Press, 1983.

Schroeder, J.W. 'Spenser's Erotic Drama: The Orgoglio Episode.' *ELH* 29 (1962): 140–59.

Scrivano, Riccardo. 'Platonic and Cabalistic Elements in the Hebrew Culture of Renaissance Italy: Leone Ebreo and his *Dialoghi d'amore*.' In *Ficino and Renaissance Neoplatonism*, ed. Eisenbichler and Pugliese, 123–39.

Sedgwick, Eve Kosofsky. *Between Men: English Literature and Male Homosocial Desire*. New York: Columbia University Press, 1985.

Sharratt, Peter, ed. *French Renaissance Studies, 1540–70: Humanism and the Encyclopedia*. Edinburgh: Edinburgh University Press, 1976.

Shearman, John. *Mannerism*. Harmondsworth: Penguin, 1967.

Silberman, Lauren. 'Singing Unsung Heroines: Androgynous Discourse in Book 3 of *The Faerie Queene*.' In *Rewriting the Renaissance: The Discourses of Sexual Difference in Early Modern Europe*, ed. Margaret W. Ferguson, Maureen Quilligan, and Nancy Vickers, 259–71. Chicago: University of Chicago Press, 1986.

– *Transforming Desire: Erotic Knowledge in Books III and IV of* The Faerie Queene. Berkeley and Los Angeles: University of California Press, 1995.

Smith, Bruce R. *Homosexual Desire in Shakespeare's England: A Cultural Poetics*. Chicago: University of Chicago Press, 1991.

Snare, Gerald. 'Satire, Logic, and Rhetoric in Harvey's Earthquake Letter to Spenser.' *Tulane Studies in English* 18 (1970): 17–33.

Spenser, Edmund. *Edmund Spenser's Poetry*. Norton Critical Editions. 3rd edition. Ed. Hugh Maclean and Anne Lake Prescott. New York: W.W. Norton, 1993.

Speroni, Sperone. *Dialoghi di M. S. Speroni: Nuouamente ristampati, & con molta diligenza riueduti, & corretti*. Venice: Figlivoli di Aldo, 1543.

Staten, Henry. *Eros in Mourning: Homer to Lacan*. Baltimore: Johns Hopkins University Press, 1995.

Staub, Hans. *Le Curieux désir: Scève et Peletier du Mans, poètes de la connaissance*. Geneva: Droz, 1967.

Stephens, Dorothy. *The Limits of Eroticism in Post-Petrarchan Narrative: Conditional Pleasure from Spenser to Marvell*. Cambridge: Cambridge University Press, 1998.

Stern, Virginia. *Gabriel Harvey: His Life, Marginalia, and Library*. Oxford: Clarendon Press, 1979.

Stirling, Brents. 'The Philosophy of Spenser's "Garden of Adonis."' *PMLA* 49 (1934): 501–38.

– 'Spenser's "Platonic" Garden.' *JEPG* 41 (1942): 482–6.

Tasso, Torquato. *Discourses on the Heroic Poem*. Trans. Mariella Cavalchini and Irene Samuel. Oxford: Clarendon Press, 1973.

Teskey, Gordon. *Allegory and Violence*. Ithaca: Cornell University Press, 1996.

– 'From Allegory to Dialectic: Imagining Error in Spenser and Milton.' *PMLA* 101 (1986): 9–23.

Tigerstedt, E.N. 'The Poet as Creator: Origins of a Metaphor.' *Comparative Literature Studies* 5 (1968): 455–88.

Tomlinson, Gary. *Music in Renaissance Magic: Toward a Historiography of Others*. Chicago: University of Chicago Press, 1993.

Topitsch, Ernst. 'World Interpretation and Self-Interpretation: Some Basic Patterns.' In *Myth and Myth-Making*, ed. Henry A. Murray, 157–73. Boston: Beacon Press, 1968.

Trinkaus, Charles. *In Our Image and Likeness: Humanity and Divinity in Italian Humanist Thought.* 2 vols. Chicago: University of Chicago Press, 1970.

– *The Poet as Philosopher: Petrarch and the Formation of Renaissance Consciousness.* New Haven: Yale University Press, 1979.

– 'Renaissance Problems in Calvin's Theology.' *Studies in the Renaissance* 1 (1954): 59–80.

Tripet, Arnaud. 'Aspects de l'analogie à la renaissance.' *BHR* 39 (1977): 7–21.

Tuan, Yi-Fu. *Topophilia: A Study of Environmental Perception, Attitudes, and Values.* Englewood Cliffs: Prentice-Hall, 1974.

Tuve, Rosemond. *Essays by Rosemond Tuve: Spenser, Herbert, Milton.* Ed. Thomas P. Roche, Jr. Princeton: Princeton University Press, 1970.

Vickers, Brian. 'On the Function of Analogy in the Occult.' In *Hermeticism and the Renaissance,* ed. Ingrid Merkel and Allen G. Debus, 265–92. Washington, D.C.: Folger Books and Associated University Presses, 1988.

Vickers, Brian, ed. *Occult and Scientific Mentalities in the Renaissance.* Cambridge: Cambridge University Press, 1984.

Virgil (Publius Vergilius Maro). *Virgilius cum commentariis quinque.* Lyon: Jacques Sachon, 1499.

Walker, D.P. *The Ancient Theology: Studies in Christian Platonism from the Fifteenth to the Eighteenth Centuries.* Ithaca: Cornell University Press, 1972.

– 'The Astral Body in Renaissance Medicine.' *JWCI* 21 (1958): 119–33.

– 'Francis Bacon and *Spiritus.*' In *Music, Spirit and Language in the Renaissance.* Ed. Penelope Gouk. London: Variorum Reprints, 1985.

– *Spiritual and Demonic Magic from Ficino to Campanella.* London: Warburg Institute, 1958.

Weatherby, Harold L. *Mirrors of Celestial Grace: Patristic Theology in Spenser's Allegory.* Toronto: University of Toronto Press, 1994.

Weil, Kari. *Androgyny and the Denial of Difference.* Charlottesville: University Press of Virginia, 1992.

Whigham, Frank. *Ambition and Privilege: The Social Tropes of Elizabethan Courtesy Theory.* Berkeley and Los Angeles: University of California Press, 1984.

Williams, Kathleen. '"Eterne in Mutabilitie": The Unified World of *The Faerie Queene.*' *ELH* 19 (1952): 115–30.

– *Spenser's World of Glass: A Reading of* The Faerie Queene. Berkeley and Los Angeles: University of California Press, 1966.

Wind, Edgar. *Pagan Mysteries in the Renaissance.* Revised edition. Harmondsworth: Penguin, 1967.

Wofford, Susanne Lindgren. *The Choice of Achilles: The Ideology of Figure in the Epic.* Stanford: Stanford University Press, 1992.

Wölfflin, Heinrich. *Principles of Art History*. Trans. M.D. Hottinger. N.p.:
    Dover, n.d.
Yates, Frances A. *Giordano Bruno and the Hermetic Tradition*. Chicago: Univer-
    sity of Chicago Press, 1964.
– 'Giovanni Pico della Mirandola and Magic.' In *L'Opera e il pensiero di
    Giovanni Pico della Mirandola nella storia dell'umanesimo ...* Vol. I: *Relazioni*,
    159–203. Florence: Instituto Nazionale di Studi sul Rinascimento, 1965.
– *Theatre of the World*. Chicago: University of Chicago Press, 1969.
Yavneh, Naomi. 'The Spiritual Eroticism of Leone's Hermaphrodite.' In *Playing
    with Gender: A Renaissance Pursuit*, ed. Jean R. Brink, Maryanne C. Horo-
    witz, and Allison P. Coudert, 85–95. Urbana: University of Illinois Press,
    1991.
Zetzel, James E.G. 'Re-creating the Canon: Augustan Poetry and the
    Alexandrian Past.' *CI* 10 (1983): 83–105.

General Index

Names of scholars are indexed when cited in the text or notes. Canonical authors are indexed where more than a passing reference is to be found; titles appear under authors' names. Characters and places in *The Faerie Queene* are indexed separately.

Index of Names and Places in *The Faerie Queene*